TOKYO DAYS BANGKOK NIGHTS

Tokyo

Jonathan Vankin
Writer

Seth Fisher
Artist

Comicraft
Letters

Chris Chuckry
Colors

Seth Fisher
Original Series Covers

Rian Hughes
Logo Design

Special thanks to **Masami
"Goro" Shimano,
Aki Yanagi** &
Nozomi Yazawa

Vertigo Pop! Tokyo created
by **Vankin** & **Fisher**

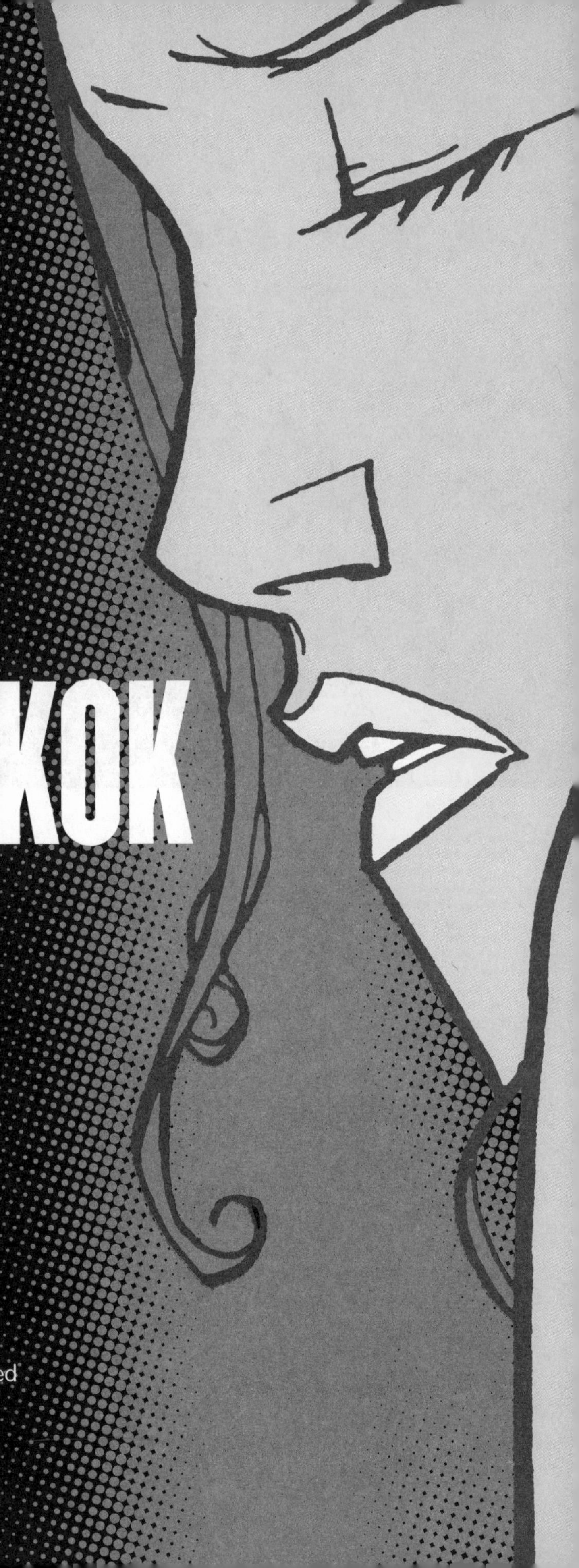

BANGKOK

Jonathan Vankin
Writer

Giuseppe Camuncoli
Penciller

Shawn Martinbrough
Inker

Comicraft
Letters

Hi-Fi
Colors

Seth Fisher
Original Series Covers

Louis Prandi
Logo Design

Vertigo Pop! Bangkok created
by **Vankin** & **Camuncoli**

In Memory of Seth Fisher, 1972 - 2006

Karen Berger Senior VP-Executive Editor
Shelly Bond Editor-original series
Maria Huehner Assistant Editor-original series
Sean Mackiewicz Editor-collected edition
Robbin Brosterman Senior Art Director
Louis Prandi Art Director
Paul Levitz President & Publisher
Georg Brewer VP-Design & DC Direct Creative
Richard Bruning Senior VP-Creative Director
Patrick Caldon Executive VP-Finance & Operations
Chris Caramalis VP-Finance
John Cunningham VP-Marketing
Terri Cunningham VP-Managing Editor
Amy Genkins Senior VP-Business & Legal Affairs
Alison Gill VP-Manufacturing
David Hyde VP-Publicity
Hank Kanalz VP-General Manager, WildStorm
Jim Lee Editorial Director-WildStorm
Gregory Noveck Senior VP-Creative Affairs
Sue Pohja VP-Book Trade Sales
Steve Rotterdam Senior VP-Sales & Marketing
Cheryl Rubin Senior VP-Brand Management
Alysse Soll VP-Advertising & Custom Publishing
Jeff Trojan VP-Business Development, DC Direct
Bob Wayne VP-Sales

Cover by Seth Fisher and Giuseppe Camuncoli with Shawn Martinbrough.

TOKYO DAYS, BANGKOK NIGHTS
Published by DC Comics. Cover, text and compilation Copyright © 2009 DC Comics. All Rights Reserved.
Originally published in single magazine form in VERTIGO POP! TOKYO 1-4, VERTIGO POP! BANGKOK 1-4. Copyright © 2002, 2003 Jonathan Vankin,
Seth Fisher and Giuseppe Camuncoli. All Rights Reserved. All characters, their distinctive likenesses and related elements featured in this publication
are trademarks of Jonathan Vankin, Seth Fisher and Giuseppe Camuncoli. The stories, characters and incidents featured in this publication are entirely
fictional. Vertigo is a trademark of DC Comics. DC Comics does not read or accept unsolicited submissions of ideas, stories or artwork.
DC Comics, 1700 Broadway, New York, NY 10019
A Warner Bros. Entertainment Company
Printed in Canada. First Printing.
ISBN: 978-1-4012-2189-8

SFI
CERTIFIED SOURCING
Fiber used in this product line meets the
sourcing requirements of the SFI program.
www.sfiprogram.org
PWC-SFICOC-260

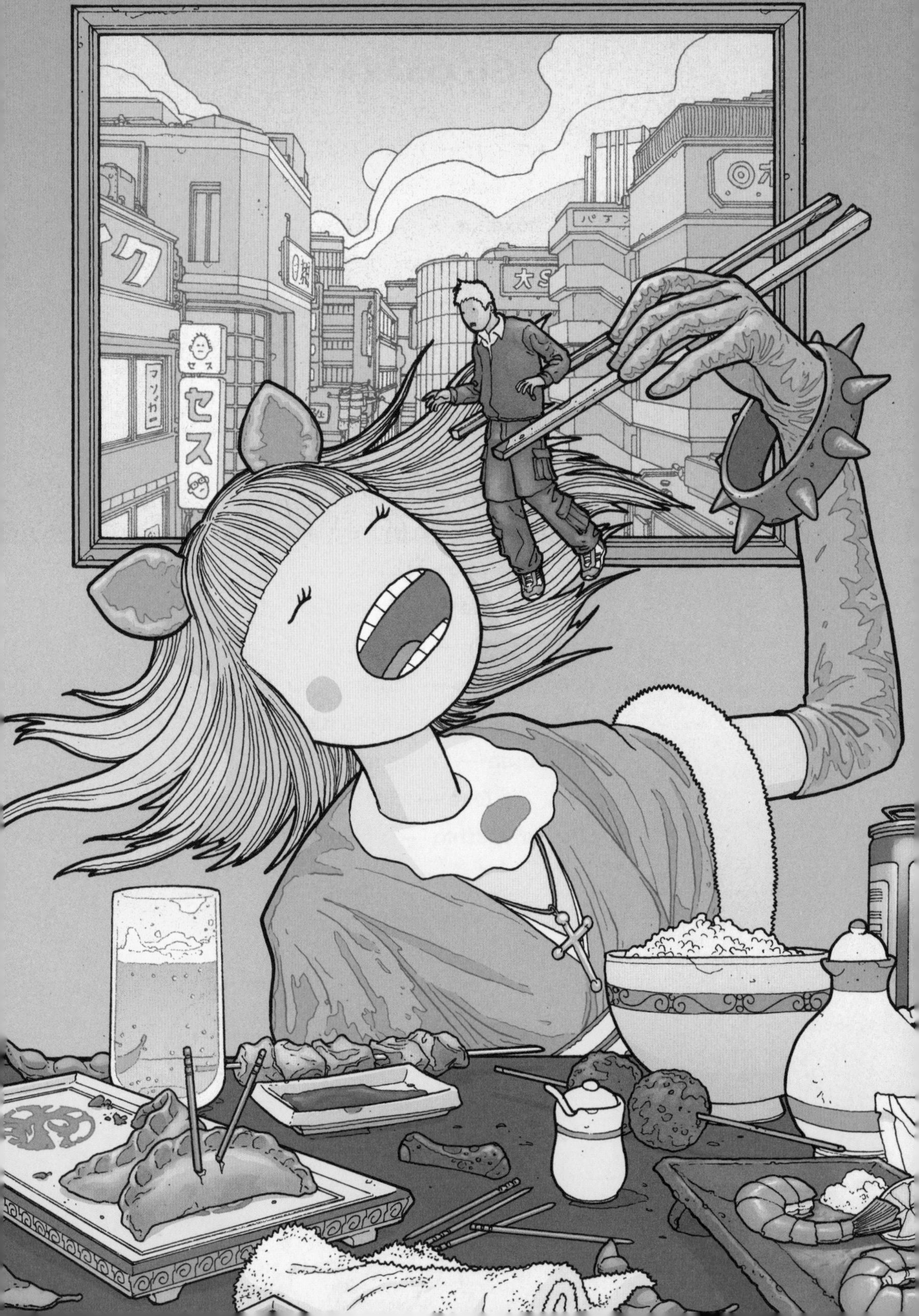
セス
セス

GLOSSARY

Are wa? — What's that?

Baka — stupid

Bakatare — stupid jerk

Bento — box lunch

Daijobu — It's okay

Genki — Feeling energetic

Gumi — Gang

Ikimasho — Let's go!

Itai — It hurts! (pain)

Kawai so — That's too bad

Konnichiwa — Hello (in the afternoon)

Kuso Yaro — Dumb Shif

Naruhodo — I see; indeed

Oi shi — Delicious

Osewa ni narimashita — Thank you for your help

Shabu — amphetamines (slang)

Sumimasen — Excuse me, I'm sorry

Toire — toilet

Wakari Mashta — I understand

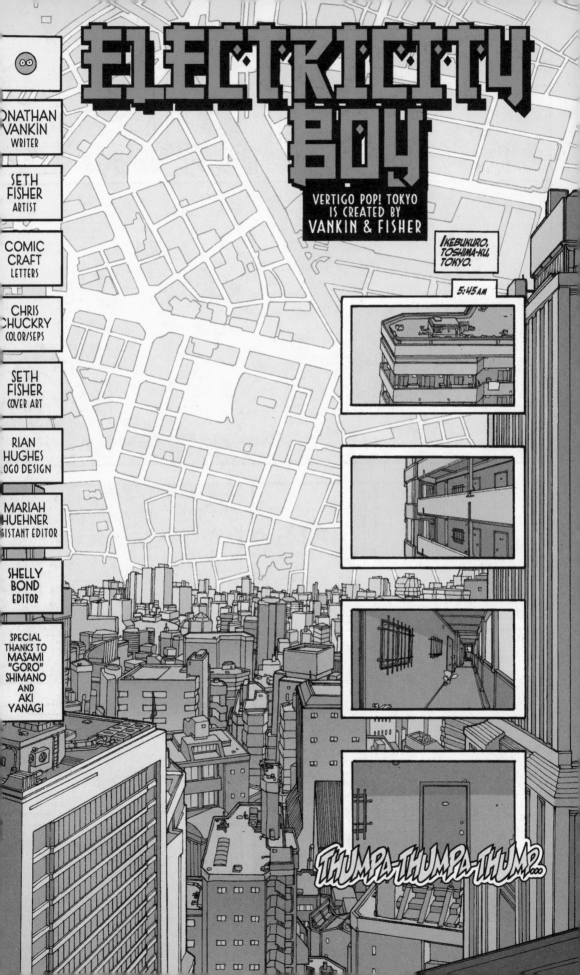

ELECTRICITY BOY

VERTIGO POP! TOKYO
IS CREATED BY
VANKIN & FISHER

JONATHAN VANKIN
WRITER

SETH FISHER
ARTIST

COMIC CRAFT
LETTERS

CHRIS CHUCKRY
COLOR/SEPS

SETH FISHER
COVER ART

RIAN HUGHES
LOGO DESIGN

MARIAH HUEHNER
ASSISTANT EDITOR

SHELLY BOND
EDITOR

SPECIAL THANKS TO MASAMI "GORO" SHIMANO AND AKI YANAGI

IKEBUKURO, TOSHIMA-KU, TOKYO.

5:45 AM

THUMPA-THUMPA-THUMP...

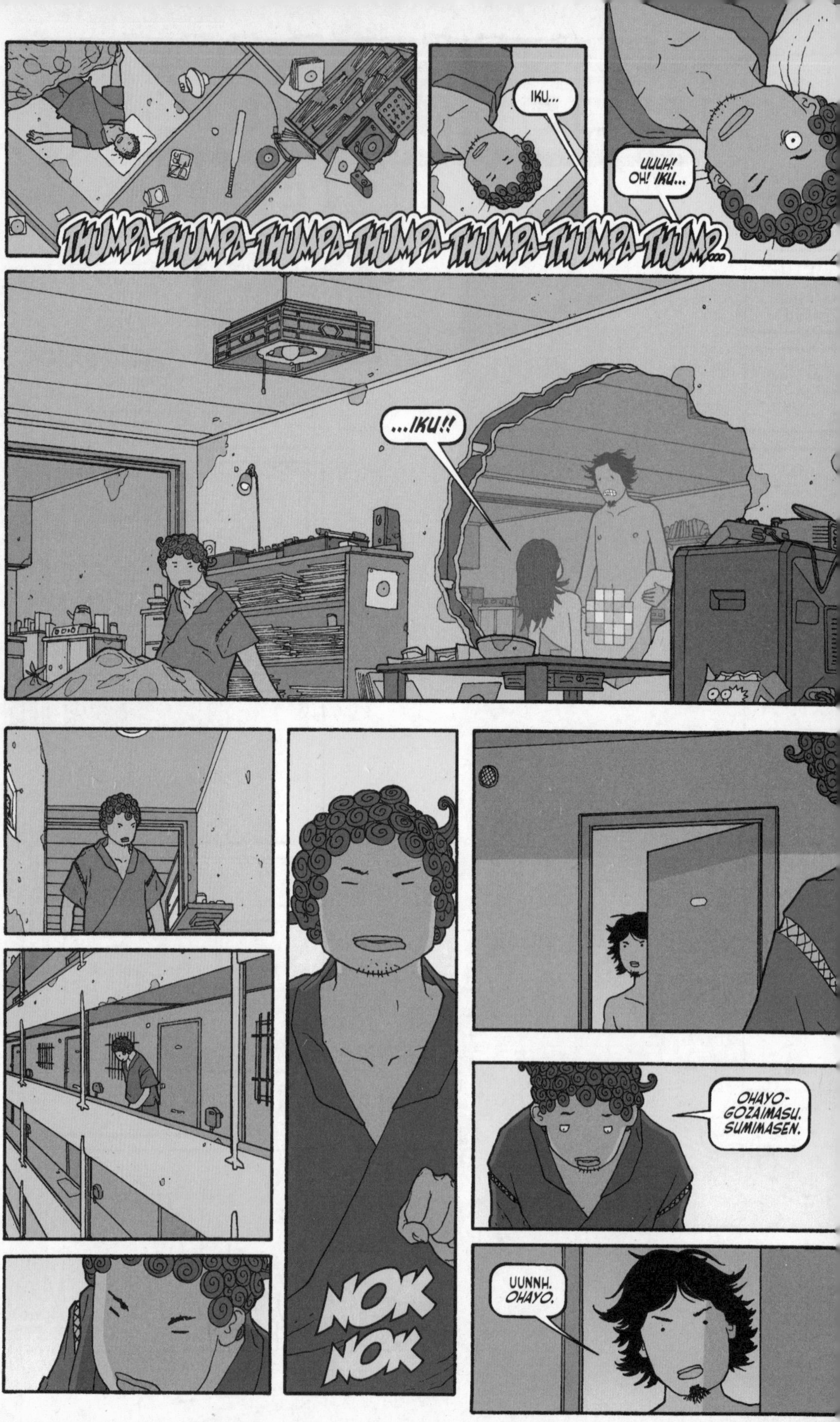
IKU...
UUUH! OH! IKU...
THUMPA-THUMPA-THUMPA-THUMPA-THUMPA-THUMPA-THUMP...
...IKU!!
NOK NOK
OHAYO-GOZAIMASU. SUMIMASEN.
UUNNH. OHAYO.

SUMIMASEN. I AM TERRIBLY SORRY TO DISTURB SUCH AN ESTEEMED PERSON AS YOURSELF AT THIS EARLY HOUR. I CAN SEE YOU ARE VERY BUSY.

NANI?

MY INTERFERENCE IN YOUR HONORABLE AFFAIRS IS AN INEXCUSABLE INTRUSION. BUT AS TO THE MATTER AT HAND...

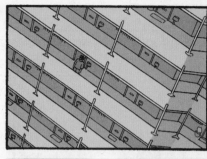

SORE DE?

...I MUST HUMBLY ASK THAT YOU KEEP THE NOISE DOWN BECAUSE I FEAR THAT FOR THE RESIDENTS OF THE BUILDING, THIS MAY BECOME -- A MEIWAKU.

UUNNH.

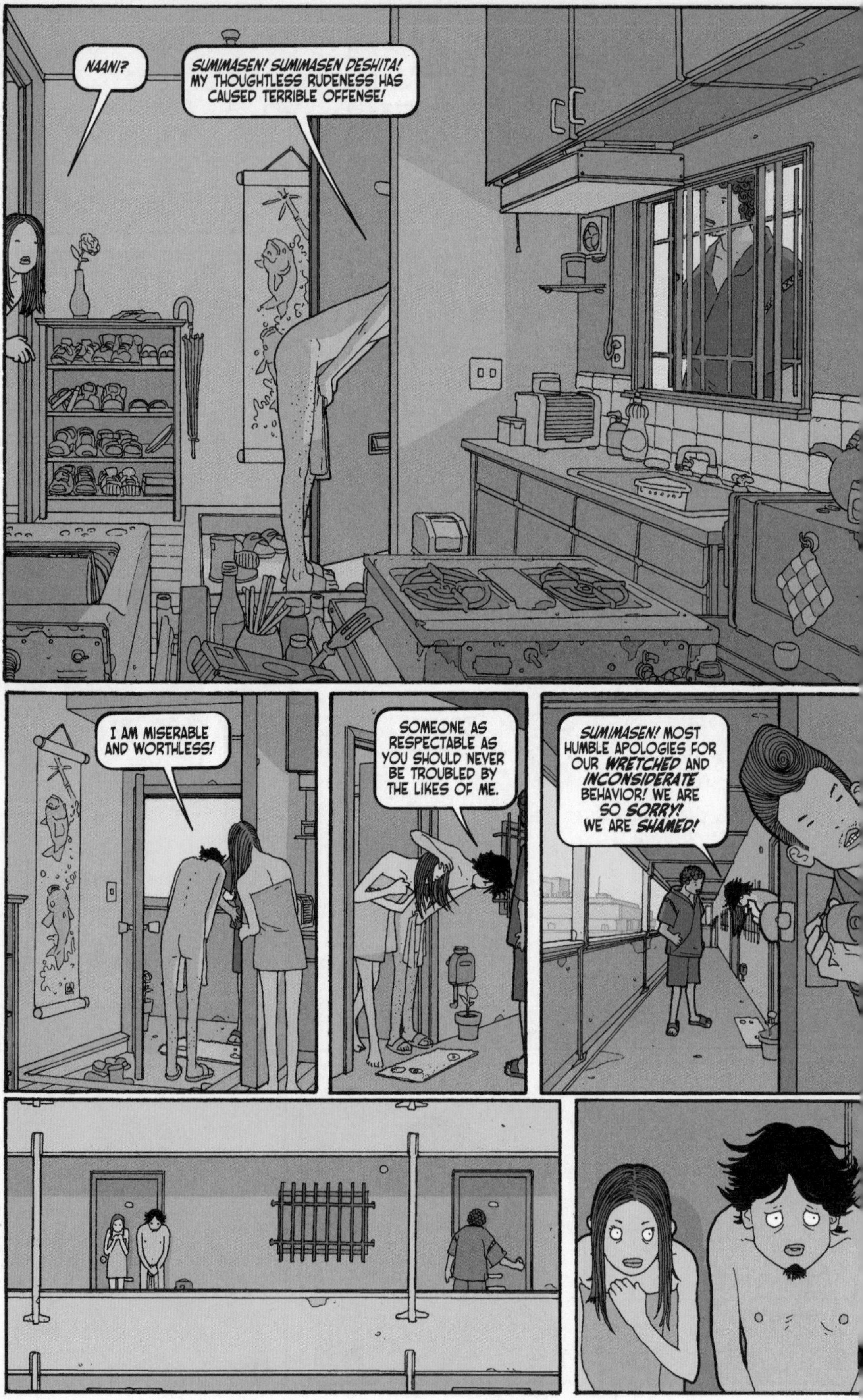
NAANI?
SUMIMASEN! SUMIMASEN DESHITA! MY THOUGHTLESS RUDENESS HAS CAUSED TERRIBLE OFFENSE!
I AM MISERABLE AND WORTHLESS!
SOMEONE AS RESPECTABLE AS YOU SHOULD NEVER BE TROUBLED BY THE LIKES OF ME.
SUMIMASEN! MOST HUMBLE APOLOGIES FOR OUR WRETCHED AND INCONSIDERATE BEHAVIOR! WE ARE SO SORRY! WE ARE SHAMED!

#!#@

OOOPH!

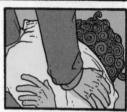

HAHAHAHA! RYUJI-KUN! YOUR NEIGHBOR *INSULTS* YOU AND YOU LET HIM OFF WITHOUT A BEATING!

SOME *GANGSTER!* I SHOULD HAVE SNUFFED YOU WITH THIS PILLOW! *HAHAHAHA!*

THIS IS YOUR ONLY WEAPON? DISGRACEFUL! WHERE'S YOUR *GUN?* YOUR *SWORD?*

ASK THE BOSS.

YOU SHOULD HAVE TAUGHT THAT NEIGHBOR A *LESSON.*

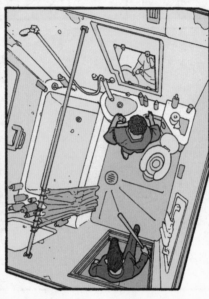

WHAT ARE YOU, AN *OYAJI?* NO ONE UNDER THE AGE OF FORTY-FOUR WEARS A *PUNCH-PERM* THESE DAYS.

THE *SUKI-GUMI* IS YOUR FAMILY NOW, *RYUJI-KUN.* DO *NOT* EMBARRASS US!

ESPECIALLY NOT NOW.

AGAINST MY BETTER JUDGMENT, THE BOSS HAS A *VERY IMPORTANT* JOB FOR YOU.

AAAYY? WHY ME?

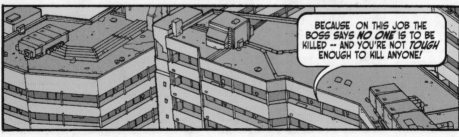

BECAUSE ON THIS JOB THE BOSS SAYS *NO ONE* IS TO BE KILLED -- AND YOU'RE NOT *TOUGH* ENOUGH TO KILL ANYONE!

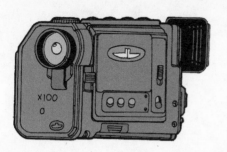

I AM MANAGER. WHAT IS -- PROBLEM?

I'M TRYING TO BUY THIS STUFF ON MY VISA.

AH, SO-KA.

AAY?

NAN-DA?

HMM. MISTER STE-BU.

STEVE.

DAIJOBU, STE-BU-SAN. MAYBE IT'S OKAY.

AFTER ALL THAT.

IT'S OKAY. SHE WILL HELP YOU. THANK YOU.

HEY, WHAT? LET GO OF THAT...

THEY'RE NOT HAPPY UNLESS THEY GIFT WRAP EVERYTHING.

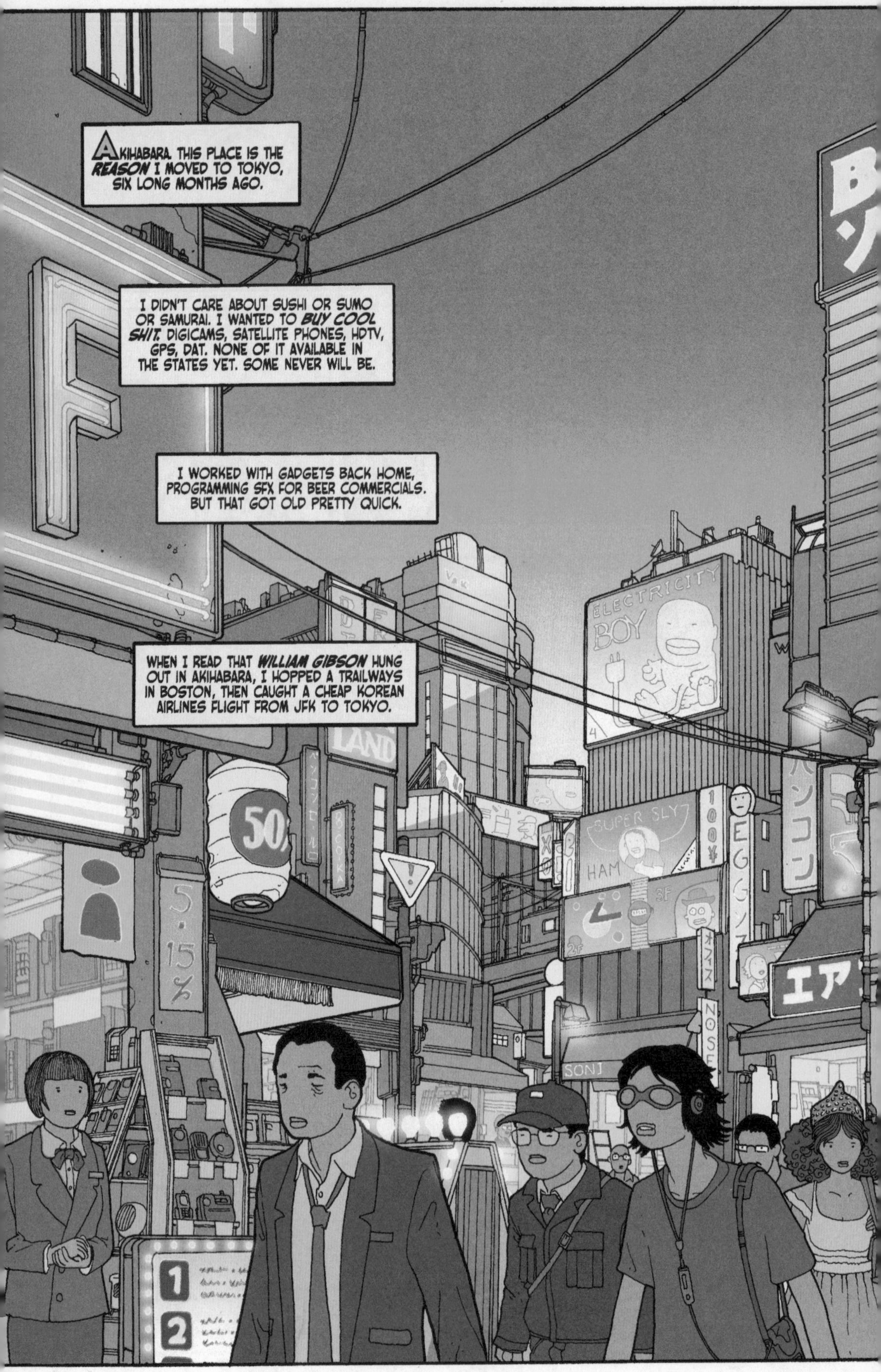
AKIHABARA. THIS PLACE IS THE *REASON* I MOVED TO TOKYO, SIX LONG MONTHS AGO.
I DIDN'T CARE ABOUT SUSHI OR SUMO OR SAMURAI. I WANTED TO *BUY COOL SHIT.* DIGICAMS, SATELLITE PHONES, HDTV, GPS, DAT. NONE OF IT AVAILABLE IN THE STATES YET. SOME NEVER WILL BE.
I WORKED WITH GADGETS BACK HOME, PROGRAMMING SFX FOR BEER COMMERCIALS. BUT THAT GOT OLD PRETTY QUICK.
WHEN I READ THAT *WILLIAM GIBSON* HUNG OUT IN AKIHABARA, I HOPPED A TRAILWAYS IN BOSTON, THEN CAUGHT A CHEAP KOREAN AIRLINES FLIGHT FROM JFK TO TOKYO.
ELECTRICITY BOY
SUPER SLY
HAM
LAND
パソコン
EGG
SONJ
エア

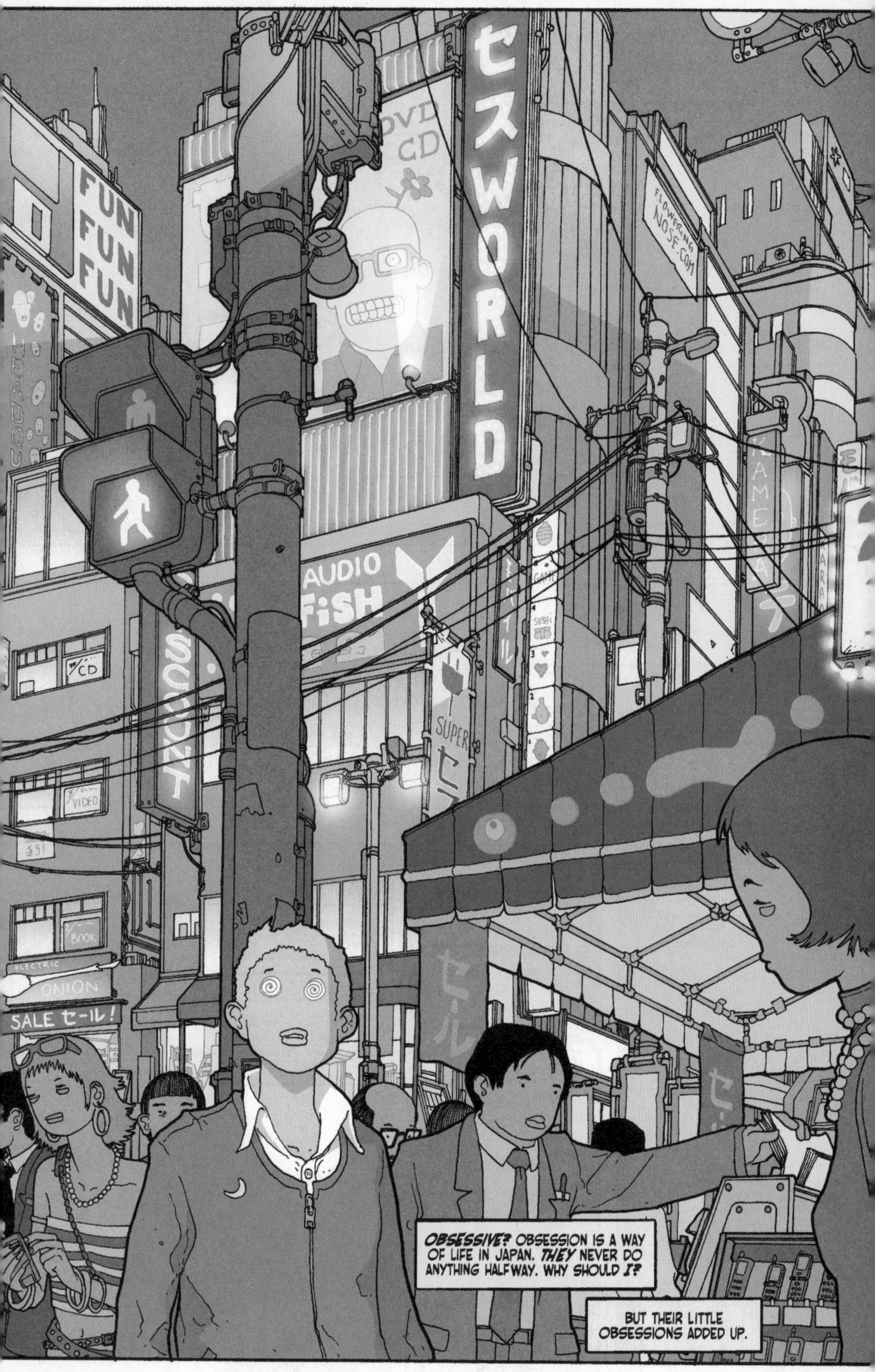
OBSESSIVE? OBSESSION IS A WAY OF LIFE IN JAPAN. THEY NEVER DO ANYTHING HALFWAY. WHY SHOULD I?
BUT THEIR LITTLE OBSESSIONS ADDED UP.

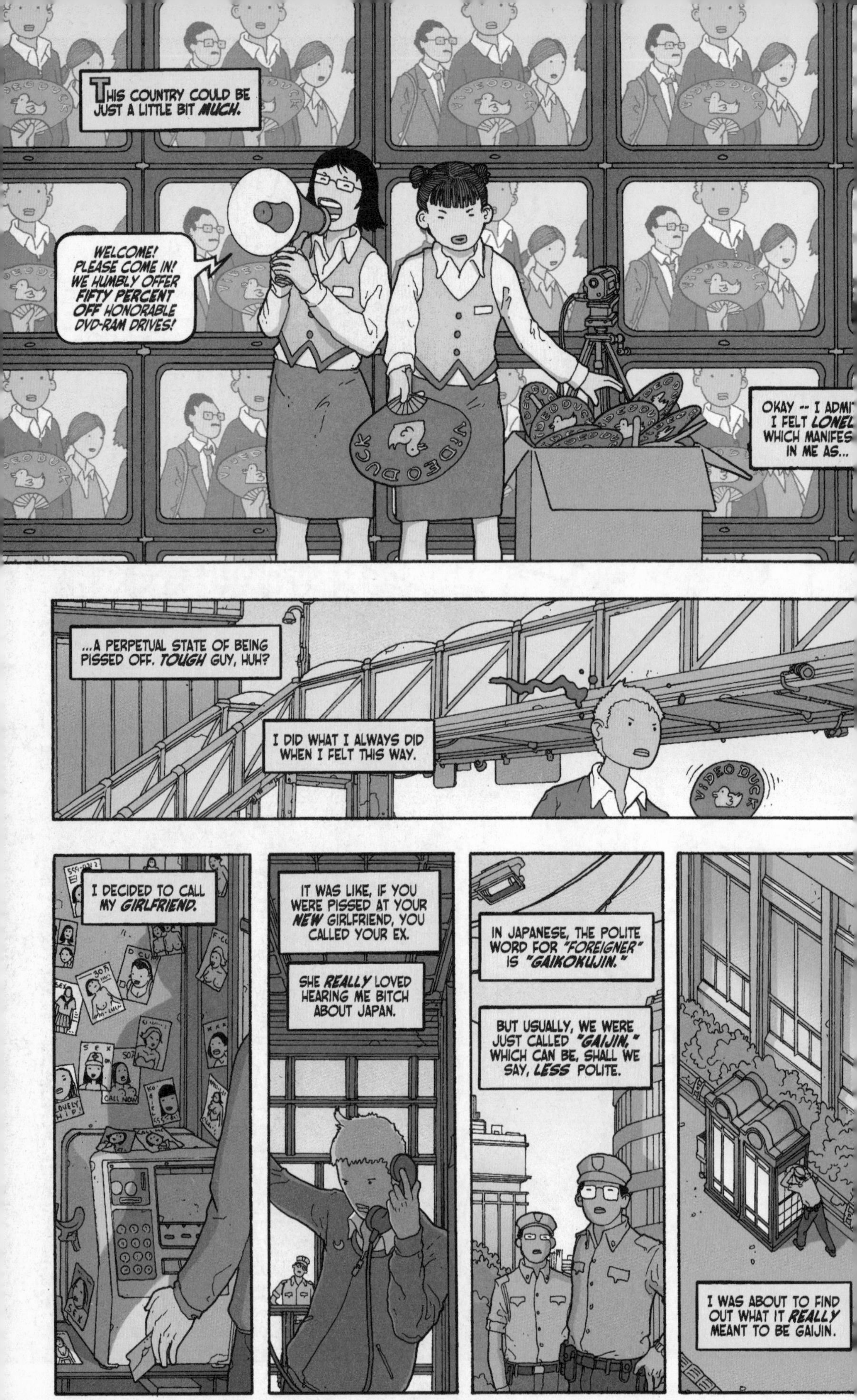
THIS COUNTRY COULD BE JUST A LITTLE BIT MUCH.
WELCOME! PLEASE COME IN! WE HUMBLY OFFER FIFTY PERCENT OFF HONORABLE DVD-RAM DRIVES!
VIDEODUCK
OKAY -- I ADMI I FELT LONEL WHICH MANIFES IN ME AS...
...A PERPETUAL STATE OF BEING PISSED OFF. TOUGH GUY, HUH?
I DID WHAT I ALWAYS DID WHEN I FELT THIS WAY.
VIDEODUCK
I DECIDED TO CALL MY GIRLFRIEND.
IT WAS LIKE, IF YOU WERE PISSED AT YOUR NEW GIRLFRIEND, YOU CALLED YOUR EX.
SHE REALLY LOVED HEARING ME BITCH ABOUT JAPAN.
IN JAPANESE, THE POLITE WORD FOR "FOREIGNER" IS "GAIKOKUJIN."
BUT USUALLY, WE WERE JUST CALLED "GAIJIN," WHICH CAN BE, SHALL WE SAY, LESS POLITE.
I WAS ABOUT TO FIND OUT WHAT IT REALLY MEANT TO BE GAIJIN.

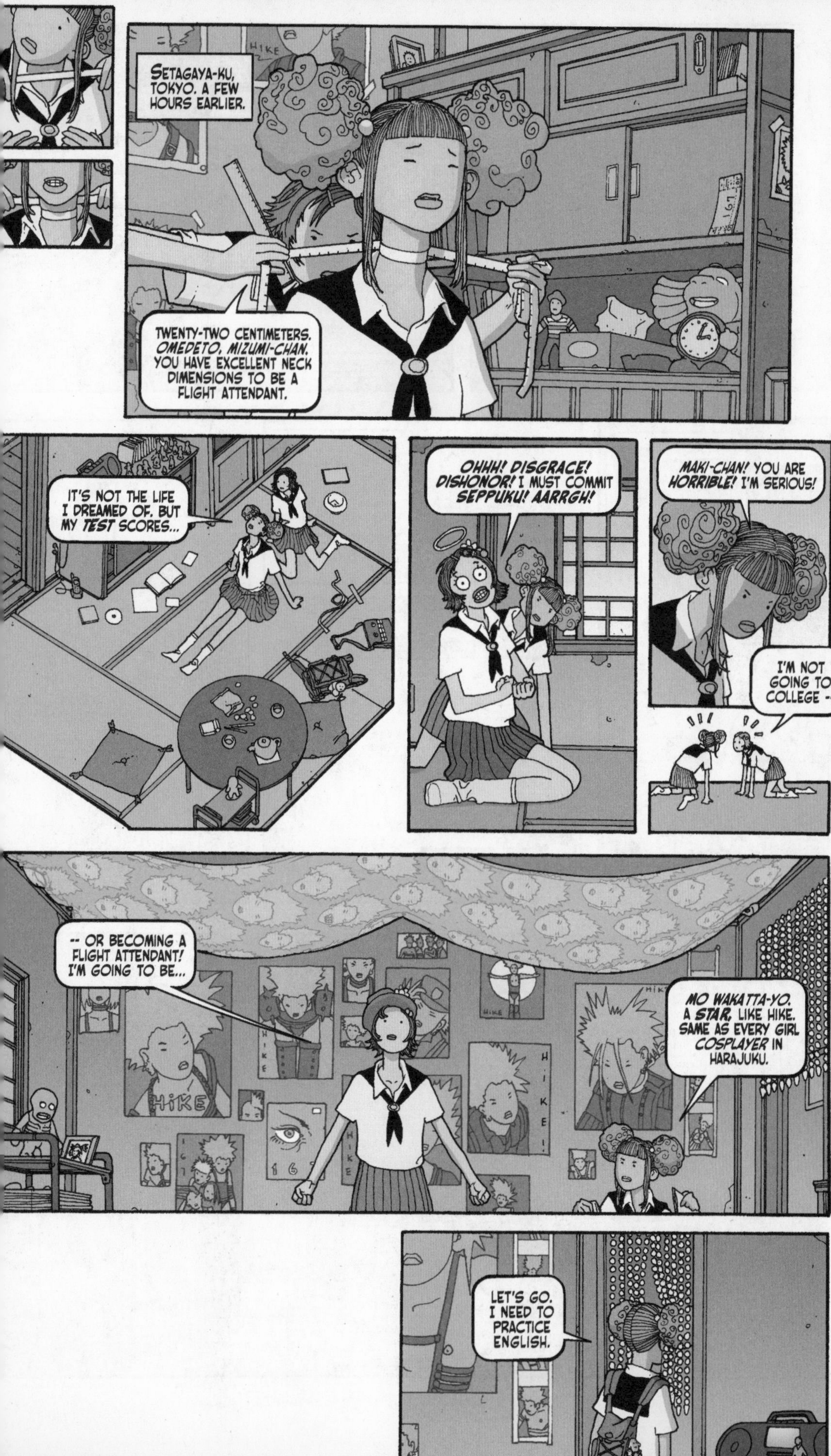
SETAGAYA-KU, TOKYO. A FEW HOURS EARLIER.
TWENTY-TWO CENTIMETERS. OMEDETO, MIZUMI-CHAN. YOU HAVE EXCELLENT NECK DIMENSIONS TO BE A FLIGHT ATTENDANT.
IT'S NOT THE LIFE I DREAMED OF. BUT MY TEST SCORES...
OHHH! DISGRACE! DISHONOR! I MUST COMMIT SEPPUKU! AARRGH!
MAKI-CHAN! YOU ARE HORRIBLE! I'M SERIOUS!
I'M NOT GOING TO COLLEGE --
-- OR BECOMING A FLIGHT ATTENDANT! I'M GOING TO BE...
MO WAKATTA-YO. A STAR, LIKE HIKE. SAME AS EVERY GIRL COSPLAYER IN HARAJUKU.
LET'S GO. I NEED TO PRACTICE ENGLISH.

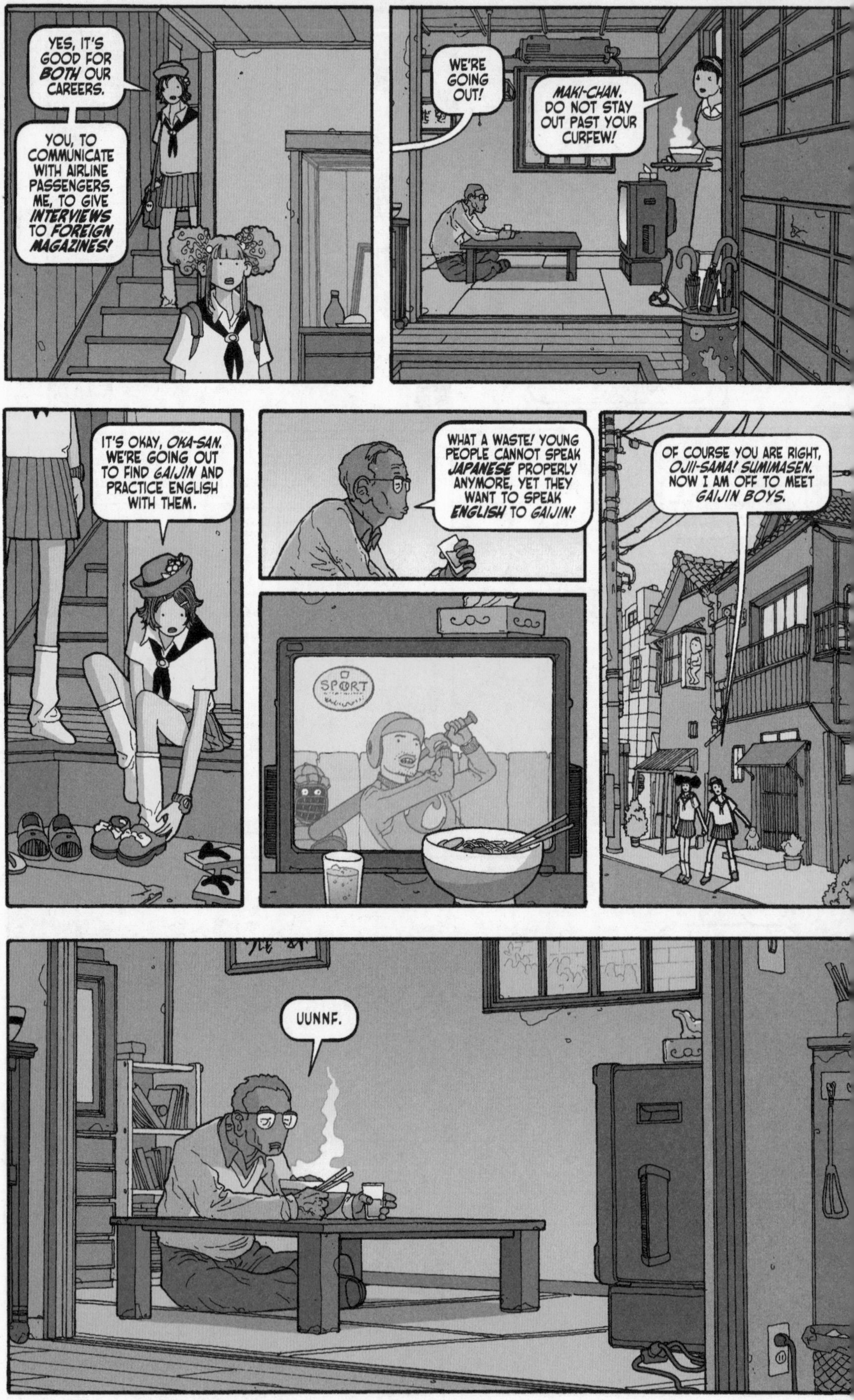

YES, IT'S GOOD FOR *BOTH* OUR CAREERS.
YOU, TO COMMUNICATE WITH AIRLINE PASSENGERS. ME, TO GIVE *INTERVIEWS* TO *FOREIGN MAGAZINES!*
WE'RE GOING OUT!
MAKI-CHAN. DO NOT STAY OUT PAST YOUR CURFEW!
IT'S OKAY, *OKA-SAN.* WE'RE GOING OUT TO FIND *GAIJIN* AND PRACTICE ENGLISH WITH THEM.
WHAT A WASTE! YOUNG PEOPLE CANNOT SPEAK *JAPANESE* PROPERLY ANYMORE, YET THEY WANT TO SPEAK *ENGLISH* TO *GAIJIN!*
SPORT
OF COURSE YOU ARE RIGHT, *OJII-SAMA! SUMIMASEN.* NOW I AM OFF TO MEET *GAIJIN BOYS.*
UUNNF.

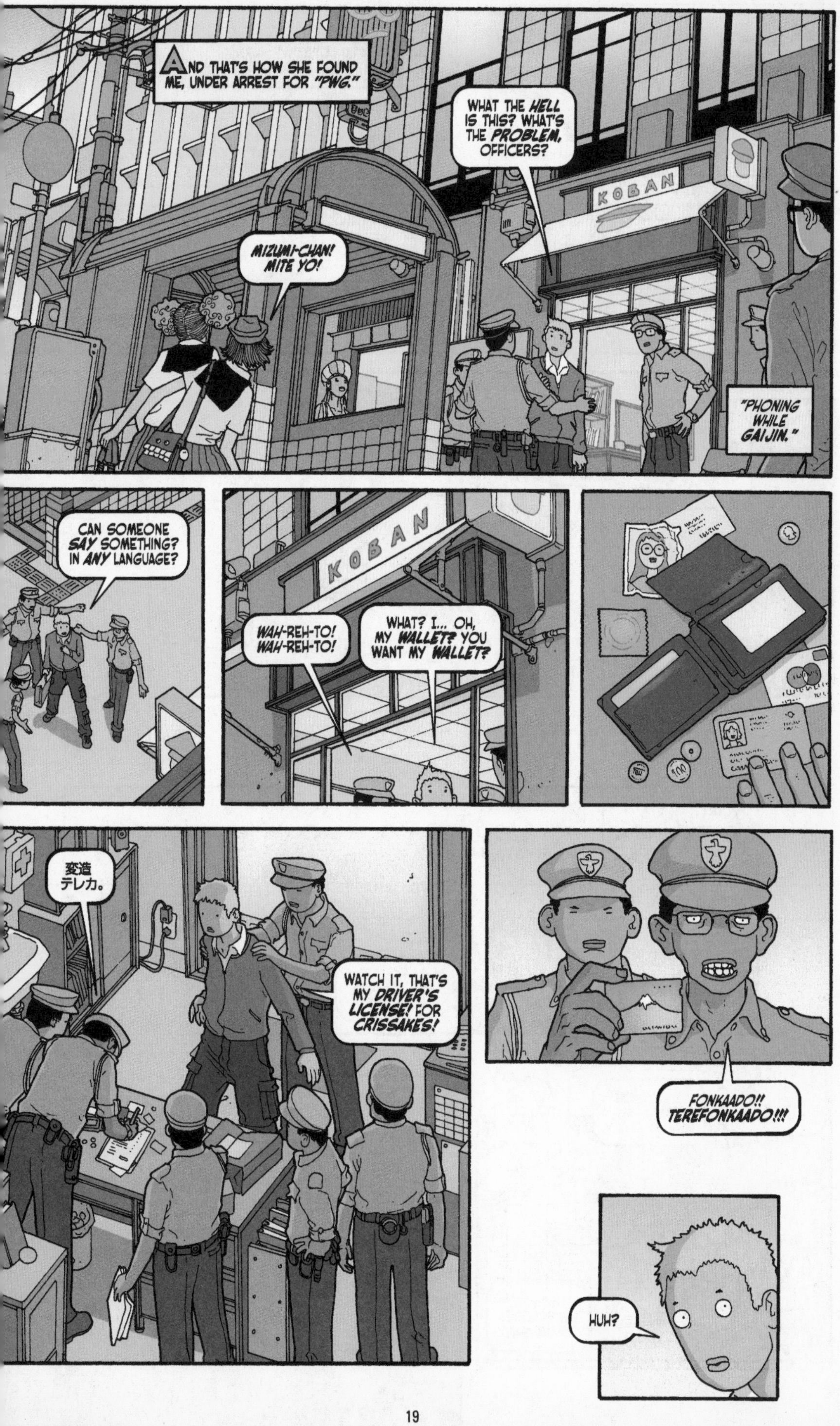

AND THAT'S HOW SHE FOUND ME, UNDER ARREST FOR "PWG."
KOBAN
WHAT THE HELL IS THIS? WHAT'S THE PROBLEM, OFFICERS?
MIZUMI-CHAN! MITE YO!
"PHONING WHILE GAIJIN."
CAN SOMEONE SAY SOMETHING? IN ANY LANGUAGE?
KOBAN
WAH-REH-TO! WAH-REH-TO!
WHAT? I... OH, MY WALLET? YOU WANT MY WALLET?
変造
テレカ。
WATCH IT, THAT'S MY DRIVER'S LICENSE! FOR CRISSAKES!
FONKAADO!! TEREFONKAADO!!!
HUH?

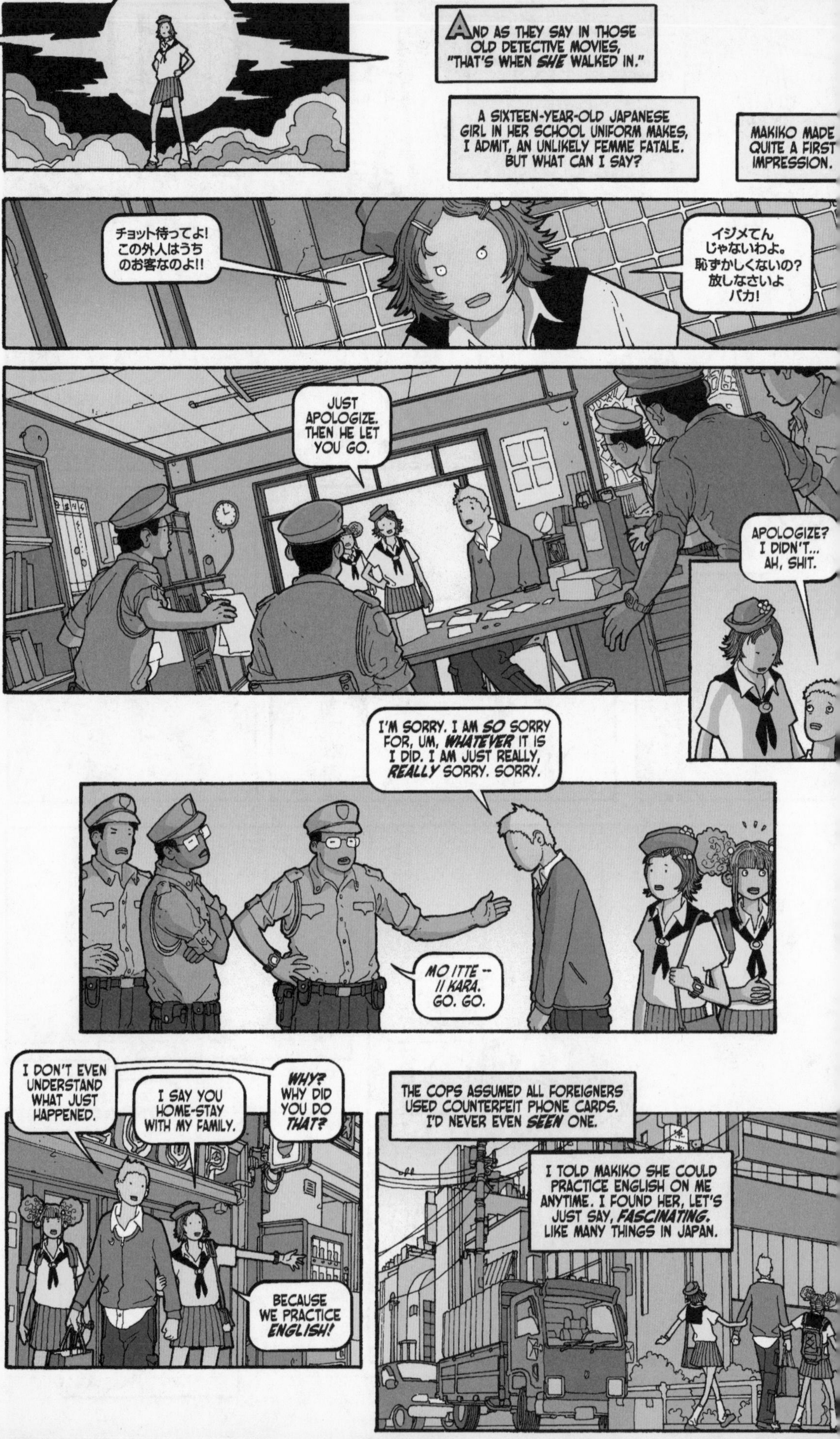

AND AS THEY SAY IN THOSE OLD DETECTIVE MOVIES, "THAT'S WHEN SHE WALKED IN."
A SIXTEEN-YEAR-OLD JAPANESE GIRL IN HER SCHOOL UNIFORM MAKES, I ADMIT, AN UNLIKELY FEMME FATALE. BUT WHAT CAN I SAY?
MAKIKO MADE QUITE A FIRST IMPRESSION.
チョット待ってよ! この外人はうちのお客なのよ!!
イジメてんじゃないわよ。恥ずかしくないの? 放しなさいよ バカ!
JUST APOLOGIZE. THEN HE LET YOU GO.
APOLOGIZE? I DIDN'T... AH, SHIT.
I'M SORRY. I AM SO SORRY FOR, UM, WHATEVER IT IS I DID. I AM JUST REALLY, REALLY SORRY. SORRY.
MO ITTE -- II KARA. GO. GO.
I DON'T EVEN UNDERSTAND WHAT JUST HAPPENED.
WHY? WHY DID YOU DO THAT?
I SAY YOU HOME-STAY WITH MY FAMILY.
BECAUSE WE PRACTICE ENGLISH!
THE COPS ASSUMED ALL FOREIGNERS USED COUNTERFEIT PHONE CARDS. I'D NEVER EVEN SEEN ONE.
I TOLD MAKIKO SHE COULD PRACTICE ENGLISH ON ME ANYTIME. I FOUND HER, LET'S JUST SAY, FASCINATING. LIKE MANY THINGS IN JAPAN.

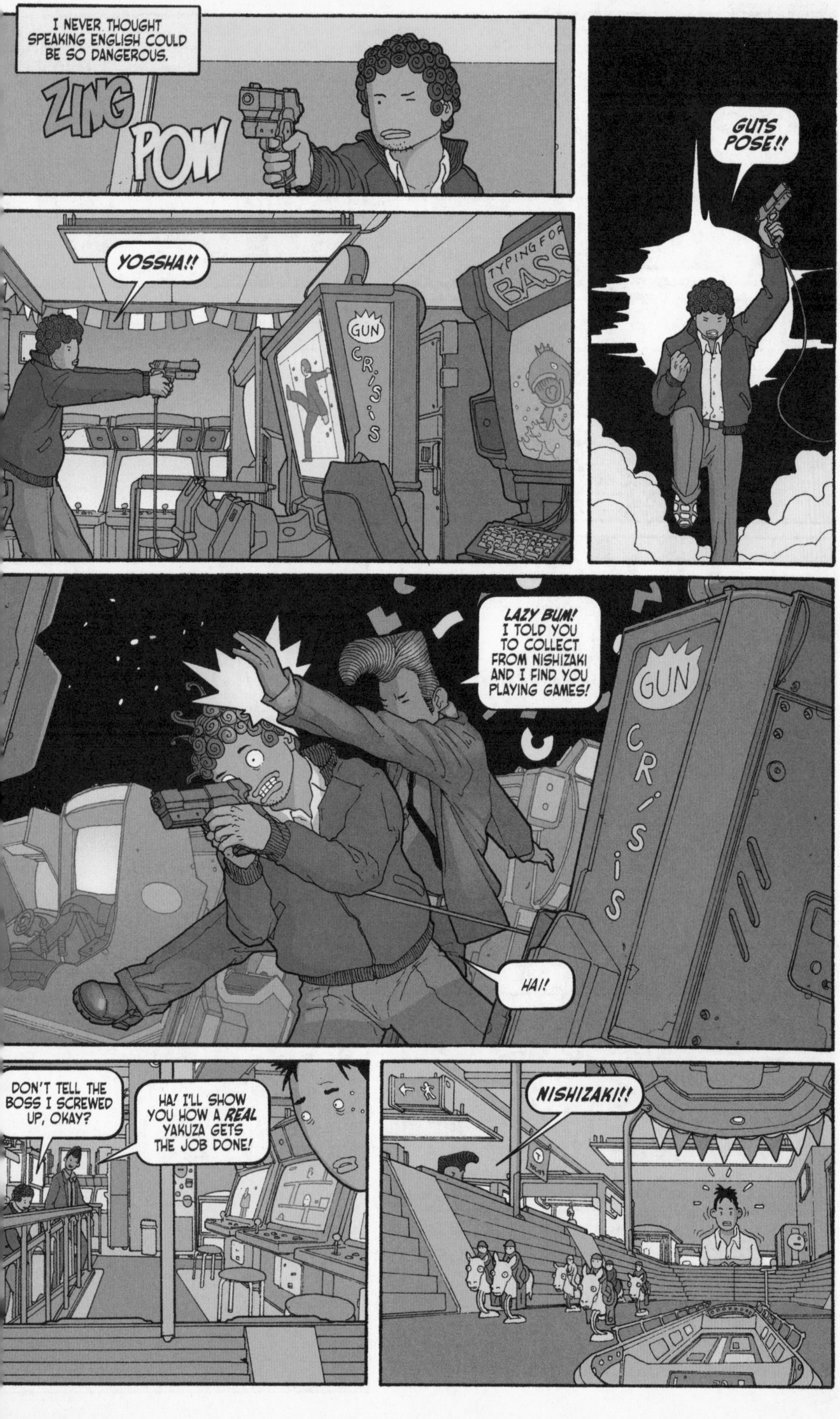
I NEVER THOUGHT SPEAKING ENGLISH COULD BE SO DANGEROUS.
ZING
POW
YOSSHA!!
TYPING FOR BASS
GUN CRISIS
GUTS POSE!!
LAZY BUM! I TOLD YOU TO COLLECT FROM NISHIZAKI AND I FIND YOU PLAYING GAMES!
GUN CRISIS
HAI!
DON'T TELL THE BOSS I SCREWED UP, OKAY?
HA! I'LL SHOW YOU HOW A *REAL* YAKUZA GETS THE JOB DONE!
NISHIZAKI!!

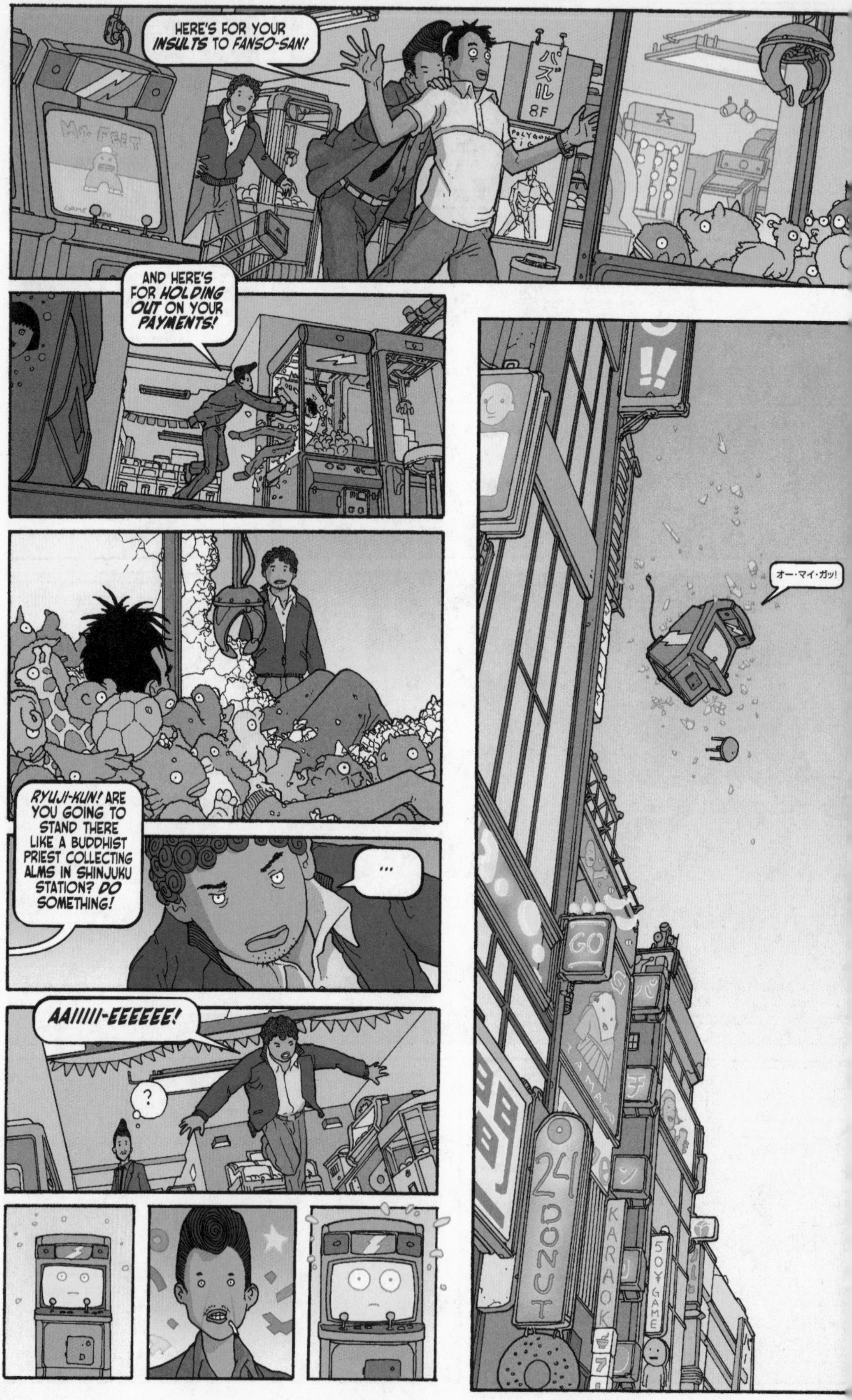
HERE'S FOR YOUR *INSULTS* TO FANSO-SAN!
パズル 8F
AND HERE'S FOR *HOLDING OUT* ON YOUR *PAYMENTS!*
RYUJI-KUN! ARE YOU GOING TO STAND THERE LIKE A BUDDHIST PRIEST COLLECTING ALMS IN SHINJUKU STATION? *DO* SOMETHING!
...
AAIIIII-EEEEEE!
?
オー・マイ・ガッ!
GO
TAMAGO
24 DONUT
KARAOKE
50¥ GAME

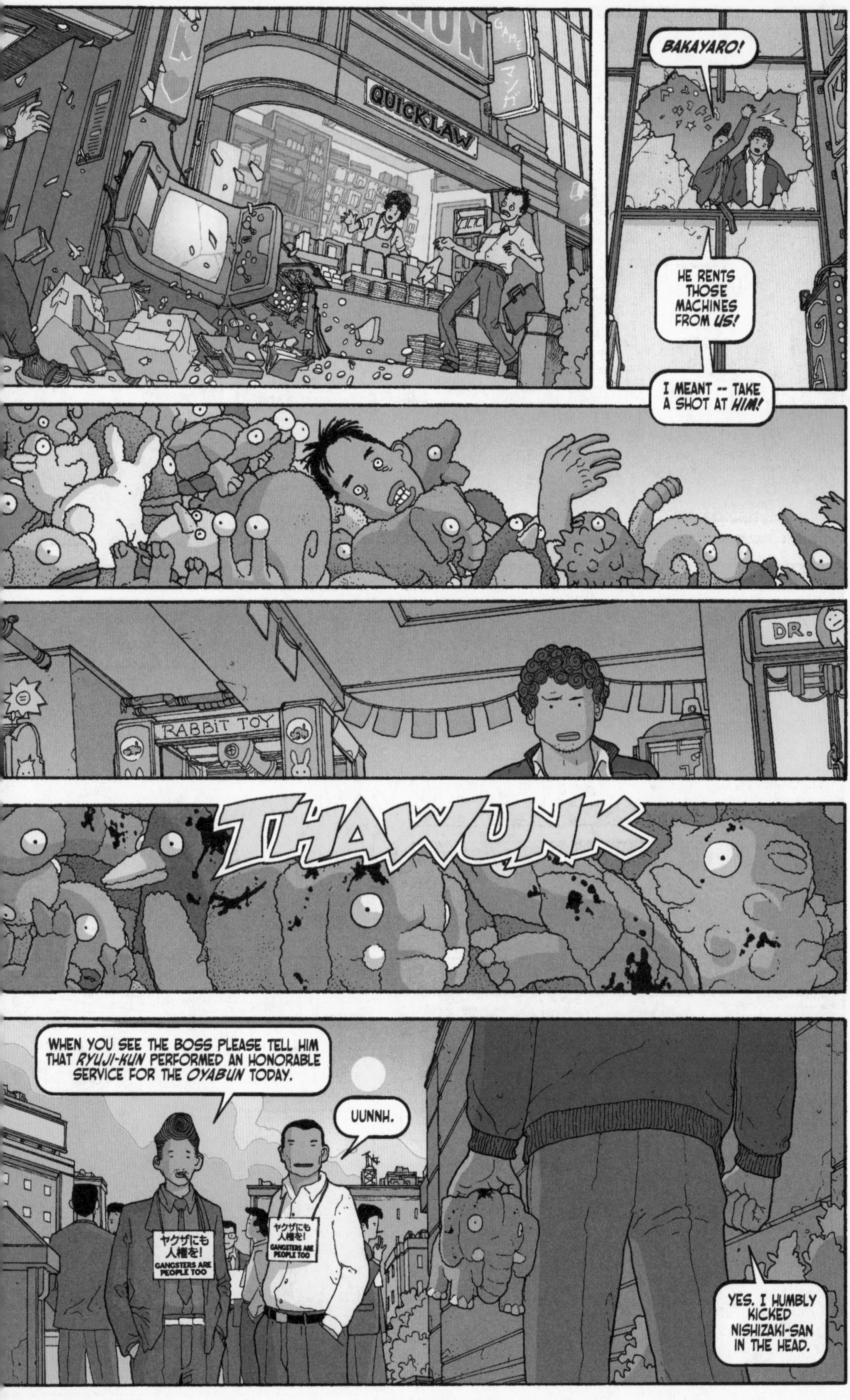
QUICKLAW
GAME
マンガ
BAKAYARO!
HE RENTS THOSE MACHINES FROM US!
I MEANT -- TAKE A SHOT AT HIM!
DR.
RABBIT TOY
THAWUNK
WHEN YOU SEE THE BOSS PLEASE TELL HIM THAT RYUJI-KUN PERFORMED AN HONORABLE SERVICE FOR THE OYABUN TODAY.
UUNNH.
ヤクザにも人権を! GANGSTERS ARE PEOPLE TOO
ヤクザにも人権を! GANGSTERS ARE PEOPLE TOO
YES. I HUMBLY KICKED NISHIZAKI-SAN IN THE HEAD.

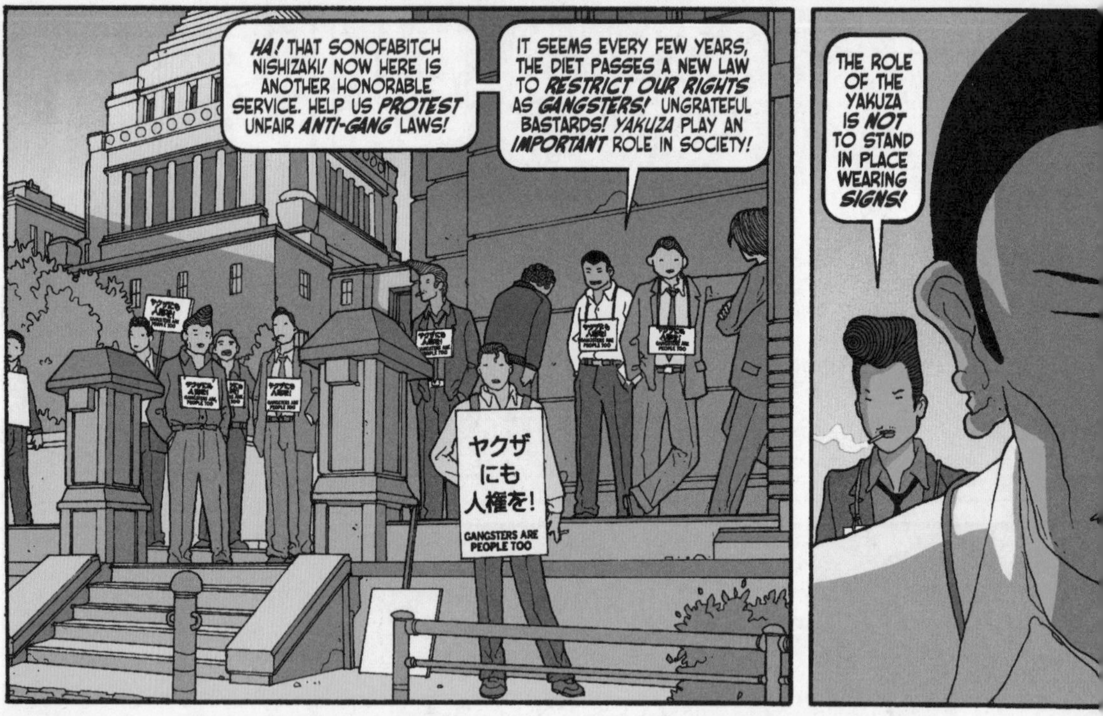
HA! THAT SONOFABITCH NISHIZAKI! NOW HERE IS ANOTHER HONORABLE SERVICE. HELP US PROTEST UNFAIR ANTI-GANG LAWS!
IT SEEMS EVERY FEW YEARS, THE DIET PASSES A NEW LAW TO RESTRICT OUR RIGHTS AS GANGSTERS! UNGRATEFUL BASTARDS! YAKUZA PLAY AN IMPORTANT ROLE IN SOCIETY!
ヤクザにも人権を!
GANGSTERS ARE PEOPLE TOO
THE ROLE OF THE YAKUZA IS NOT TO STAND IN PLACE WEARING SIGNS!

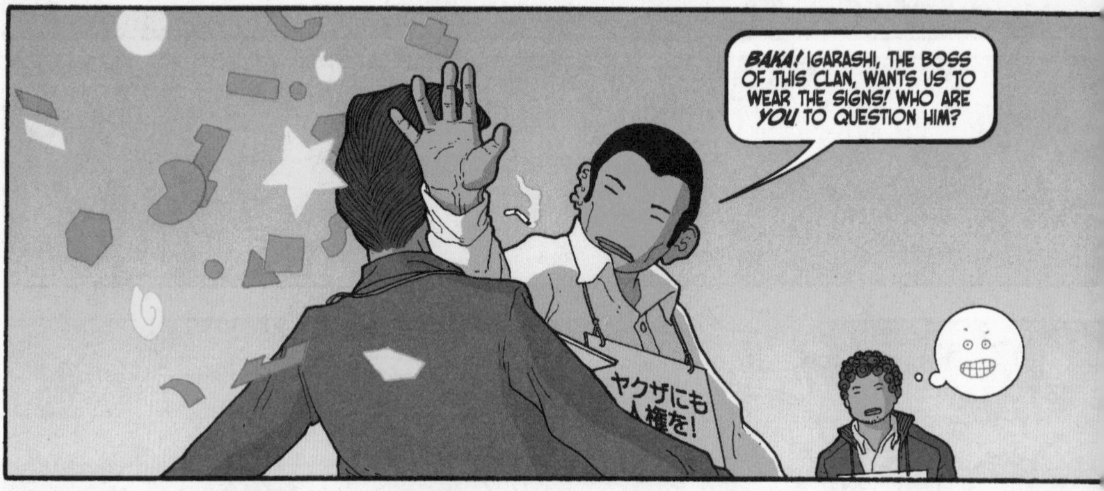
BAKA! IGARASHI, THE BOSS OF THIS CLAN, WANTS US TO WEAR THE SIGNS! WHO ARE YOU TO QUESTION HIM?
ヤクザにも人権を!

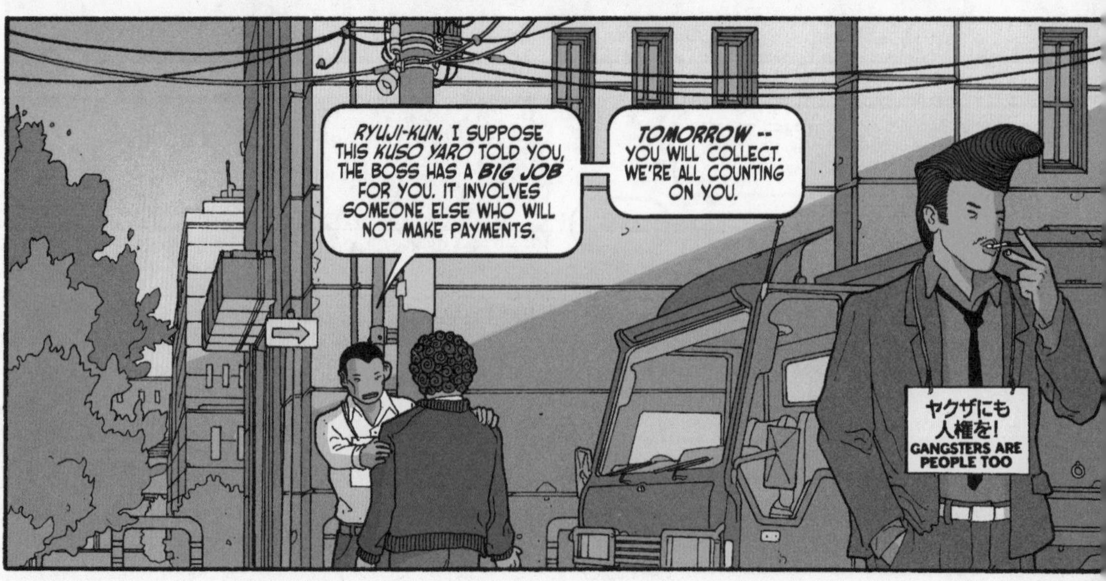
RYUJI-KUN, I SUPPOSE THIS KUSO YARO TOLD YOU, THE BOSS HAS A BIG JOB FOR YOU. IT INVOLVES SOMEONE ELSE WHO WILL NOT MAKE PAYMENTS.
TOMORROW -- YOU WILL COLLECT. WE'RE ALL COUNTING ON YOU.
ヤクザにも人権を!
GANGSTERS ARE PEOPLE TOO

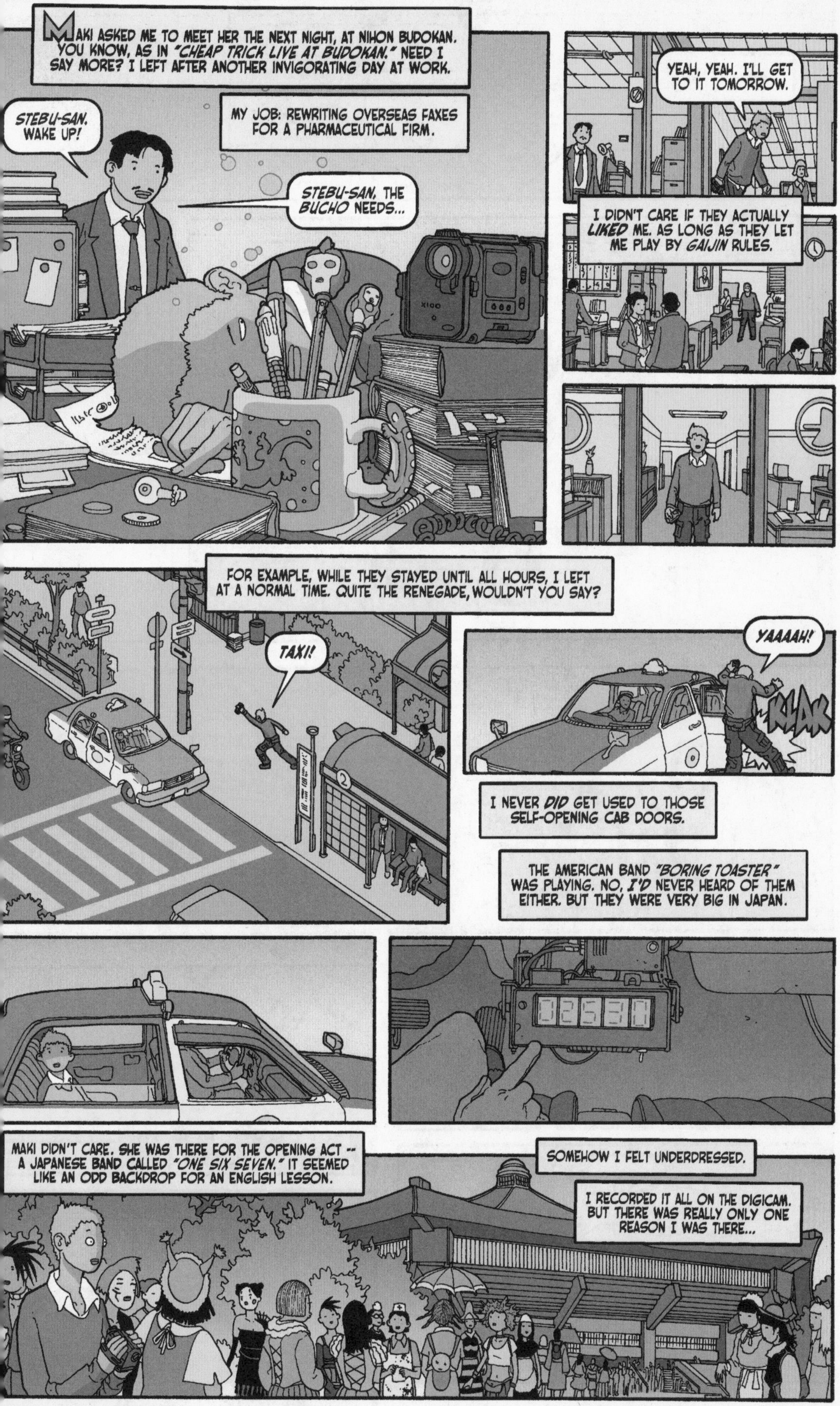

MAKI ASKED ME TO MEET HER THE NEXT NIGHT, AT NIHON BUDOKAN. YOU KNOW, AS IN *"CHEAP TRICK LIVE AT BUDOKAN."* NEED I SAY MORE? I LEFT AFTER ANOTHER INVIGORATING DAY AT WORK.
STEBU-SAN. WAKE UP!
MY JOB: REWRITING OVERSEAS FAXES FOR A PHARMACEUTICAL FIRM.
STEBU-SAN, THE *BUCHO* NEEDS...
YEAH, YEAH. I'LL GET TO IT TOMORROW.
I DIDN'T CARE IF THEY ACTUALLY *LIKED* ME. AS LONG AS THEY LET ME PLAY BY *GAIJIN* RULES.
FOR EXAMPLE, WHILE THEY STAYED UNTIL ALL HOURS, I LEFT AT A NORMAL TIME. QUITE THE RENEGADE, WOULDN'T YOU SAY?
TAXI!
YAAAAH!
KLAK
I NEVER *DID* GET USED TO THOSE SELF-OPENING CAB DOORS.
THE AMERICAN BAND *"BORING TOASTER"* WAS PLAYING. NO, *I'D* NEVER HEARD OF THEM EITHER. BUT THEY WERE VERY BIG IN JAPAN.
MAKI DIDN'T CARE. SHE WAS THERE FOR THE OPENING ACT -- A JAPANESE BAND CALLED *"ONE SIX SEVEN."* IT SEEMED LIKE AN ODD BACKDROP FOR AN ENGLISH LESSON.
SOMEHOW I FELT UNDERDRESSED.
I RECORDED IT ALL ON THE DIGICAM. BUT THERE WAS REALLY ONLY ONE REASON I WAS THERE...

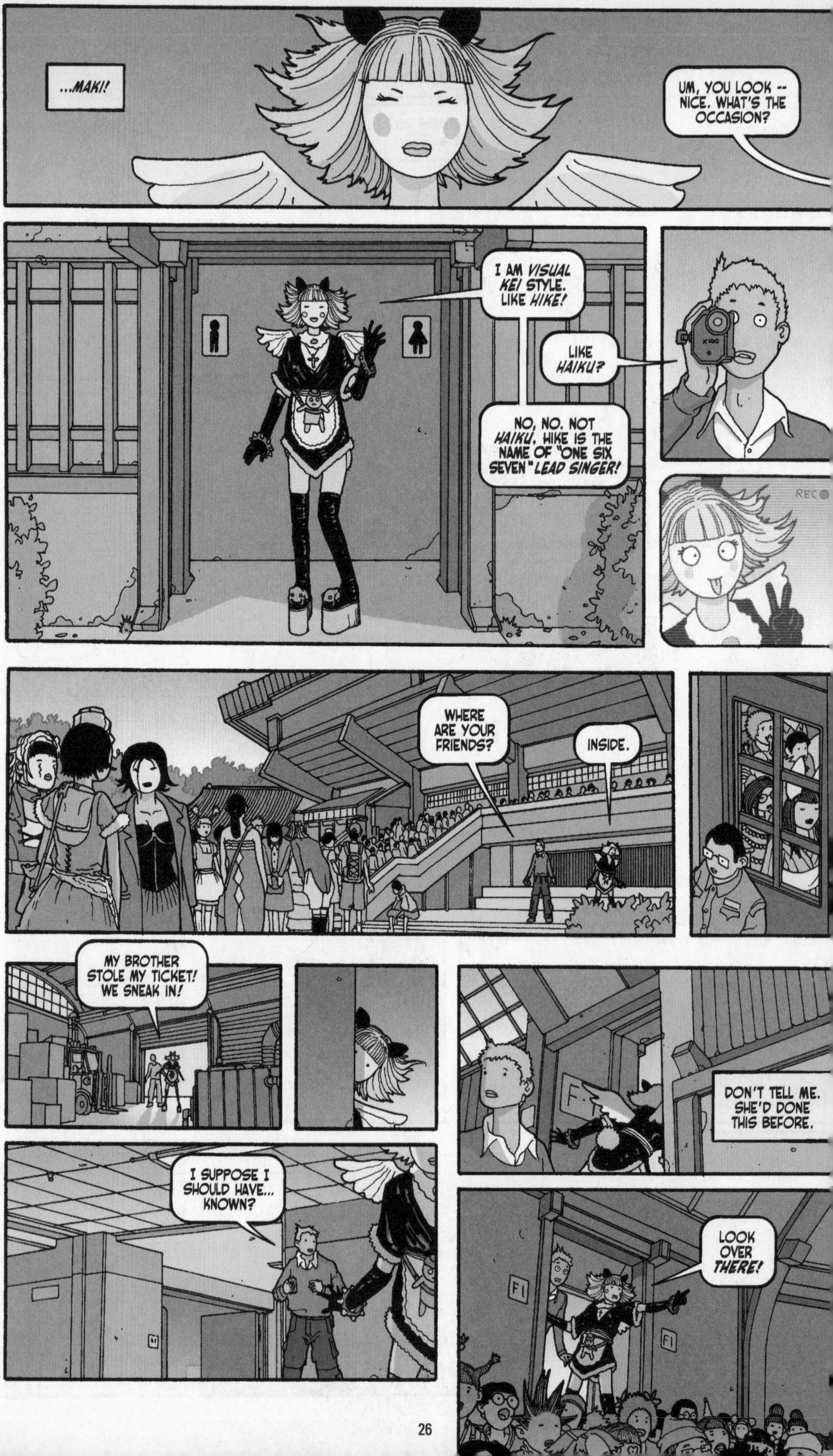

...MAKI!
UM, YOU LOOK -- NICE. WHAT'S THE OCCASION?
I AM VISUAL KEI STYLE. LIKE HIKE!
LIKE HAIKU?
NO, NO. NOT HAIKU. HIKE IS THE NAME OF "ONE SIX SEVEN" LEAD SINGER!
REC
WHERE ARE YOUR FRIENDS?
INSIDE.
MY BROTHER STOLE MY TICKET! WE SNEAK IN!
DON'T TELL ME. SHE'D DONE THIS BEFORE.
I SUPPOSE I SHOULD HAVE... KNOWN?
LOOK OVER THERE!

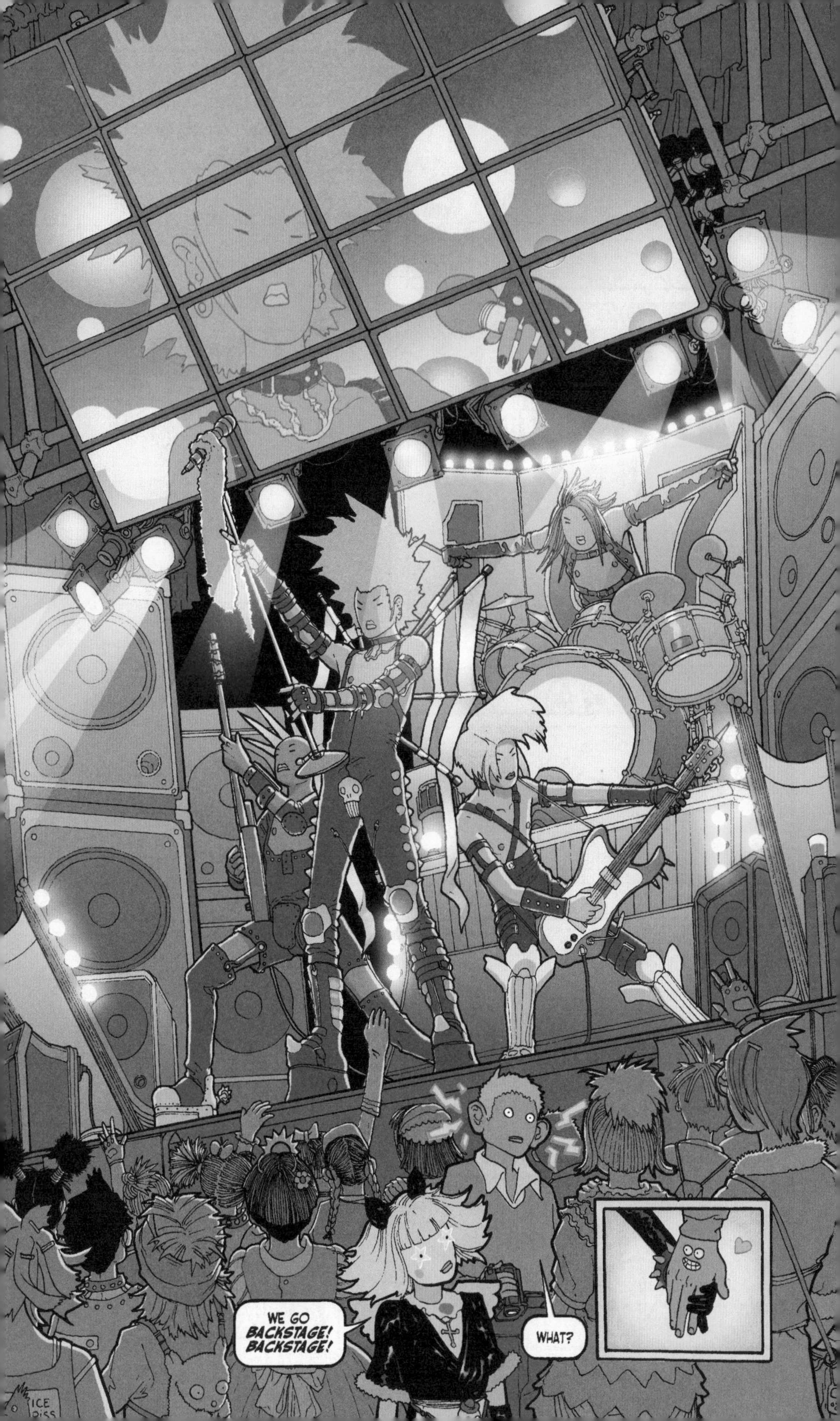
WE GO BACKSTAGE! BACKSTAGE!
WHAT?

SO, WHAT'S YOUR PLAN FOR GETTING PAST SECURITY?

I SAY YOU ARE *FAMOUS FOREIGN JOURNALIST.*

OH.

WHAT??

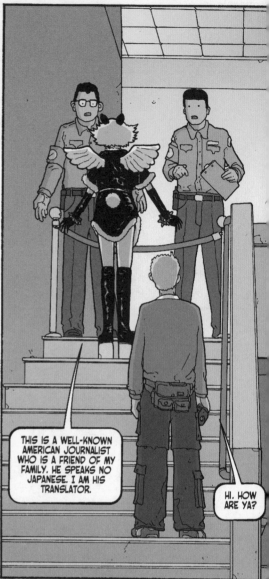

THIS IS A WELL-KNOWN AMERICAN JOURNALIST WHO IS A FRIEND OF MY FAMILY. HE SPEAKS NO JAPANESE. I AM HIS TRANSLATOR.

HI. HOW ARE YA?

PU-REH-SU PAHSS, ONEGAISHIMASU?

UM, *NIHONGO TABE MASEN!* TABE MASEN!

HEAR THAT? I TOLD THEM I DON'T SPEAK JAPANESE!

NO, YOU SAY, "I DON'T *EAT* JAPANESE!"

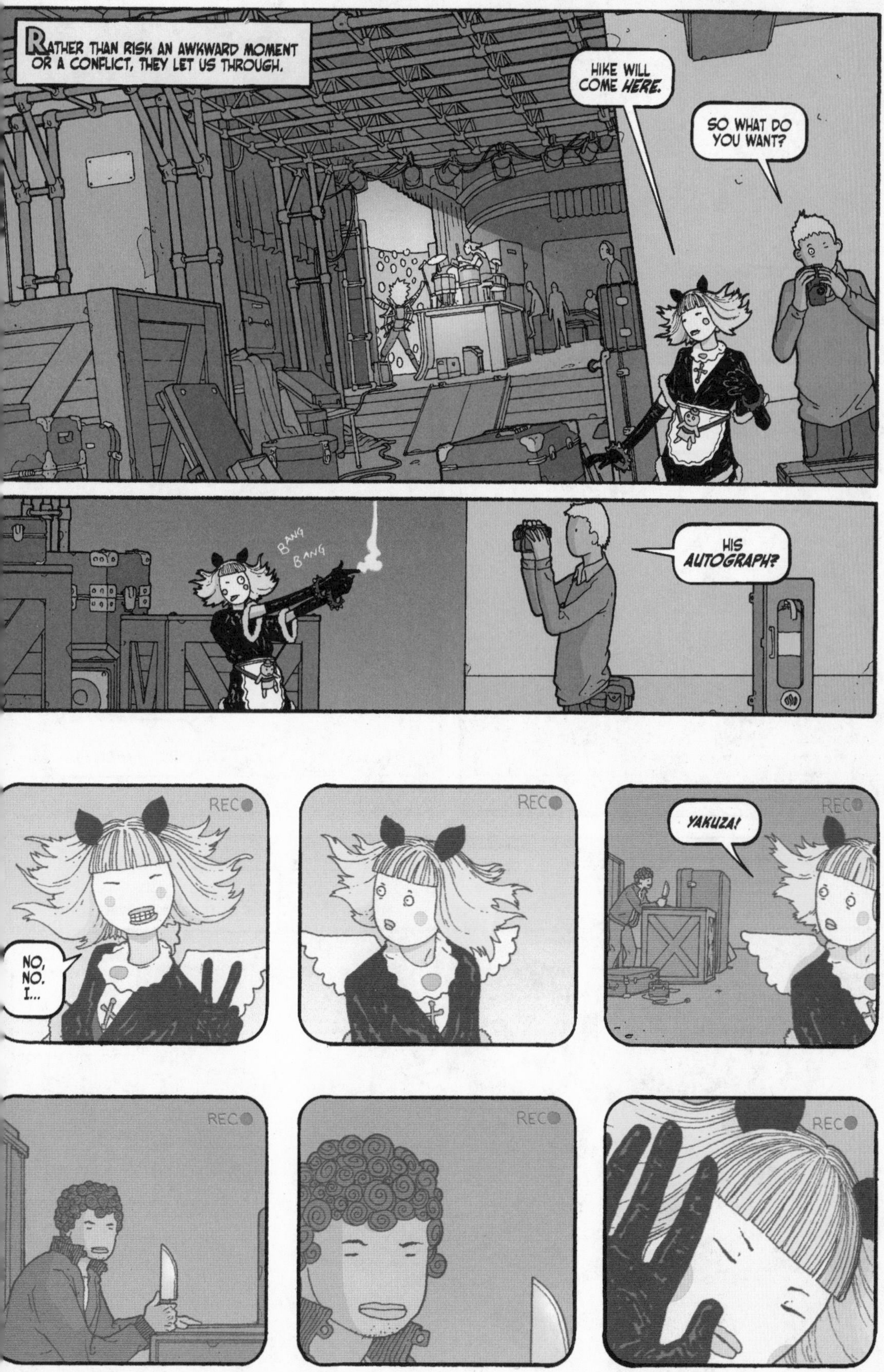
RATHER THAN RISK AN AWKWARD MOMENT OR A CONFLICT, THEY LET US THROUGH.
HIKE WILL COME *HERE.*
SO WHAT DO YOU WANT?
BANG BANG
HIS *AUTOGRAPH?*
REC
NO, NO. I...
REC
REC
YAKUZA!
REC
REC
REC

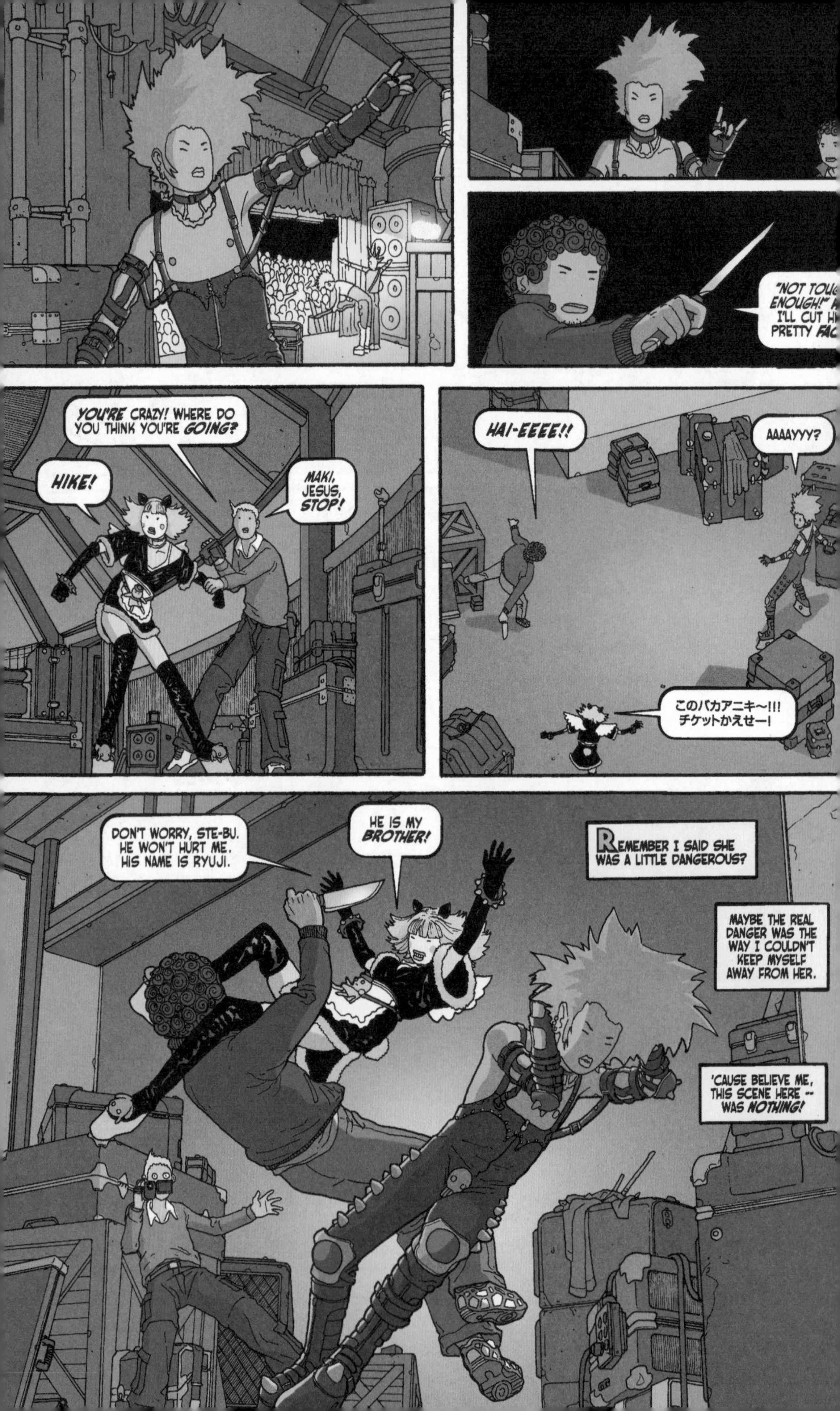
"NOT TOUG
ENOUGH!"
I'LL CUT H
PRETTY FAC
YOU'RE CRAZY! WHERE DO YOU THINK YOU'RE GOING?
HIKE!
MAKI, JESUS, STOP!
HAI-EEEE!!
AAAAYYY?
このバカアニキ〜!!!
チケットかえせー!
DON'T WORRY, STE-BU. HE WON'T HURT ME. HIS NAME IS RYUJI.
HE IS MY BROTHER!
REMEMBER I SAID SHE WAS A LITTLE DANGEROUS?
MAYBE THE REAL DANGER WAS THE WAY I COULDN'T KEEP MYSELF AWAY FROM HER.
'CAUSE BELIEVE ME, THIS SCENE HERE -- WAS NOTHING!

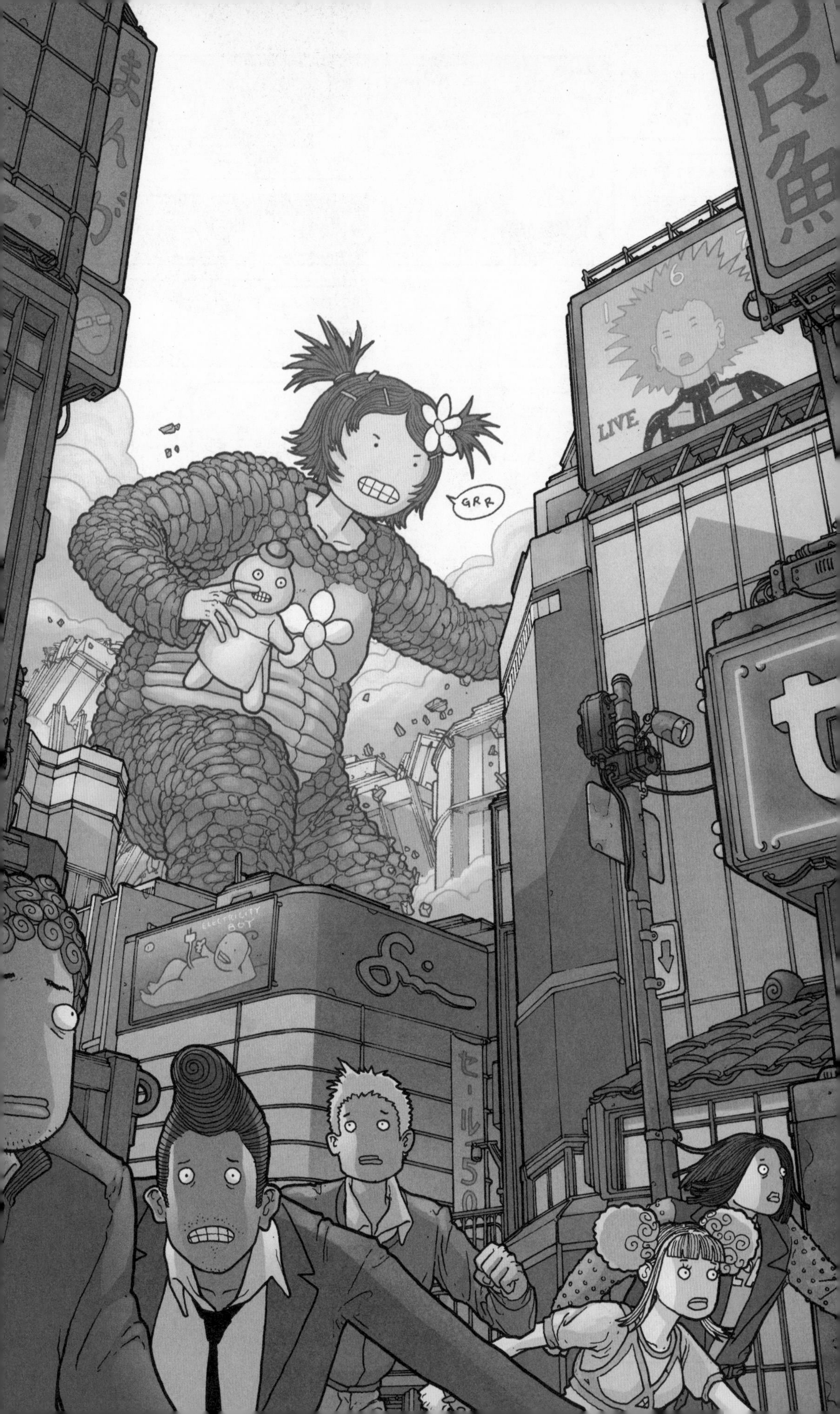
DR魚
LIVE
GRR
ELECTRICITY BOT
セール50

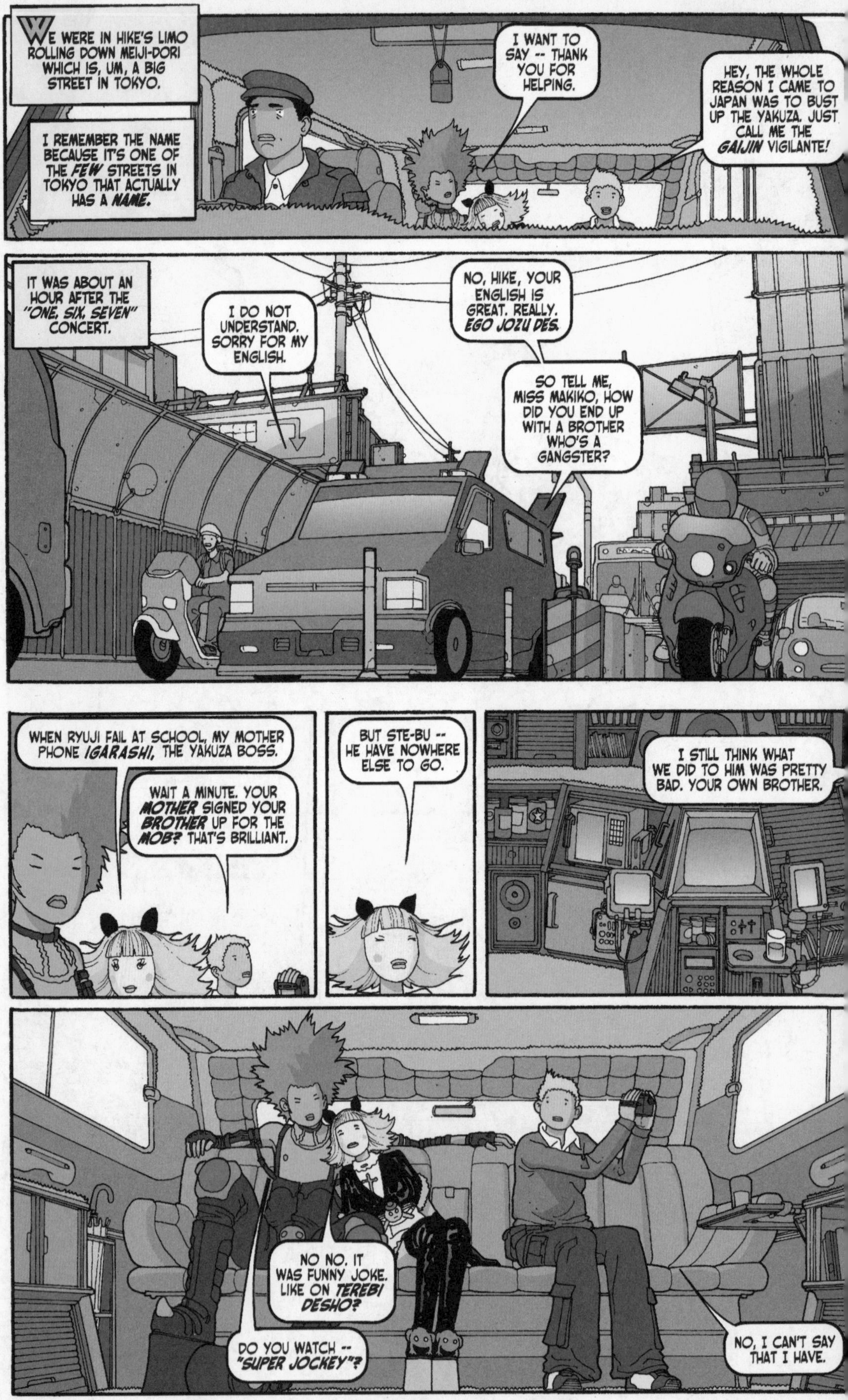
WE WERE IN HIKE'S LIMO ROLLING DOWN MEIJI-DORI WHICH IS, UM, A BIG STREET IN TOKYO.
I REMEMBER THE NAME BECAUSE IT'S ONE OF THE FEW STREETS IN TOKYO THAT ACTUALLY HAS A NAME.
I WANT TO SAY -- THANK YOU FOR HELPING.
HEY, THE WHOLE REASON I CAME TO JAPAN WAS TO BUST UP THE YAKUZA. JUST CALL ME THE GAIJIN VIGILANTE!
IT WAS ABOUT AN HOUR AFTER THE "ONE, SIX, SEVEN" CONCERT.
I DO NOT UNDERSTAND. SORRY FOR MY ENGLISH.
NO, HIKE, YOUR ENGLISH IS GREAT. REALLY. EGO JOZU DES.
SO TELL ME, MISS MAKIKO, HOW DID YOU END UP WITH A BROTHER WHO'S A GANGSTER?
WHEN RYUJI FAIL AT SCHOOL, MY MOTHER PHONE IGARASHI, THE YAKUZA BOSS.
WAIT A MINUTE. YOUR MOTHER SIGNED YOUR BROTHER UP FOR THE MOB? THAT'S BRILLIANT.
BUT STE-BU -- HE HAVE NOWHERE ELSE TO GO.
I STILL THINK WHAT WE DID TO HIM WAS PRETTY BAD. YOUR OWN BROTHER.
NO NO. IT WAS FUNNY JOKE. LIKE ON TEREBI DESHO?
DO YOU WATCH -- "SUPER JOCKEY"?
NO, I CAN'T SAY THAT I HAVE.

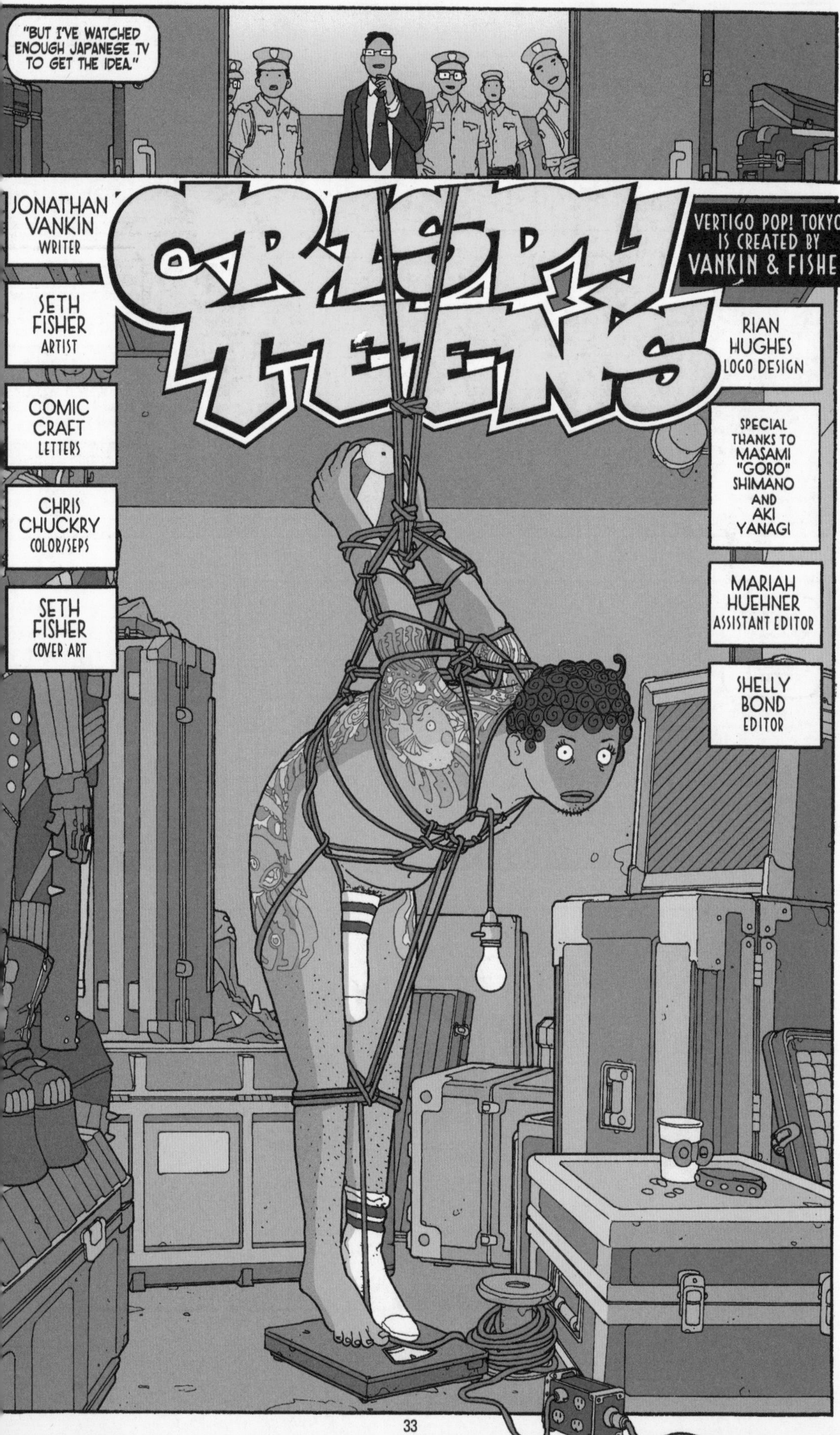
"BUT I'VE WATCHED ENOUGH JAPANESE TV TO GET THE IDEA."
CRISPY TEENS
JONATHAN VANKIN WRITER
SETH FISHER ARTIST
COMIC CRAFT LETTERS
CHRIS CHUCKRY COLOR/SEPS
SETH FISHER COVER ART
VERTIGO POP! TOKYO IS CREATED BY VANKIN & FISHER
RIAN HUGHES LOGO DESIGN
SPECIAL THANKS TO MASAMI "GORO" SHIMANO AND AKI YANAGI
MARIAH HUEHNER ASSISTANT EDITOR
SHELLY BOND EDITOR

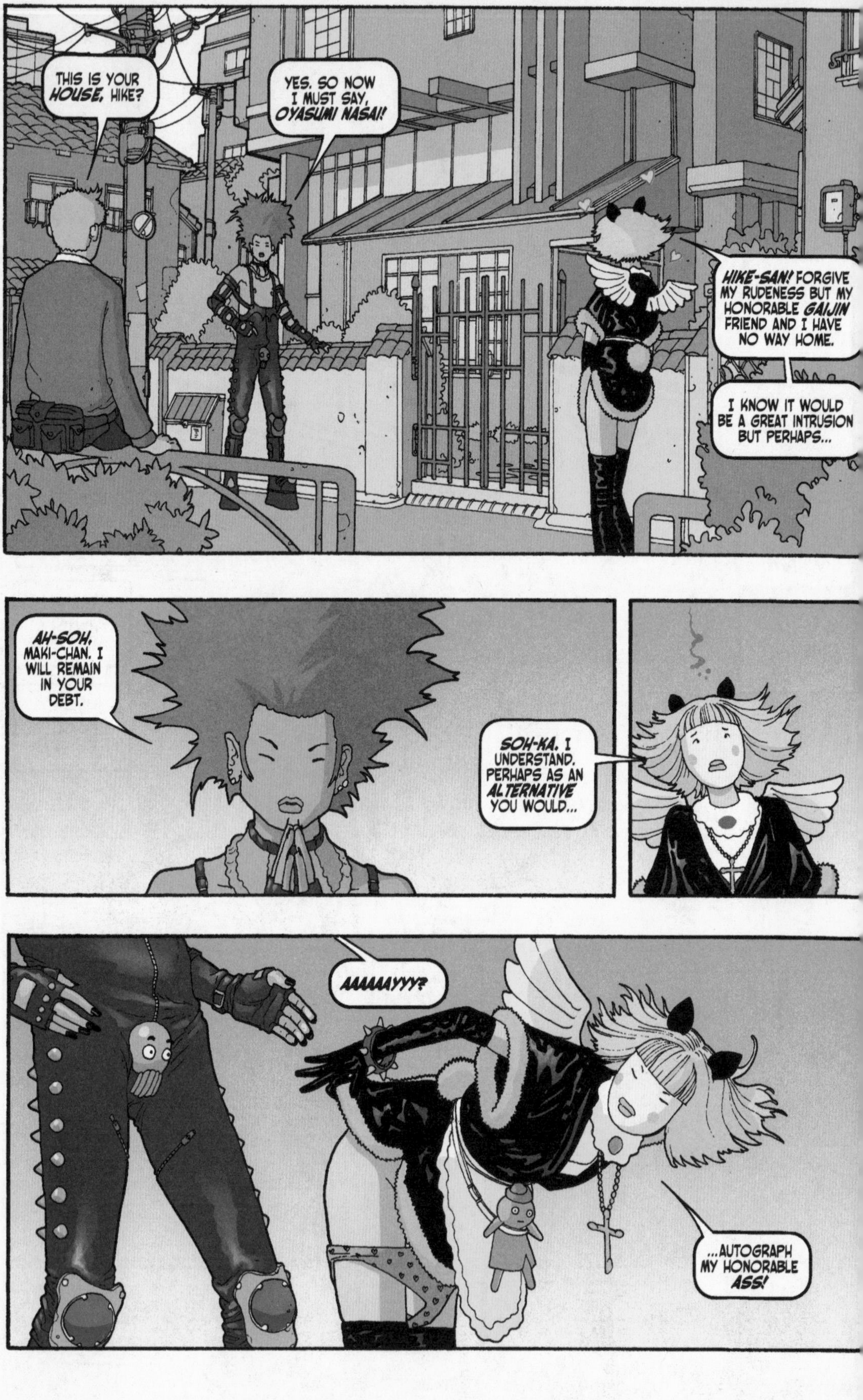

THIS IS YOUR HOUSE, HIKE?
YES. SO NOW I MUST SAY, OYASUMI NASAI!
HIKE-SAN! FORGIVE MY RUDENESS BUT MY HONORABLE GAIJIN FRIEND AND I HAVE NO WAY HOME.
I KNOW IT WOULD BE A GREAT INTRUSION BUT PERHAPS...
AH-SOH, MAKI-CHAN. I WILL REMAIN IN YOUR DEBT.
SOH-KA. I UNDERSTAND. PERHAPS AS AN ALTERNATIVE YOU WOULD...
AAAAAAYYY?
...AUTOGRAPH MY HONORABLE ASS!

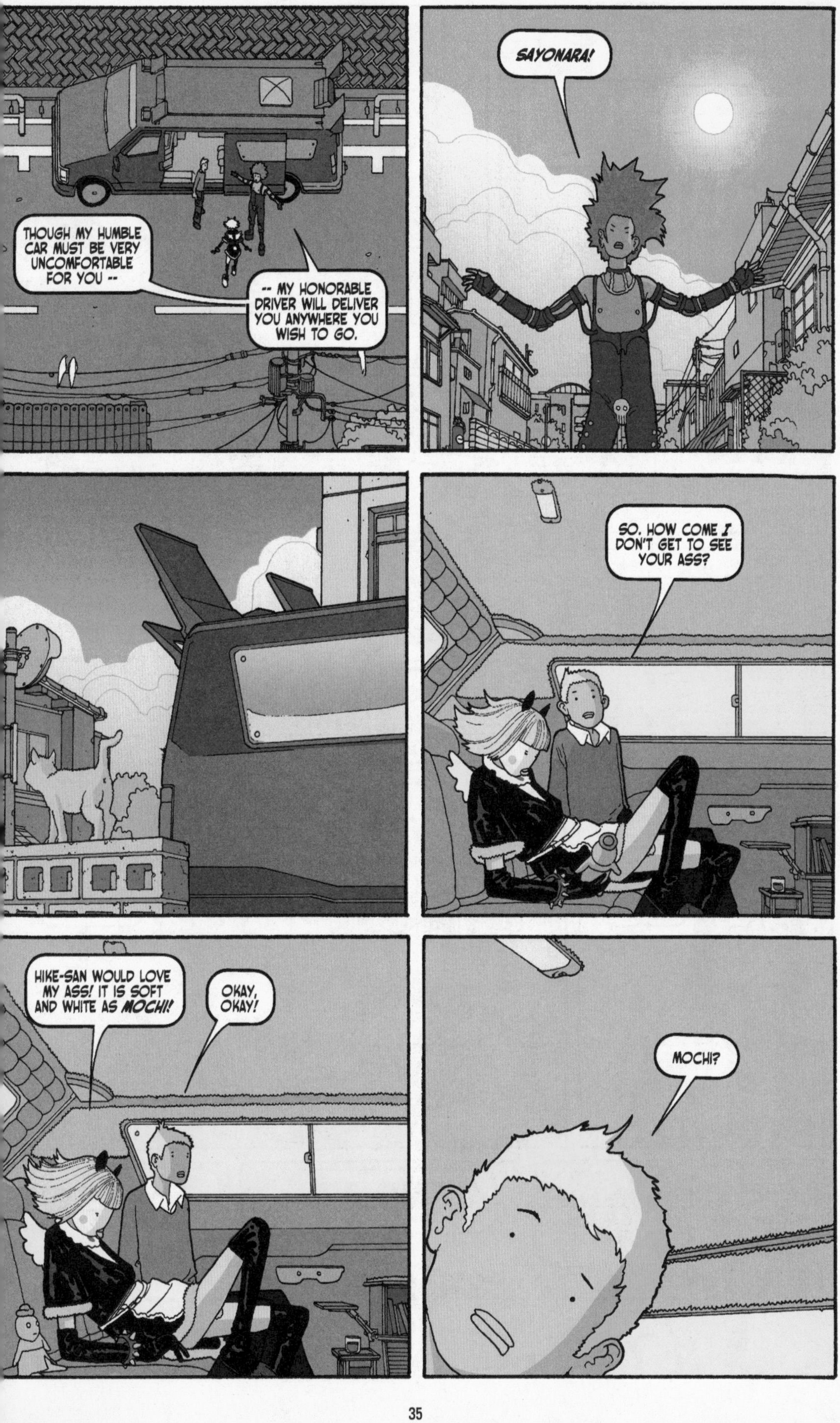
THOUGH MY HUMBLE CAR MUST BE VERY UNCOMFORTABLE FOR YOU --
-- MY HONORABLE DRIVER WILL DELIVER YOU ANYWHERE YOU WISH TO GO.
SAYONARA!
SO. HOW COME *I* DON'T GET TO SEE YOUR ASS?
HIKE-SAN WOULD LOVE MY ASS! IT IS SOFT AND WHITE AS *MOCHI!*
OKAY, OKAY!
MOCHI?

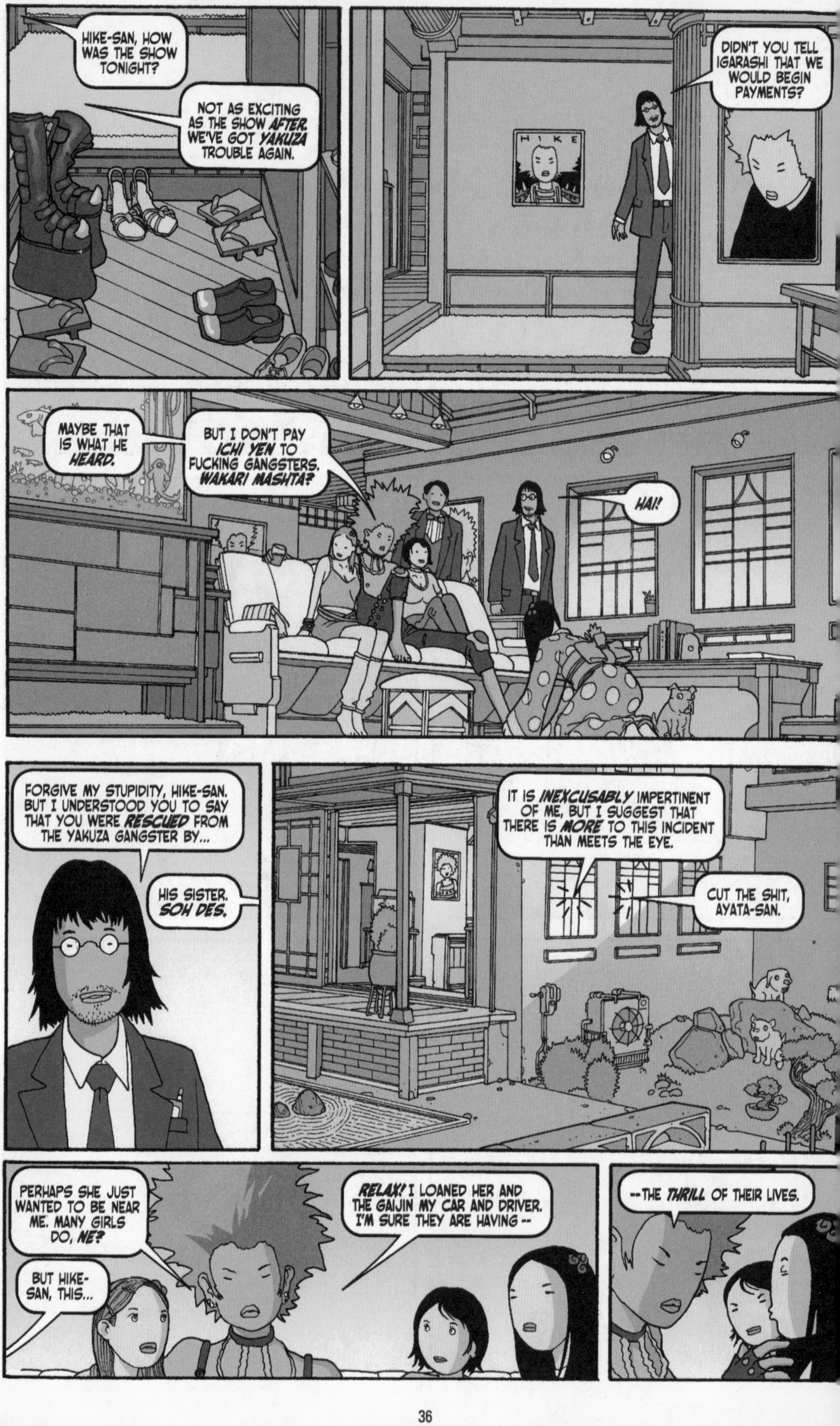
HIKE-SAN, HOW WAS THE SHOW TONIGHT?
NOT AS EXCITING AS THE SHOW AFTER. WE'VE GOT YAKUZA TROUBLE AGAIN.
DIDN'T YOU TELL IGARASHI THAT WE WOULD BEGIN PAYMENTS?
HIKE
MAYBE THAT IS WHAT HE HEARD.
BUT I DON'T PAY ICHI YEN TO FUCKING GANGSTERS. WAKARI MASHTA?
HAI!
FORGIVE MY STUPIDITY, HIKE-SAN. BUT I UNDERSTOOD YOU TO SAY THAT YOU WERE RESCUED FROM THE YAKUZA GANGSTER BY...
HIS SISTER. SOH DES.
IT IS INEXCUSABLY IMPERTINENT OF ME, BUT I SUGGEST THAT THERE IS MORE TO THIS INCIDENT THAN MEETS THE EYE.
CUT THE SHIT, AYATA-SAN.
PERHAPS SHE JUST WANTED TO BE NEAR ME. MANY GIRLS DO, NE?
BUT HIKE-SAN, THIS...
RELAX! I LOANED HER AND THE GAIJIN MY CAR AND DRIVER. I'M SURE THEY ARE HAVING --
--THE THRILL OF THEIR LIVES.

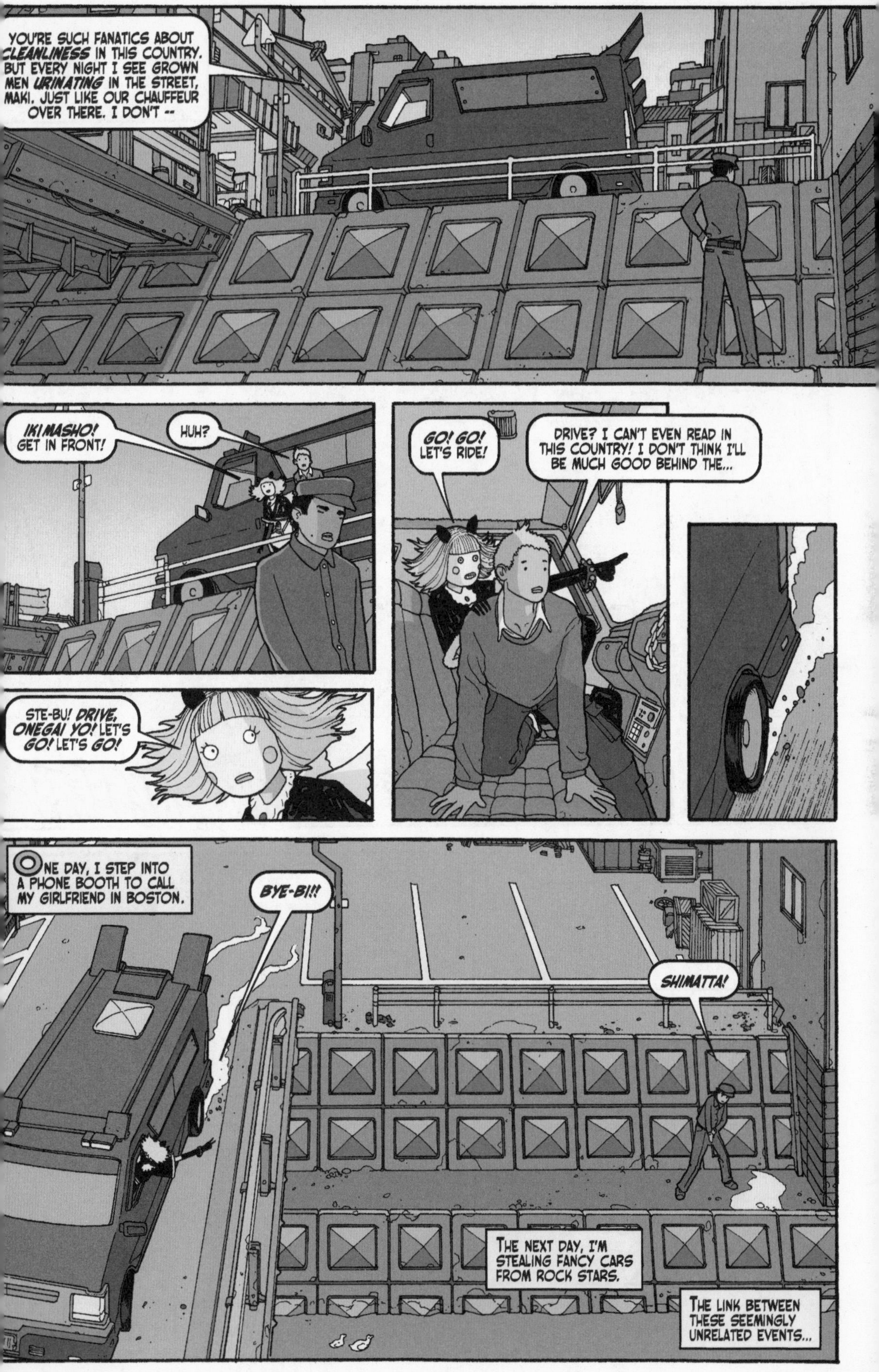
YOU'RE SUCH FANATICS ABOUT *CLEANLINESS* IN THIS COUNTRY. BUT EVERY NIGHT I SEE GROWN MEN *URINATING* IN THE STREET, MAKI. JUST LIKE OUR CHAUFFEUR OVER THERE. I DON'T --
IKIMASHO! GET IN FRONT!
HUH?
GO! GO! LET'S RIDE!
DRIVE? I CAN'T EVEN READ IN THIS COUNTRY! I DON'T THINK I'LL BE MUCH GOOD BEHIND THE...
STE-BU! *DRIVE, ONEGAI YO!* LET'S *GO!* LET'S *GO!*
ONE DAY, I STEP INTO A PHONE BOOTH TO CALL MY GIRLFRIEND IN BOSTON.
BYE-BI!!
SHIMATTA!
THE NEXT DAY, I'M STEALING FANCY CARS FROM ROCK STARS.
THE LINK BETWEEN THESE SEEMINGLY UNRELATED EVENTS...

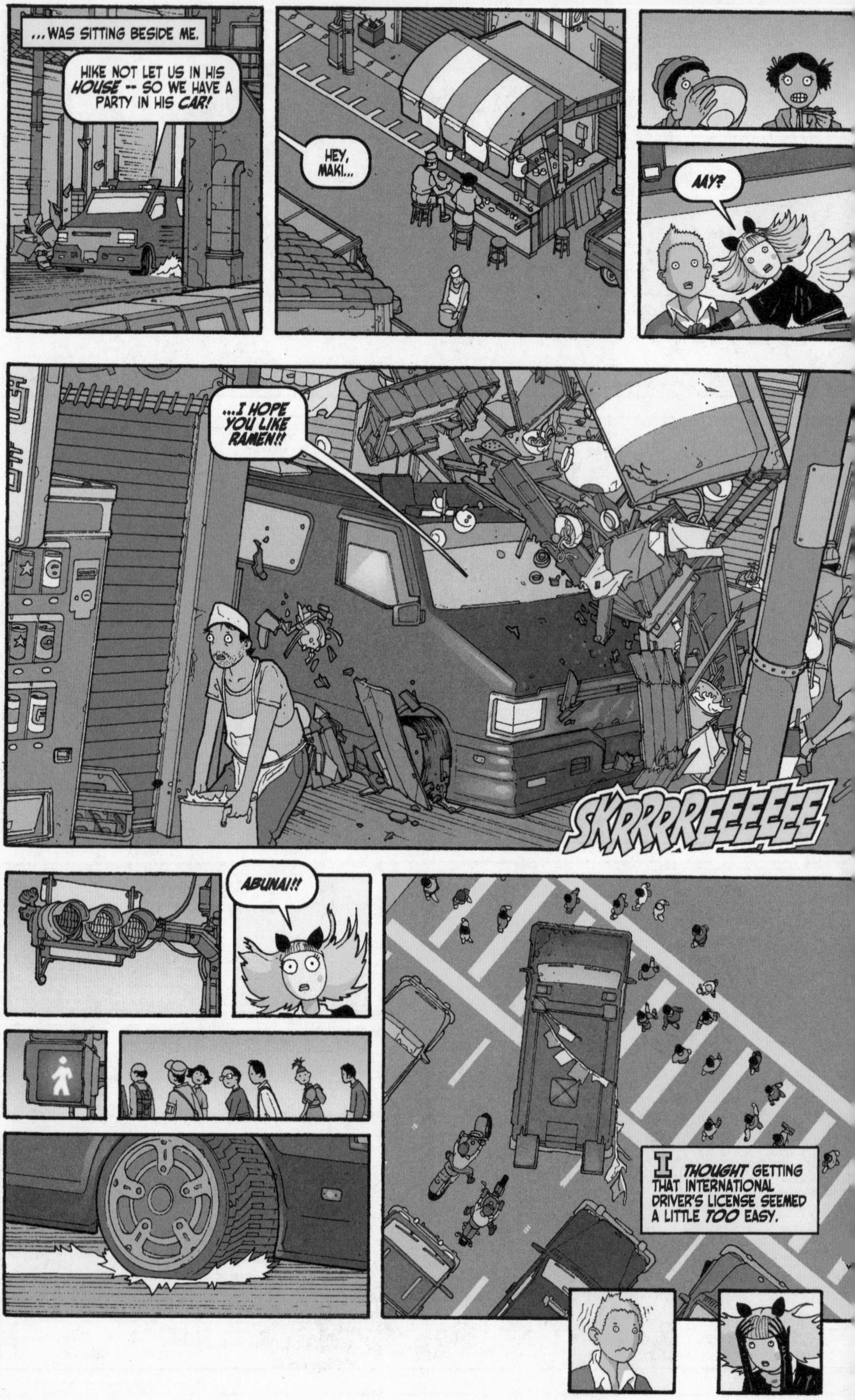
...WAS SITTING BESIDE ME.
HIKE NOT LET US IN HIS HOUSE -- SO WE HAVE A PARTY IN HIS CAR!
HEY, MAKI...
AAY?
...I HOPE YOU LIKE RAMEN!!
SKRRRREEEEEE
ABUNAI!!
I THOUGHT GETTING THAT INTERNATIONAL DRIVER'S LICENSE SEEMED A LITTLE TOO EASY.

MAKI TRASHED THE BACK OF THAT LIMO. WHAT A SHAME.

IT WAS LIKE THE BRIDGE OF THE *ENTERPRISE* BACK THERE.

SAIKO!

THAT MEANS, *"THIS IS GREAT!"*

I THOUGHT YOU MEANT A DIFFERENT KIND OF *"PSYCHO."*

LET'S GO TO *TOP* OF TOKYO TOWER!

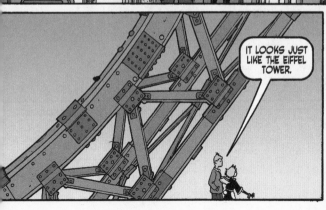

IT LOOKS JUST LIKE THE EIFFEL TOWER.

NO, TOKYO TOWER IS *TALLER.* 333 METERS.

IRASSHAIMASE!

I KNEW I COULD BE DEPORTED FOR THE THINGS THAT HAPPENED THAT NIGHT.

BUT WITH THE CITY 333 METERS BELOW ME, FOR THE FIRST TIME AFTER SIX MONTHS IN TOKYO...

...I FELT AT HOME.

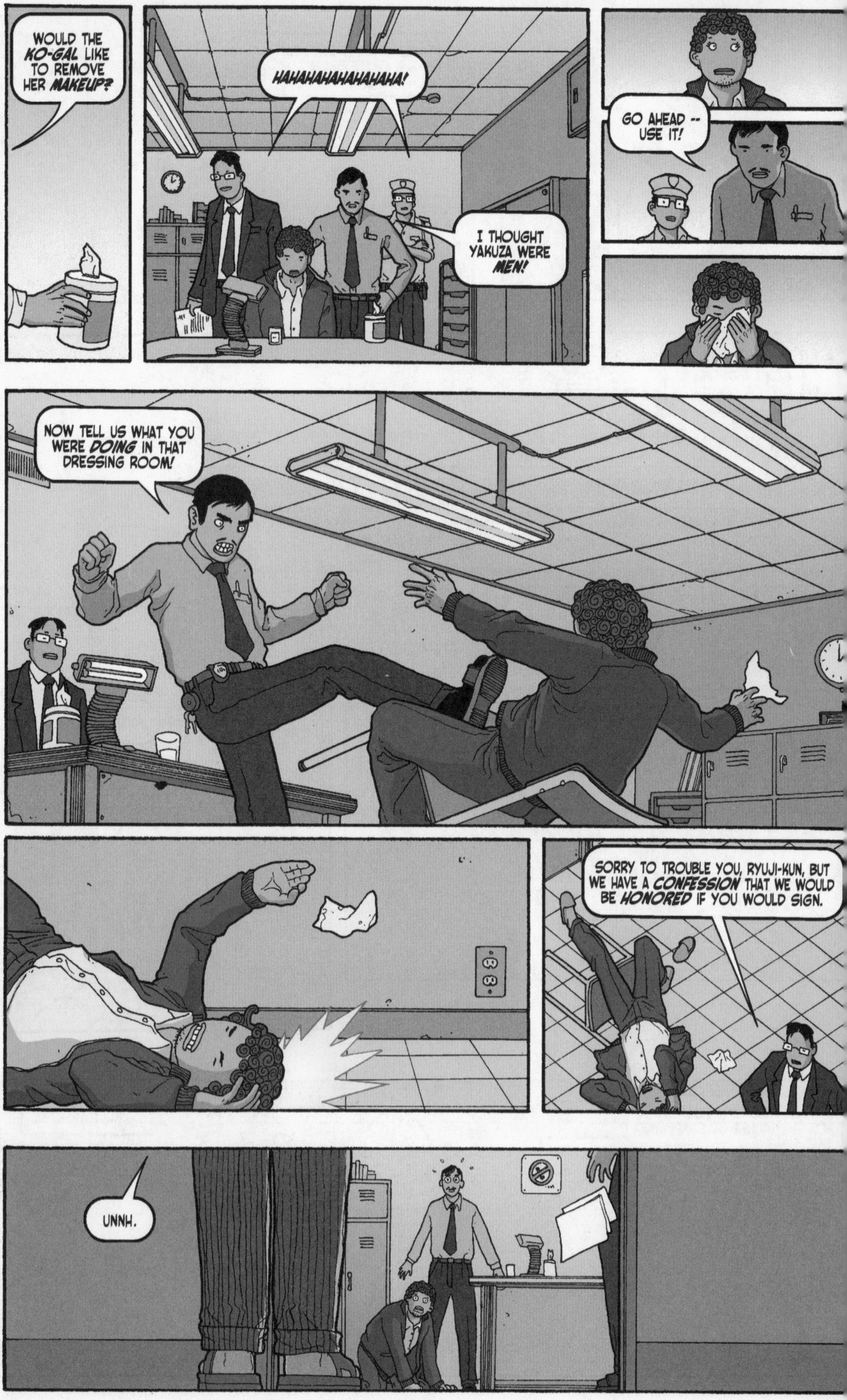
WOULD THE KO-GAL LIKE TO REMOVE HER MAKEUP?
HAHAHAHAHAHAHAHA!
I THOUGHT YAKUZA WERE MEN!
GO AHEAD -- USE IT!
NOW TELL US WHAT YOU WERE DOING IN THAT DRESSING ROOM!
SORRY TO TROUBLE YOU, RYUJI-KUN, BUT WE HAVE A CONFESSION THAT WE WOULD BE HONORED IF YOU WOULD SIGN.
UNNH.

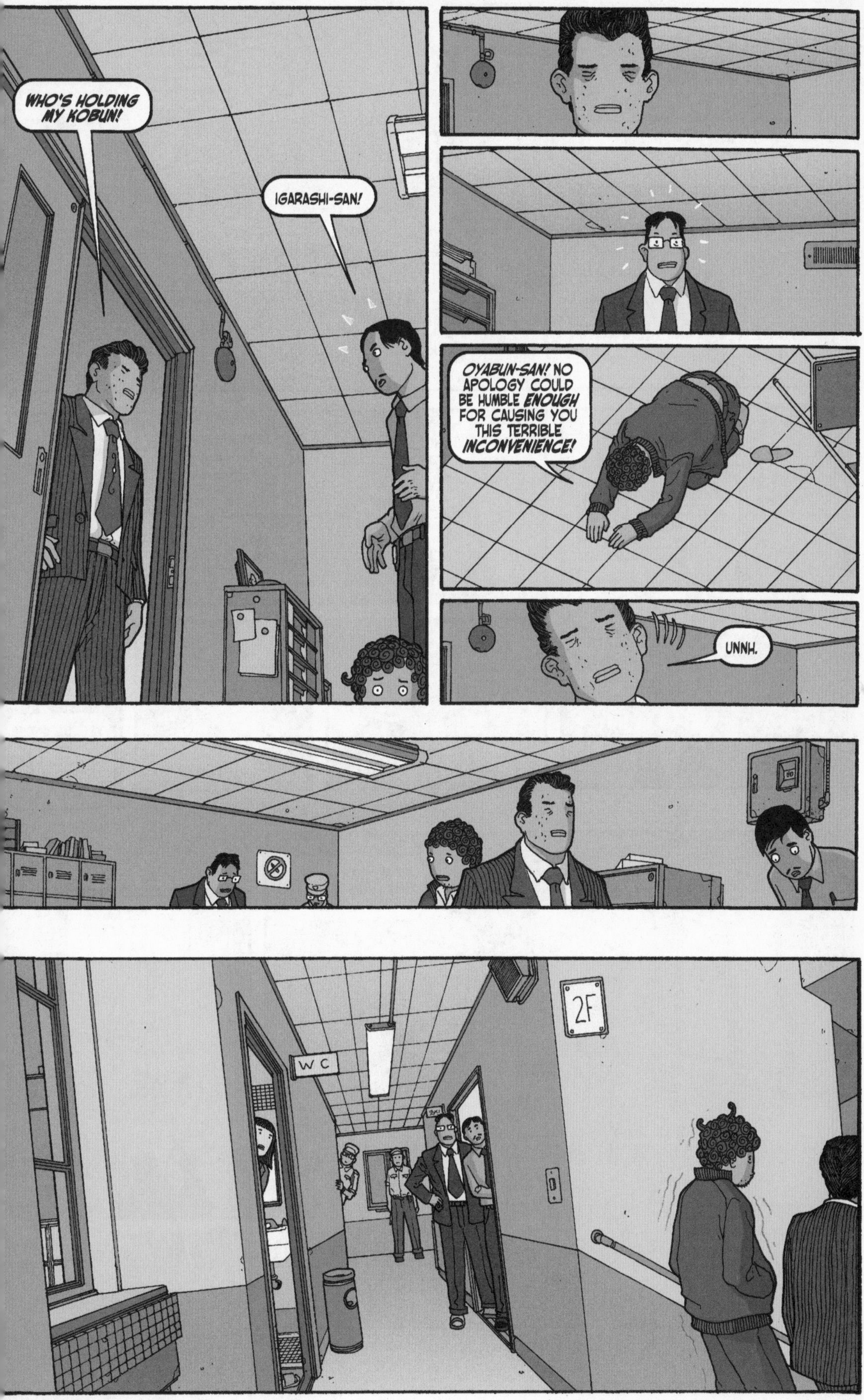
WHO'S HOLDING MY KOBUN!
IGARASHI-SAN!
OYABUN-SAN! NO APOLOGY COULD BE HUMBLE ENOUGH FOR CAUSING YOU THIS TERRIBLE INCONVENIENCE!
UNNH.
WC
2F

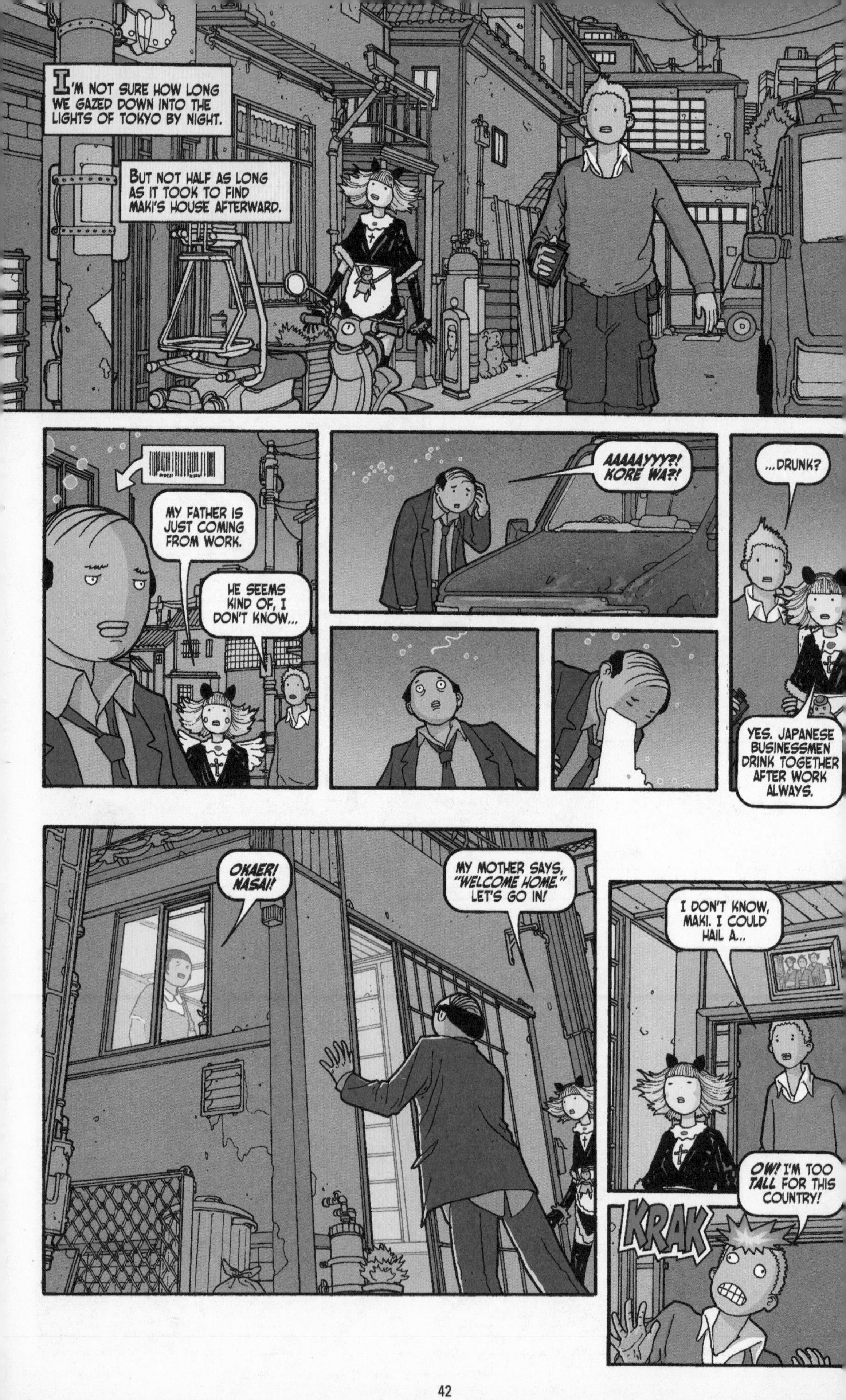

I'M NOT SURE HOW LONG WE GAZED DOWN INTO THE LIGHTS OF TOKYO BY NIGHT.
BUT NOT HALF AS LONG AS IT TOOK TO FIND MAKI'S HOUSE AFTERWARD.
MY FATHER IS JUST COMING FROM WORK.
HE SEEMS KIND OF, I DON'T KNOW...
AAAAAYYY?! KORE WA?!
...DRUNK?
YES. JAPANESE BUSINESSMEN DRINK TOGETHER AFTER WORK ALWAYS.
OKAERI NASAI!
MY MOTHER SAYS, "WELCOME HOME." LET'S GO IN!
I DON'T KNOW, MAKI. I COULD HAIL A...
KRAK
OW! I'M TOO TALL FOR THIS COUNTRY!

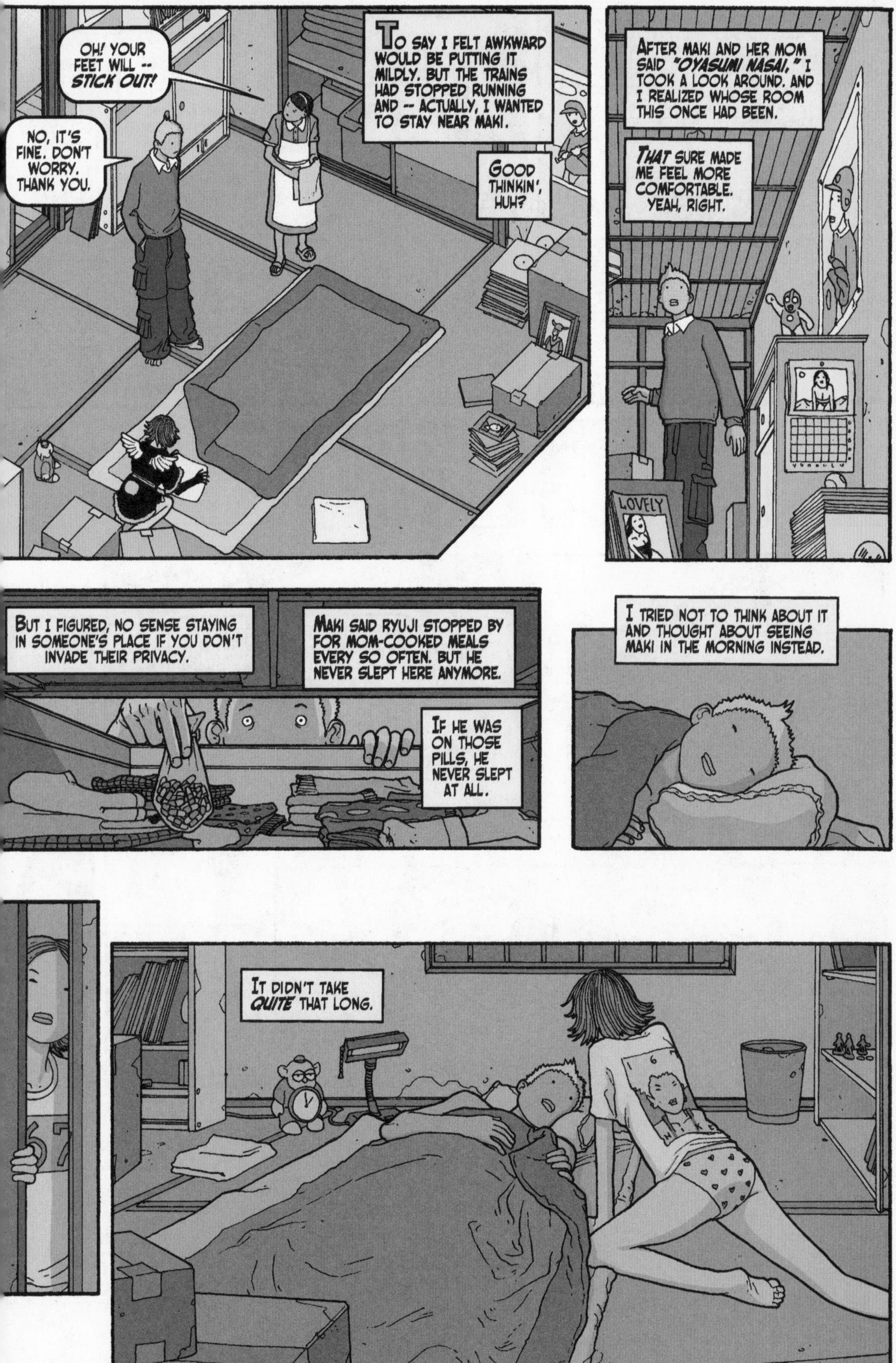
OH! YOUR FEET WILL -- STICK OUT!
NO, IT'S FINE. DON'T WORRY. THANK YOU.
TO SAY I FELT AWKWARD WOULD BE PUTTING IT MILDLY. BUT THE TRAINS HAD STOPPED RUNNING AND -- ACTUALLY, I WANTED TO STAY NEAR MAKI.
GOOD THINKIN', HUH?
AFTER MAKI AND HER MOM SAID "OYASUMI NASAI," I TOOK A LOOK AROUND. AND I REALIZED WHOSE ROOM THIS ONCE HAD BEEN.
THAT SURE MADE ME FEEL MORE COMFORTABLE. YEAH, RIGHT.
LOVELY
BUT I FIGURED, NO SENSE STAYING IN SOMEONE'S PLACE IF YOU DON'T INVADE THEIR PRIVACY.
MAKI SAID RYUJI STOPPED BY FOR MOM-COOKED MEALS EVERY SO OFTEN. BUT HE NEVER SLEPT HERE ANYMORE.
IF HE WAS ON THOSE PILLS, HE NEVER SLEPT AT ALL.
I TRIED NOT TO THINK ABOUT IT AND THOUGHT ABOUT SEEING MAKI IN THE MORNING INSTEAD.
IT DIDN'T TAKE QUITE THAT LONG.

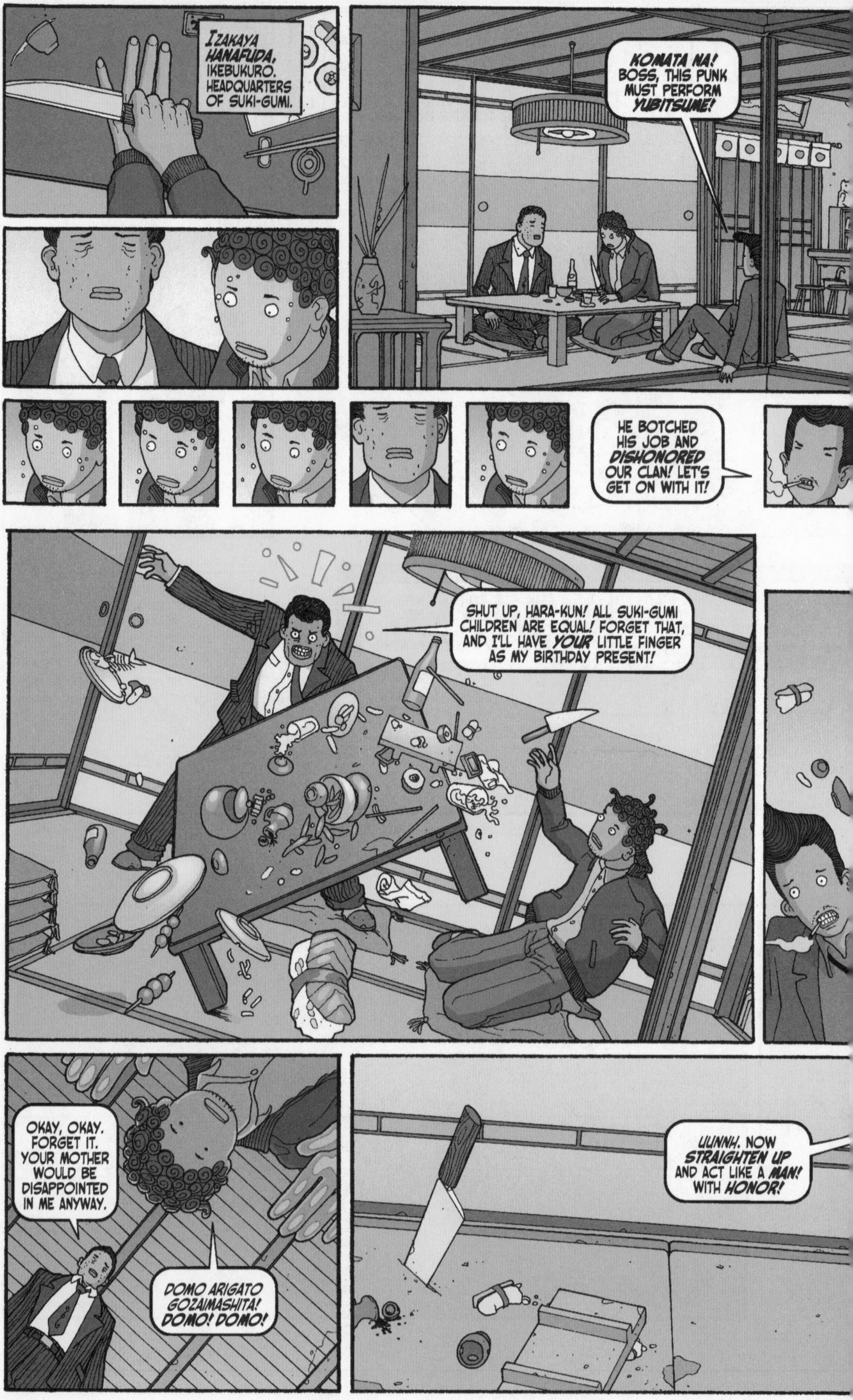

IZAKAYA HANAFUDA, IKEBUKURO. HEADQUARTERS OF SUKI-GUMI.
KOMATA NA! BOSS, THIS PUNK MUST PERFORM YUBITSUME!
HE BOTCHED HIS JOB AND DISHONORED OUR CLAN! LET'S GET ON WITH IT!
SHUT UP, HARA-KUN! ALL SUKI-GUMI CHILDREN ARE EQUAL! FORGET THAT, AND I'LL HAVE YOUR LITTLE FINGER AS MY BIRTHDAY PRESENT!
OKAY, OKAY. FORGET IT. YOUR MOTHER WOULD BE DISAPPOINTED IN ME ANYWAY.
DOMO ARIGATO GOZAIMASHITA! DOMO! DOMO!
UUNNH. NOW STRAIGHTEN UP AND ACT LIKE A MAN! WITH HONOR!

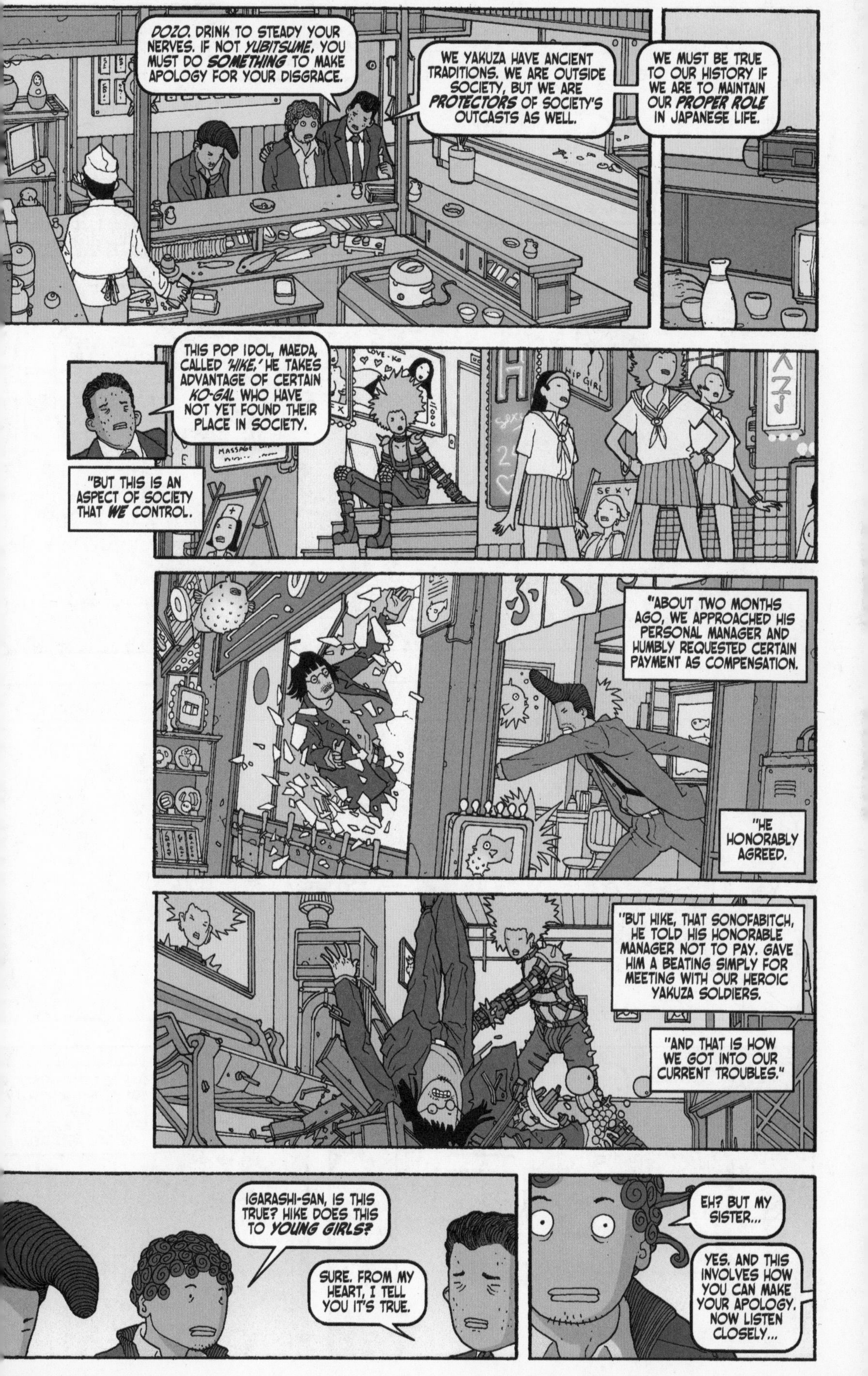

DOZO. DRINK TO STEADY YOUR NERVES. IF NOT YUBITSUME, YOU MUST DO SOMETHING TO MAKE APOLOGY FOR YOUR DISGRACE.
WE YAKUZA HAVE ANCIENT TRADITIONS. WE ARE OUTSIDE SOCIETY, BUT WE ARE PROTECTORS OF SOCIETY'S OUTCASTS AS WELL.
WE MUST BE TRUE TO OUR HISTORY IF WE ARE TO MAINTAIN OUR PROPER ROLE IN JAPANESE LIFE.
THIS POP IDOL, MAEDA, CALLED 'HIKE,' HE TAKES ADVANTAGE OF CERTAIN KO-GAL WHO HAVE NOT YET FOUND THEIR PLACE IN SOCIETY.
"BUT THIS IS AN ASPECT OF SOCIETY THAT WE CONTROL.
"ABOUT TWO MONTHS AGO, WE APPROACHED HIS PERSONAL MANAGER AND HUMBLY REQUESTED CERTAIN PAYMENT AS COMPENSATION.
"HE HONORABLY AGREED.
"BUT HIKE, THAT SONOFABITCH, HE TOLD HIS HONORABLE MANAGER NOT TO PAY. GAVE HIM A BEATING SIMPLY FOR MEETING WITH OUR HEROIC YAKUZA SOLDIERS.
"AND THAT IS HOW WE GOT INTO OUR CURRENT TROUBLES."
IGARASHI-SAN, IS THIS TRUE? HIKE DOES THIS TO YOUNG GIRLS?
SURE. FROM MY HEART, I TELL YOU IT'S TRUE.
EH? BUT MY SISTER...
YES. AND THIS INVOLVES HOW YOU CAN MAKE YOUR APOLOGY. NOW LISTEN CLOSELY...

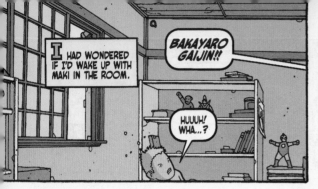

I HAD WONDERED IF I'D WAKE UP WITH MAKI IN THE ROOM.

HUUUH! WHA...?

BAKAYARO GAIJIN!!

RYUJI-KUN! YOU HAVE THE MANNERS OF A DOG! FORGET LAST NIGHT!

BUT THIS WASN'T *EXACTLY* WHAT I HAD IN MIND.

<WHEN THIS JOB IS FINISHED, I'M GOING TO *KILL* YOU FOR DISGRACING ME!>

WHAT'D HE SAY?

HE SAY, HE IS SORRY, BUT HE ASKS YOU TO APOLOGIZE FOR PAINTING *MAKEUP* ON HIM.

BELIEVE ME. I'M SORRY. NOW -- CAN WE JUST BRING THAT CAR BACK?

NOT NOW. LATER. ALL TOGETHER.

WHY NOT NOW? I MEAN, IT IS *STOLEN* AFTER ALL...

NOW I MUST GO TO *SCHOOL!*

THIS KEPT GETTING BETTER AND BETTER. HOPEFULLY, I COULD LAST UNTIL THE AFTERNOON WITHOUT GETTING ARRESTED.

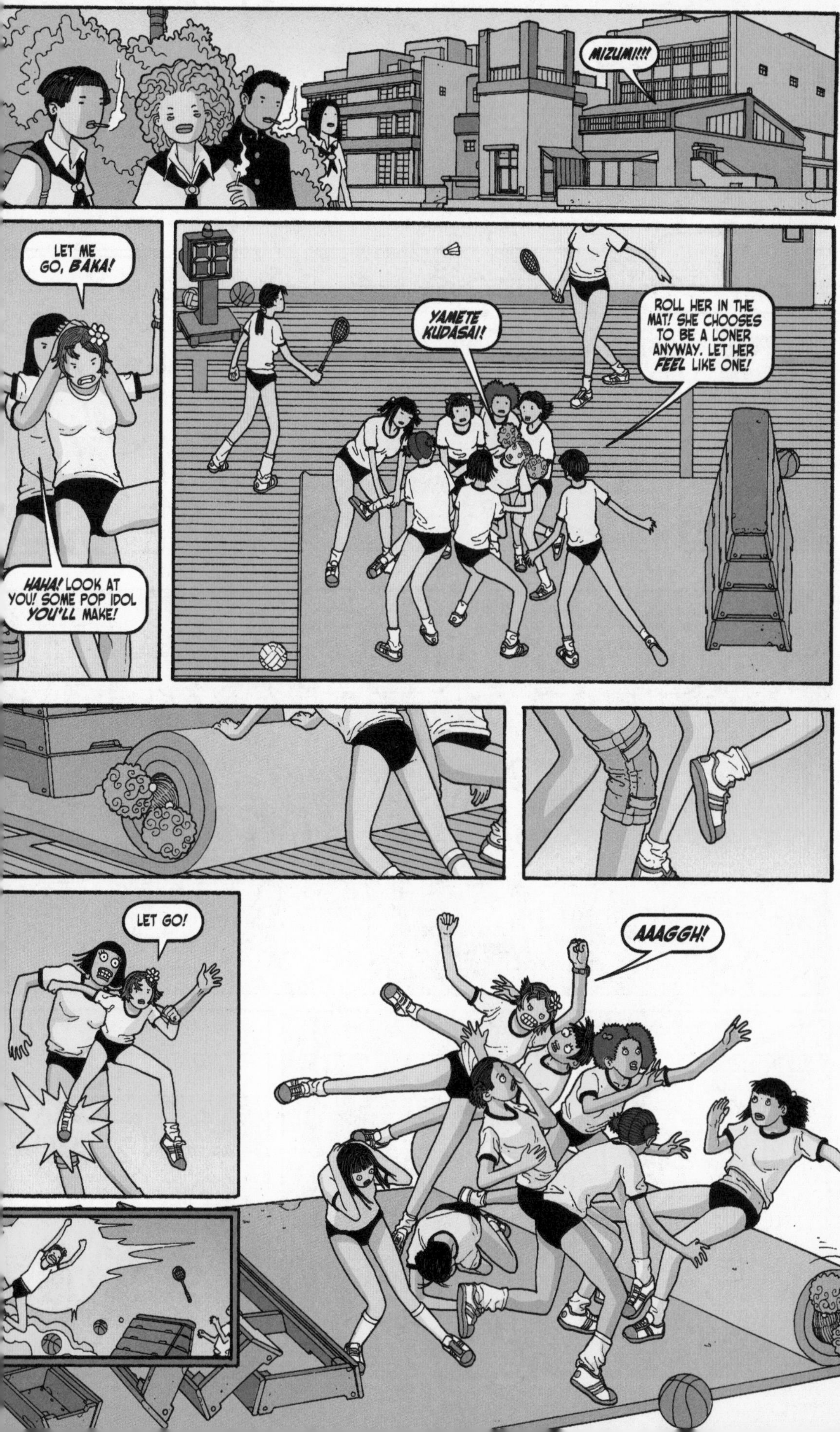
MIZUMI!!!
LET ME GO, BAKA!
HAHA! LOOK AT YOU! SOME POP IDOL YOU'LL MAKE!
YAMETE KUDASAI!
ROLL HER IN THE MAT! SHE CHOOSES TO BE A LONER ANYWAY. LET HER FEEL LIKE ONE!
LET GO!
AAAGGH!

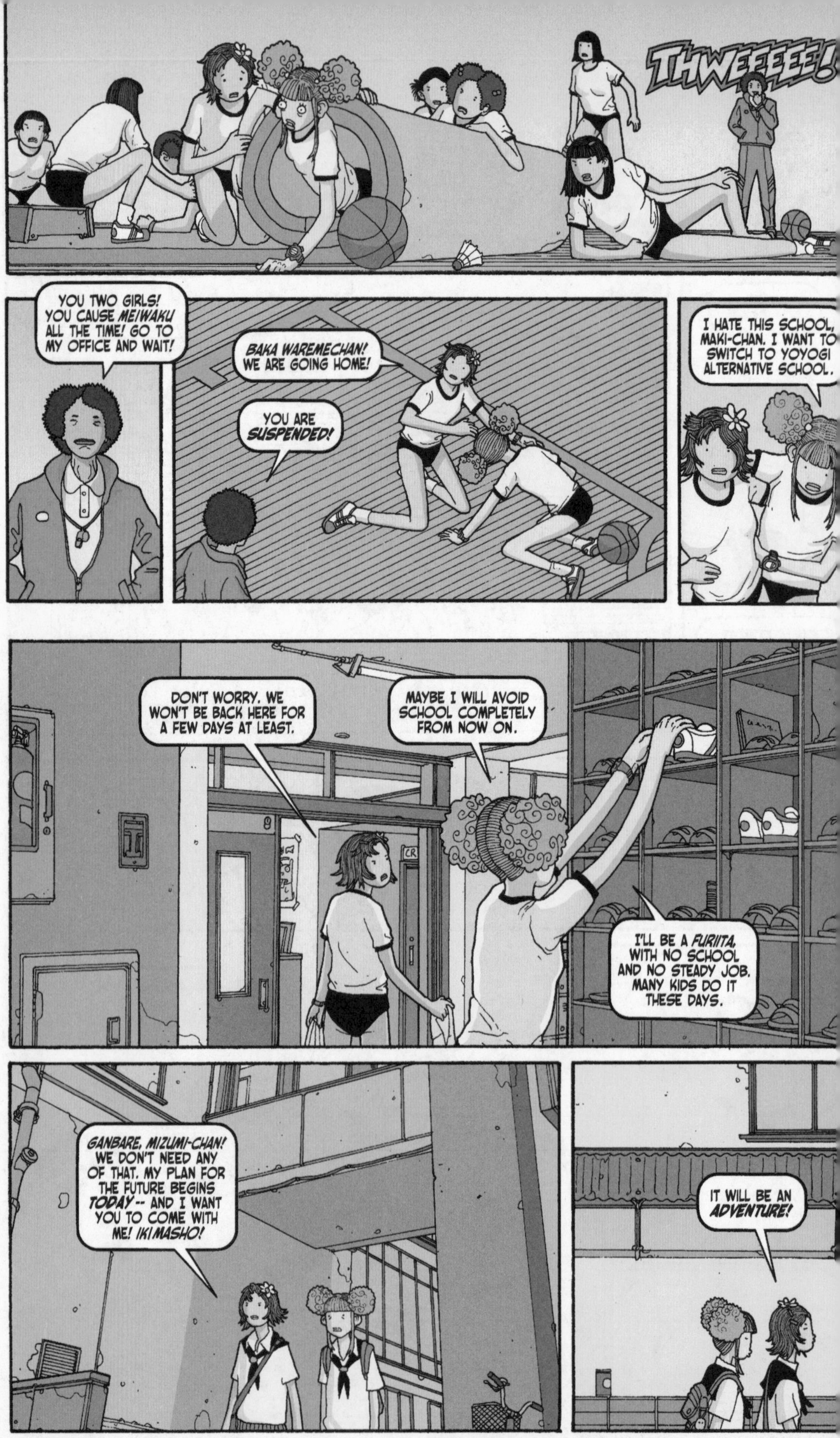
THWEEEEE!
YOU TWO GIRLS! YOU CAUSE MEIWAKU ALL THE TIME! GO TO MY OFFICE AND WAIT!
BAKA WAREMECHAN! WE ARE GOING HOME!
YOU ARE SUSPENDED!
I HATE THIS SCHOOL, MAKI-CHAN. I WANT TO SWITCH TO YOYOGI ALTERNATIVE SCHOOL.
DON'T WORRY. WE WON'T BE BACK HERE FOR A FEW DAYS AT LEAST.
MAYBE I WILL AVOID SCHOOL COMPLETELY FROM NOW ON.
I'LL BE A FURIITA, WITH NO SCHOOL AND NO STEADY JOB. MANY KIDS DO IT THESE DAYS.
GANBARE, MIZUMI-CHAN! WE DON'T NEED ANY OF THAT. MY PLAN FOR THE FUTURE BEGINS TODAY -- AND I WANT YOU TO COME WITH ME! IKIMASHO!
IT WILL BE AN ADVENTURE!

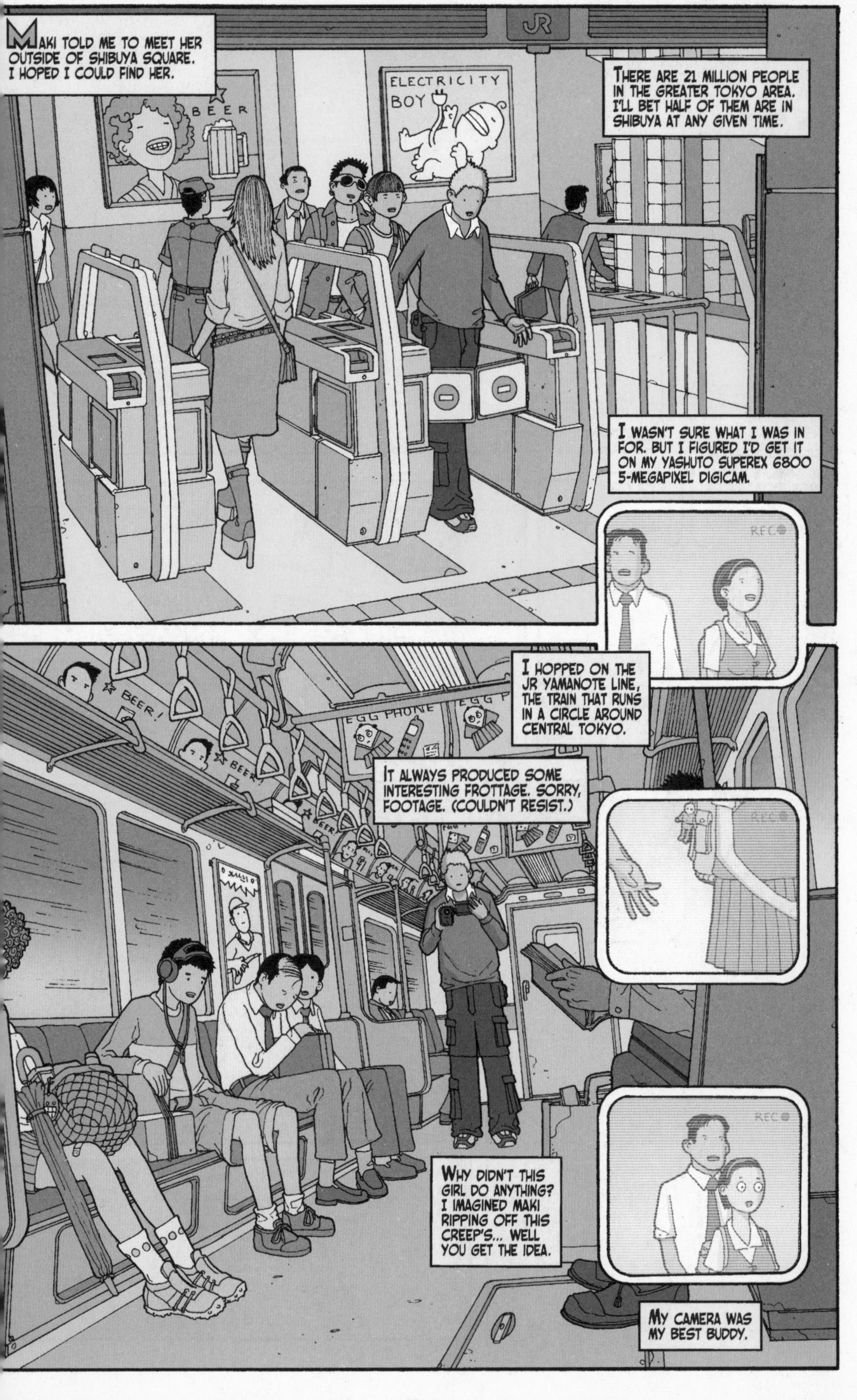
MAKI TOLD ME TO MEET HER OUTSIDE OF SHIBUYA SQUARE. I HOPED I COULD FIND HER.
JR
BEER
ELECTRICITY BOY
THERE ARE 21 MILLION PEOPLE IN THE GREATER TOKYO AREA. I'LL BET HALF OF THEM ARE IN SHIBUYA AT ANY GIVEN TIME.
I WASN'T SURE WHAT I WAS IN FOR. BUT I FIGURED I'D GET IT ON MY YASHUTO SUPEREX 6800 5-MEGAPIXEL DIGICAM.
REC
I HOPPED ON THE JR YAMANOTE LINE, THE TRAIN THAT RUNS IN A CIRCLE AROUND CENTRAL TOKYO.
BEER!
EGG PHONE
IT ALWAYS PRODUCED SOME INTERESTING FROTTAGE. SORRY, FOOTAGE. (COULDN'T RESIST.)
REC
WHY DIDN'T THIS GIRL DO ANYTHING? I IMAGINED MAKI RIPPING OFF THIS CREEP'S... WELL YOU GET THE IDEA.
REC
MY CAMERA WAS MY BEST BUDDY.

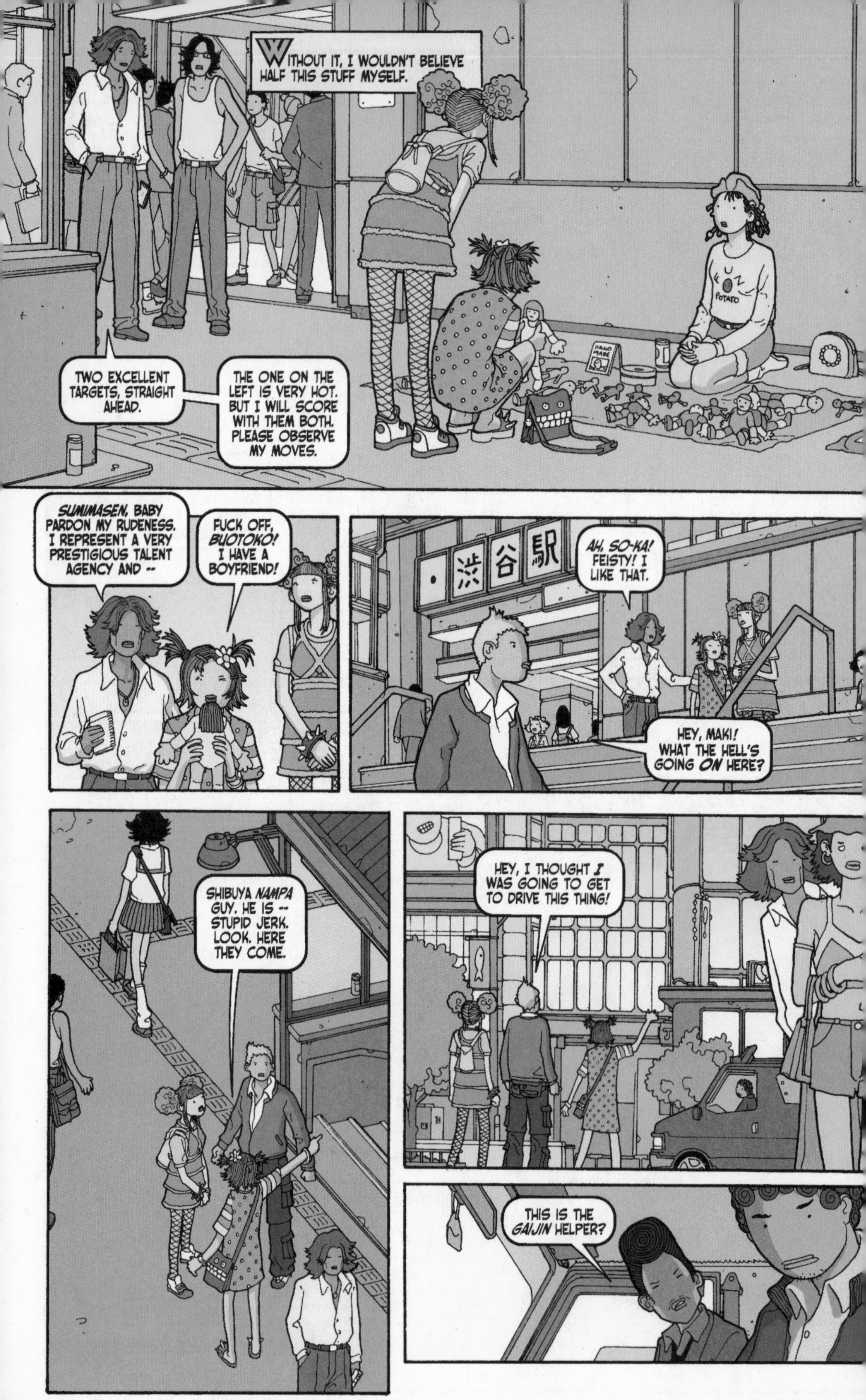
WITHOUT IT, I WOULDN'T BELIEVE HALF THIS STUFF MYSELF.
HAND MADE
POTATO
TWO EXCELLENT TARGETS, STRAIGHT AHEAD.
THE ONE ON THE LEFT IS VERY HOT. BUT I WILL SCORE WITH THEM BOTH. PLEASE OBSERVE MY MOVES.
SUMIMASEN, BABY PARDON MY RUDENESS. I REPRESENT A VERY PRESTIGIOUS TALENT AGENCY AND --
FUCK OFF, *BUOTOKO!* I HAVE A BOYFRIEND!
渋谷駅
AH, SO-KA! FEISTY! I LIKE THAT.
HEY, MAKI! WHAT THE HELL'S GOING *ON* HERE?
SHIBUYA *NAMPA* GUY. HE IS -- STUPID JERK. LOOK. HERE THEY COME.
HEY, I THOUGHT *I* WAS GOING TO GET TO DRIVE THIS THING!
THIS IS THE *GAIJIN* HELPER?

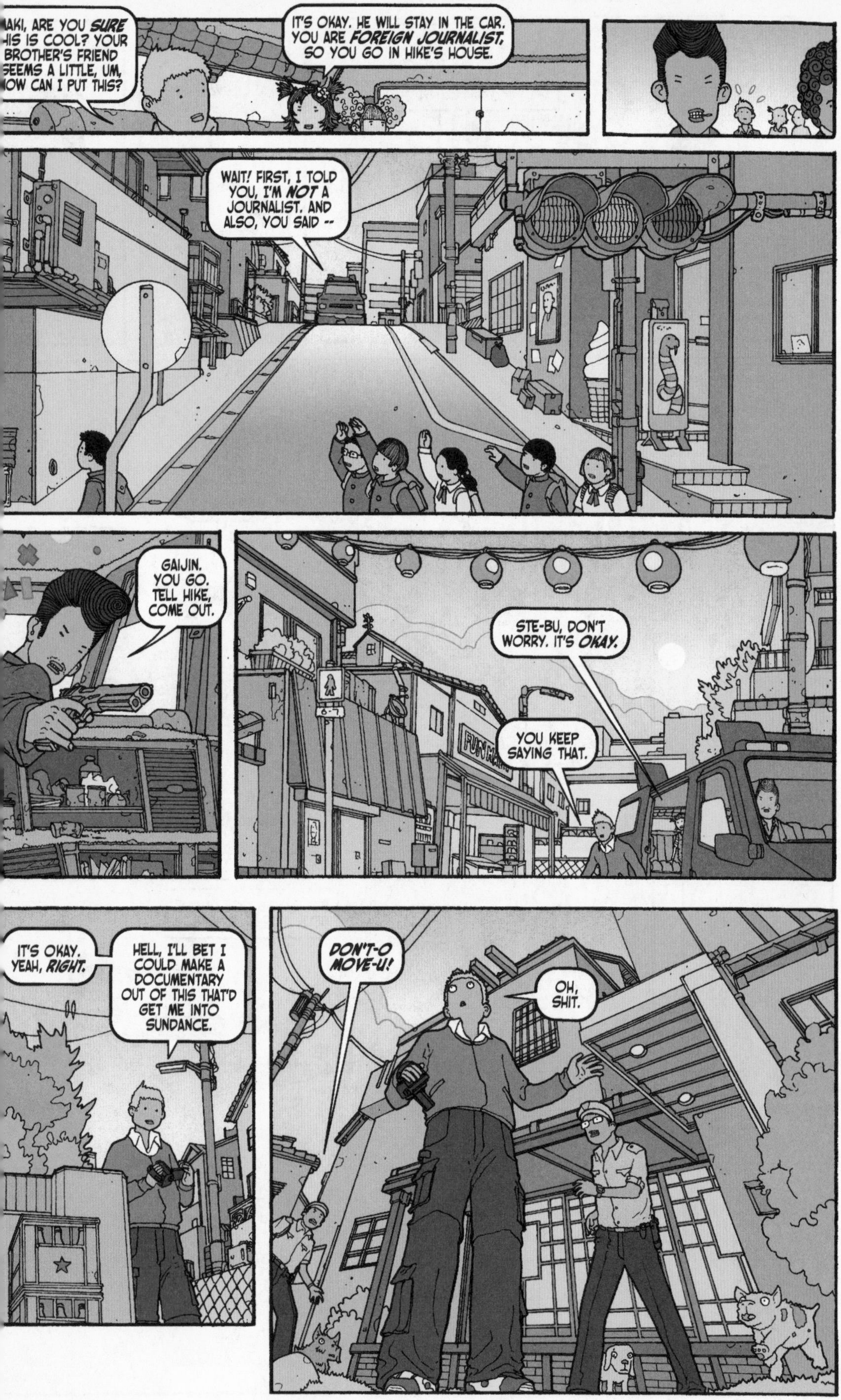
AKI, ARE YOU SURE THIS IS COOL? YOUR BROTHER'S FRIEND SEEMS A LITTLE, UM, HOW CAN I PUT THIS?
IT'S OKAY. HE WILL STAY IN THE CAR. YOU ARE FOREIGN JOURNALIST, SO YOU GO IN HIKE'S HOUSE.
WAIT! FIRST, I TOLD YOU, I'M NOT A JOURNALIST. AND ALSO, YOU SAID --
GAIJIN. YOU GO. TELL HIKE, COME OUT.
STE-BU, DON'T WORRY. IT'S OKAY.
YOU KEEP SAYING THAT.
IT'S OKAY. YEAH, RIGHT.
HELL, I'LL BET I COULD MAKE A DOCUMENTARY OUT OF THIS THAT'D GET ME INTO SUNDANCE.
DON'T-O MOVE-U!
OH, SHIT.

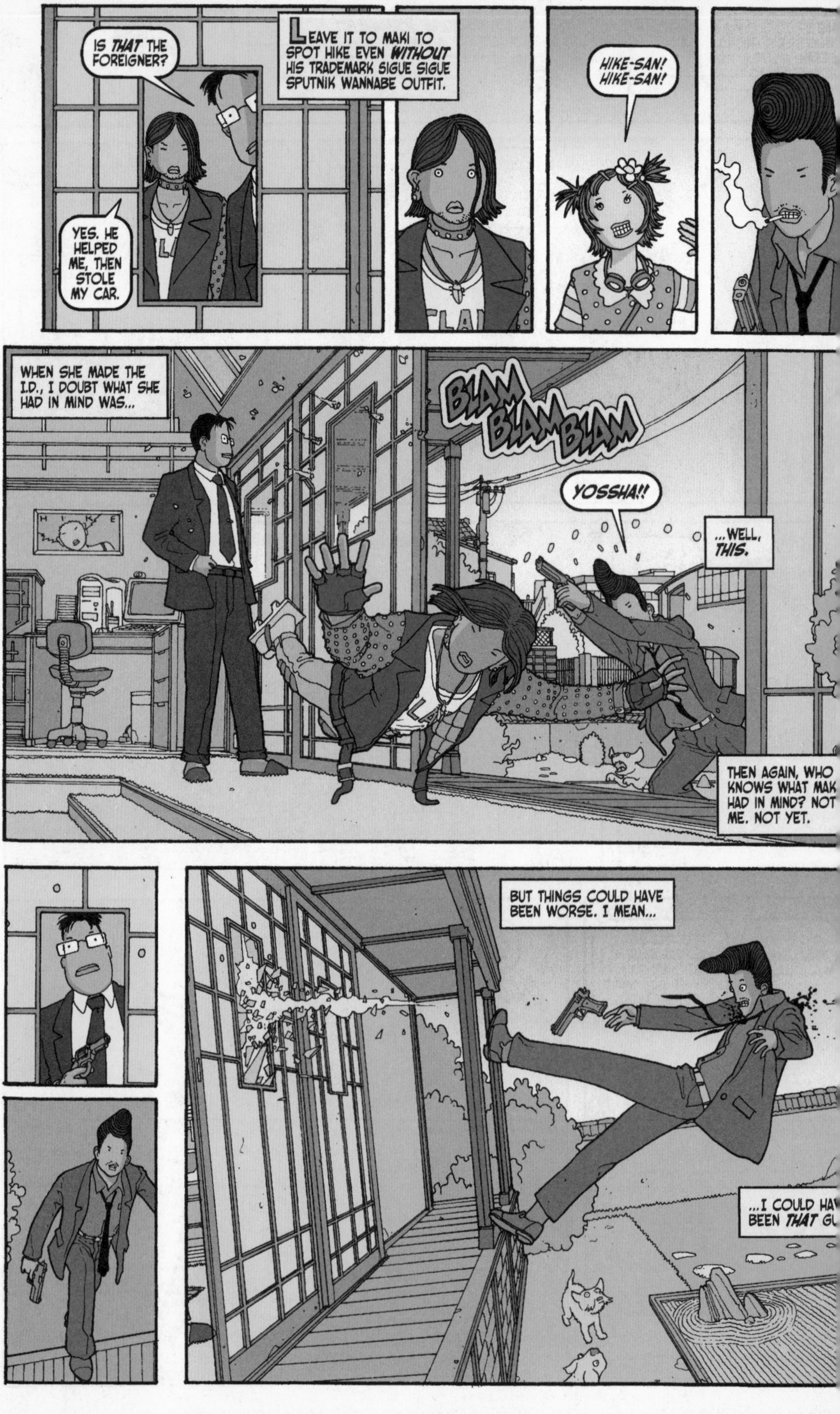
IS *THAT* THE FOREIGNER?
YES. HE HELPED ME, THEN STOLE MY CAR.
LEAVE IT TO MAKI TO SPOT HIKE EVEN *WITHOUT* HIS TRADEMARK SIGUE SIGUE SPUTNIK WANNABE OUTFIT.
HIKE-SAN! HIKE-SAN!
WHEN SHE MADE THE I.D., I DOUBT WHAT SHE HAD IN MIND WAS...
BLAM BLAM BLAM
YOSSHA!!
...WELL, *THIS.*
THEN AGAIN, WHO KNOWS WHAT MAK
HAD IN MIND? NOT
ME. NOT YET.
BUT THINGS COULD HAVE BEEN WORSE. I MEAN...
...I COULD HA
BEEN *THAT* G

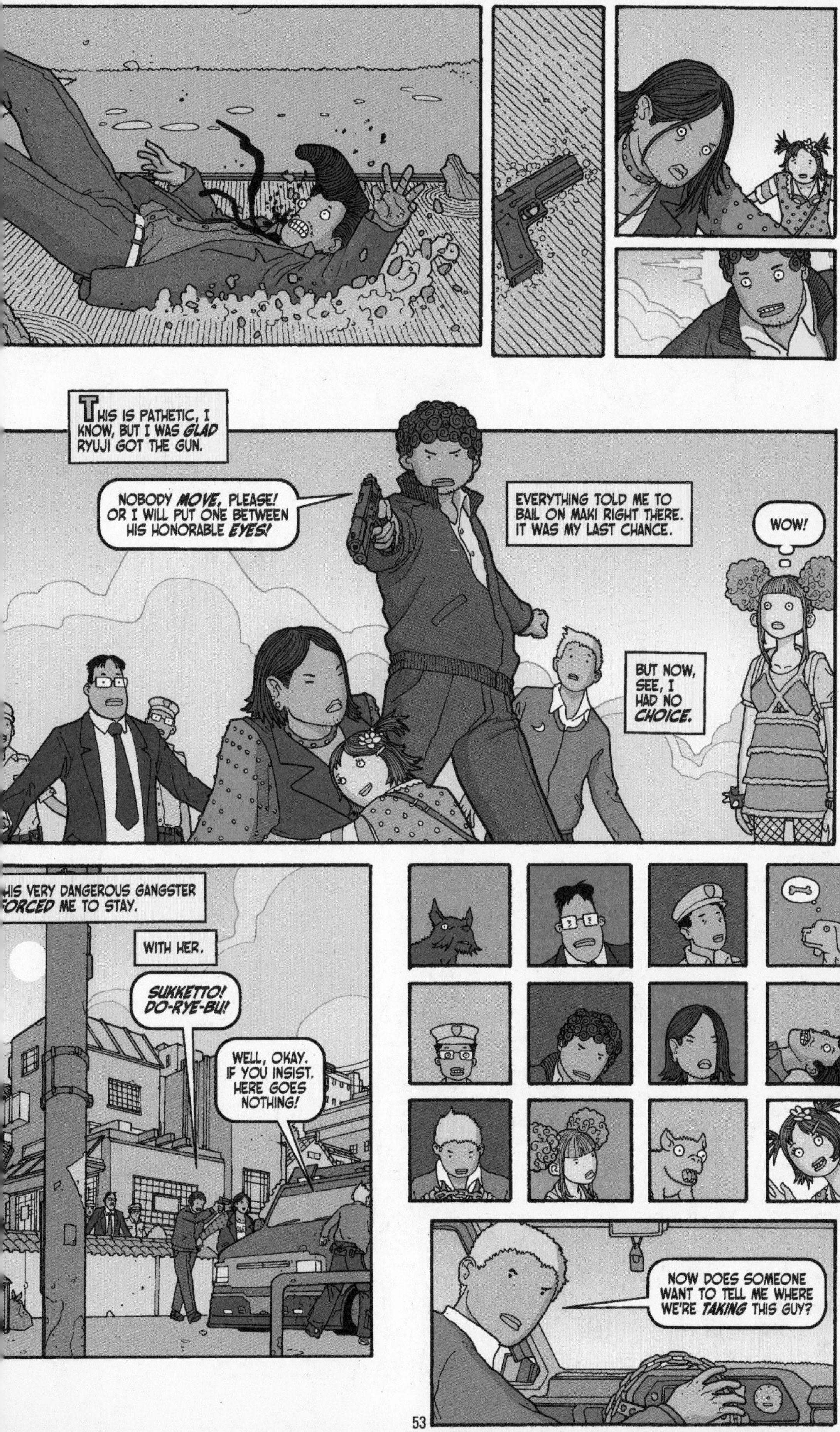
THIS IS PATHETIC, I KNOW, BUT I WAS GLAD RYUJI GOT THE GUN.
NOBODY MOVE, PLEASE! OR I WILL PUT ONE BETWEEN HIS HONORABLE EYES!
EVERYTHING TOLD ME TO BAIL ON MAKI RIGHT THERE. IT WAS MY LAST CHANCE.
WOW!
BUT NOW, SEE, I HAD NO CHOICE.
THIS VERY DANGEROUS GANGSTER FORCED ME TO STAY.
WITH HER.
SUKKETTO! DO-RYE-BU!
WELL, OKAY. IF YOU INSIST. HERE GOES NOTHING!
NOW DOES SOMEONE WANT TO TELL ME WHERE WE'RE TAKING THIS GUY?

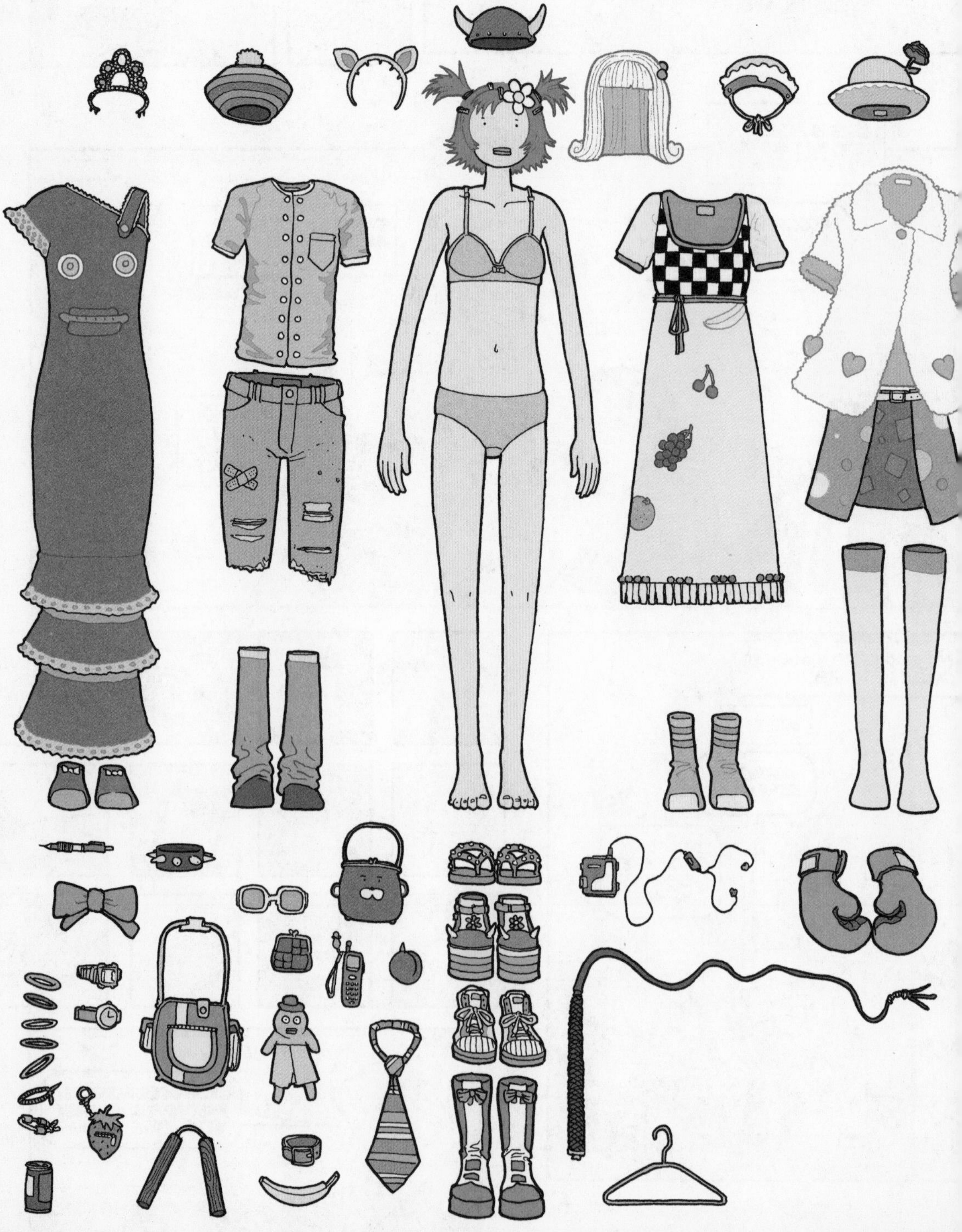

AAAII! ITAI!

BASTARD COP! IGARASHI WILL *RUIN* YOU!

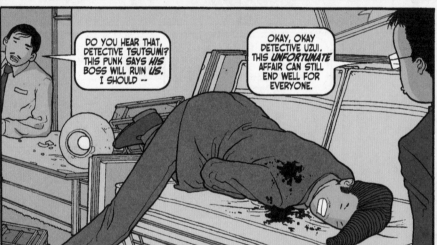

DO YOU HEAR THAT, DETECTIVE TSUTSUMI? THIS PUNK SAYS *HIS* BOSS WILL RUIN *US.* I SHOULD --

OKAY, OKAY DETECTIVE UZUI. THIS *UNFORTUNATE* AFFAIR CAN STILL END WELL FOR EVERYONE.

GET HIM A BANDAGE! THAT SOFA COST *ONE MILLION YEN!*

パニック

THIS WILL CAUSE *FRICTION* BETWEEN ME AND HIKE-SAN!

AN AMBULANCE WILL ARRIVE SOON WITH A BANDAGE.

SORRY TO BE SO MUCH TROUBLE. WE ARE UNDER *CONSIDERABLE* PRESSURE. IF YOU COULD, HARA-SAN, PLEASE TELL US THE DESTINATION OF YOUR FELLOW *CRIMINALS.*

INVESTIGATIVE TIP: IF YOU'RE SEARCHING FOR A BAND OF TEENAGE JAPANESE OUTLAWS AND THEIR MOTLEY GAIJIN HANGER-ON...

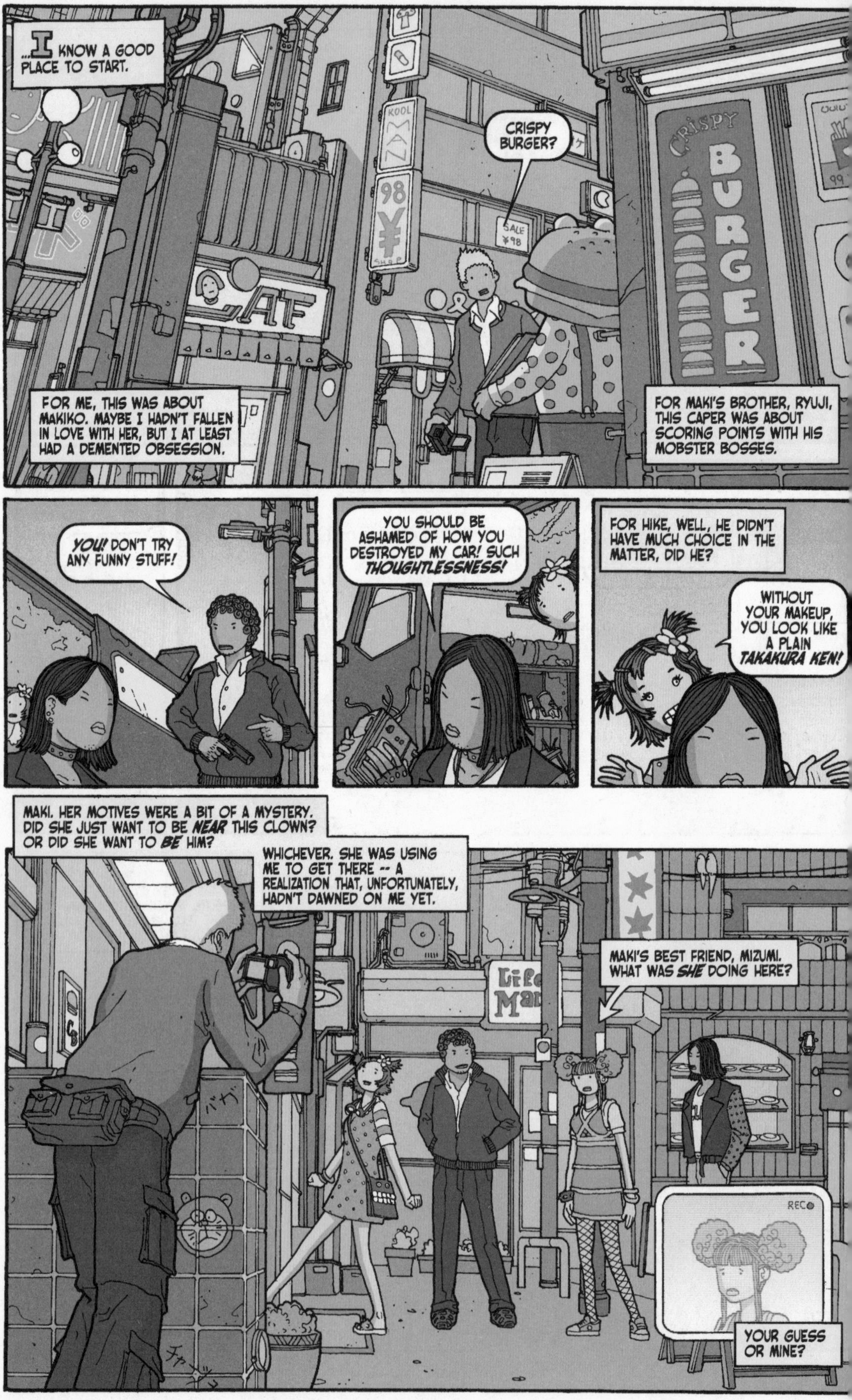

...I KNOW A GOOD PLACE TO START.
KOOL MAN
98 ¥
SALE ¥98
CRISPY BURGER?
Crispy BURGER
FOR ME, THIS WAS ABOUT MAKIKO. MAYBE I HADN'T FALLEN IN LOVE WITH HER, BUT I AT LEAST HAD A DEMENTED OBSESSION.
FOR MAKI'S BROTHER, RYUJI, THIS CAPER WAS ABOUT SCORING POINTS WITH HIS MOBSTER BOSSES.
YOU! DON'T TRY ANY FUNNY STUFF!
YOU SHOULD BE ASHAMED OF HOW YOU DESTROYED MY CAR! SUCH THOUGHTLESSNESS!
FOR HIKE, WELL, HE DIDN'T HAVE MUCH CHOICE IN THE MATTER, DID HE?
WITHOUT YOUR MAKEUP, YOU LOOK LIKE A PLAIN TAKAKURA KEN!
MAKI. HER MOTIVES WERE A BIT OF A MYSTERY. DID SHE JUST WANT TO BE NEAR THIS CLOWN? OR DID SHE WANT TO BE HIM?
WHICHEVER. SHE WAS USING ME TO GET THERE -- A REALIZATION THAT, UNFORTUNATELY, HADN'T DAWNED ON ME YET.
MAKI'S BEST FRIEND, MIZUMI. WHAT WAS SHE DOING HERE?
REC
YOUR GUESS OR MINE?

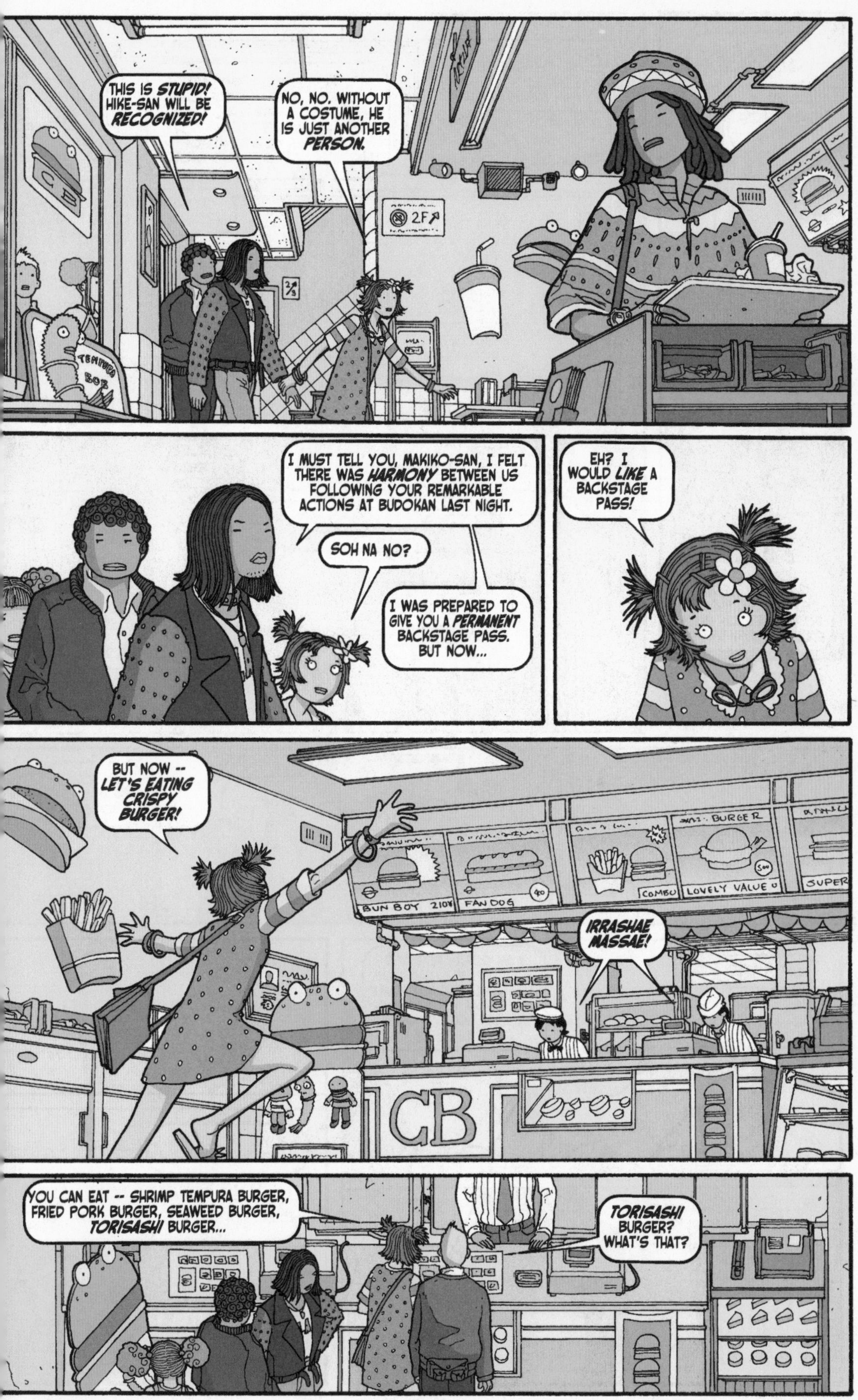
THIS IS STUPID! HIKE-SAN WILL BE RECOGNIZED!
NO, NO. WITHOUT A COSTUME, HE IS JUST ANOTHER PERSON.
2F
TEMPURA BOB
I MUST TELL YOU, MAKIKO-SAN, I FELT THERE WAS HARMONY BETWEEN US FOLLOWING YOUR REMARKABLE ACTIONS AT BUDOKAN LAST NIGHT.
SOH NA NO?
I WAS PREPARED TO GIVE YOU A PERMANENT BACKSTAGE PASS. BUT NOW...
EH? I WOULD LIKE A BACKSTAGE PASS!
BUT NOW -- LET'S EATING CRISPY BURGER!
BUN BOY 210¥
FAN DOG
COMBO
BURGER
LOVELY VALUE
SUPER
IRRASHAE MASSAE!
CB
YOU CAN EAT -- SHRIMP TEMPURA BURGER, FRIED PORK BURGER, SEAWEED BURGER, TORISASHI BURGER...
TORISASHI BURGER? WHAT'S THAT?

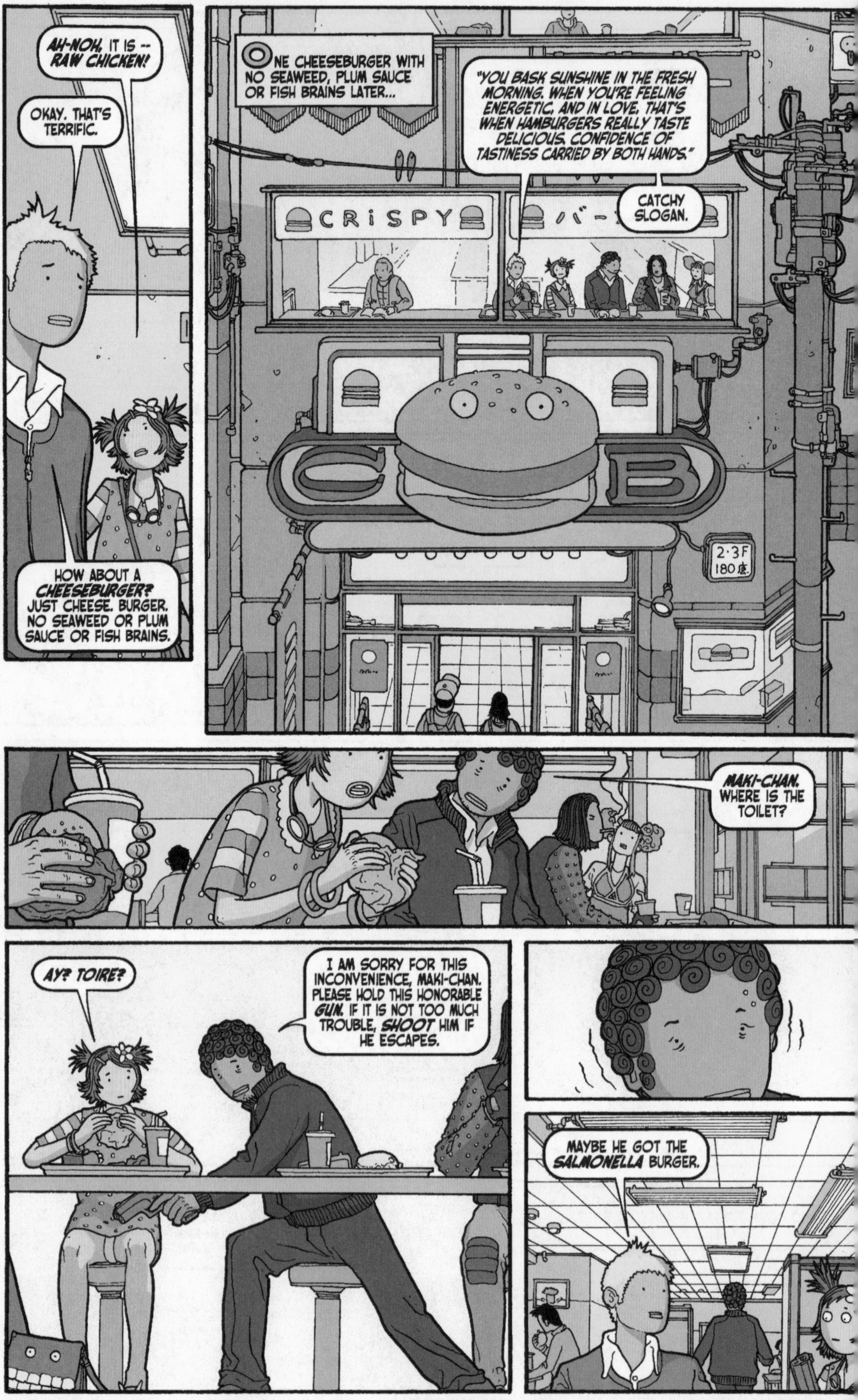
AH-NOH, IT IS -- RAW CHICKEN!
OKAY. THAT'S TERRIFIC.
HOW ABOUT A CHEESEBURGER? JUST CHEESE. BURGER. NO SEAWEED OR PLUM SAUCE OR FISH BRAINS.
ONE CHEESEBURGER WITH NO SEAWEED, PLUM SAUCE OR FISH BRAINS LATER...
"YOU BASK SUNSHINE IN THE FRESH MORNING. WHEN YOU'RE FEELING ENERGETIC, AND IN LOVE, THAT'S WHEN HAMBURGERS REALLY TASTE DELICIOUS. CONFIDENCE OF TASTINESS CARRIED BY BOTH HANDS."
CATCHY SLOGAN.
CRiSPY
CB
2·3F
180席
MAKI-CHAN. WHERE IS THE TOILET?
AY? TOIRE?
I AM SORRY FOR THIS INCONVENIENCE, MAKI-CHAN. PLEASE HOLD THIS HONORABLE GUN. IF IT IS NOT TOO MUCH TROUBLE, SHOOT HIM IF HE ESCAPES.
MAYBE HE GOT THE SALMONELLA BURGER.

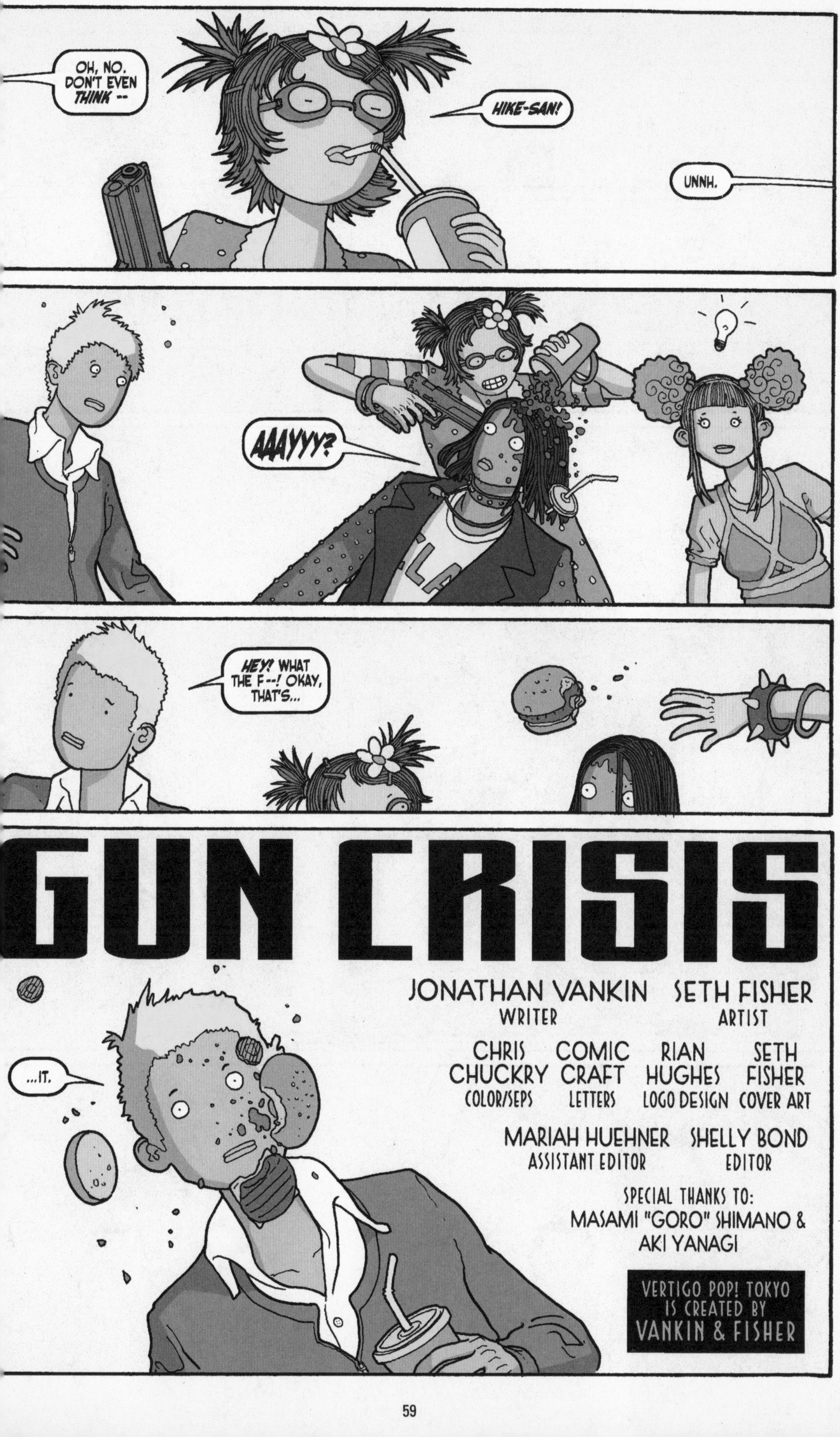
OH, NO. DON'T EVEN THINK --
HIKE-SAN!
UNNH.
AAAYYY?
HEY! WHAT THE F--! OKAY, THAT'S...
...IT.
GUN CRISIS
JONATHAN VANKIN WRITER
SETH FISHER ARTIST
CHRIS CHUCKRY COLOR/SEPS
COMIC CRAFT LETTERS
RIAN HUGHES LOGO DESIGN
SETH FISHER COVER ART
MARIAH HUEHNER ASSISTANT EDITOR
SHELLY BOND EDITOR
SPECIAL THANKS TO: MASAMI "GORO" SHIMANO & AKI YANAGI
VERTIGO POP! TOKYO IS CREATED BY VANKIN & FISHER

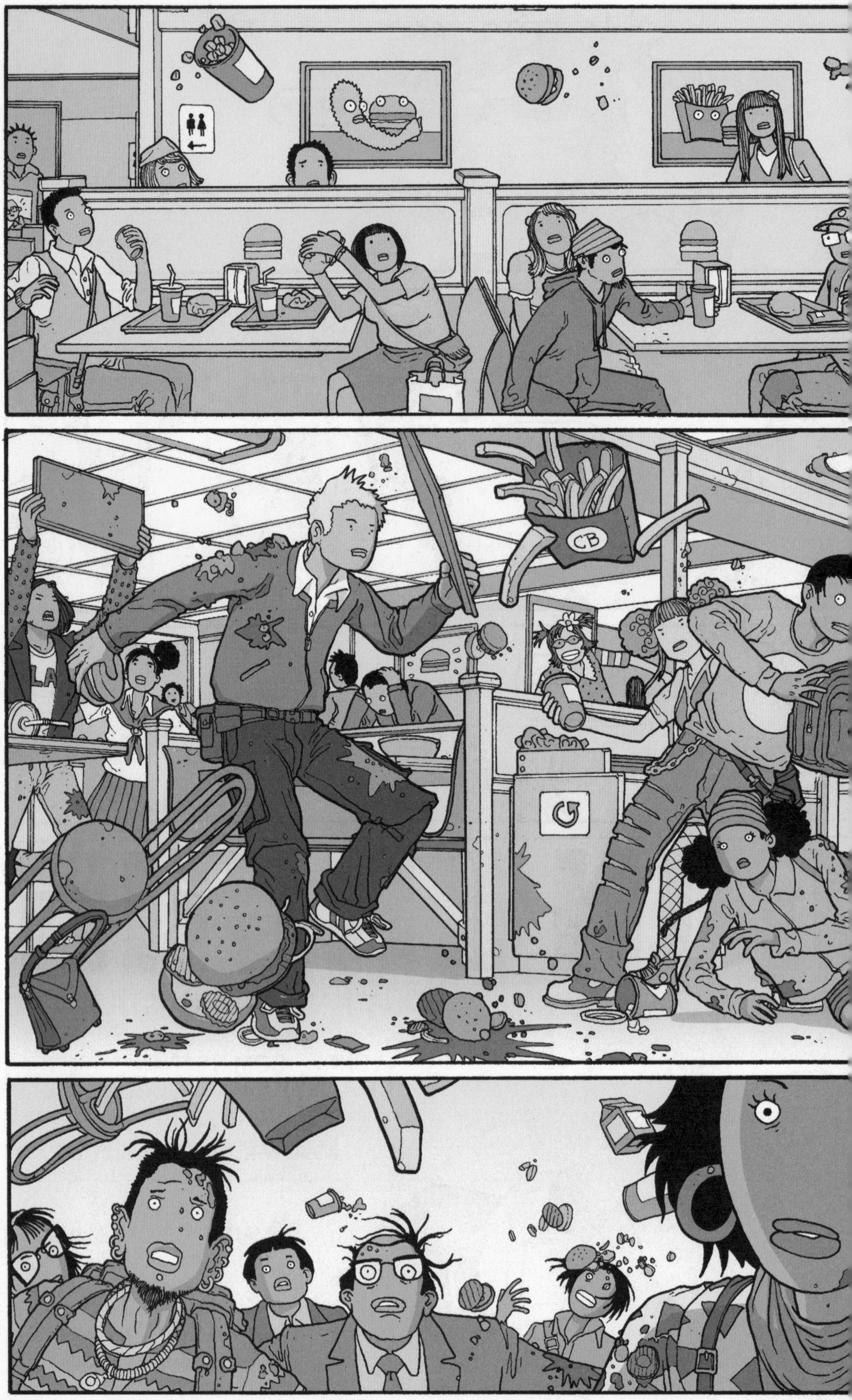
CB
LA

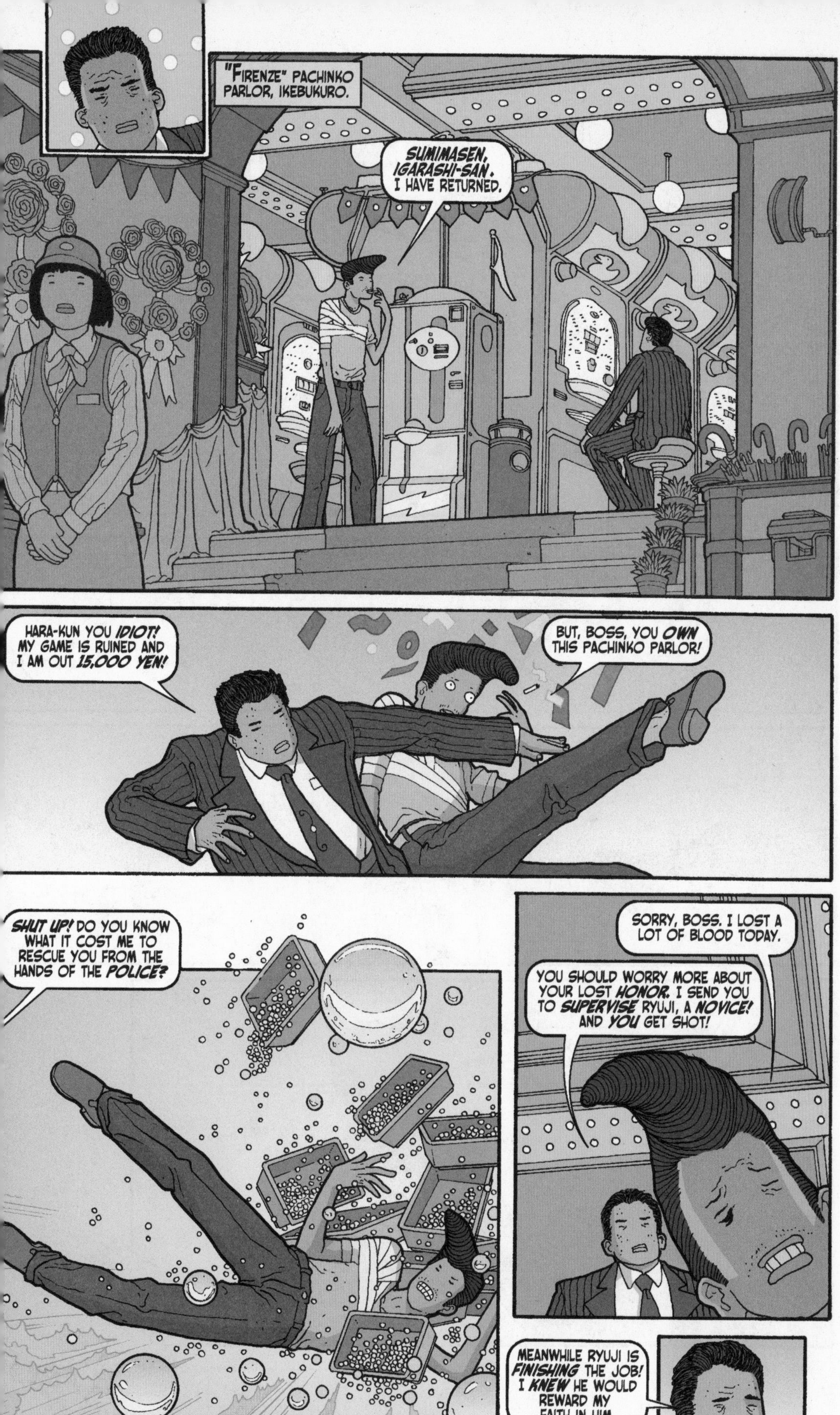

"FIRENZE" PACHINKO PARLOR, IKEBUKURO.
SUMIMASEN, IGARASHI-SAN. I HAVE RETURNED.
HARA-KUN YOU IDIOT! MY GAME IS RUINED AND I AM OUT 15,000 YEN!
BUT, BOSS, YOU OWN THIS PACHINKO PARLOR!
SHUT UP! DO YOU KNOW WHAT IT COST ME TO RESCUE YOU FROM THE HANDS OF THE POLICE?
SORRY, BOSS. I LOST A LOT OF BLOOD TODAY.
YOU SHOULD WORRY MORE ABOUT YOUR LOST HONOR. I SEND YOU TO SUPERVISE RYUJI, A NOVICE! AND YOU GET SHOT!
MEANWHILE RYUJI IS FINISHING THE JOB! I KNEW HE WOULD REWARD MY FAITH IN HIM.

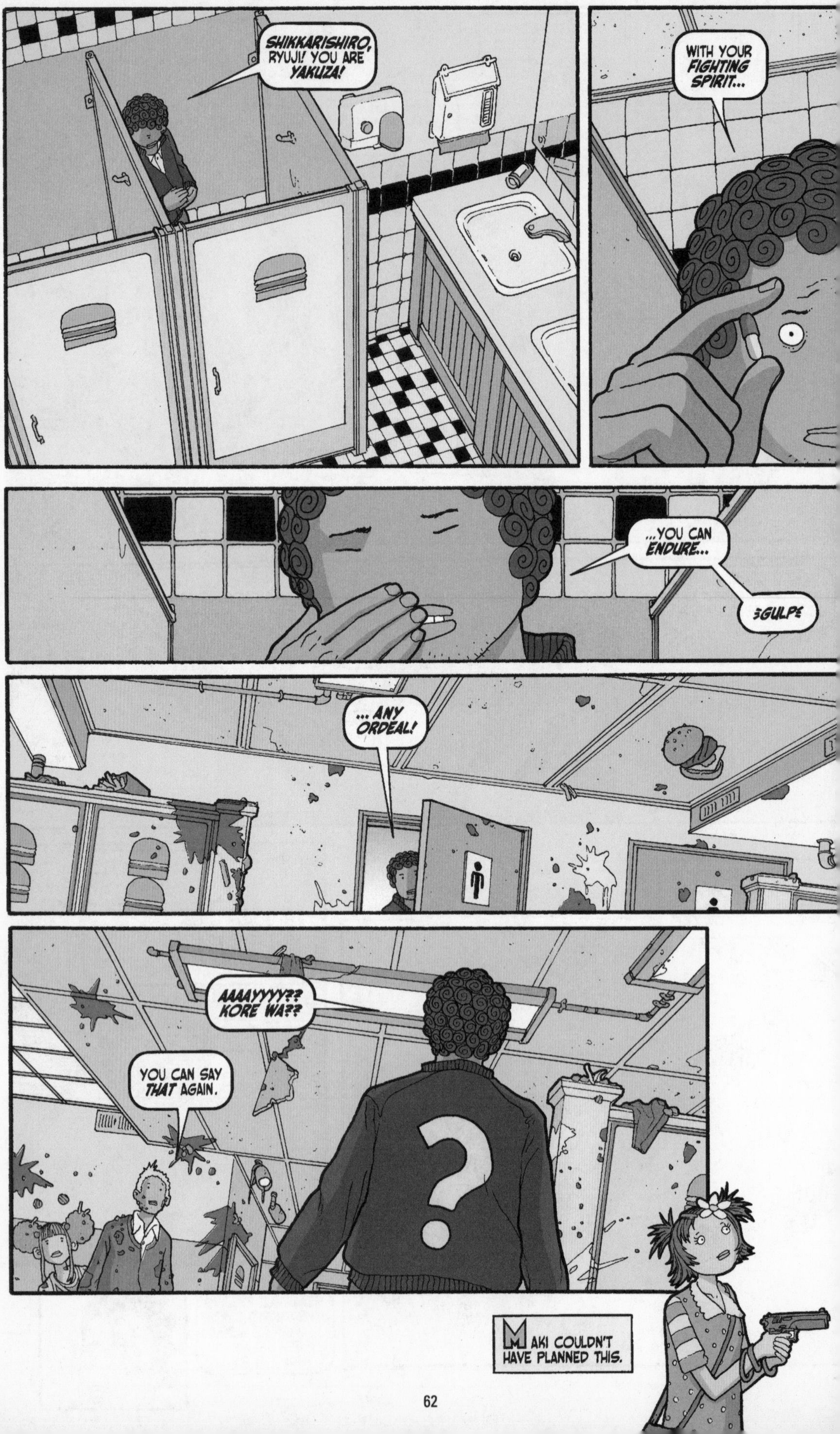
SHIKKARISHIRO, RYUJI! YOU ARE YAKUZA!
WITH YOUR FIGHTING SPIRIT...
...YOU CAN ENDURE...
GULP
...ANY ORDEAL!
AAAAYYYY?? KORE WA??
YOU CAN SAY THAT AGAIN.
MAKI COULDN'T HAVE PLANNED THIS.

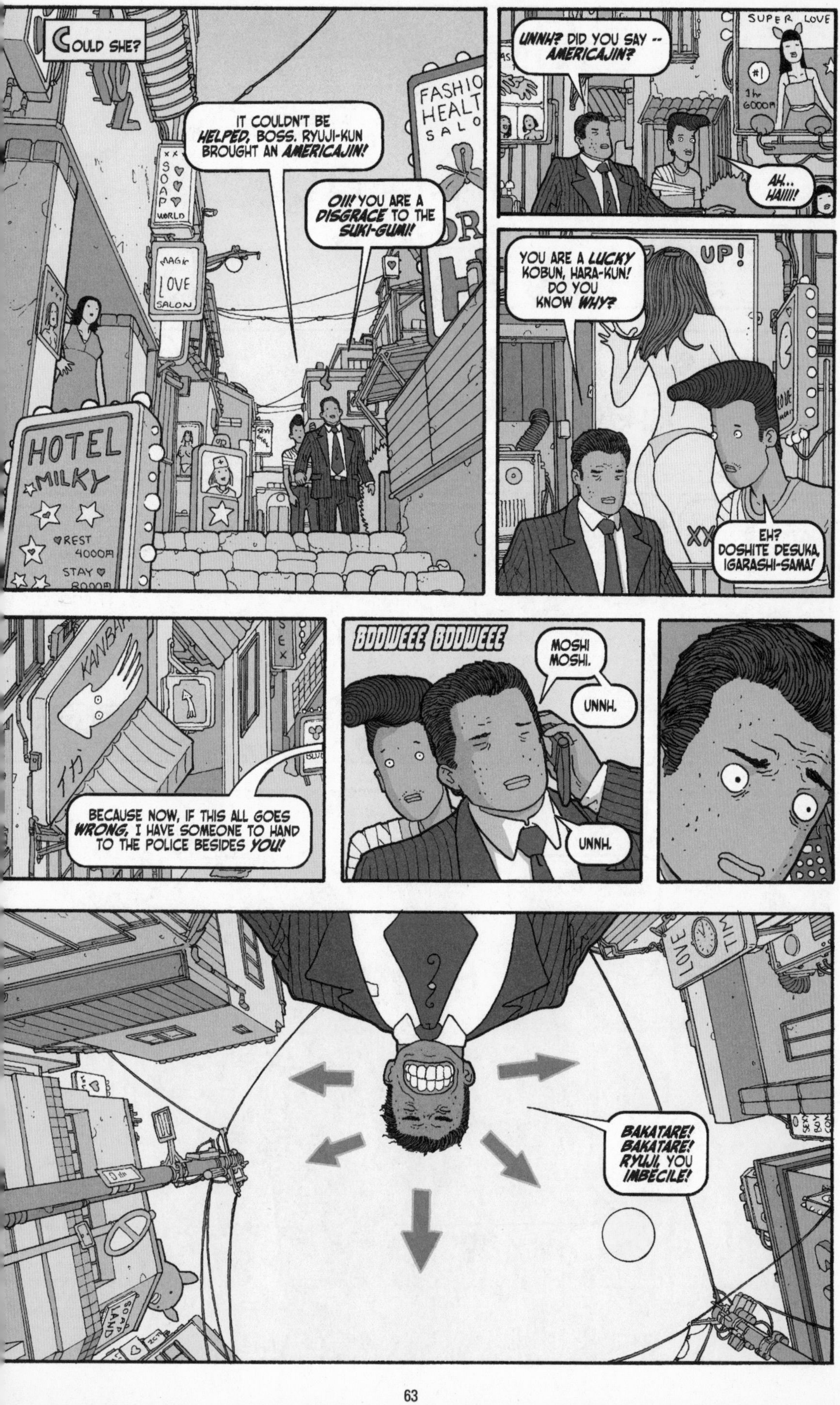

COULD SHE?
IT COULDN'T BE HELPED, BOSS. RYUJI-KUN BROUGHT AN AMERICAJIN!
OII! YOU ARE A DISGRACE TO THE SUKI-GUMI!
HOTEL MILKY
REST 4000円
STAY
SOAP WORLD
MAGIC LOVE SALON
FASHION HEALTH SALON
UNNH? DID YOU SAY -- AMERICAJIN?
AH.. HAIIII!
SUPER LOVE
#1
1 hr 6000円
YOU ARE A LUCKY KOBUN, HARA-KUN! DO YOU KNOW WHY?
UP!
EH? DOSHITE DESUKA, IGARASHI-SAMA!
BECAUSE NOW, IF THIS ALL GOES WRONG, I HAVE SOMEONE TO HAND TO THE POLICE BESIDES YOU!
SEX
BDDWEEE BDDWEEE
MOSHI MOSHI.
UNNH.
UNNH.
BAKATARE! BAKATARE! RYUJI, YOU IMBECILE!
LOVE
SOAP LAND

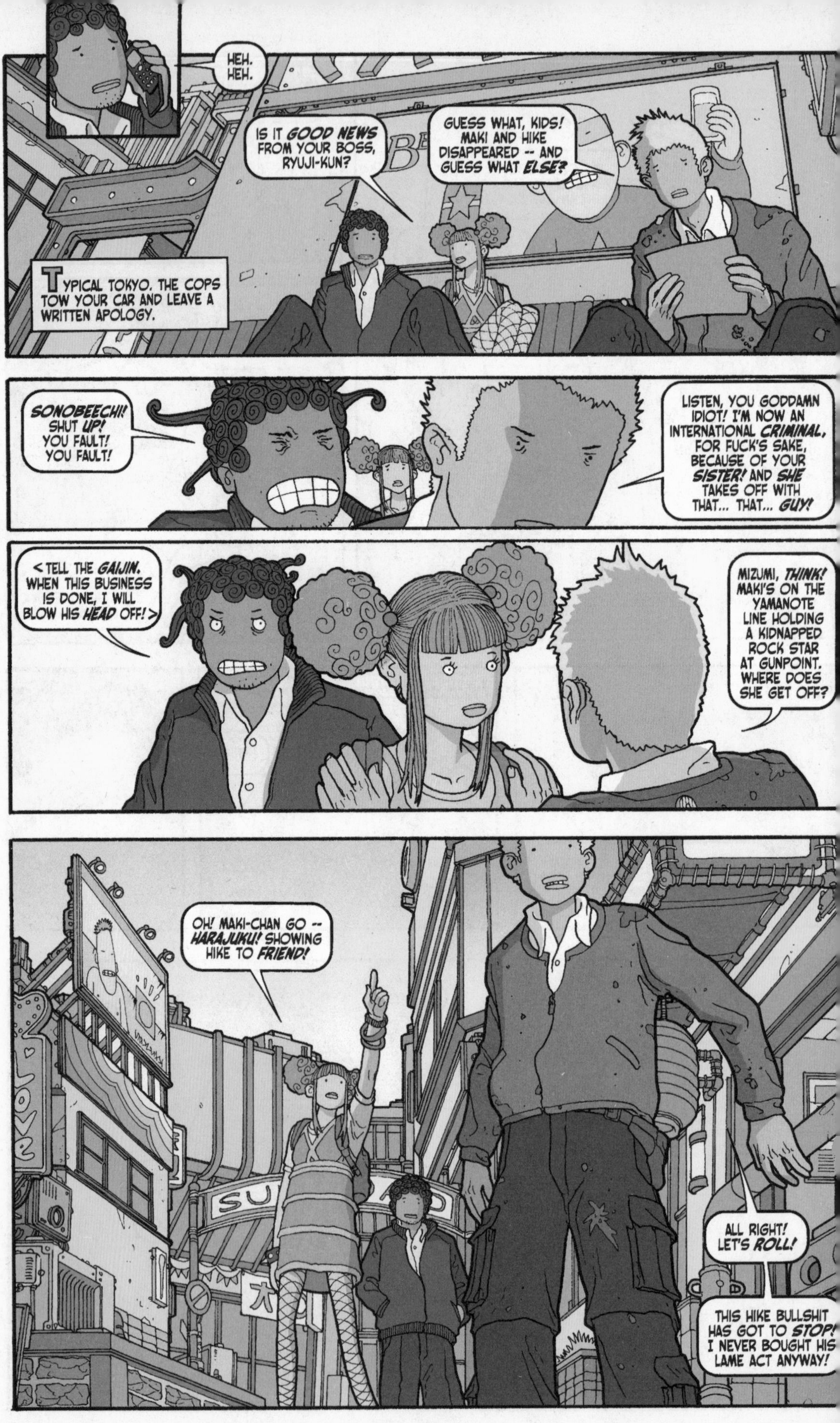
HEH. HEH.
IS IT GOOD NEWS FROM YOUR BOSS, RYUJI-KUN?
GUESS WHAT, KIDS! MAKI AND HIKE DISAPPEARED -- AND GUESS WHAT ELSE?
TYPICAL TOKYO. THE COPS TOW YOUR CAR AND LEAVE A WRITTEN APOLOGY.
SONOBEECHI! SHUT UP! YOU FAULT! YOU FAULT!
LISTEN, YOU GODDAMN IDIOT! I'M NOW AN INTERNATIONAL CRIMINAL, FOR FUCK'S SAKE, BECAUSE OF YOUR SISTER! AND SHE TAKES OFF WITH THAT... THAT... GUY!
<TELL THE GAIJIN. WHEN THIS BUSINESS IS DONE, I WILL BLOW HIS HEAD OFF!>
MIZUMI, THINK! MAKI'S ON THE YAMANOTE LINE HOLDING A KIDNAPPED ROCK STAR AT GUNPOINT. WHERE DOES SHE GET OFF?
OH! MAKI-CHAN GO -- HARAJUKU! SHOWING HIKE TO FRIEND!
ALL RIGHT! LET'S ROLL!
THIS HIKE BULLSHIT HAS GOT TO STOP! I NEVER BOUGHT HIS LAME ACT ANYWAY!

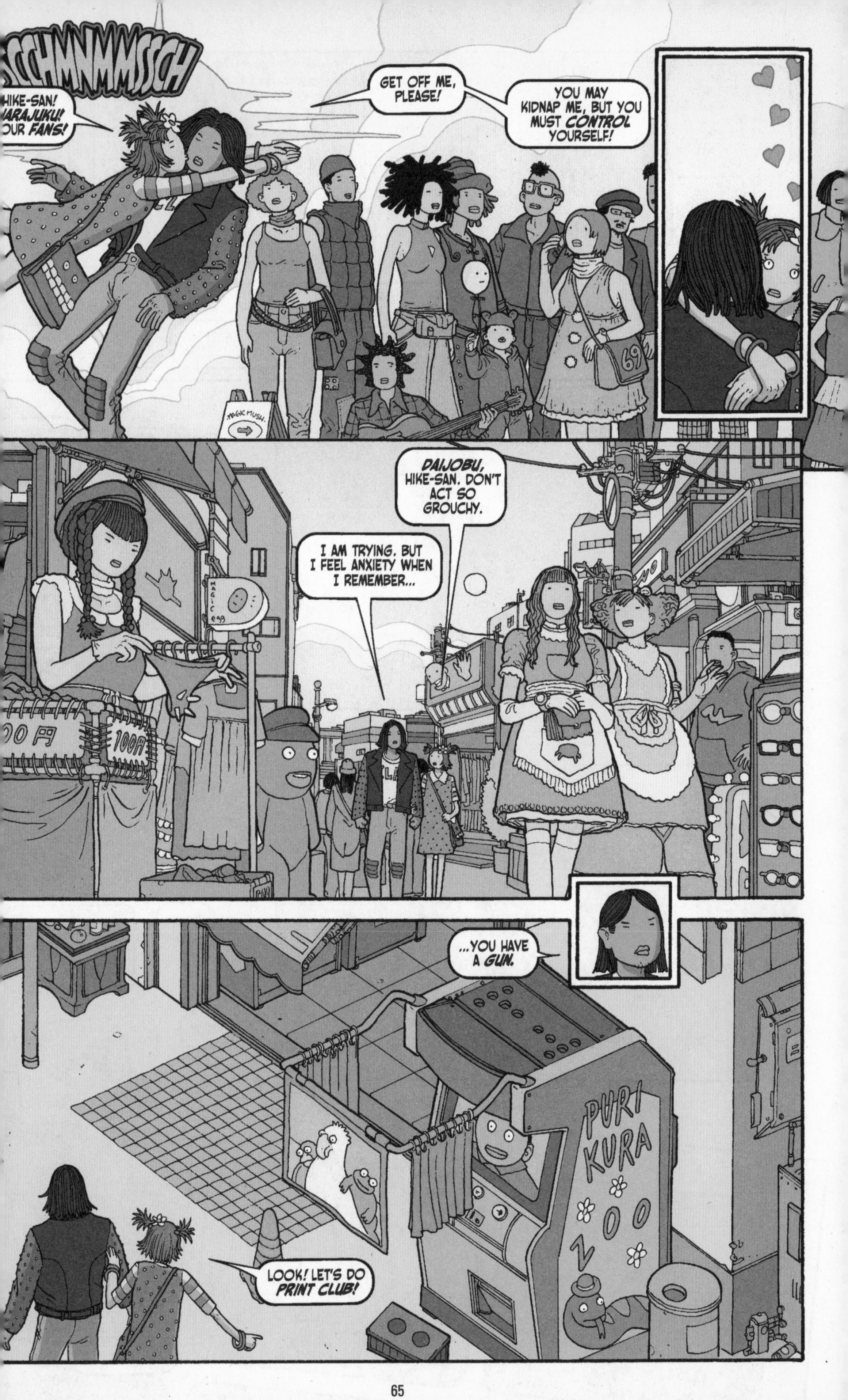
SCHMNMMSSCH
HIKE-SAN! HARAJUKU! YOUR FANS!
GET OFF ME, PLEASE!
YOU MAY KIDNAP ME, BUT YOU MUST CONTROL YOURSELF!
MAGIC MUSH
DAIJOBU, HIKE-SAN. DON'T ACT SO GROUCHY.
I AM TRYING. BUT I FEEL ANXIETY WHEN I REMEMBER...
MAGIC egg
100円
...YOU HAVE A GUN.
LOOK! LET'S DO PRINT CLUB!
PURI KURA ZOO

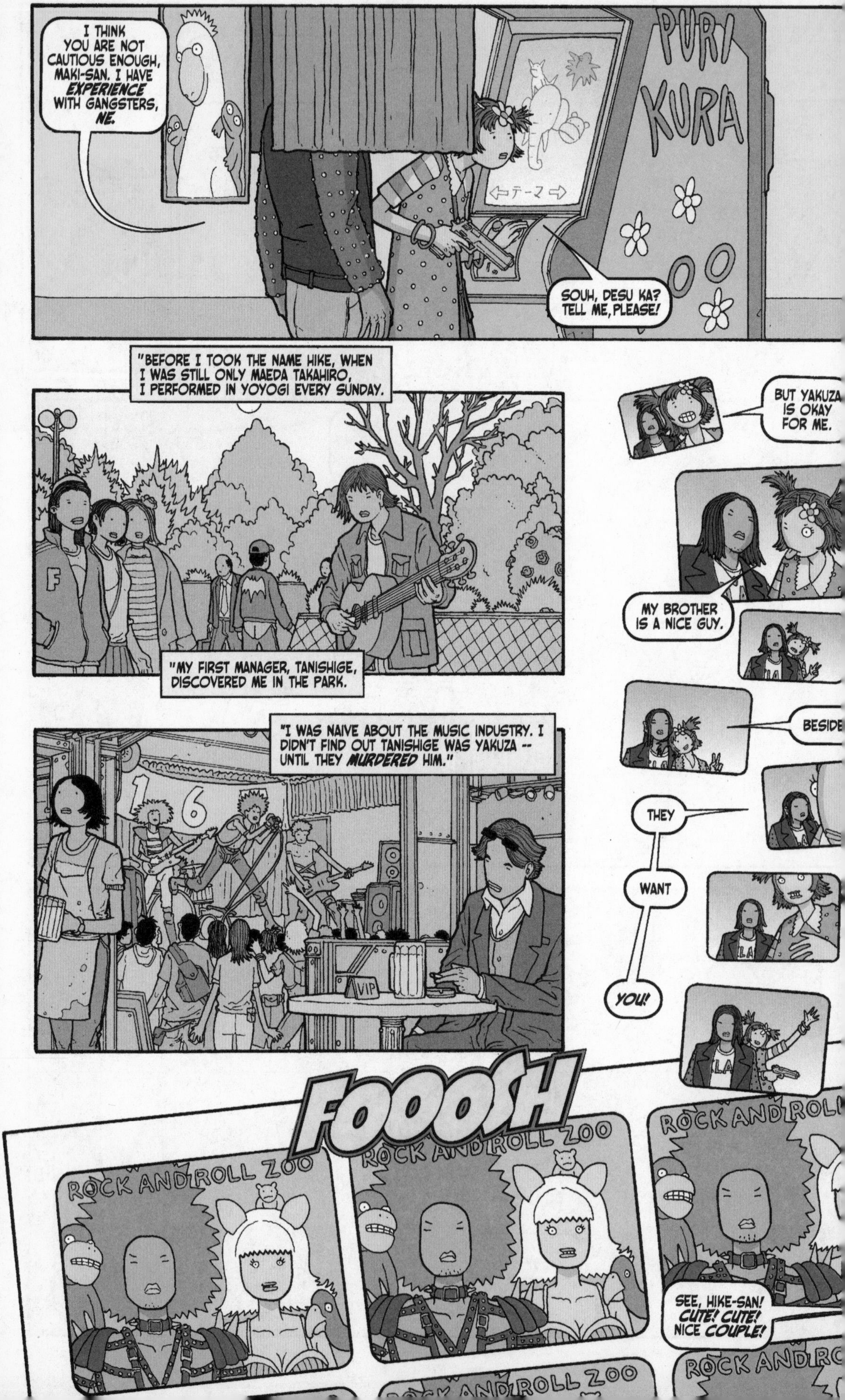
PURI KURA
I THINK YOU ARE NOT CAUTIOUS ENOUGH, MAKI-SAN. I HAVE *EXPERIENCE* WITH GANGSTERS, *NE.*
⇦テーマ⇨
SOUH, DESU KA? TELL ME, PLEASE!
"BEFORE I TOOK THE NAME HIKE, WHEN I WAS STILL ONLY MAEDA TAKAHIRO, I PERFORMED IN YOYOGI EVERY SUNDAY.
"MY FIRST MANAGER, TANISHIGE, DISCOVERED ME IN THE PARK.
"I WAS NAIVE ABOUT THE MUSIC INDUSTRY. I DIDN'T FIND OUT TANISHIGE WAS YAKUZA -- UNTIL THEY *MURDERED* HIM."
VIP
BUT YAKUZA IS OKAY FOR ME.
MY BROTHER IS A NICE GUY.
BESIDE
THEY
WANT
YOU!
FOOOSH
ROCK AND ROLL ZOO
SEE, HIKE-SAN! *CUTE! CUTE!* NICE *COUPLE!*

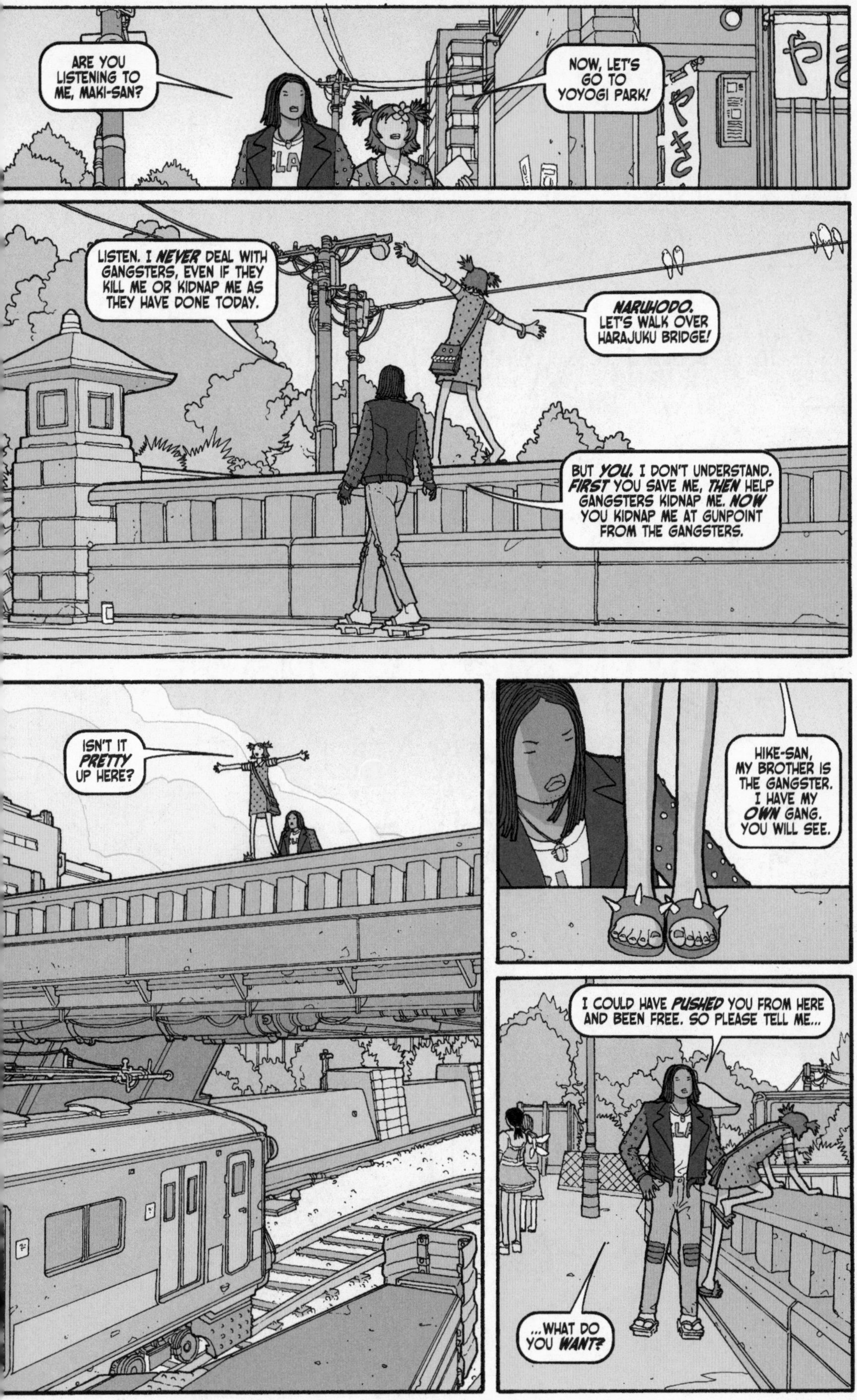

ARE YOU LISTENING TO ME, MAKI-SAN?
NOW, LET'S GO TO YOYOGI PARK!
LISTEN. I NEVER DEAL WITH GANGSTERS, EVEN IF THEY KILL ME OR KIDNAP ME AS THEY HAVE DONE TODAY.
NARUHODO. LET'S WALK OVER HARAJUKU BRIDGE!
BUT YOU. I DON'T UNDERSTAND. FIRST YOU SAVE ME, THEN HELP GANGSTERS KIDNAP ME. NOW YOU KIDNAP ME AT GUNPOINT FROM THE GANGSTERS.
ISN'T IT PRETTY UP HERE?
HIKE-SAN, MY BROTHER IS THE GANGSTER. I HAVE MY OWN GANG. YOU WILL SEE.
I COULD HAVE PUSHED YOU FROM HERE AND BEEN FREE. SO PLEASE TELL ME...
...WHAT DO YOU WANT?

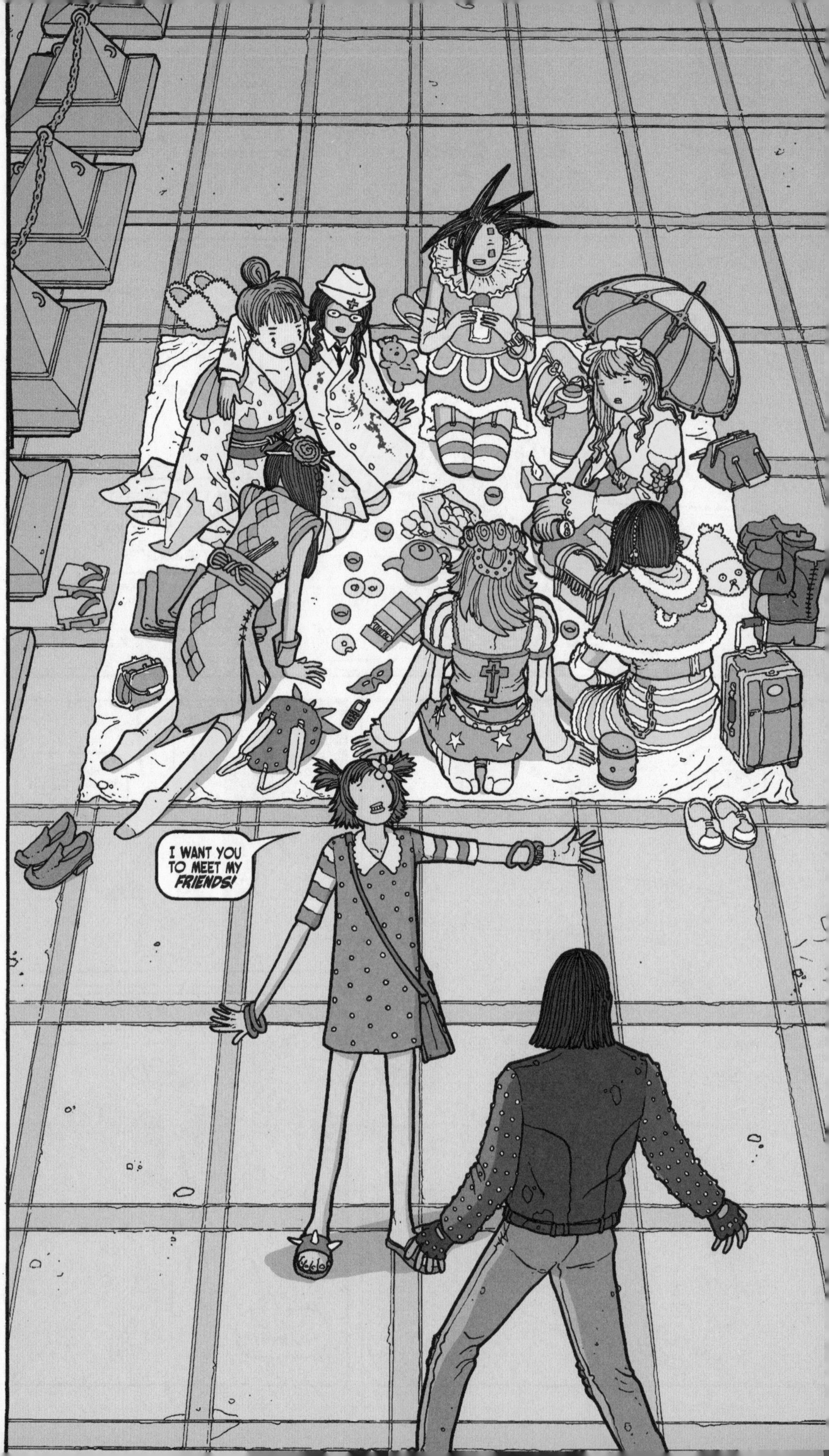
I WANT YOU TO MEET MY FRIENDS!

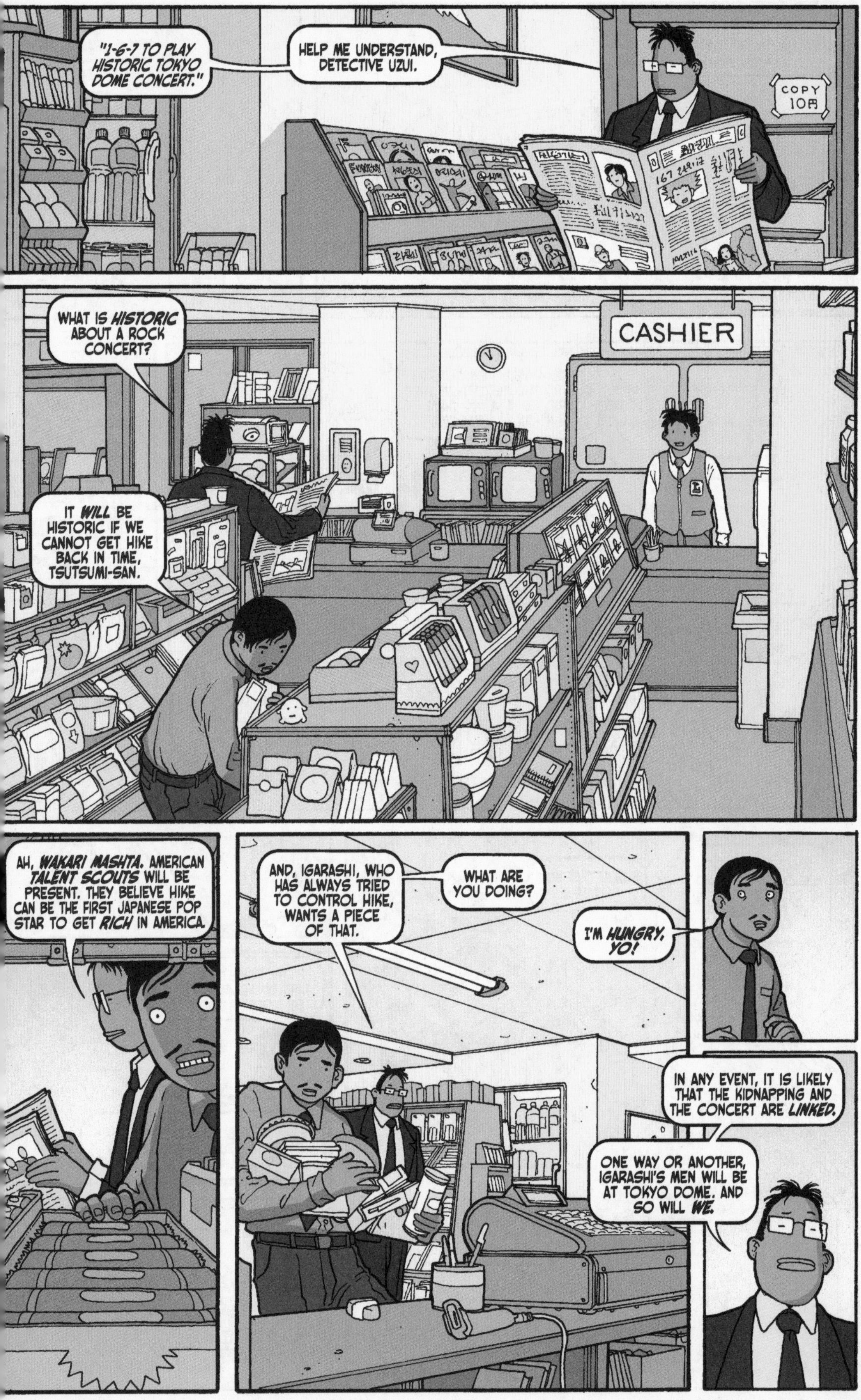
"1-6-7 TO PLAY HISTORIC TOKYO DOME CONCERT."
HELP ME UNDERSTAND, DETECTIVE UZUI.
COPY 10円
WHAT IS HISTORIC ABOUT A ROCK CONCERT?
CASHIER
IT WILL BE HISTORIC IF WE CANNOT GET HIKE BACK IN TIME, TSUTSUMI-SAN.
AH, WAKARI MASHTA. AMERICAN TALENT SCOUTS WILL BE PRESENT. THEY BELIEVE HIKE CAN BE THE FIRST JAPANESE POP STAR TO GET RICH IN AMERICA.
AND, IGARASHI, WHO HAS ALWAYS TRIED TO CONTROL HIKE, WANTS A PIECE OF THAT.
WHAT ARE YOU DOING?
I'M HUNGRY, YO!
IN ANY EVENT, IT IS LIKELY THAT THE KIDNAPPING AND THE CONCERT ARE LINKED.
ONE WAY OR ANOTHER, IGARASHI'S MEN WILL BE AT TOKYO DOME. AND SO WILL WE.

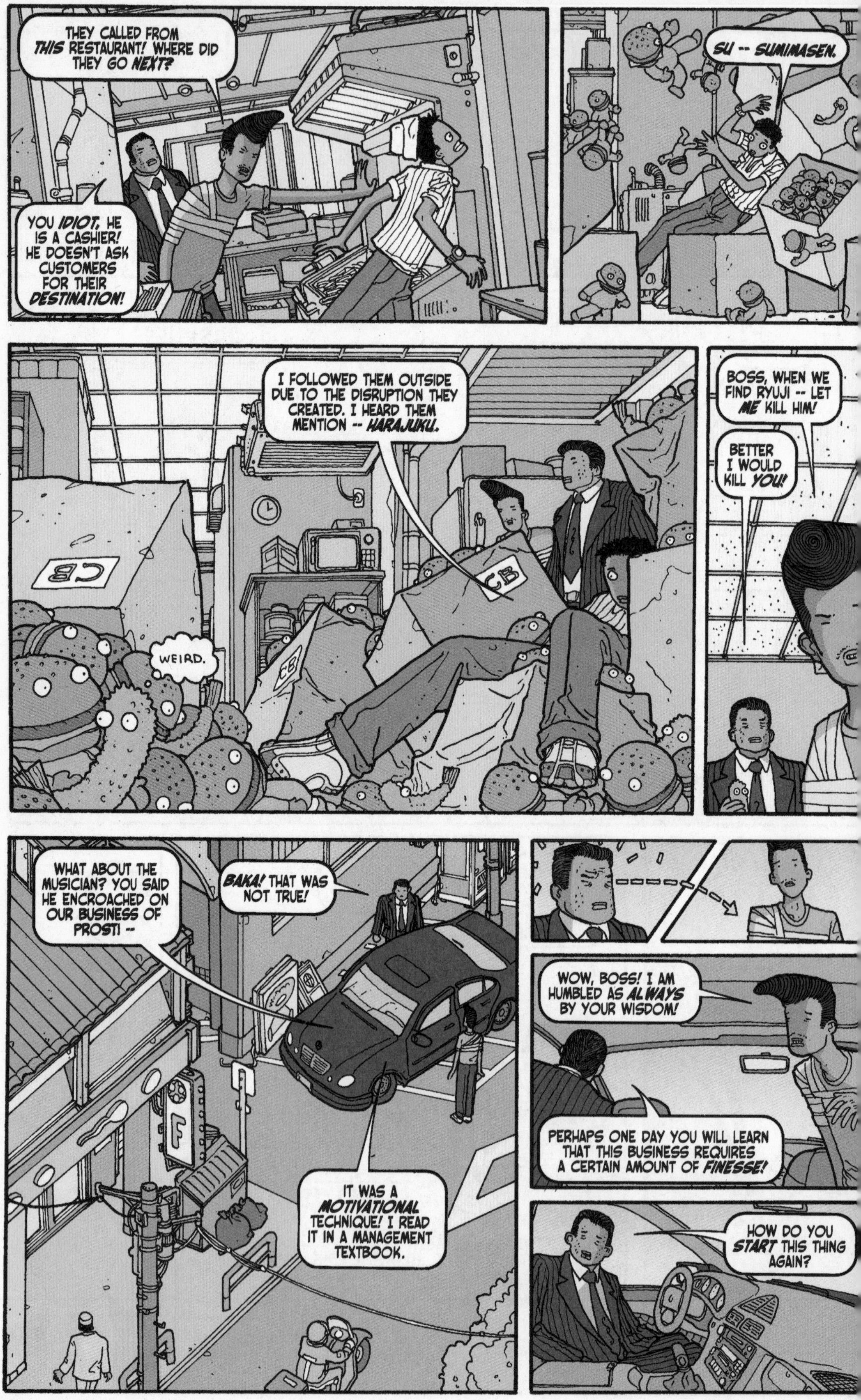
THEY CALLED FROM THIS RESTAURANT! WHERE DID THEY GO NEXT?
YOU IDIOT, HE IS A CASHIER! HE DOESN'T ASK CUSTOMERS FOR THEIR DESTINATION!
SU -- SUMIMASEN.
I FOLLOWED THEM OUTSIDE DUE TO THE DISRUPTION THEY CREATED. I HEARD THEM MENTION -- HARAJUKU.
CB
CB
CB
WEIRD.
BOSS, WHEN WE FIND RYUJI -- LET ME KILL HIM!
BETTER I WOULD KILL YOU!
WHAT ABOUT THE MUSICIAN? YOU SAID HE ENCROACHED ON OUR BUSINESS OF PROSTI --
BAKA! THAT WAS NOT TRUE!
IT WAS A MOTIVATIONAL TECHNIQUE! I READ IT IN A MANAGEMENT TEXTBOOK.
F
WOW, BOSS! I AM HUMBLED AS ALWAYS BY YOUR WISDOM!
PERHAPS ONE DAY YOU WILL LEARN THAT THIS BUSINESS REQUIRES A CERTAIN AMOUNT OF FINESSE!
HOW DO YOU START THIS THING AGAIN?

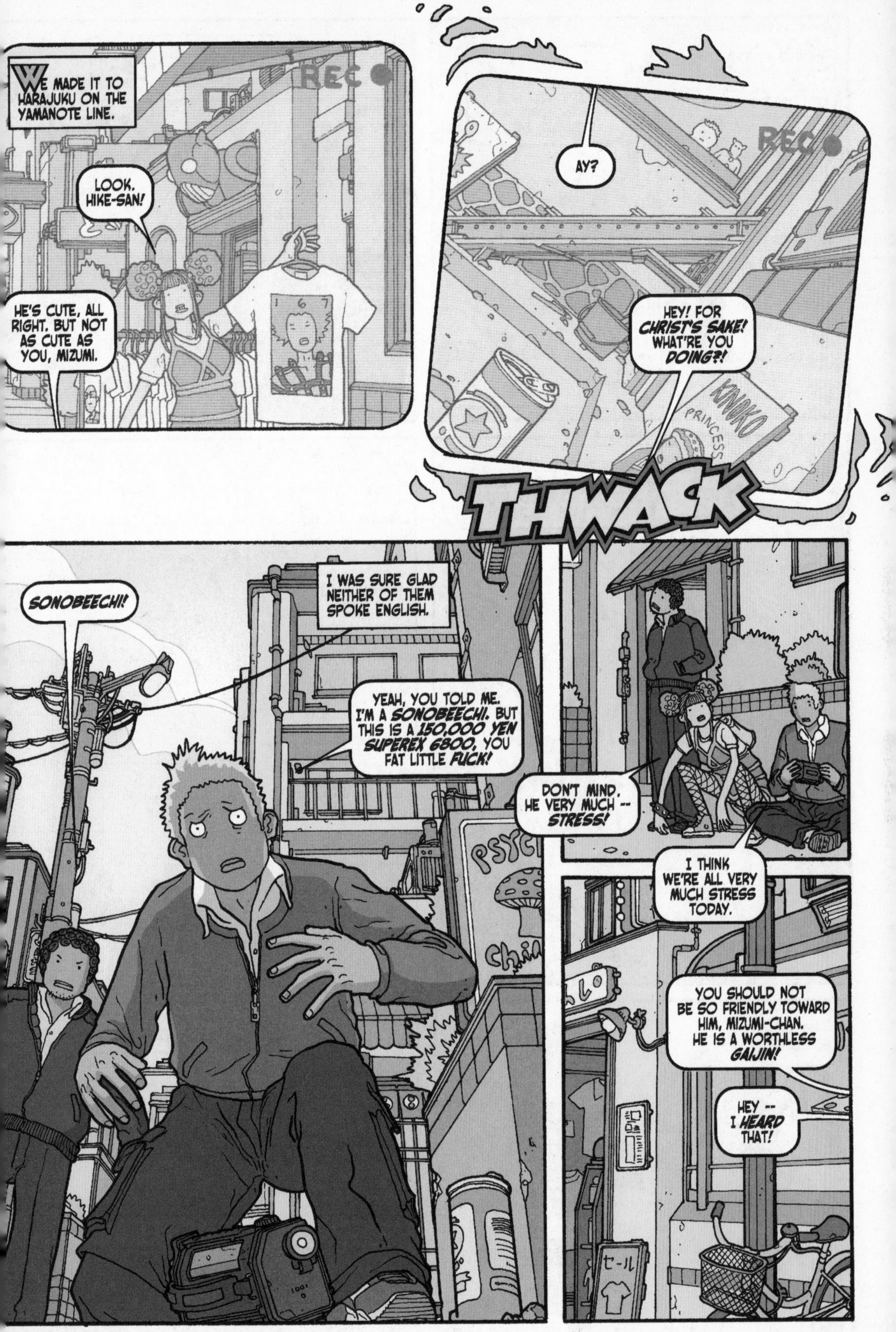
WE MADE IT TO HARAJUKU ON THE YAMANOTE LINE.
REC
LOOK, HIKE-SAN!
HE'S CUTE, ALL RIGHT. BUT NOT AS CUTE AS YOU, MIZUMI.
AY?
REC
HEY! FOR CHRIST'S SAKE! WHAT'RE YOU DOING?!
KINOKO PRINCESS
THWACK
SONOBEECHI!
I WAS SURE GLAD NEITHER OF THEM SPOKE ENGLISH.
YEAH, YOU TOLD ME. I'M A SONOBEECHI. BUT THIS IS A 150,000 YEN SUPEREX 6800, YOU FAT LITTLE FUCK!
DON'T MIND. HE VERY MUCH -- STRESS!
I THINK WE'RE ALL VERY MUCH STRESS TODAY.
YOU SHOULD NOT BE SO FRIENDLY TOWARD HIM, MIZUMI-CHAN. HE IS A WORTHLESS GAIJIN!
HEY -- I HEARD THAT!
セール

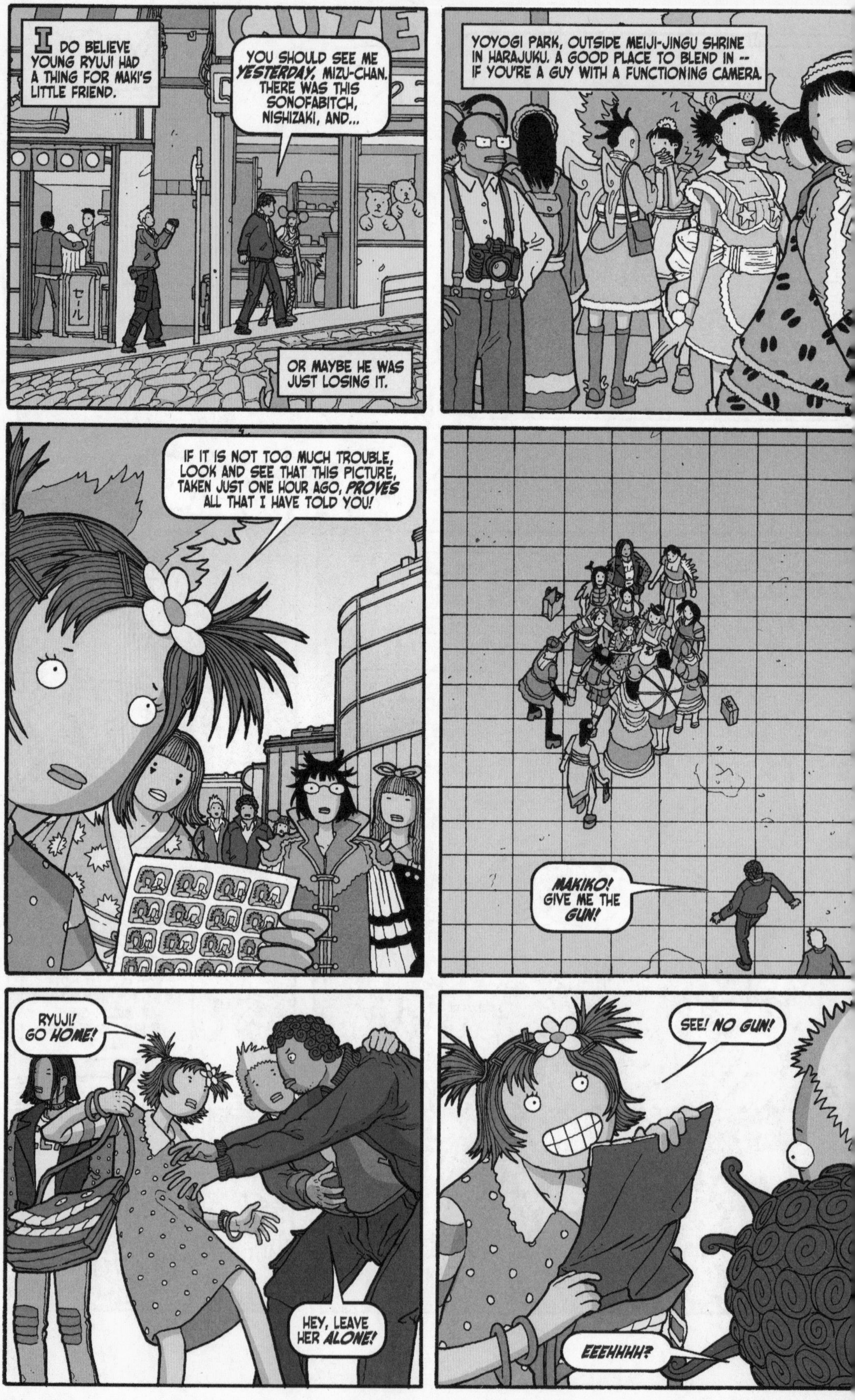
I DO BELIEVE YOUNG RYUJI HAD A THING FOR MAKI'S LITTLE FRIEND.
YOU SHOULD SEE ME YESTERDAY, MIZU-CHAN. THERE WAS THIS SONOFABITCH, NISHIZAKI, AND...
OR MAYBE HE WAS JUST LOSING IT.
YOYOGI PARK, OUTSIDE MEIJI-JINGU SHRINE IN HARAJUKU. A GOOD PLACE TO BLEND IN -- IF YOU'RE A GUY WITH A FUNCTIONING CAMERA.
IF IT IS NOT TOO MUCH TROUBLE, LOOK AND SEE THAT THIS PICTURE, TAKEN JUST ONE HOUR AGO, PROVES ALL THAT I HAVE TOLD YOU!
MAKIKO! GIVE ME THE GUN!
RYUJI! GO HOME!
HEY, LEAVE HER ALONE!
SEE! NO GUN!
EEEHHHH?

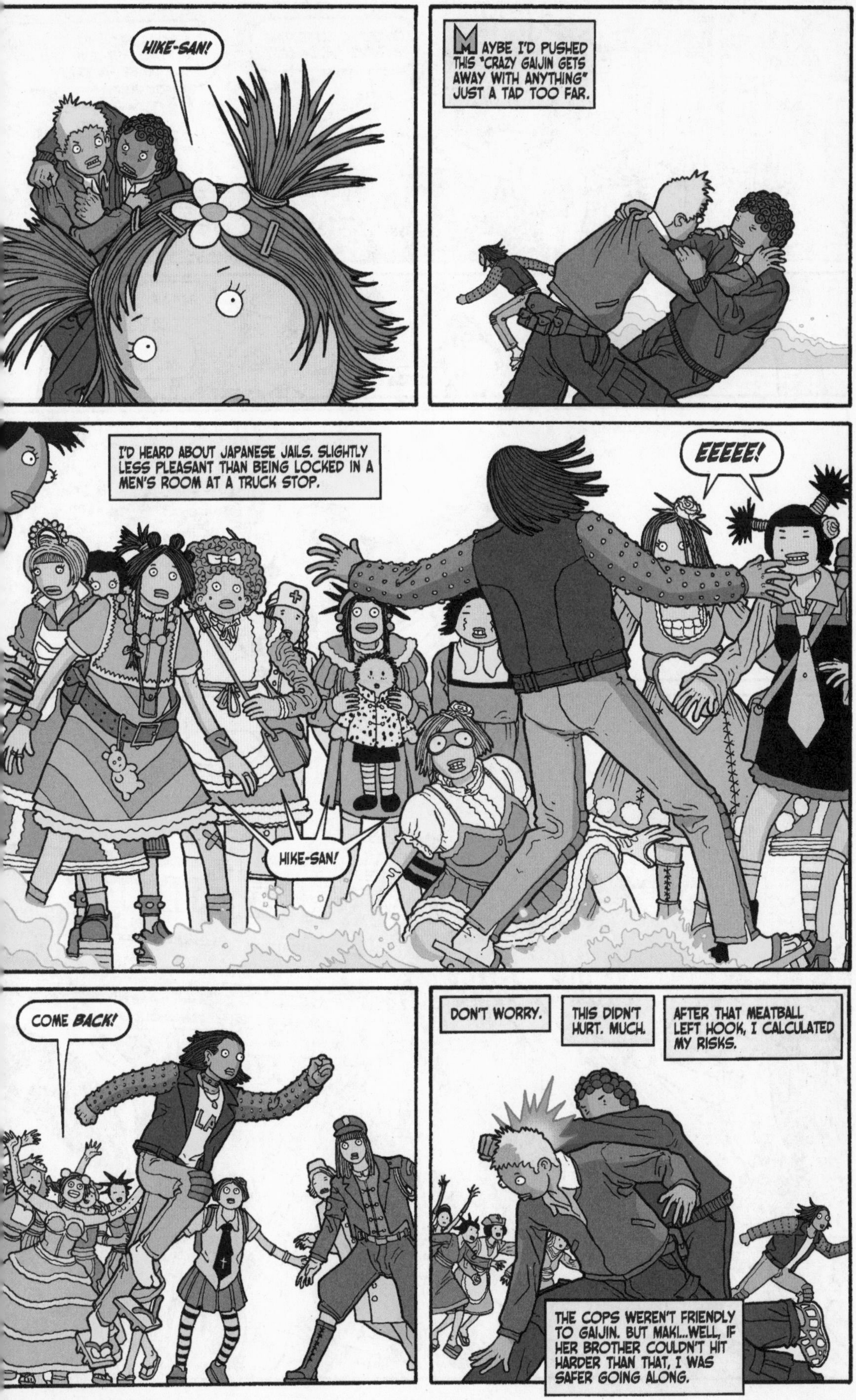
HIKE-SAN!
MAYBE I'D PUSHED THIS "CRAZY GAIJIN GETS AWAY WITH ANYTHING" JUST A TAD TOO FAR.
I'D HEARD ABOUT JAPANESE JAILS. SLIGHTLY LESS PLEASANT THAN BEING LOCKED IN A MEN'S ROOM AT A TRUCK STOP.
EEEEE!
HIKE-SAN!
COME BACK!
DON'T WORRY.
THIS DIDN'T HURT. MUCH.
AFTER THAT MEATBALL LEFT HOOK, I CALCULATED MY RISKS.
THE COPS WEREN'T FRIENDLY TO GAIJIN. BUT MAKI...WELL, IF HER BROTHER COULDN'T HIT HARDER THAN THAT, I WAS SAFER GOING ALONG.

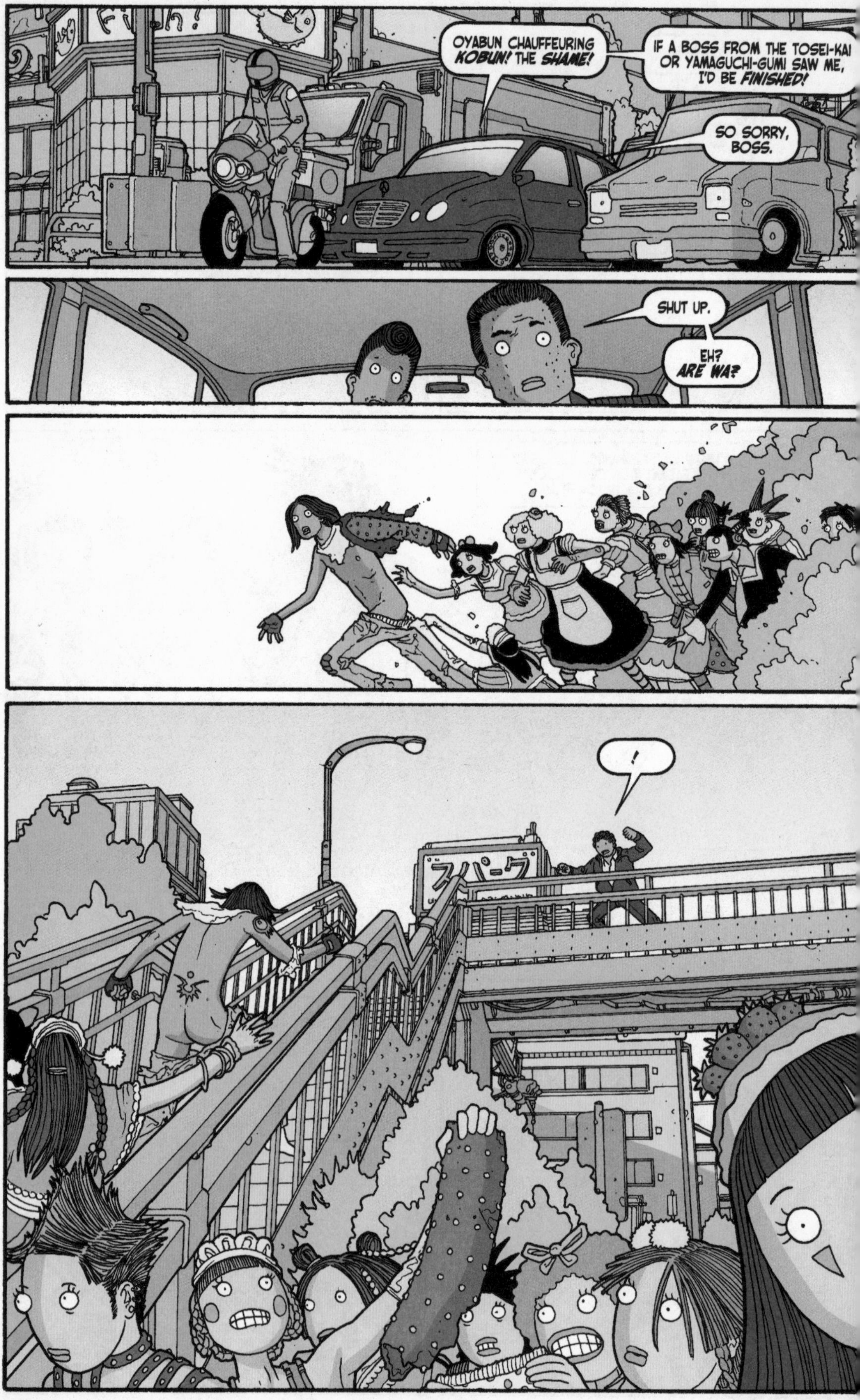

OYABUN CHAUFFEURING KOBUN! THE SHAME!
IF A BOSS FROM THE TOSEI-KAI OR YAMAGUCHI-GUMI SAW ME, I'D BE FINISHED!
SO SORRY, BOSS.
SHUT UP.
EH? ARE WA?
!

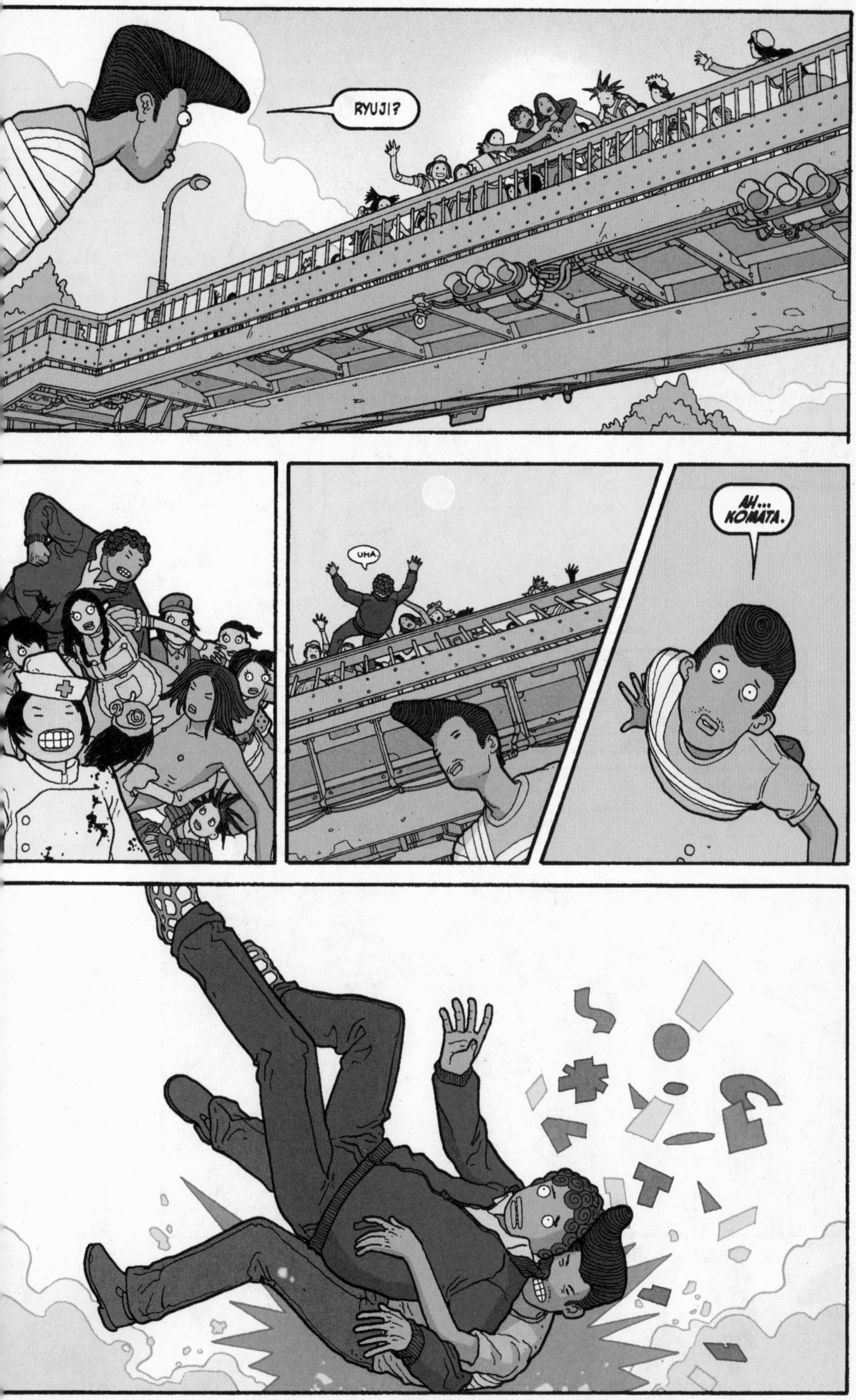
RYUJI?
UHA.
AH... KOMATA.

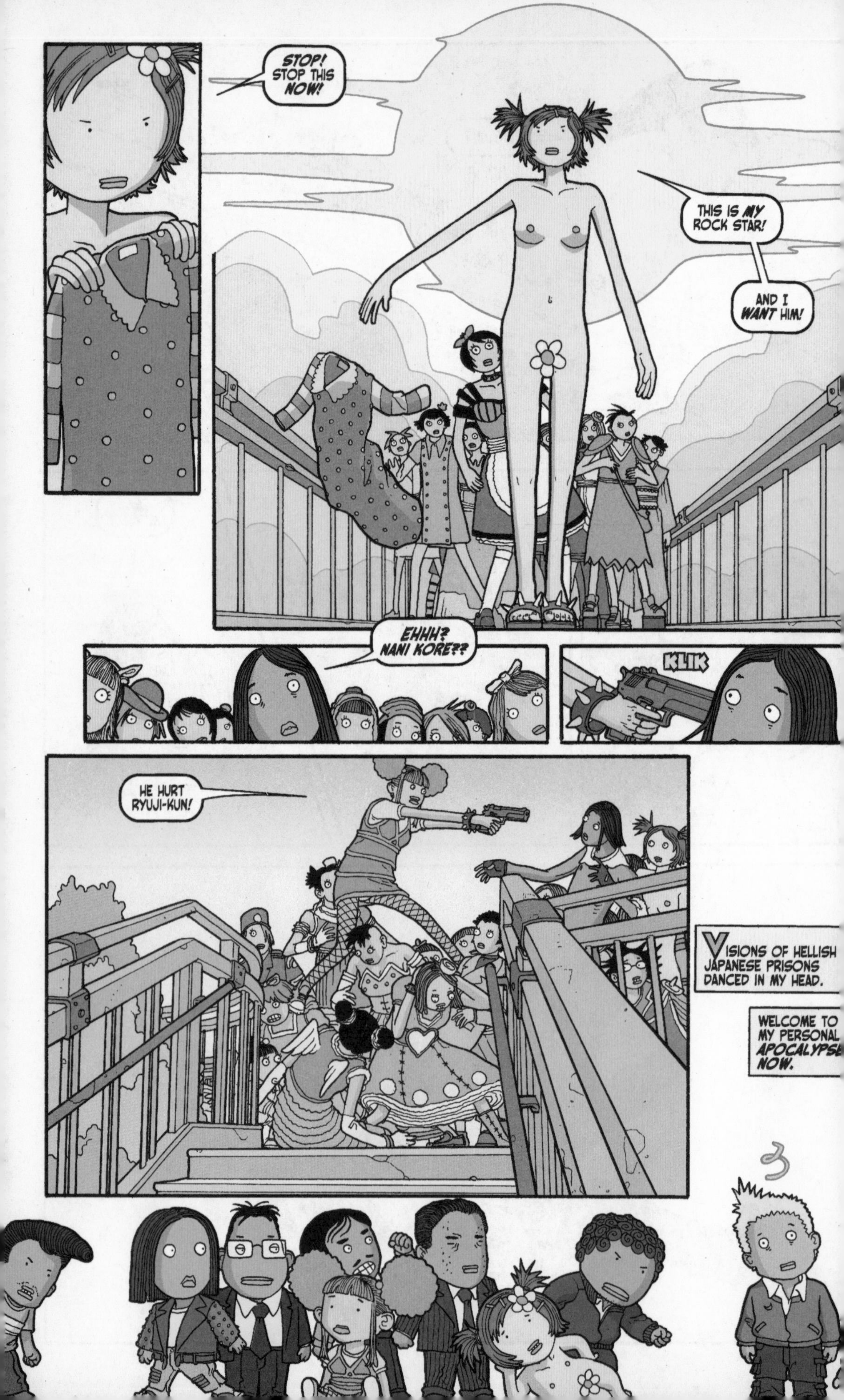
STOP! STOP THIS NOW!
THIS IS MY ROCK STAR!
AND I WANT HIM!
EHHH? NANI KORE??
KLIK
HE HURT RYUJI-KUN!
VISIONS OF HELLISH JAPANESE PRISONS DANCED IN MY HEAD.
WELCOME TO MY PERSONAL APOCALYPSE NOW.

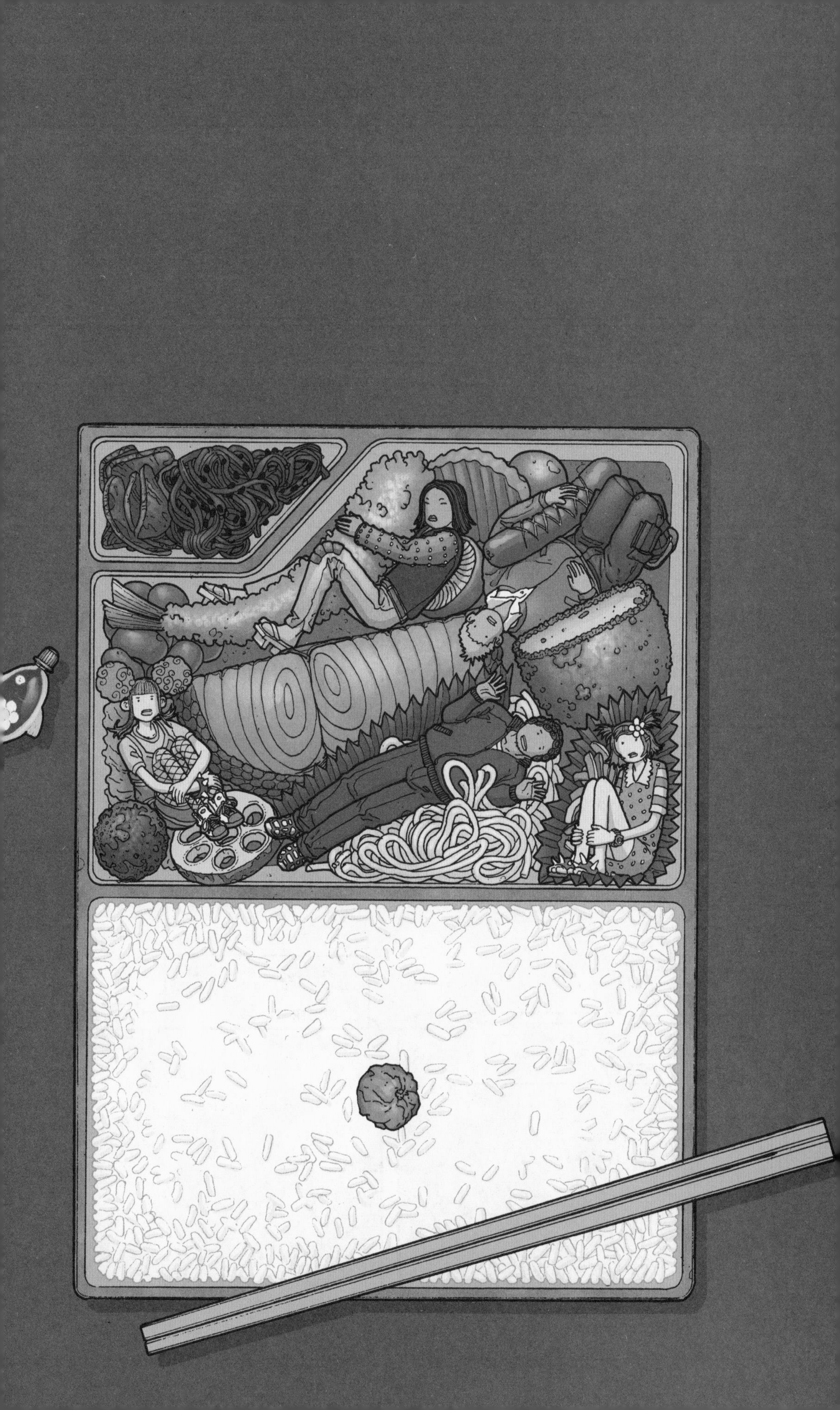

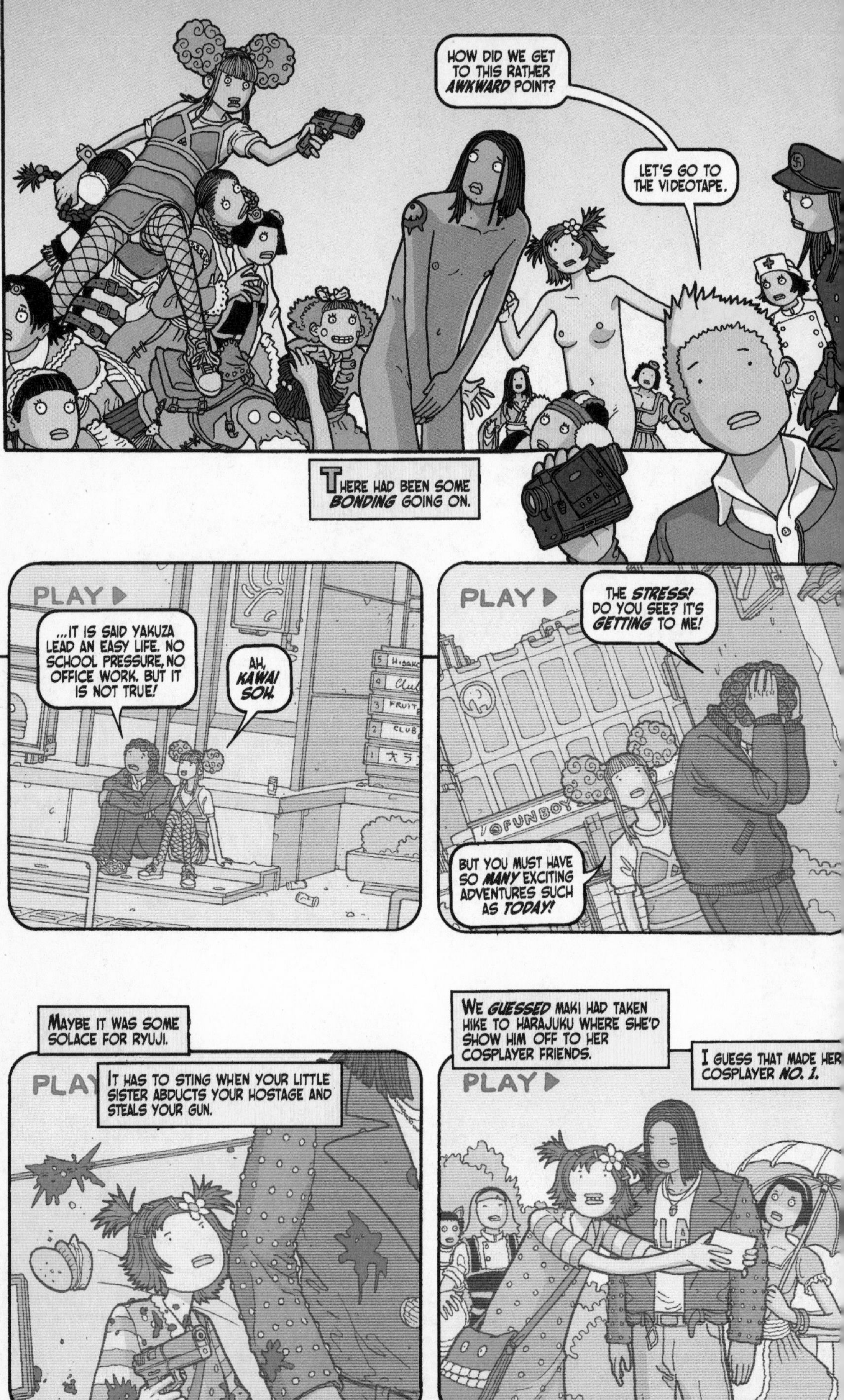

HOW DID WE GET TO THIS RATHER AWKWARD POINT?
LET'S GO TO THE VIDEOTAPE.
THERE HAD BEEN SOME BONDING GOING ON.
PLAY
...IT IS SAID YAKUZA LEAD AN EASY LIFE. NO SCHOOL PRESSURE, NO OFFICE WORK. BUT IT IS NOT TRUE!
AH, KAWAI SOH.
PLAY
THE STRESS! DO YOU SEE? IT'S GETTING TO ME!
BUT YOU MUST HAVE SO MANY EXCITING ADVENTURES SUCH AS TODAY!
FUNBOY
MAYBE IT WAS SOME SOLACE FOR RYUJI.
PLAY
IT HAS TO STING WHEN YOUR LITTLE SISTER ABDUCTS YOUR HOSTAGE AND STEALS YOUR GUN.
WE GUESSED MAKI HAD TAKEN HIKE TO HARAJUKU WHERE SHE'D SHOW HIM OFF TO HER COSPLAYER FRIENDS.
I GUESS THAT MADE HER COSPLAYER NO. 1.
PLAY

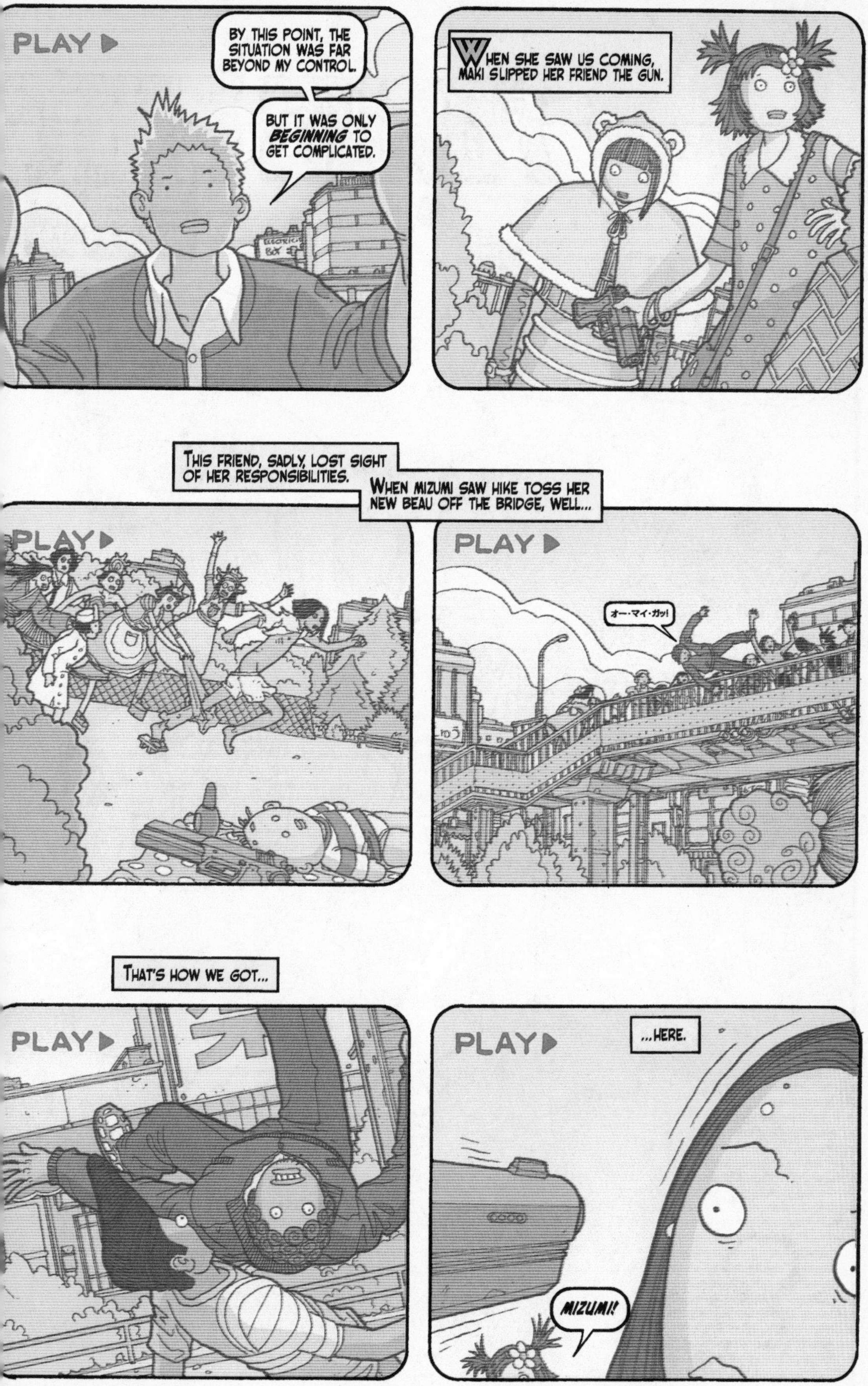
PLAY ▶
BY THIS POINT, THE SITUATION WAS FAR BEYOND MY CONTROL.
BUT IT WAS ONLY **BEGINNING** TO GET COMPLICATED.
WHEN SHE SAW US COMING, MAKI SLIPPED HER FRIEND THE GUN.
THIS FRIEND, SADLY, LOST SIGHT OF HER RESPONSIBILITIES.
WHEN MIZUMI SAW HIKE TOSS HER NEW BEAU OFF THE BRIDGE, WELL...
PLAY ▶
PLAY ▶
オー・マイ・ガッ!
THAT'S HOW WE GOT...
PLAY ▶
PLAY ▶
...HERE.
MIZUMI!

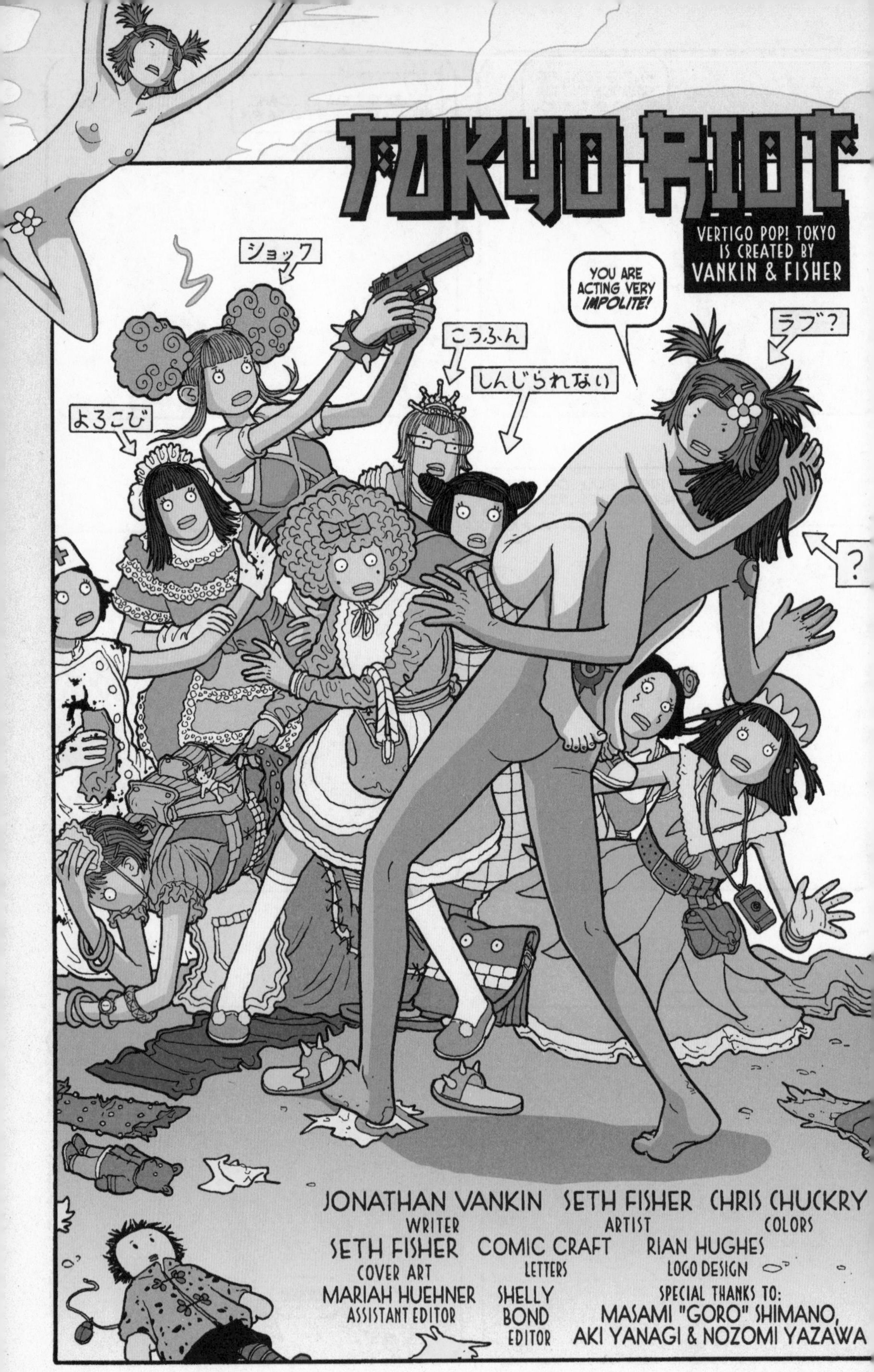
TOKYO RIOT
VERTIGO POP! TOKYO IS CREATED BY VANKIN & FISHER
ショック
こうふん
しんじられない
よろこび
YOU ARE ACTING VERY IMPOLITE!
ラブ?
?
JONATHAN VANKIN WRITER
SETH FISHER ARTIST
CHRIS CHUCKRY COLORS
SETH FISHER COVER ART
COMIC CRAFT LETTERS
RIAN HUGHES LOGO DESIGN
MARIAH HUEHNER ASSISTANT EDITOR
SHELLY BOND EDITOR
SPECIAL THANKS TO: MASAMI "GORO" SHIMANO, AKI YANAGI & NOZOMI YAZAWA

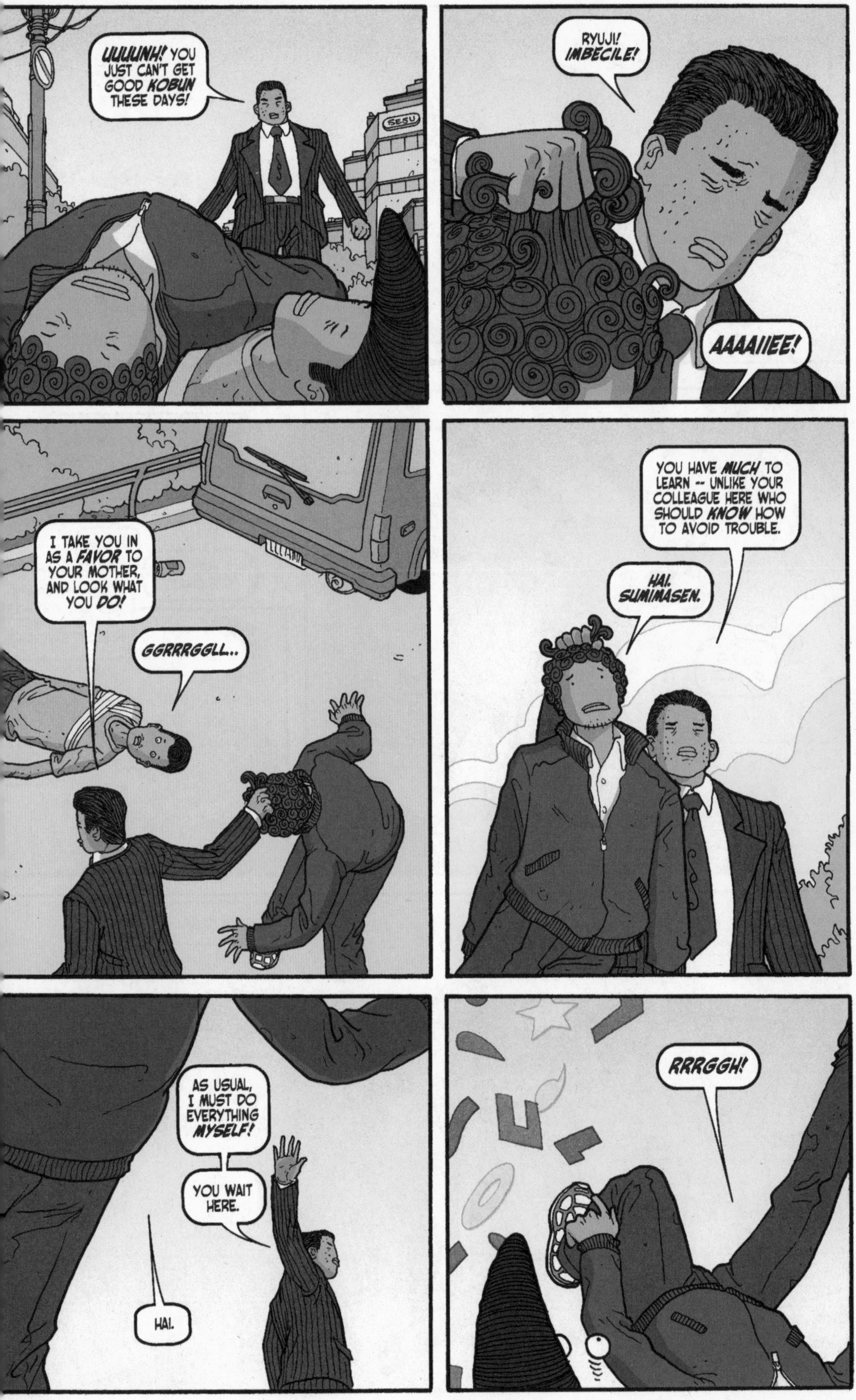
UUUUNH! YOU JUST CAN'T GET GOOD KOBUN THESE DAYS!
RYUJI! IMBECILE!
AAAAIIEE!
I TAKE YOU IN AS A FAVOR TO YOUR MOTHER, AND LOOK WHAT YOU DO!
GGRRRGGLL..
YOU HAVE MUCH TO LEARN -- UNLIKE YOUR COLLEAGUE HERE WHO SHOULD KNOW HOW TO AVOID TROUBLE.
HAI. SUMIMASEN.
AS USUAL, I MUST DO EVERYTHING MYSELF!
YOU WAIT HERE.
HAI.
RRRGGH!

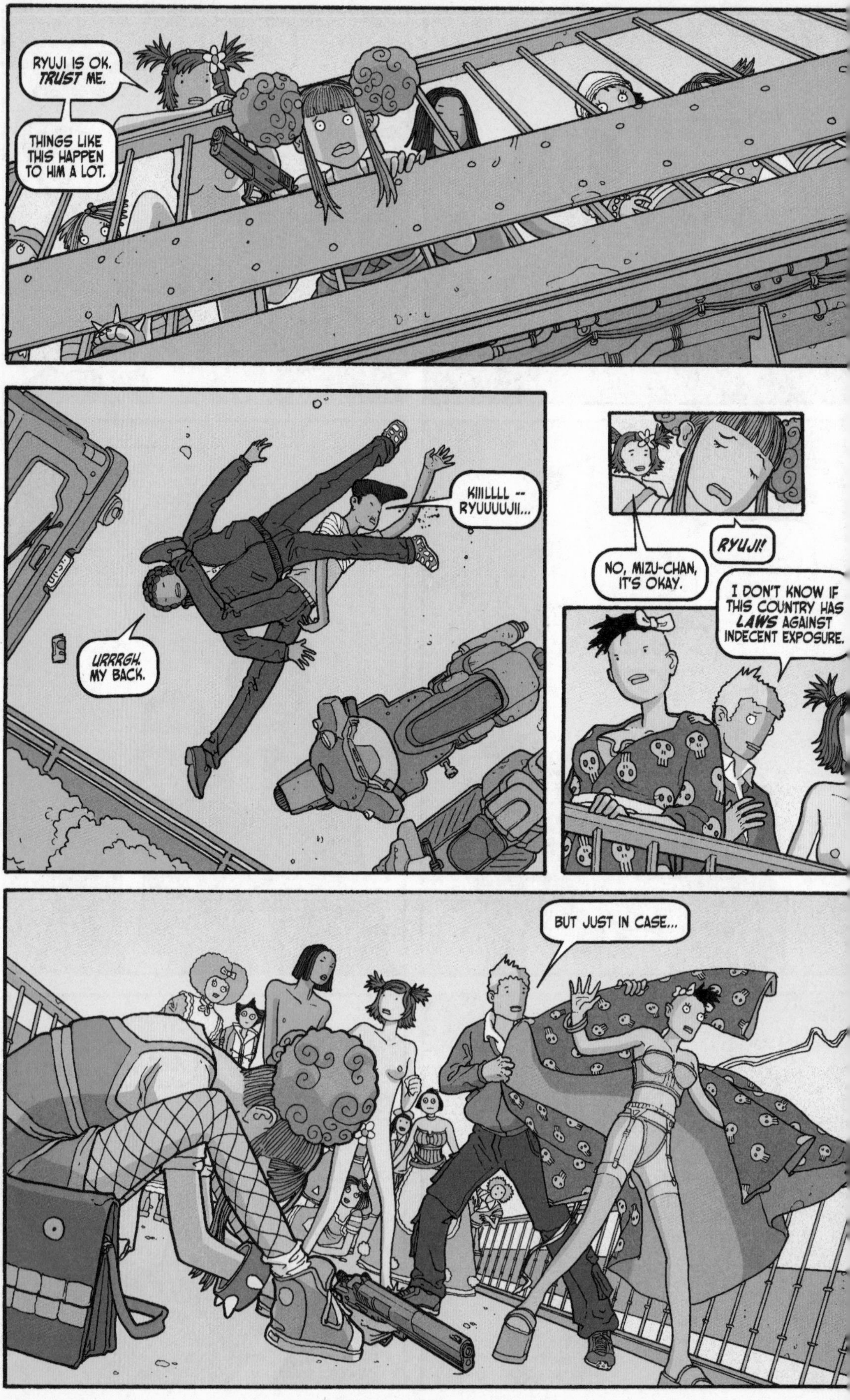
RYUJI IS OK. TRUST ME.
THINGS LIKE THIS HAPPEN TO HIM A LOT.
KIIILLLL -- RYUUUUJII...
URRRGH. MY BACK.
RYUJI!
NO, MIZU-CHAN, IT'S OKAY.
I DON'T KNOW IF THIS COUNTRY HAS LAWS AGAINST INDECENT EXPOSURE.
BUT JUST IN CASE...

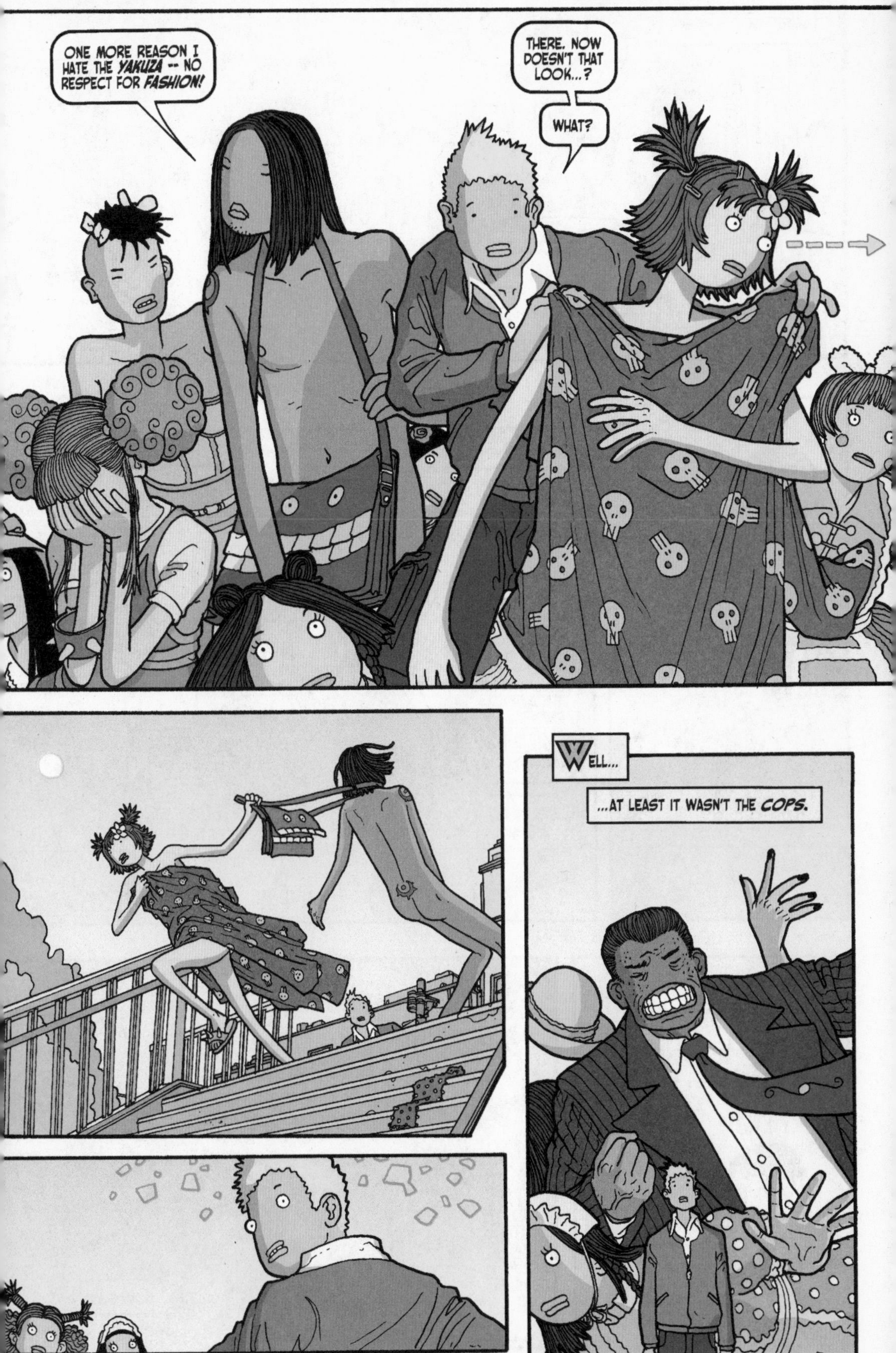
ONE MORE REASON I HATE THE YAKUZA -- NO RESPECT FOR FASHION!
THERE. NOW DOESN'T THAT LOOK...?
WHAT?
WELL...
...AT LEAST IT WASN'T THE COPS.

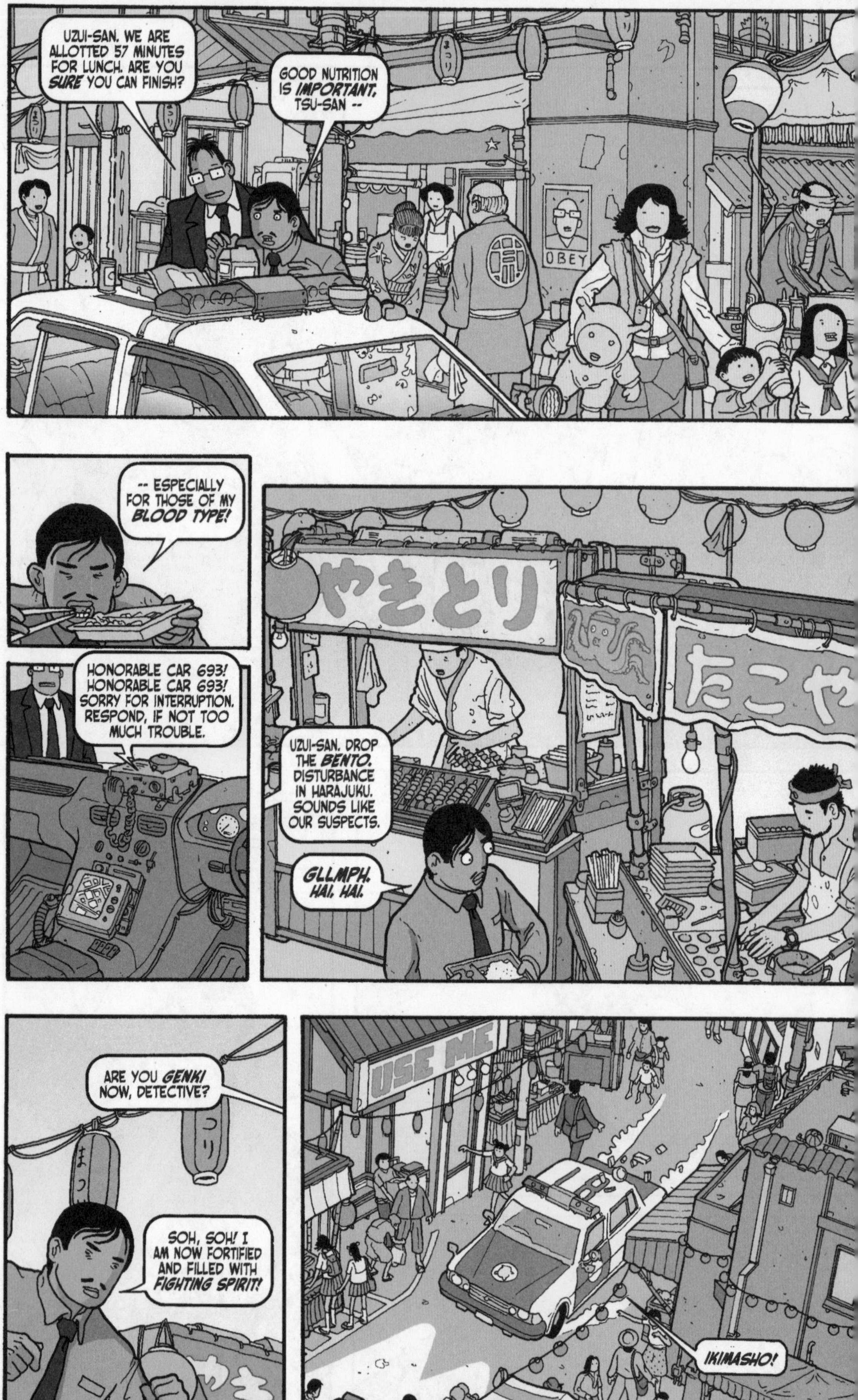
UZUI-SAN. WE ARE ALLOTTED 57 MINUTES FOR LUNCH. ARE YOU *SURE* YOU CAN FINISH?
GOOD NUTRITION IS *IMPORTANT,* TSU-SAN --
OBEY
-- ESPECIALLY FOR THOSE OF MY *BLOOD TYPE!*
やきとり
HONORABLE CAR 693! HONORABLE CAR 693! SORRY FOR INTERRUPTION. RESPOND, IF NOT TOO MUCH TROUBLE.
UZUI-SAN. DROP THE *BENTO.* DISTURBANCE IN HARAJUKU. SOUNDS LIKE OUR SUSPECTS.
GLLMPH. HAI. HAI.
ARE YOU *GENKI* NOW, DETECTIVE?
SOH, SOH! I AM NOW FORTIFIED AND FILLED WITH *FIGHTING SPIRIT!*
USE ME
IKIMASHO!

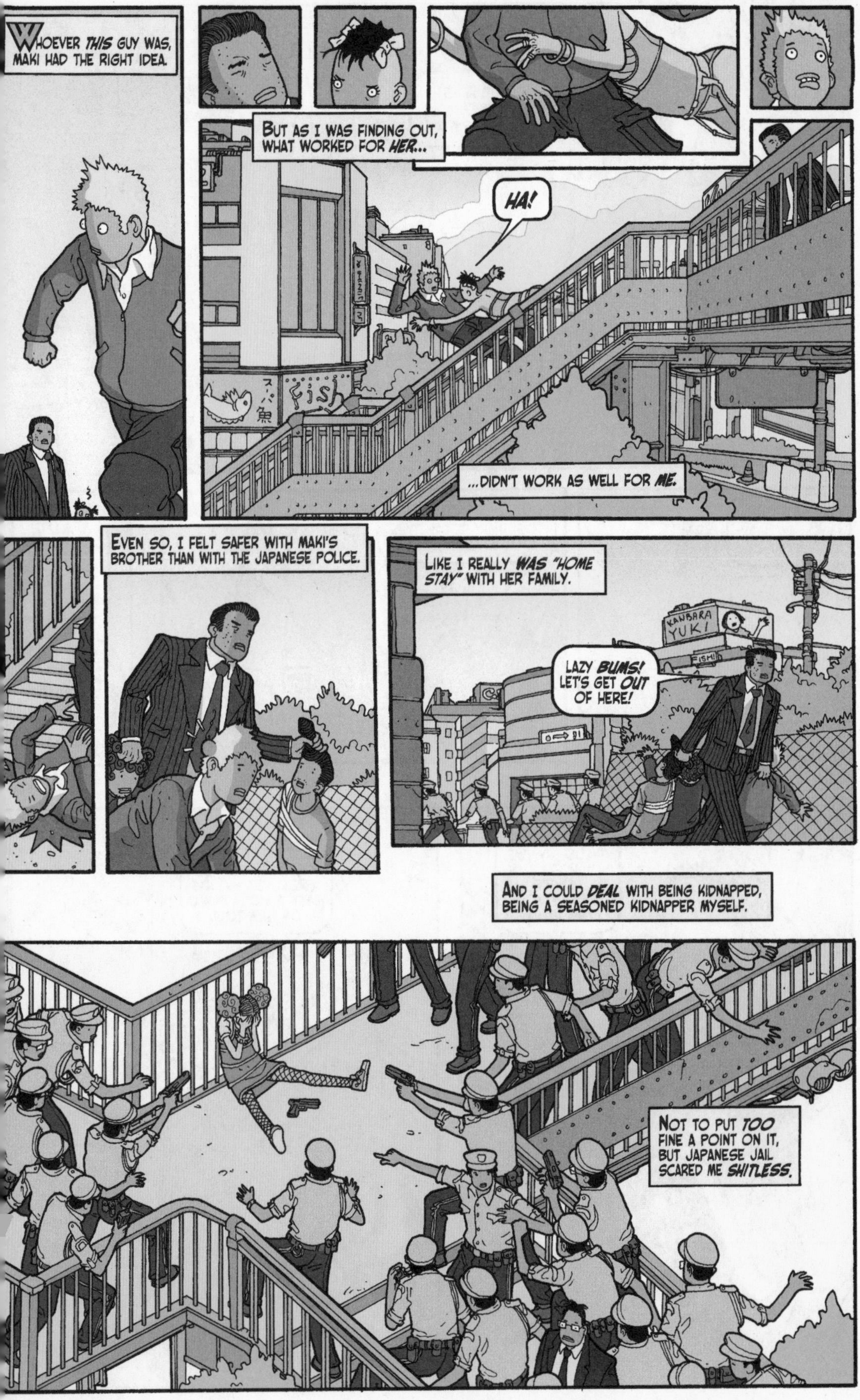
WHOEVER THIS GUY WAS, MAKI HAD THE RIGHT IDEA.
BUT AS I WAS FINDING OUT, WHAT WORKED FOR HER...
HA!
...DIDN'T WORK AS WELL FOR ME.
EVEN SO, I FELT SAFER WITH MAKI'S BROTHER THAN WITH THE JAPANESE POLICE.
LIKE I REALLY WAS "HOME STAY" WITH HER FAMILY.
KANBARA YUKI
LAZY BUMS! LET'S GET OUT OF HERE!
AND I COULD DEAL WITH BEING KIDNAPPED, BEING A SEASONED KIDNAPPER MYSELF.
NOT TO PUT TOO FINE A POINT ON IT, BUT JAPANESE JAIL SCARED ME SHITLESS.

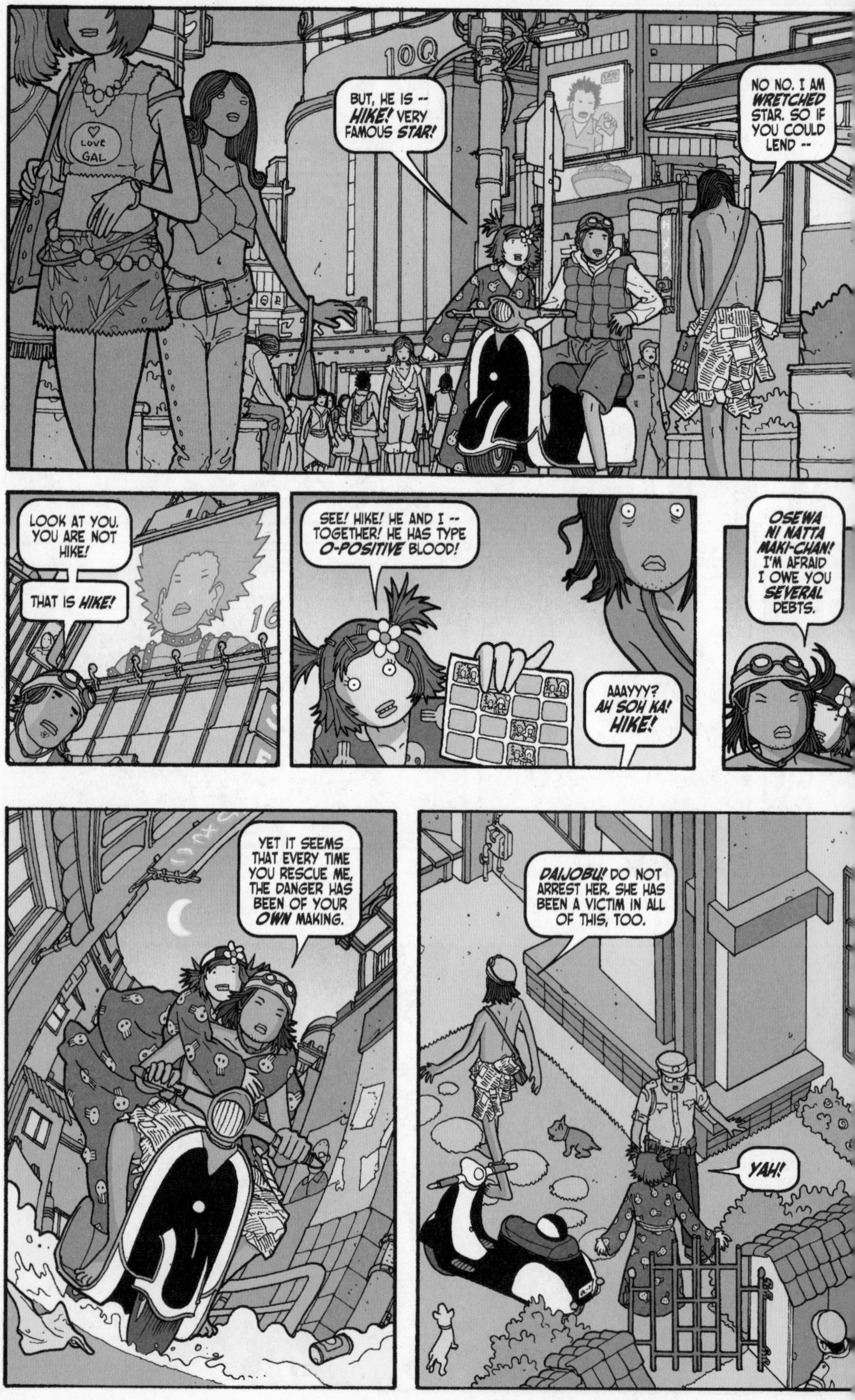

BUT, HE IS -- HIKE! VERY FAMOUS STAR!
NO NO. I AM WRETCHED STAR. SO IF YOU COULD LEND --
LOOK AT YOU. YOU ARE NOT HIKE!
THAT IS HIKE!
SEE! HIKE! HE AND I -- TOGETHER! HE HAS TYPE O-POSITIVE BLOOD!
AAAYYY? AH SOH KA! HIKE!
OSEWA NI NATTA MAKI-CHAN! I'M AFRAID I OWE YOU SEVERAL DEBTS.
YET IT SEEMS THAT EVERY TIME YOU RESCUE ME, THE DANGER HAS BEEN OF YOUR OWN MAKING.
DAIJOBU! DO NOT ARREST HER. SHE HAS BEEN A VICTIM IN ALL OF THIS, TOO.
YAH!

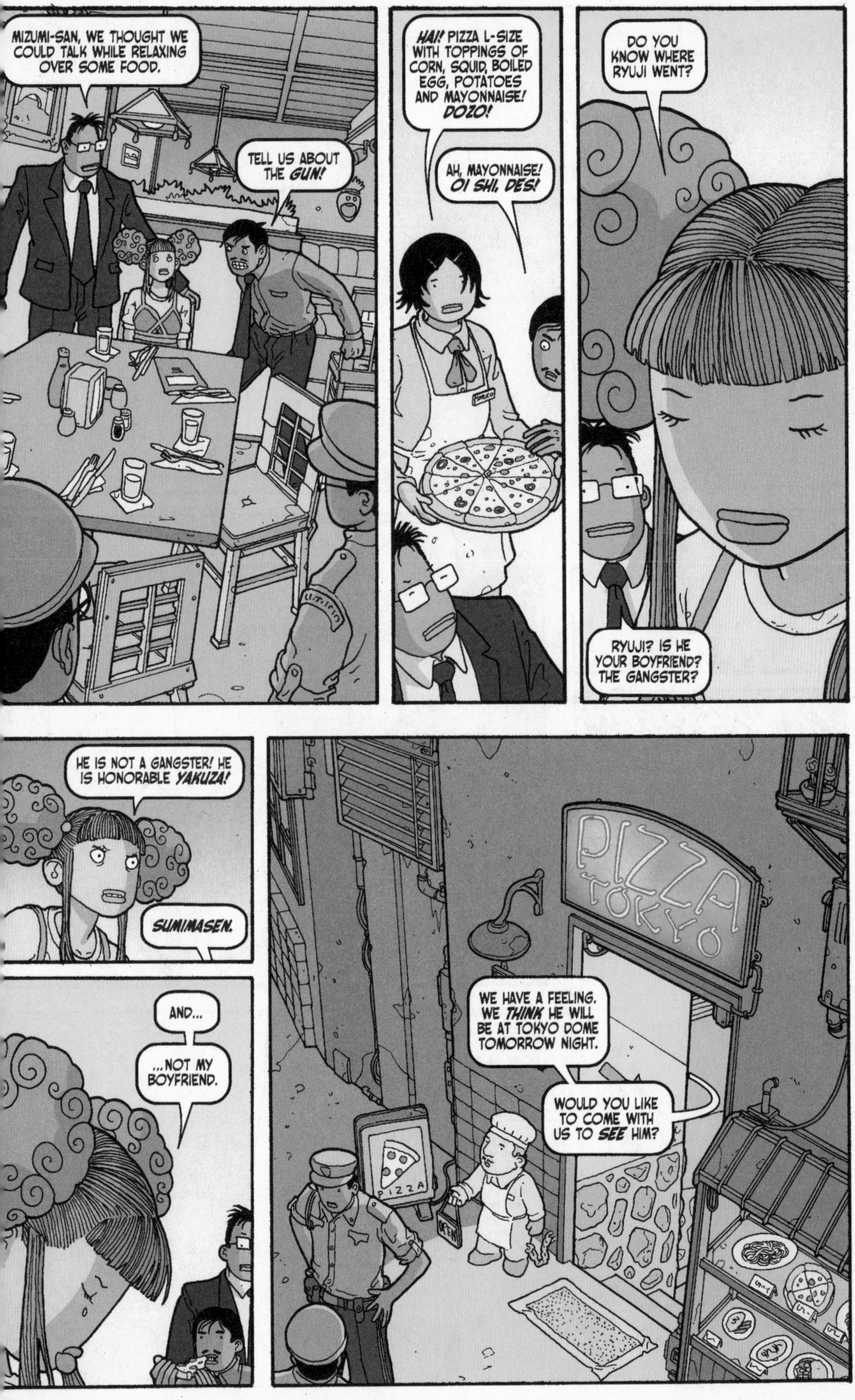
MIZUMI-SAN, WE THOUGHT WE COULD TALK WHILE RELAXING OVER SOME FOOD.
TELL US ABOUT THE GUN!
HAI! PIZZA L-SIZE WITH TOPPINGS OF CORN, SQUID, BOILED EGG, POTATOES AND MAYONNAISE! DOZO!
AH, MAYONNAISE! OI SHI, DES!
DO YOU KNOW WHERE RYUJI WENT?
RYUJI? IS HE YOUR BOYFRIEND? THE GANGSTER?
HE IS NOT A GANGSTER! HE IS HONORABLE YAKUZA!
SUMIMASEN.
AND...
...NOT MY BOYFRIEND.
PIZZA TOKYO
PIZZA
OPEN
WE HAVE A FEELING. WE THINK HE WILL BE AT TOKYO DOME TOMORROW NIGHT.
WOULD YOU LIKE TO COME WITH US TO SEE HIM?

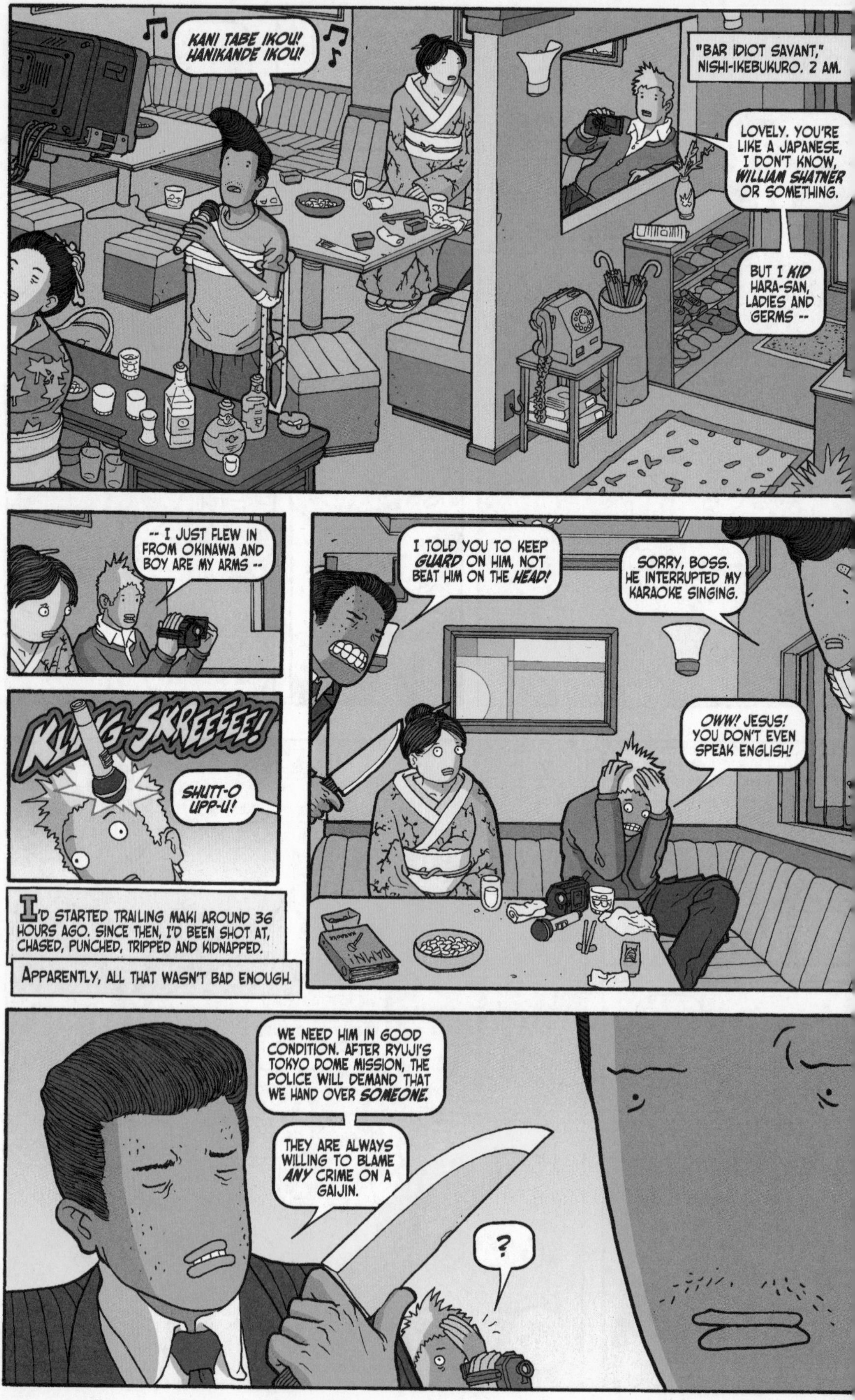

KANI TABE IKOU! HANIKANDE IKOU!
"BAR IDIOT SAVANT," NISHI-IKEBUKURO. 2 AM.
LOVELY. YOU'RE LIKE A JAPANESE, I DON'T KNOW, WILLIAM SHATNER OR SOMETHING.
BUT I KID HARA-SAN, LADIES AND GERMS --
-- I JUST FLEW IN FROM OKINAWA AND BOY ARE MY ARMS --
KLING-SKREEEEEE!
SHUTT-O UPP-U!
I'D STARTED TRAILING MAKI AROUND 36 HOURS AGO. SINCE THEN, I'D BEEN SHOT AT, CHASED, PUNCHED, TRIPPED AND KIDNAPPED.
APPARENTLY, ALL THAT WASN'T BAD ENOUGH.
I TOLD YOU TO KEEP GUARD ON HIM, NOT BEAT HIM ON THE HEAD!
SORRY, BOSS. HE INTERRUPTED MY KARAOKE SINGING.
OWW! JESUS! YOU DON'T EVEN SPEAK ENGLISH!
WE NEED HIM IN GOOD CONDITION. AFTER RYUJI'S TOKYO DOME MISSION, THE POLICE WILL DEMAND THAT WE HAND OVER SOMEONE.
THEY ARE ALWAYS WILLING TO BLAME ANY CRIME ON A GAIJIN.
?

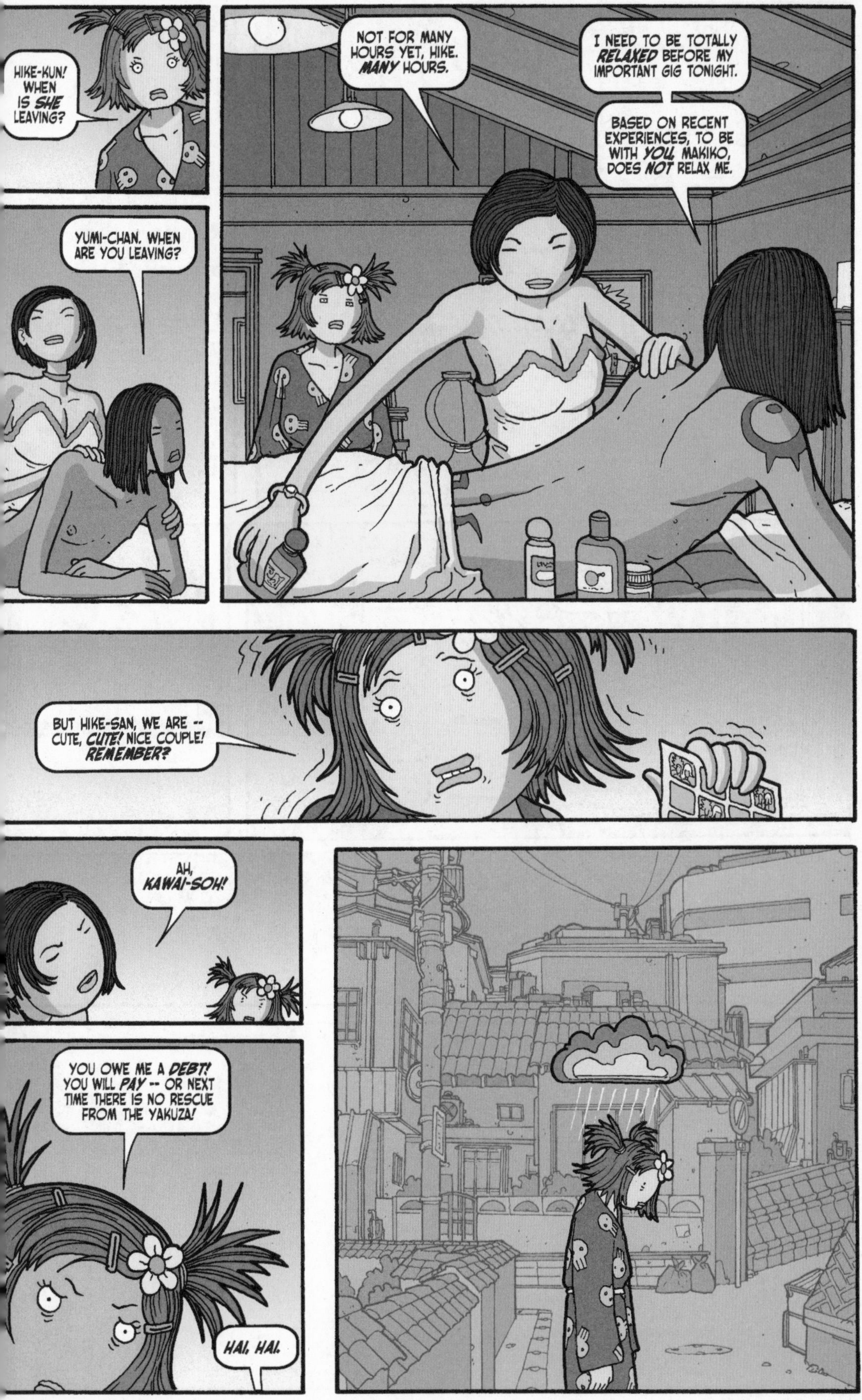
HIKE-KUN! WHEN IS SHE LEAVING?
NOT FOR MANY HOURS YET, HIKE. MANY HOURS.
I NEED TO BE TOTALLY RELAXED BEFORE MY IMPORTANT GIG TONIGHT.
BASED ON RECENT EXPERIENCES, TO BE WITH YOU, MAKIKO, DOES NOT RELAX ME.
YUMI-CHAN. WHEN ARE YOU LEAVING?
BUT HIKE-SAN, WE ARE -- CUTE, CUTE! NICE COUPLE! REMEMBER?
AH, KAWAI-SOH!
YOU OWE ME A DEBT! YOU WILL PAY -- OR NEXT TIME THERE IS NO RESCUE FROM THE YAKUZA!
HAI, HAI.

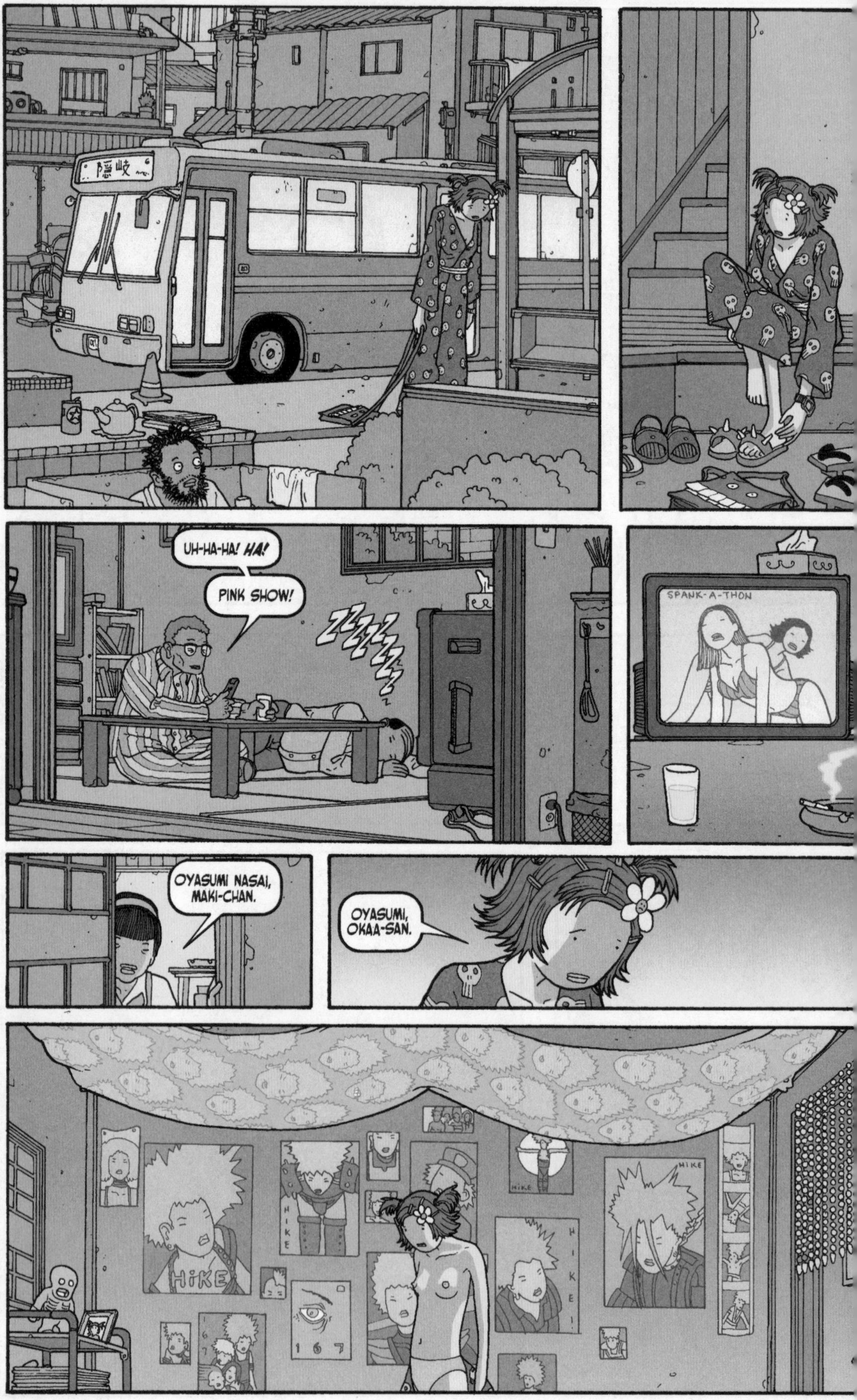

隠岐
UH-HA-HA! HA!
PINK SHOW!
ZZZZZZZZ
SPANK-A-THON
OYASUMI NASAI, MAKI-CHAN.
OYASUMI, OKAA-SAN.
HiKE
HiKE
HIKE
HIKE
HIKE!
1 6 7
167

TOKYO DOME, 17 HOURS LATER.

...THE SHOW GOES ON AFTER YESTERDAY'S BIZARRE *KIDNAPPING* OF *1-6-7* LEAD SINGER *HIKE!* THE INCIDENT IS STILL *MYSTERIOUS*.

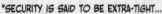

"SECURITY IS SAID TO BE EXTRA-TIGHT...

"...WITH THE KIDNAPPERS *STILL AT LARGE!*

RYUJI-KOBUN, ARE YOU READY TO REGAIN YOUR *HONOR?*

IF YOU SEE YOUR FRIEND, YOU WILL BRING HIM TO US, *NE?* ONLY *WE* CAN PROTECT HIM.

"POLICE BELIEVE THEY MAY *STRIKE AGAIN!*

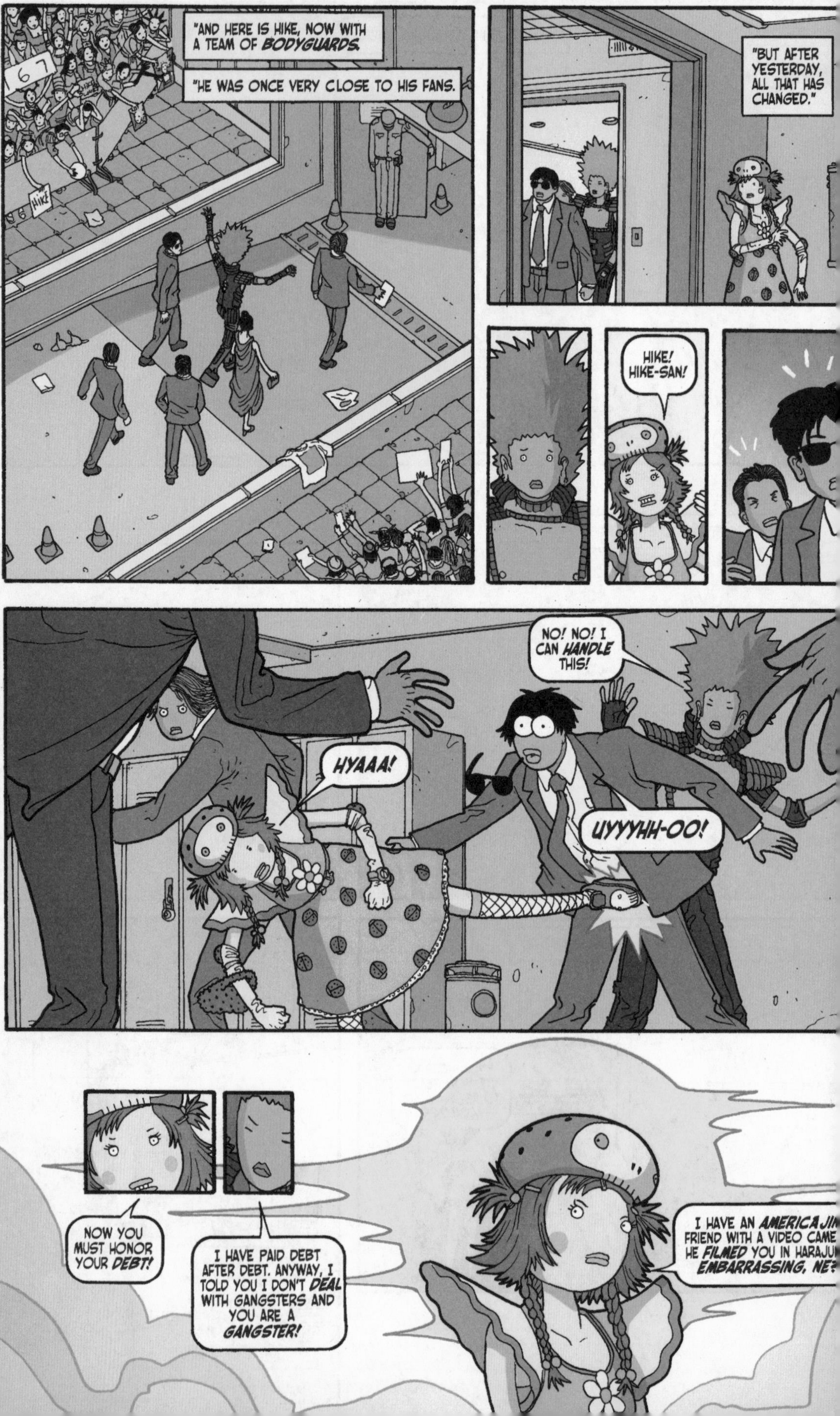
"AND HERE IS HIKE, NOW WITH A TEAM OF *BODYGUARDS.*
"HE WAS ONCE VERY CLOSE TO HIS FANS.
167
HIKE
"BUT AFTER YESTERDAY, ALL THAT HAS CHANGED."
HIKE! HIKE-SAN!
NO! NO! I CAN *HANDLE* THIS!
HYAAA!
UYYYHH-OO!
NOW YOU MUST HONOR YOUR *DEBT!*
I HAVE PAID DEBT AFTER DEBT. ANYWAY, I TOLD YOU I DON'T *DEAL* WITH GANGSTERS AND YOU ARE A *GANGSTER!*
I HAVE AN *AMERICAJIN* FRIEND WITH A VIDEO CAME HE *FILMED* YOU IN HARAJU *EMBARRASSING, NE?*

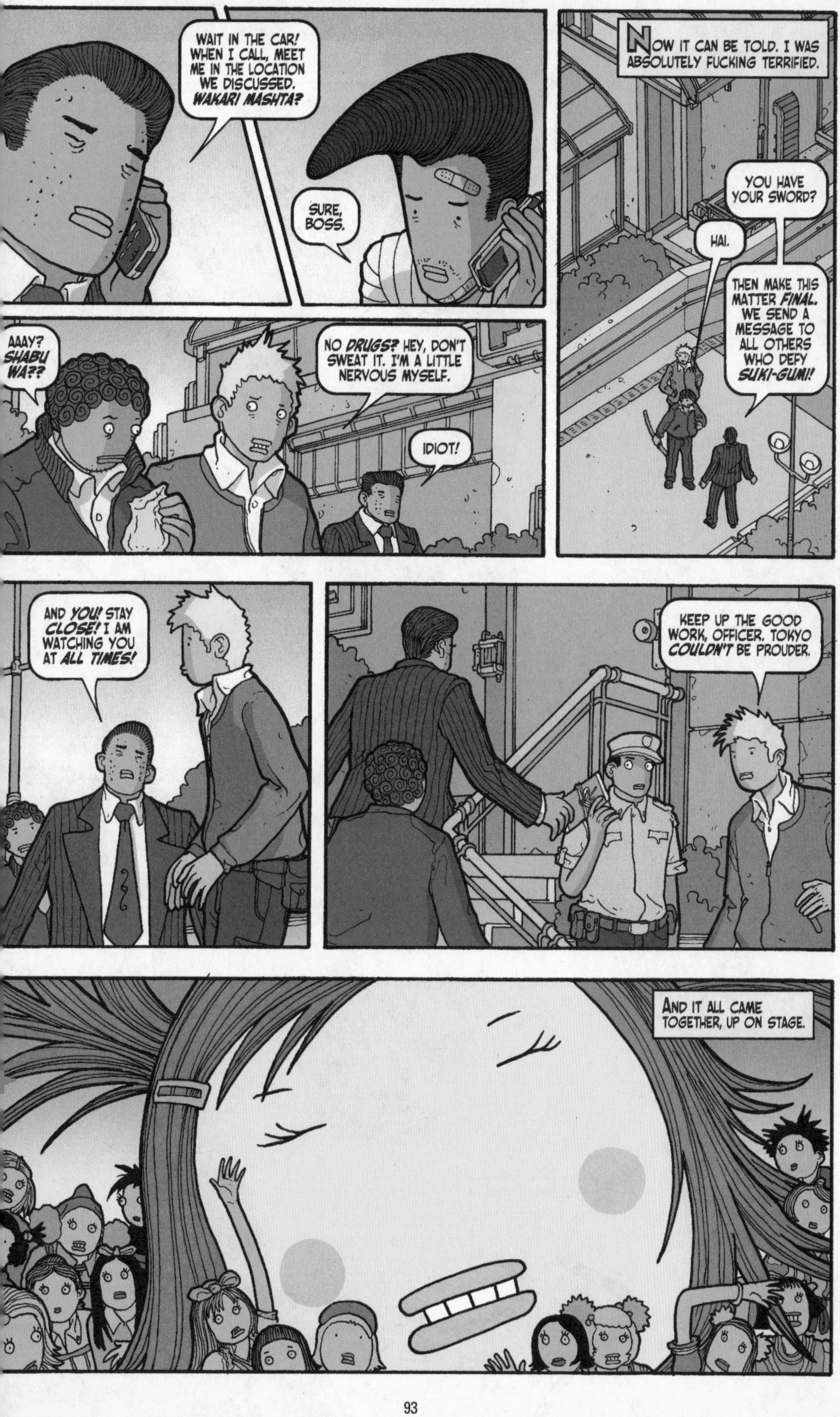
WAIT IN THE CAR! WHEN I CALL, MEET ME IN THE LOCATION WE DISCUSSED. WAKARI MASHTA?
SURE, BOSS.
NOW IT CAN BE TOLD. I WAS ABSOLUTELY FUCKING TERRIFIED.
YOU HAVE YOUR SWORD?
HAI.
THEN MAKE THIS MATTER FINAL. WE SEND A MESSAGE TO ALL OTHERS WHO DEFY SUKI-GUMI!
AAAY? SHABU WA??
NO DRUGS? HEY, DON'T SWEAT IT. I'M A LITTLE NERVOUS MYSELF.
IDIOT!
AND YOU! STAY CLOSE! I AM WATCHING YOU AT ALL TIMES!
KEEP UP THE GOOD WORK, OFFICER. TOKYO COULDN'T BE PROUDER.
AND IT ALL CAME TOGETHER, UP ON STAGE.

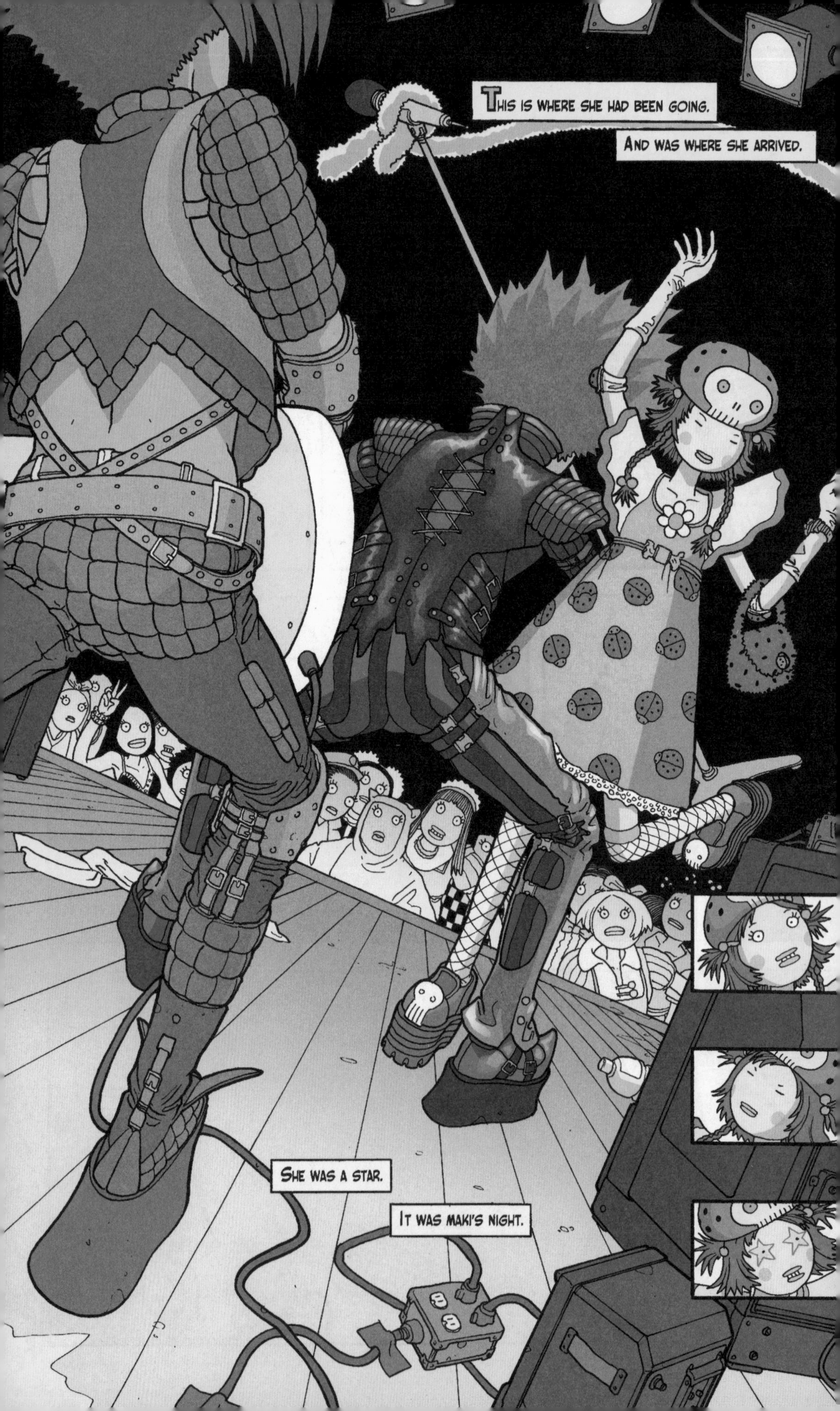

THIS IS WHERE SHE HAD BEEN GOING.
AND WAS WHERE SHE ARRIVED.
SHE WAS A STAR.
IT WAS MAKI'S NIGHT.

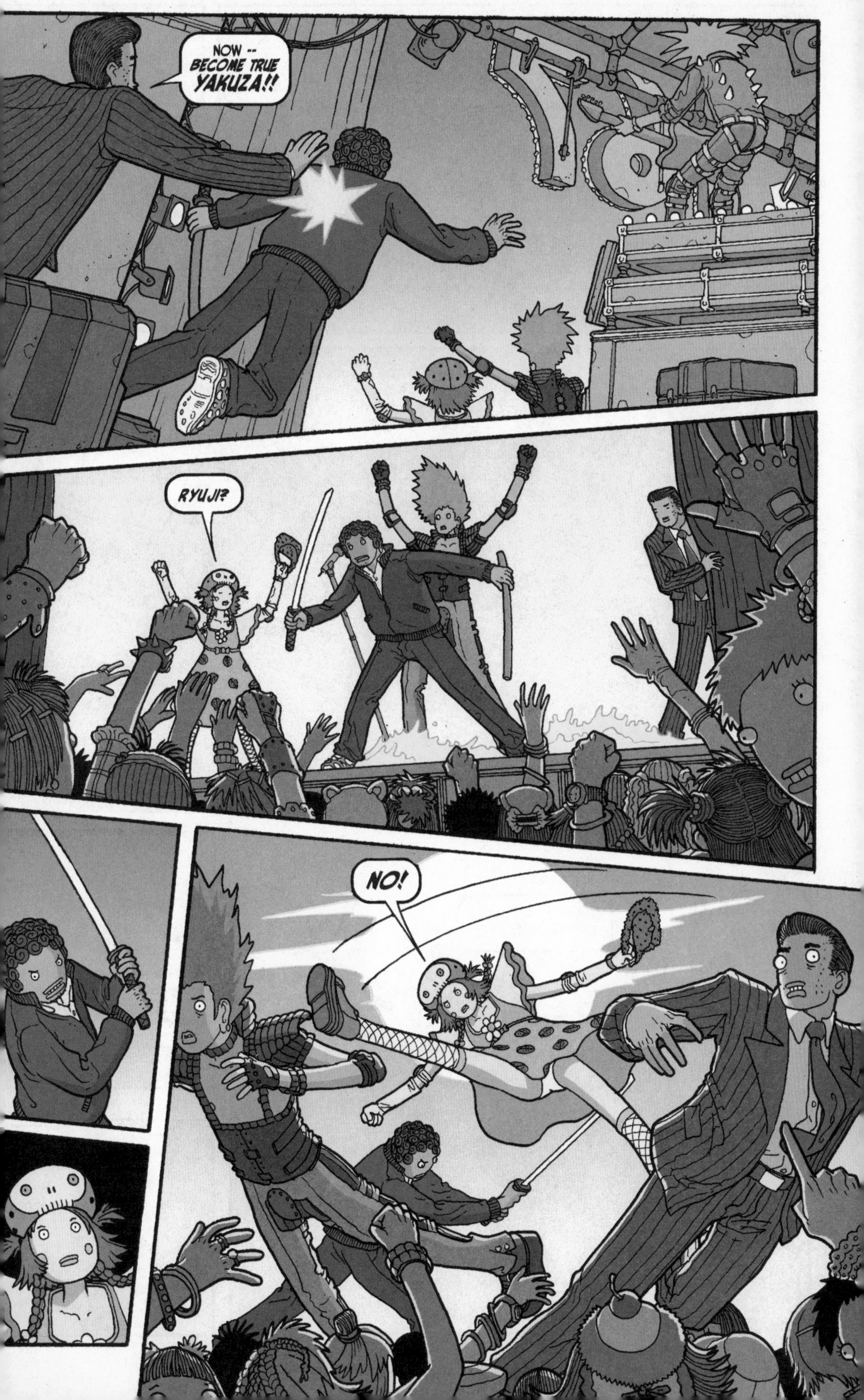
NOW -- BECOME TRUE YAKUZA!!
RYUJI?
NO!

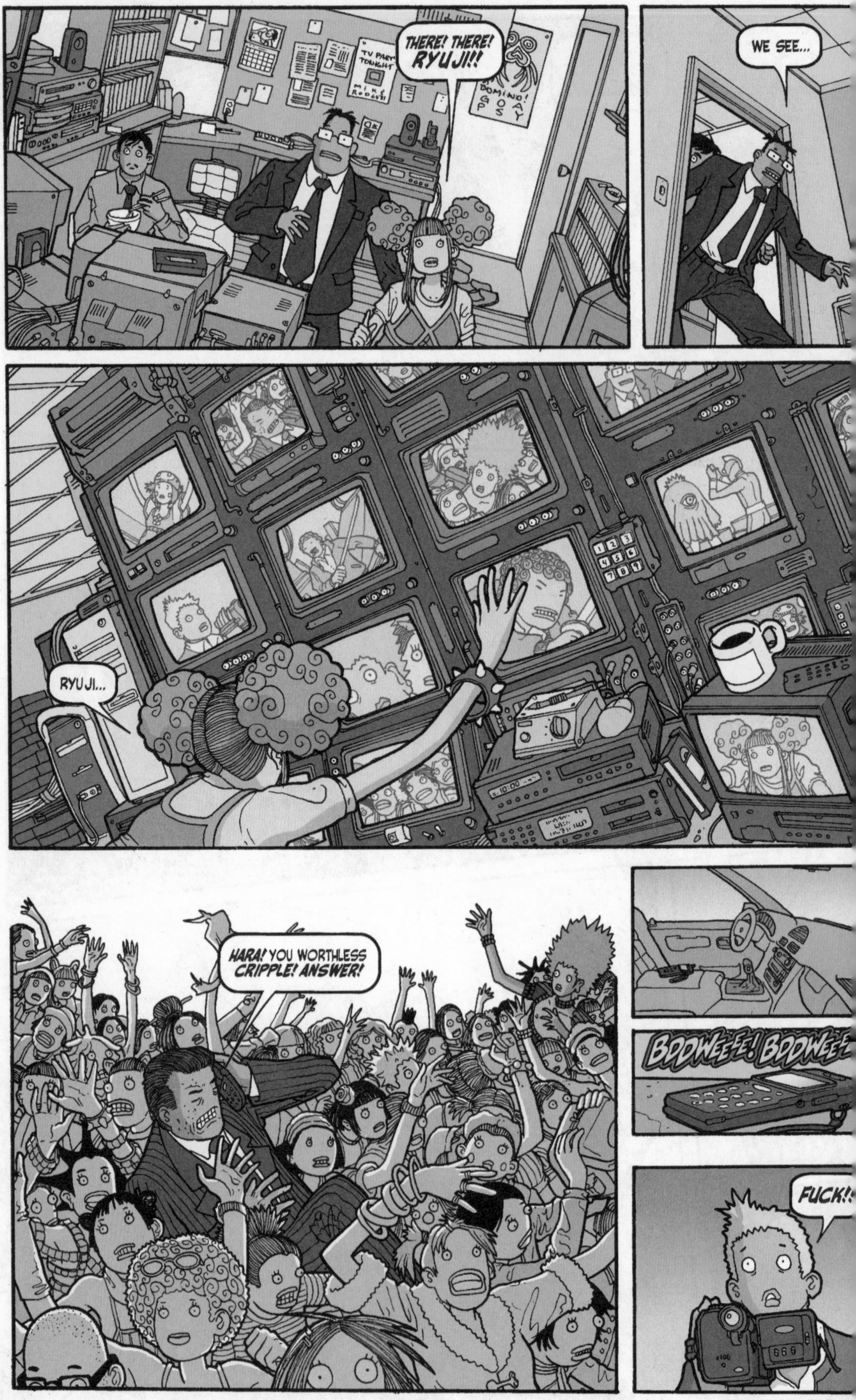
TV PARTY TONIGHT
MIKE RODGERS
DOMINO! GOA PSY
THERE! THERE! RYUJI!!
WE SEE...
RYUJI...
HARA! YOU WORTHLESS CRIPPLE! ANSWER!
BDDWEEEE! BDDWEEE
FUCK!!

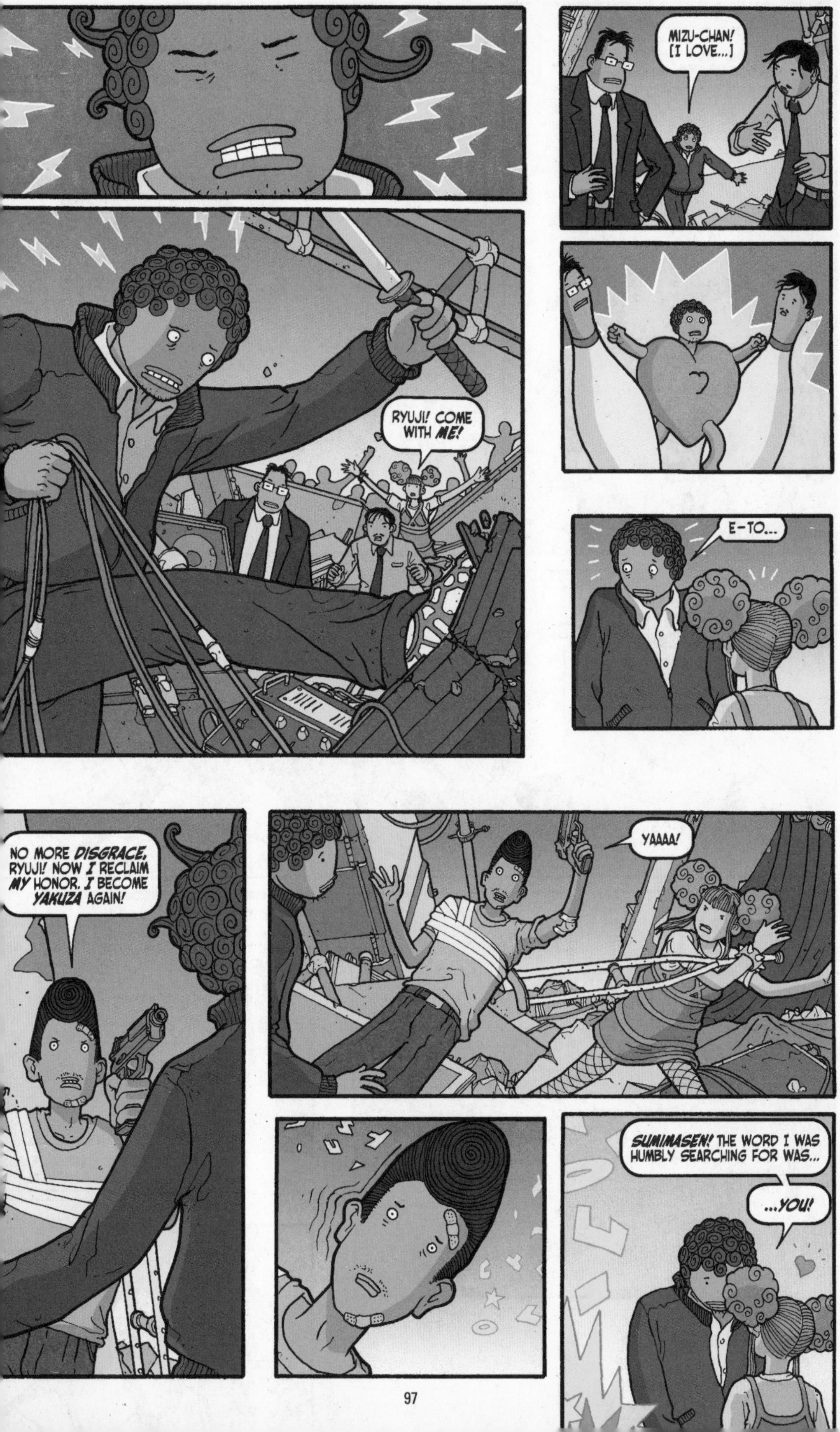

MIZU-CHAN! [I LOVE...]
RYUJI! COME WITH ME!
E-TO...
NO MORE DISGRACE, RYUJI! NOW I RECLAIM MY HONOR. I BECOME YAKUZA AGAIN!
YAAAA!
SUMIMASEN! THE WORD I WAS HUMBLY SEARCHING FOR WAS...
...YOU!

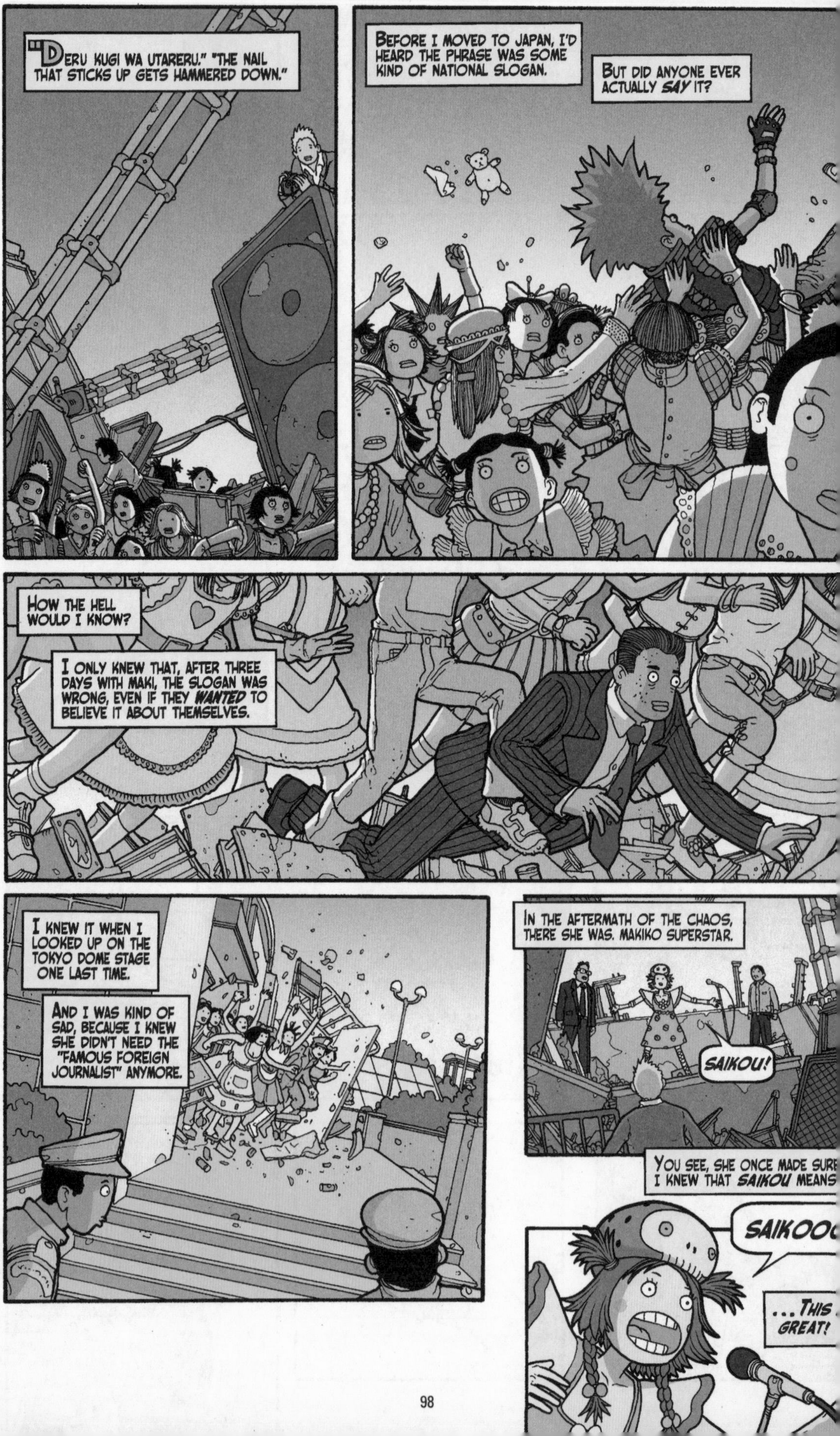
"Deru kugi wa utareru." "The nail that sticks up gets hammered down."
Before I moved to Japan, I'd heard the phrase was some kind of national slogan.
But did anyone ever actually *say* it?
How the hell would I know?
I only knew that, after three days with Maki, the slogan was wrong, even if they *wanted* to believe it about themselves.
I knew it when I looked up on the Tokyo Dome stage one last time.
And I was kind of sad, because I knew she didn't need the "famous foreign journalist" anymore.
In the aftermath of the chaos, there she was. Makiko Superstar.
Saikou!
You see, she once made sure I knew that *saikou* means
Saikoo
...This great!

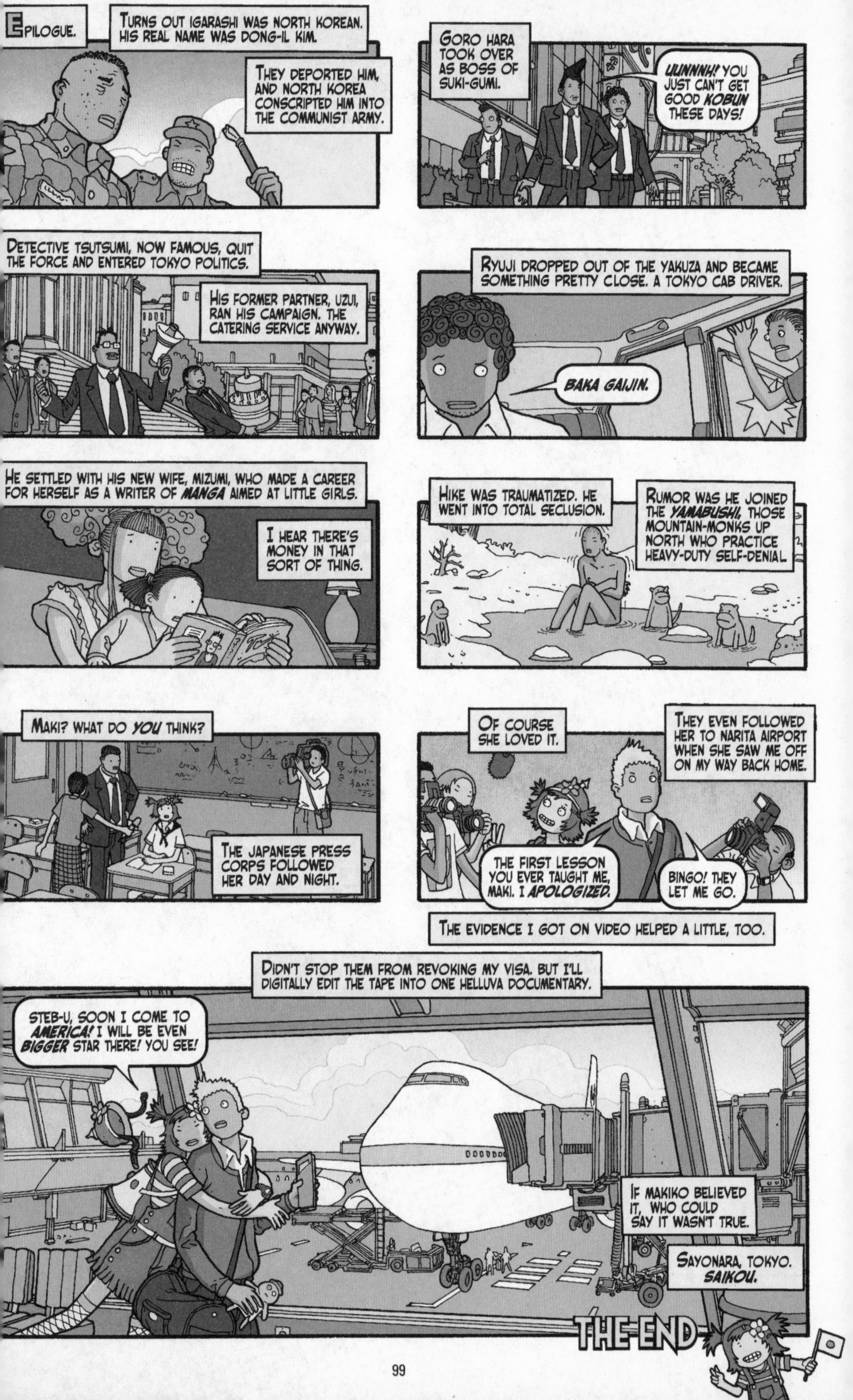
EPILOGUE.
TURNS OUT IGARASHI WAS NORTH KOREAN. HIS REAL NAME WAS DONG-IL KIM.
THEY DEPORTED HIM, AND NORTH KOREA CONSCRIPTED HIM INTO THE COMMUNIST ARMY.
GORO HARA TOOK OVER AS BOSS OF SUKI-GUMI.
UUNNNH! YOU JUST CAN'T GET GOOD KOBUN THESE DAYS!
DETECTIVE TSUTSUMI, NOW FAMOUS, QUIT THE FORCE AND ENTERED TOKYO POLITICS.
HIS FORMER PARTNER, UZUI, RAN HIS CAMPAIGN. THE CATERING SERVICE ANYWAY.
RYUJI DROPPED OUT OF THE YAKUZA AND BECAME SOMETHING PRETTY CLOSE. A TOKYO CAB DRIVER.
BAKA GAIJIN.
HE SETTLED WITH HIS NEW WIFE, MIZUMI, WHO MADE A CAREER FOR HERSELF AS A WRITER OF MANGA AIMED AT LITTLE GIRLS.
I HEAR THERE'S MONEY IN THAT SORT OF THING.
HIKE WAS TRAUMATIZED. HE WENT INTO TOTAL SECLUSION.
RUMOR WAS HE JOINED THE YAMABUSHI, THOSE MOUNTAIN-MONKS UP NORTH WHO PRACTICE HEAVY-DUTY SELF-DENIAL.
MAKI? WHAT DO YOU THINK?
THE JAPANESE PRESS CORPS FOLLOWED HER DAY AND NIGHT.
OF COURSE SHE LOVED IT.
THEY EVEN FOLLOWED HER TO NARITA AIRPORT WHEN SHE SAW ME OFF ON MY WAY BACK HOME.
THE FIRST LESSON YOU EVER TAUGHT ME, MAKI. I APOLOGIZED.
BINGO! THEY LET ME GO.
THE EVIDENCE I GOT ON VIDEO HELPED A LITTLE, TOO.
DIDN'T STOP THEM FROM REVOKING MY VISA. BUT I'LL DIGITALLY EDIT THE TAPE INTO ONE HELLUVA DOCUMENTARY.
STEB-U, SOON I COME TO AMERICA! I WILL BE EVEN BIGGER STAR THERE! YOU SEE!
IF MAKIKO BELIEVED IT, WHO COULD SAY IT WASN'T TRUE.
SAYONARA, TOKYO. SAIKOU.
THE END

You are now leaving Tokyo.
You are now entering Bangkok.

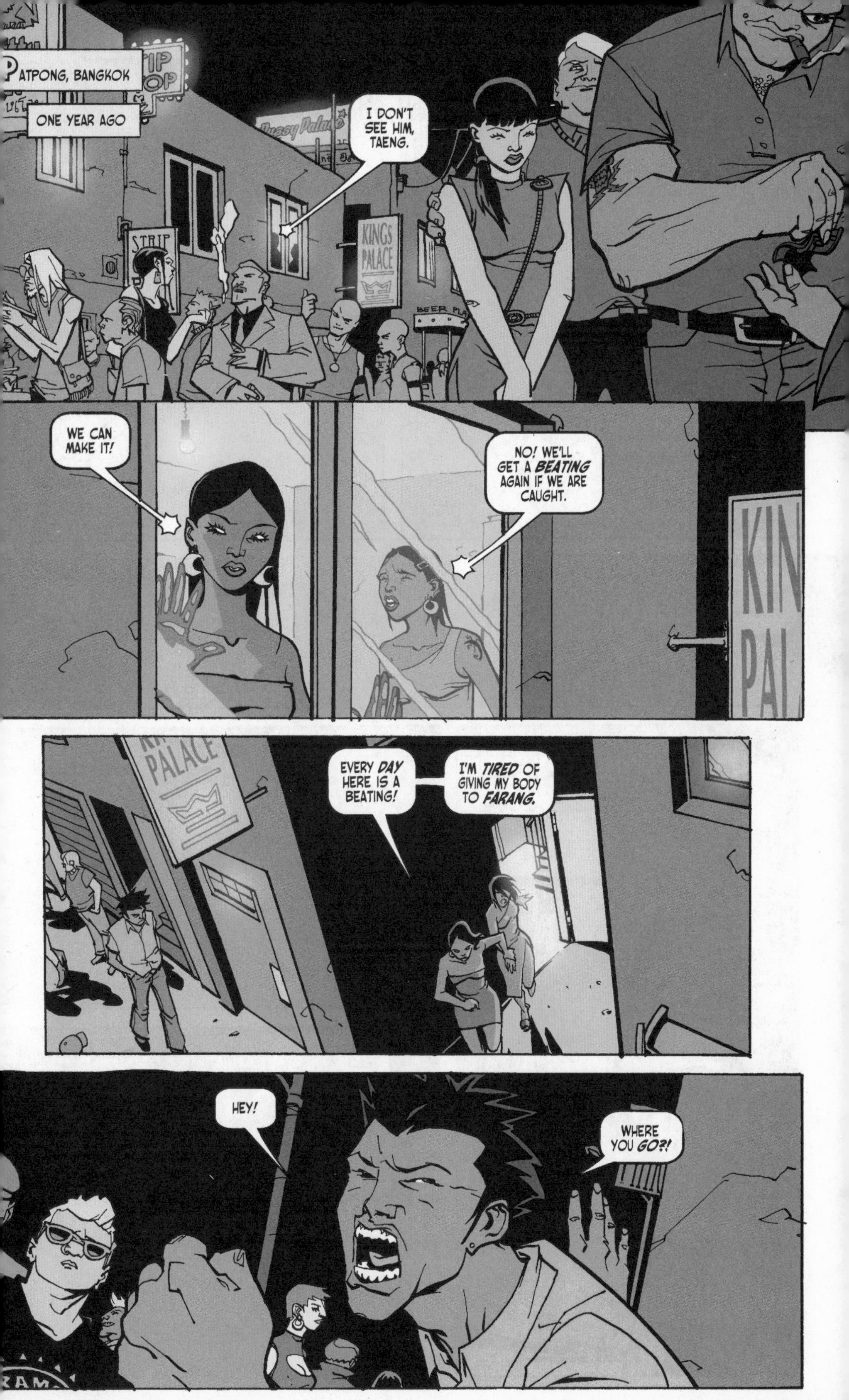
PATPONG, BANGKOK
ONE YEAR AGO
I DON'T SEE HIM, TAENG.
STRIP
KINGS PALACE
WE CAN MAKE IT!
NO! WE'LL GET A *BEATING* AGAIN IF WE ARE CAUGHT.
EVERY *DAY* HERE IS A BEATING!
I'M *TIRED* OF GIVING MY BODY TO *FARANG.*
HEY!
WHERE YOU *GO?!*

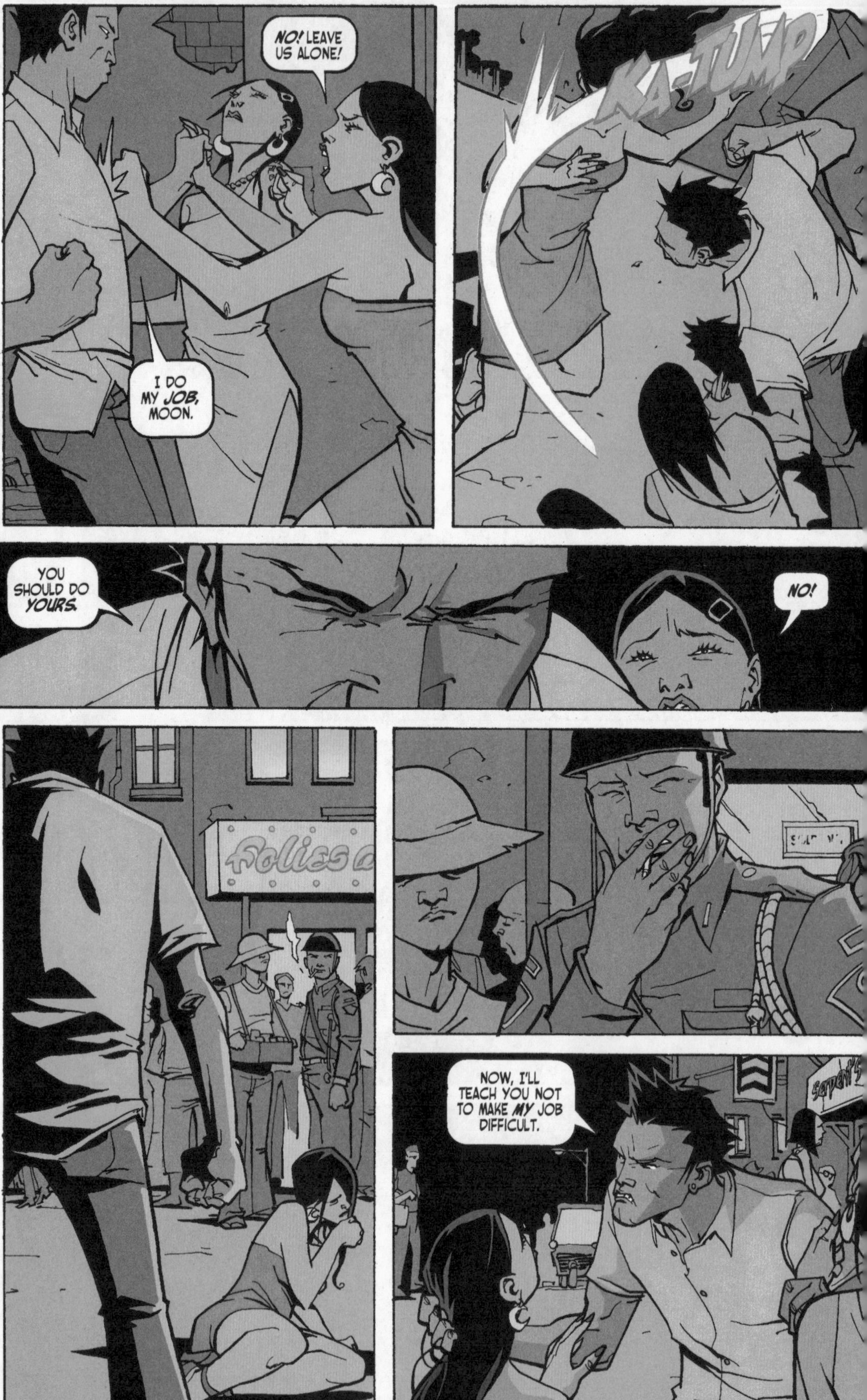
NO! LEAVE US ALONE!
I DO MY JOB, MOON.
KA-TUMP
YOU SHOULD DO YOURS.
NO!
Folies
NOW, I'LL TEACH YOU NOT TO MAKE MY JOB DIFFICULT.

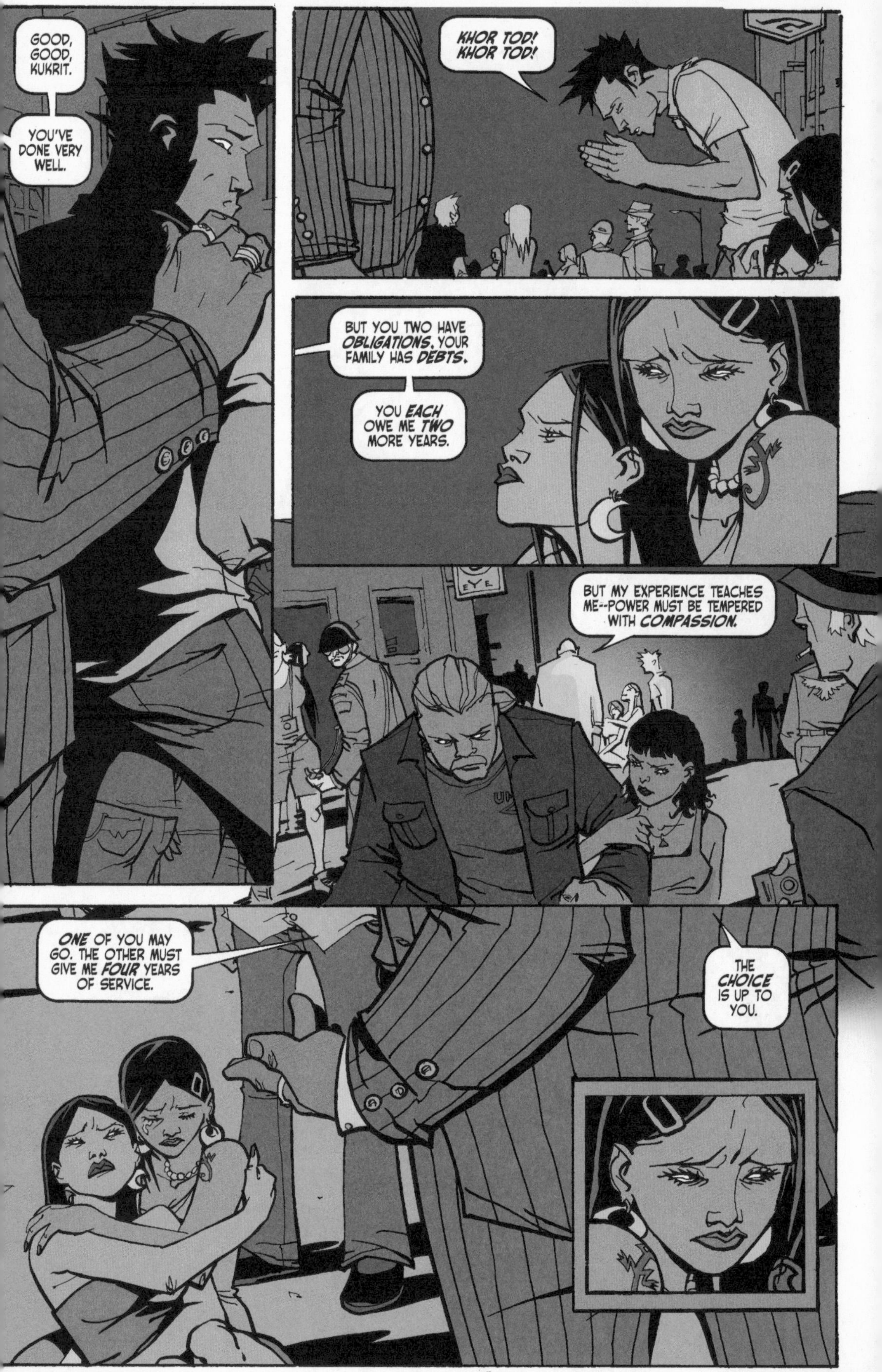
GOOD, GOOD, KUKRIT.
YOU'VE DONE VERY WELL.
KHOR TOD! KHOR TOD!
BUT YOU TWO HAVE OBLIGATIONS. YOUR FAMILY HAS DEBTS.
YOU EACH OWE ME TWO MORE YEARS.
EYE
BUT MY EXPERIENCE TEACHES ME--POWER MUST BE TEMPERED WITH COMPASSION.
ONE OF YOU MAY GO. THE OTHER MUST GIVE ME FOUR YEARS OF SERVICE.
THE CHOICE IS UP TO YOU.

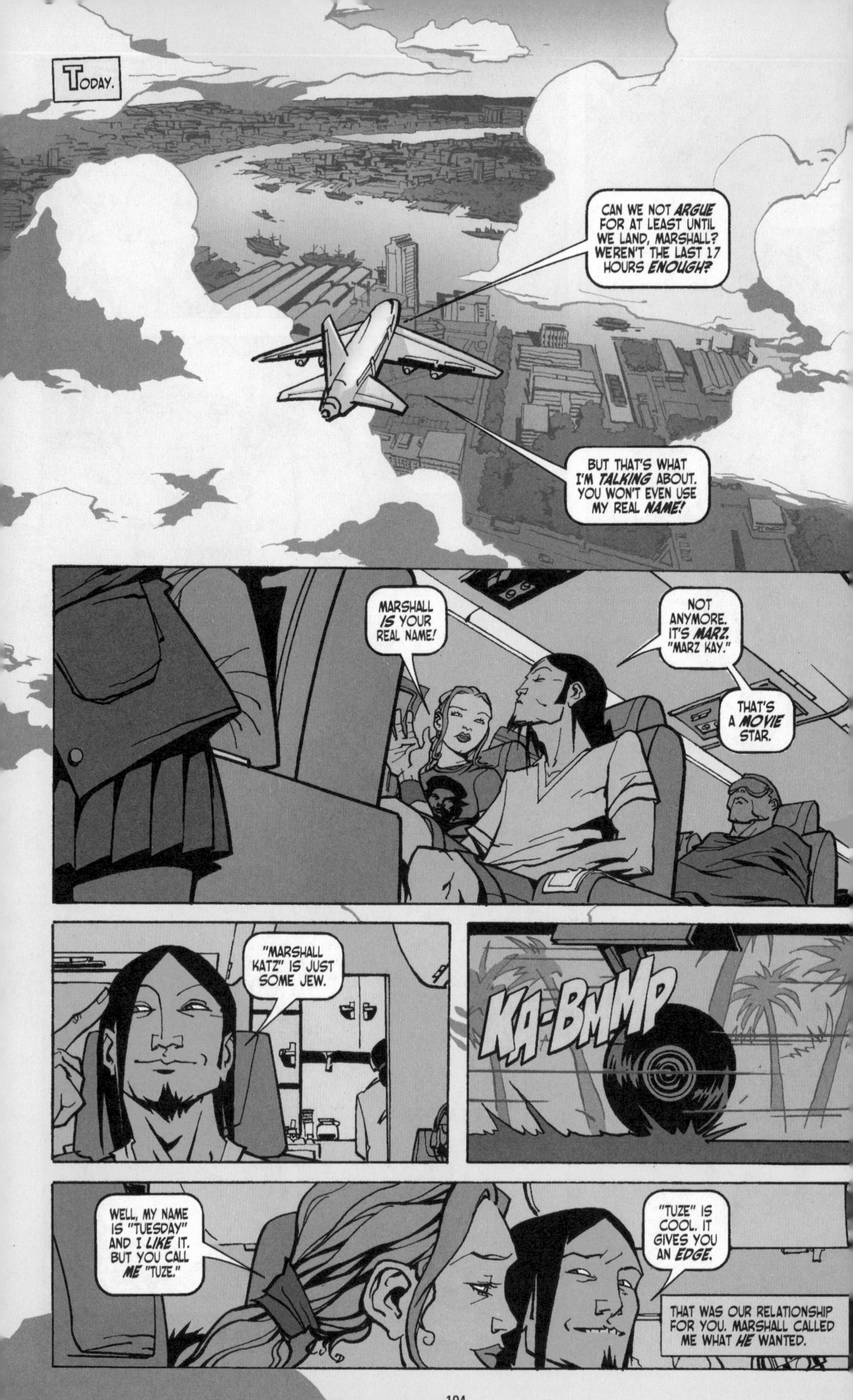
TODAY.
CAN WE NOT ARGUE FOR AT LEAST UNTIL WE LAND, MARSHALL? WEREN'T THE LAST 17 HOURS ENOUGH?
BUT THAT'S WHAT I'M TALKING ABOUT. YOU WON'T EVEN USE MY REAL NAME!
MARSHALL IS YOUR REAL NAME!
NOT ANYMORE. IT'S MARZ. "MARZ KAY."
THAT'S A MOVIE STAR.
"MARSHALL KATZ" IS JUST SOME JEW.
KA-BMMP
WELL, MY NAME IS "TUESDAY" AND I LIKE IT. BUT YOU CALL ME "TUZE."
"TUZE" IS COOL. IT GIVES YOU AN EDGE.
THAT WAS OUR RELATIONSHIP FOR YOU. MARSHALL CALLED ME WHAT HE WANTED.

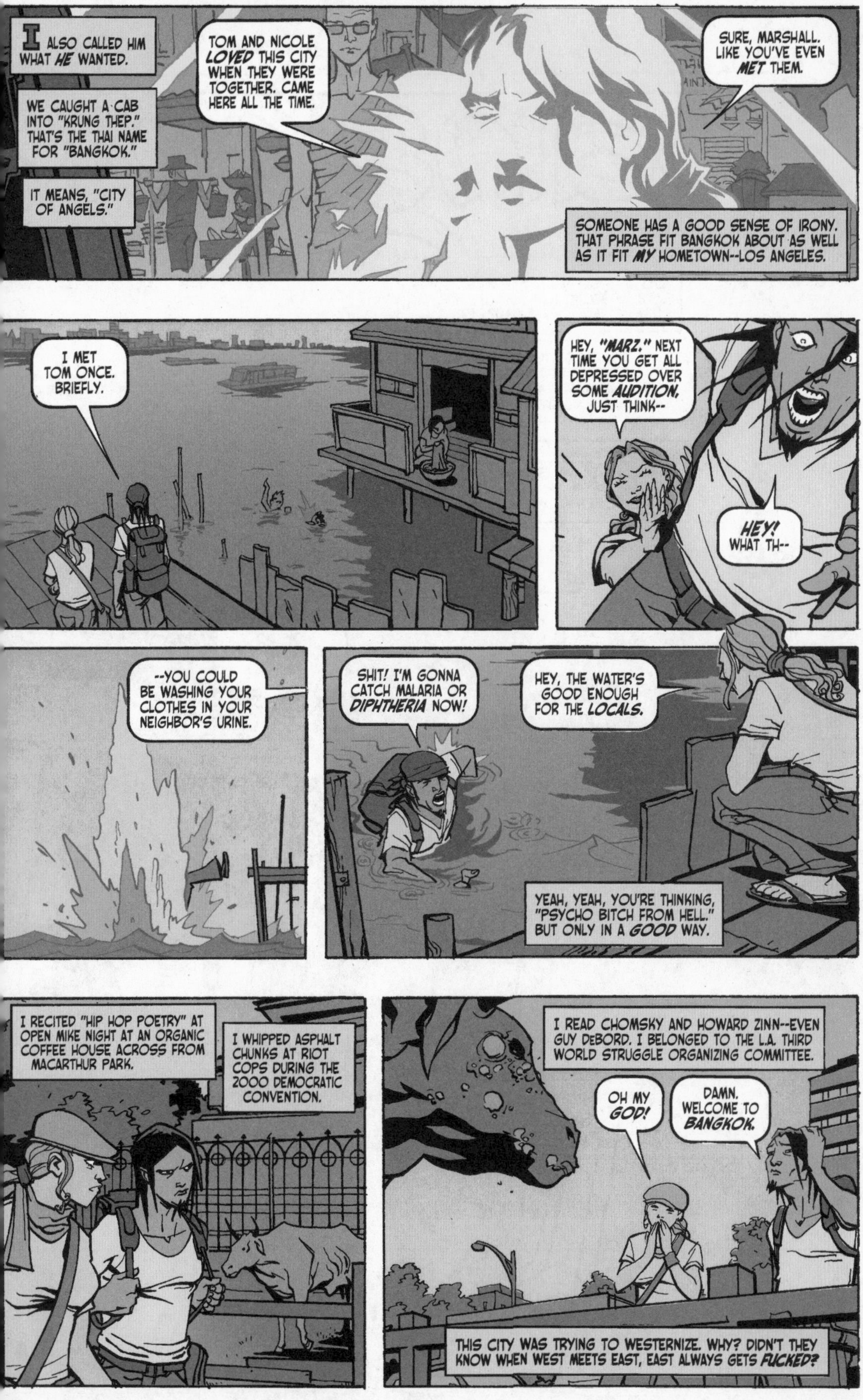
I ALSO CALLED HIM WHAT HE WANTED.
WE CAUGHT A CAB INTO "KRUNG THEP." THAT'S THE THAI NAME FOR "BANGKOK."
IT MEANS, "CITY OF ANGELS."
TOM AND NICOLE LOVED THIS CITY WHEN THEY WERE TOGETHER. CAME HERE ALL THE TIME.
SURE, MARSHALL. LIKE YOU'VE EVEN MET THEM.
SOMEONE HAS A GOOD SENSE OF IRONY. THAT PHRASE FIT BANGKOK ABOUT AS WELL AS IT FIT MY HOMETOWN--LOS ANGELES.
I MET TOM ONCE. BRIEFLY.
HEY, "MARZ." NEXT TIME YOU GET ALL DEPRESSED OVER SOME AUDITION, JUST THINK--
HEY! WHAT TH--
--YOU COULD BE WASHING YOUR CLOTHES IN YOUR NEIGHBOR'S URINE.
SHIT! I'M GONNA CATCH MALARIA OR DIPHTHERIA NOW!
HEY, THE WATER'S GOOD ENOUGH FOR THE LOCALS.
YEAH, YEAH, YOU'RE THINKING, "PSYCHO BITCH FROM HELL." BUT ONLY IN A GOOD WAY.
I RECITED "HIP HOP POETRY" AT OPEN MIKE NIGHT AT AN ORGANIC COFFEE HOUSE ACROSS FROM MACARTHUR PARK.
I WHIPPED ASPHALT CHUNKS AT RIOT COPS DURING THE 2000 DEMOCRATIC CONVENTION.
I READ CHOMSKY AND HOWARD ZINN--EVEN GUY DEBORD. I BELONGED TO THE L.A. THIRD WORLD STRUGGLE ORGANIZING COMMITTEE.
OH MY GOD!
DAMN. WELCOME TO BANGKOK.
THIS CITY WAS TRYING TO WESTERNIZE. WHY? DIDN'T THEY KNOW WHEN WEST MEETS EAST, EAST ALWAYS GETS FUCKED?

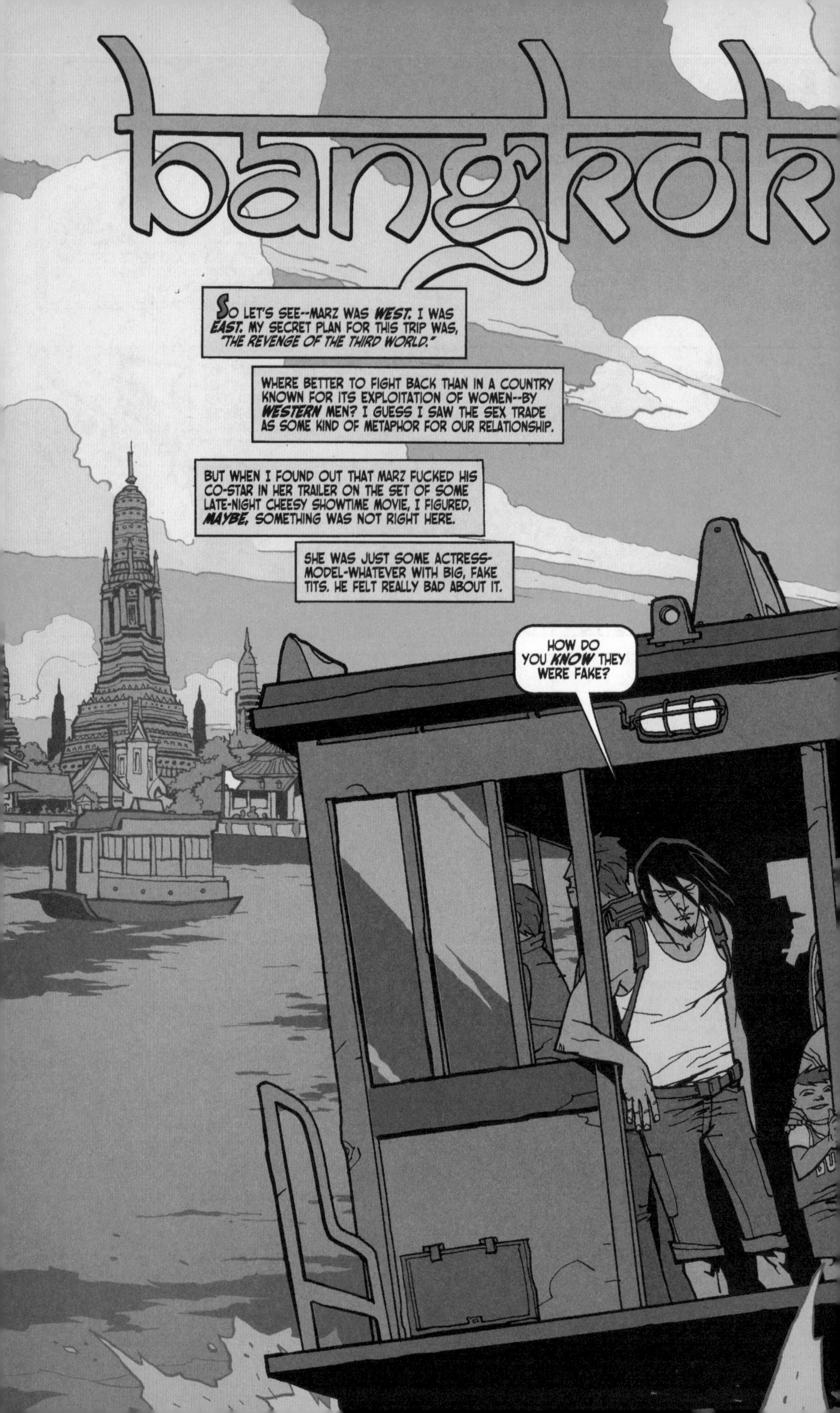

bangkok
SO LET'S SEE--MARZ WAS WEST. I WAS EAST. MY SECRET PLAN FOR THIS TRIP WAS, "THE REVENGE OF THE THIRD WORLD."
WHERE BETTER TO FIGHT BACK THAN IN A COUNTRY KNOWN FOR ITS EXPLOITATION OF WOMEN--BY WESTERN MEN? I GUESS I SAW THE SEX TRADE AS SOME KIND OF METAPHOR FOR OUR RELATIONSHIP.
BUT WHEN I FOUND OUT THAT MARZ FUCKED HIS CO-STAR IN HER TRAILER ON THE SET OF SOME LATE-NIGHT CHEESY SHOWTIME MOVIE, I FIGURED, MAYBE, SOMETHING WAS NOT RIGHT HERE.
SHE WAS JUST SOME ACTRESS-MODEL-WHATEVER WITH BIG, FAKE TITS. HE FELT REALLY BAD ABOUT IT.
HOW DO YOU KNOW THEY WERE FAKE?

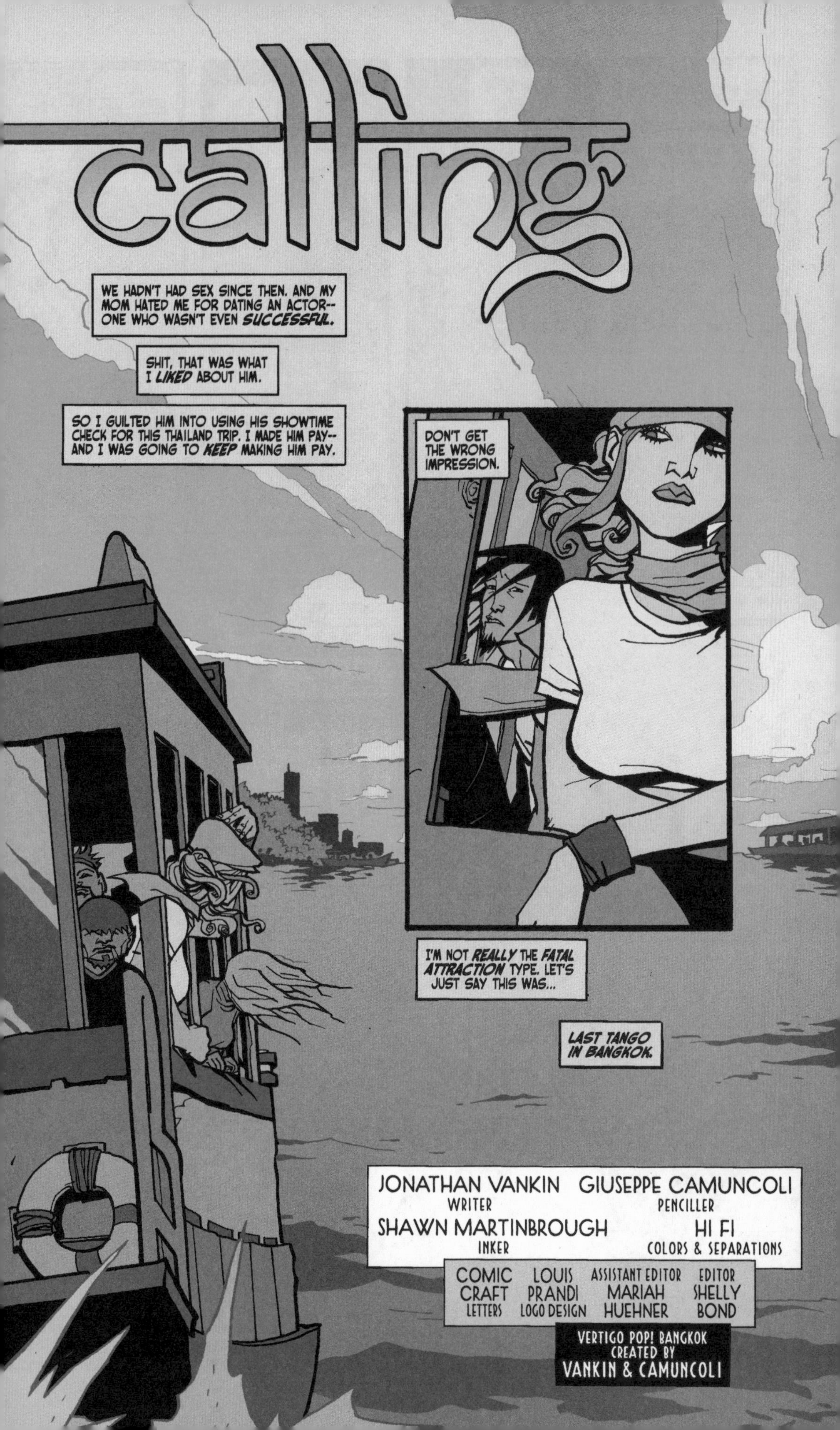
calling
WE HADN'T HAD SEX SINCE THEN. AND MY MOM HATED ME FOR DATING AN ACTOR--ONE WHO WASN'T EVEN SUCCESSFUL.
SHIT, THAT WAS WHAT I LIKED ABOUT HIM.
SO I GUILTED HIM INTO USING HIS SHOWTIME CHECK FOR THIS THAILAND TRIP. I MADE HIM PAY--AND I WAS GOING TO KEEP MAKING HIM PAY.
DON'T GET THE WRONG IMPRESSION.
I'M NOT REALLY THE FATAL ATTRACTION TYPE. LET'S JUST SAY THIS WAS...
LAST TANGO IN BANGKOK.
JONATHAN VANKIN WRITER
GIUSEPPE CAMUNCOLI PENCILLER
SHAWN MARTINBROUGH INKER
HI FI COLORS & SEPARATIONS
COMICCRAFT LETTERS
LOUIS PRANDI LOGO DESIGN
ASSISTANT EDITOR MARIAH HUEHNER
EDITOR SHELLY BOND
VERTIGO POP! BANGKOK CREATED BY VANKIN & CAMUNCOLI

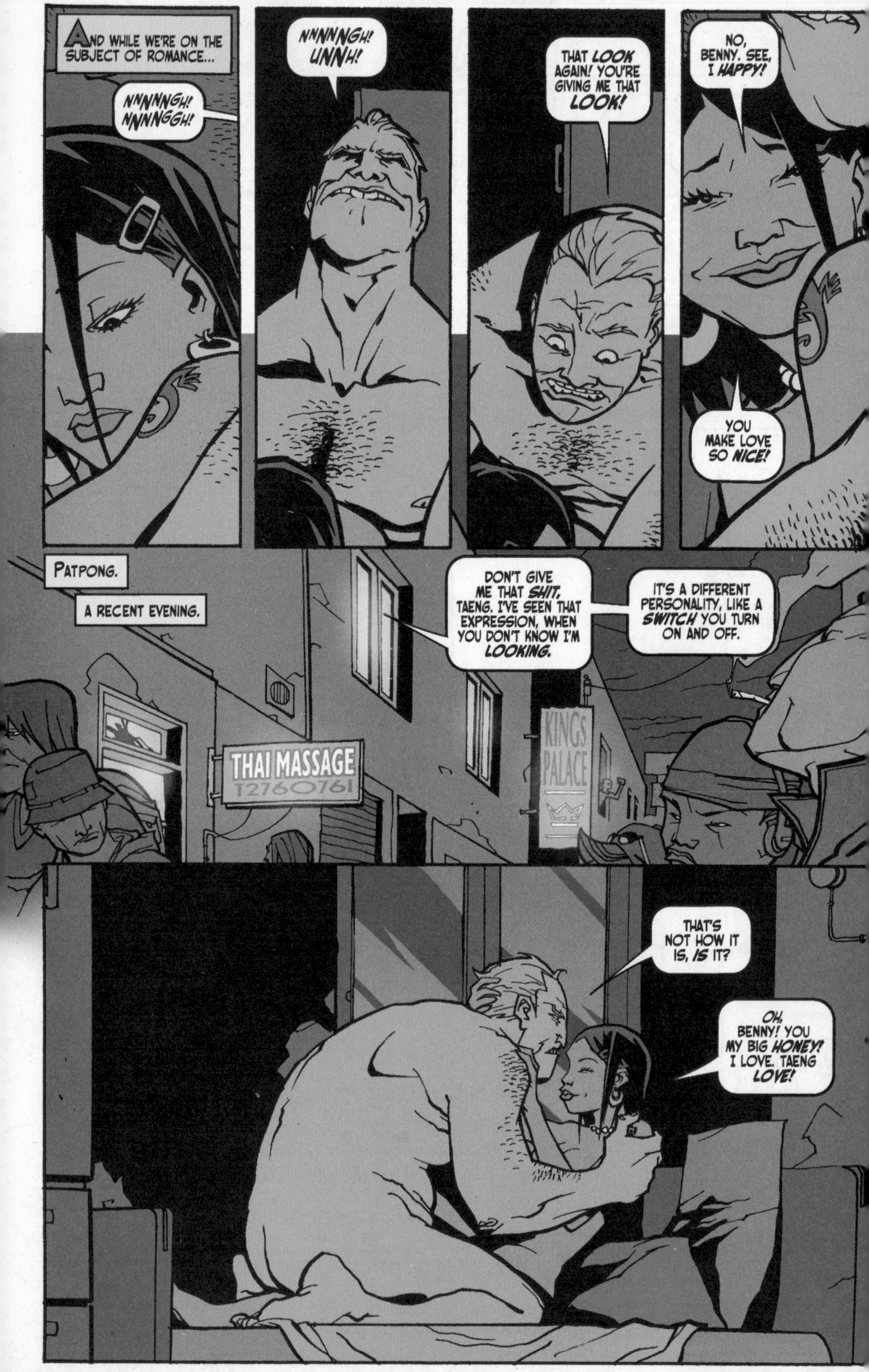
AND WHILE WE'RE ON THE SUBJECT OF ROMANCE...
NNNNNGH! NNNNGGH!
NNNNNGH! UNNH!
THAT LOOK AGAIN! YOU'RE GIVING ME THAT LOOK!
NO, BENNY. SEE, I HAPPY!
YOU MAKE LOVE SO NICE!
PATPONG.
A RECENT EVENING.
DON'T GIVE ME THAT SHIT, TAENG. I'VE SEEN THAT EXPRESSION, WHEN YOU DON'T KNOW I'M LOOKING.
IT'S A DIFFERENT PERSONALITY, LIKE A SWITCH YOU TURN ON AND OFF.
THAI MASSAGE
12760761
KINGS PALACE
THAT'S NOT HOW IT IS, IS IT?
OH, BENNY! YOU MY BIG HONEY! I LOVE. TAENG LOVE!

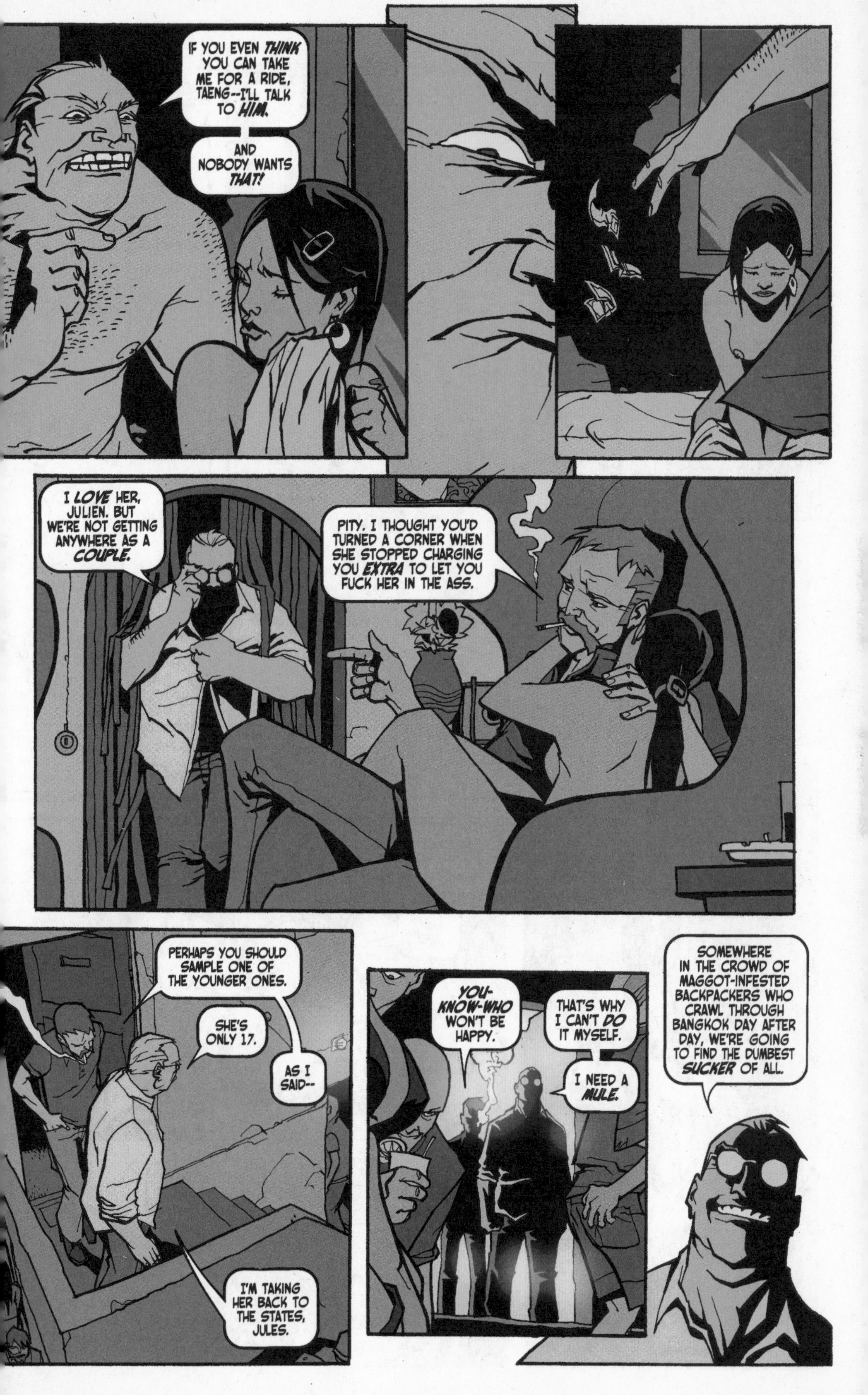
IF YOU EVEN THINK YOU CAN TAKE ME FOR A RIDE, TAENG--I'LL TALK TO HIM.
AND NOBODY WANTS THAT!
I LOVE HER, JULIEN. BUT WE'RE NOT GETTING ANYWHERE AS A COUPLE.
PITY. I THOUGHT YOU'D TURNED A CORNER WHEN SHE STOPPED CHARGING YOU EXTRA TO LET YOU FUCK HER IN THE ASS.
PERHAPS YOU SHOULD SAMPLE ONE OF THE YOUNGER ONES.
SHE'S ONLY 17.
AS I SAID--
I'M TAKING HER BACK TO THE STATES, JULES.
YOU-KNOW-WHO WON'T BE HAPPY.
THAT'S WHY I CAN'T DO IT MYSELF.
I NEED A MULE.
SOMEWHERE IN THE CROWD OF MAGGOT-INFESTED BACKPACKERS WHO CRAWL THROUGH BANGKOK DAY AFTER DAY, WE'RE GOING TO FIND THE DUMBEST SUCKER OF ALL.

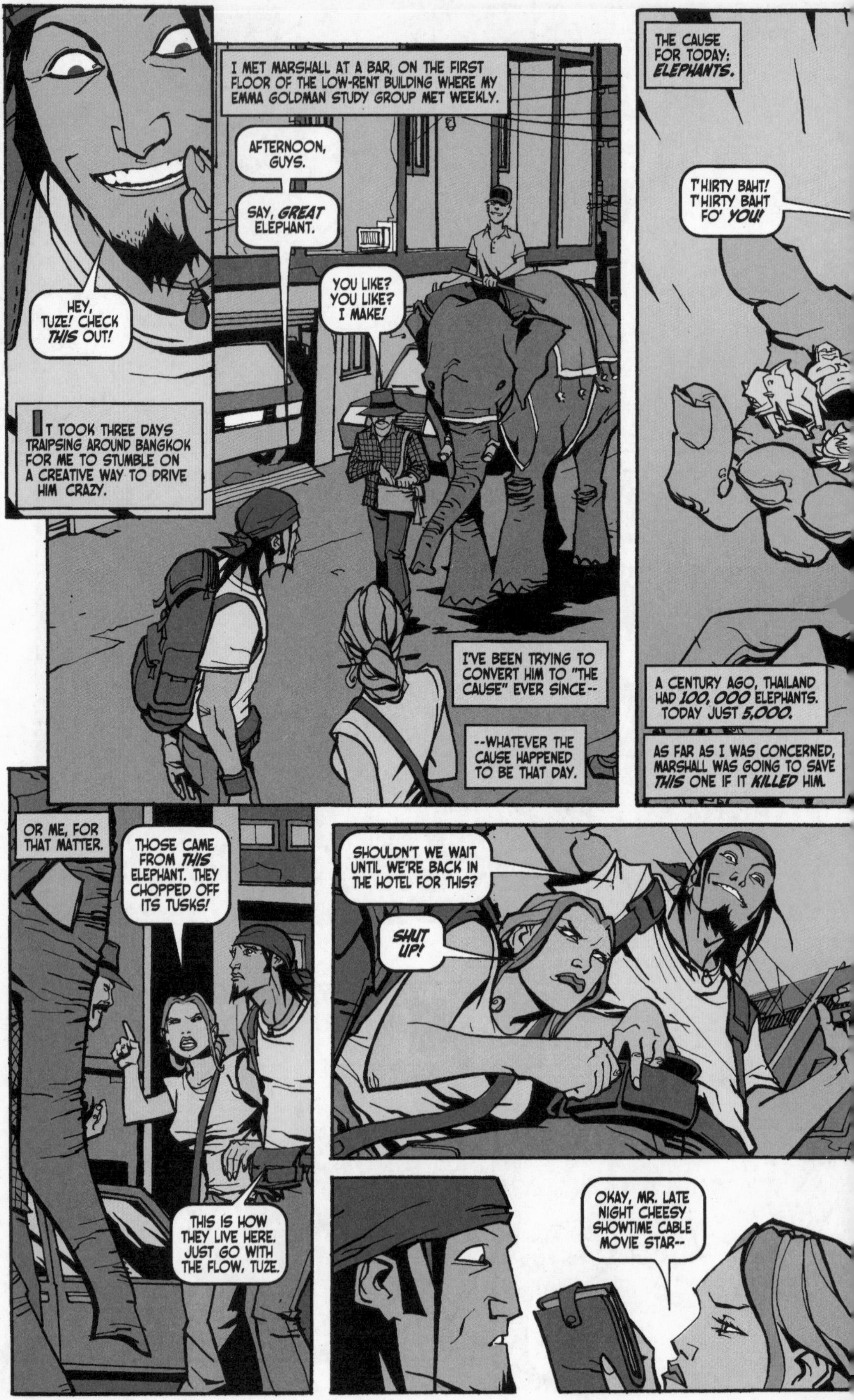
HEY, TUZE! CHECK THIS OUT!
IT TOOK THREE DAYS TRAIPSING AROUND BANGKOK FOR ME TO STUMBLE ON A CREATIVE WAY TO DRIVE HIM CRAZY.
I MET MARSHALL AT A BAR, ON THE FIRST FLOOR OF THE LOW-RENT BUILDING WHERE MY EMMA GOLDMAN STUDY GROUP MET WEEKLY.
AFTERNOON, GUYS.
SAY, GREAT ELEPHANT.
YOU LIKE? YOU LIKE? I MAKE!
I'VE BEEN TRYING TO CONVERT HIM TO "THE CAUSE" EVER SINCE--
--WHATEVER THE CAUSE HAPPENED TO BE THAT DAY.
THE CAUSE FOR TODAY: ELEPHANTS.
T'HIRTY BAHT! T'HIRTY BAHT FO' YOU!
A CENTURY AGO, THAILAND HAD 100,000 ELEPHANTS. TODAY JUST 5,000.
AS FAR AS I WAS CONCERNED, MARSHALL WAS GOING TO SAVE THIS ONE IF IT KILLED HIM.
OR ME, FOR THAT MATTER.
THOSE CAME FROM THIS ELEPHANT. THEY CHOPPED OFF ITS TUSKS!
THIS IS HOW THEY LIVE HERE. JUST GO WITH THE FLOW, TUZE.
SHOULDN'T WE WAIT UNTIL WE'RE BACK IN THE HOTEL FOR THIS?
SHUT UP!
OKAY, MR. LATE NIGHT CHEESY SHOWTIME CABLE MOVIE STAR--

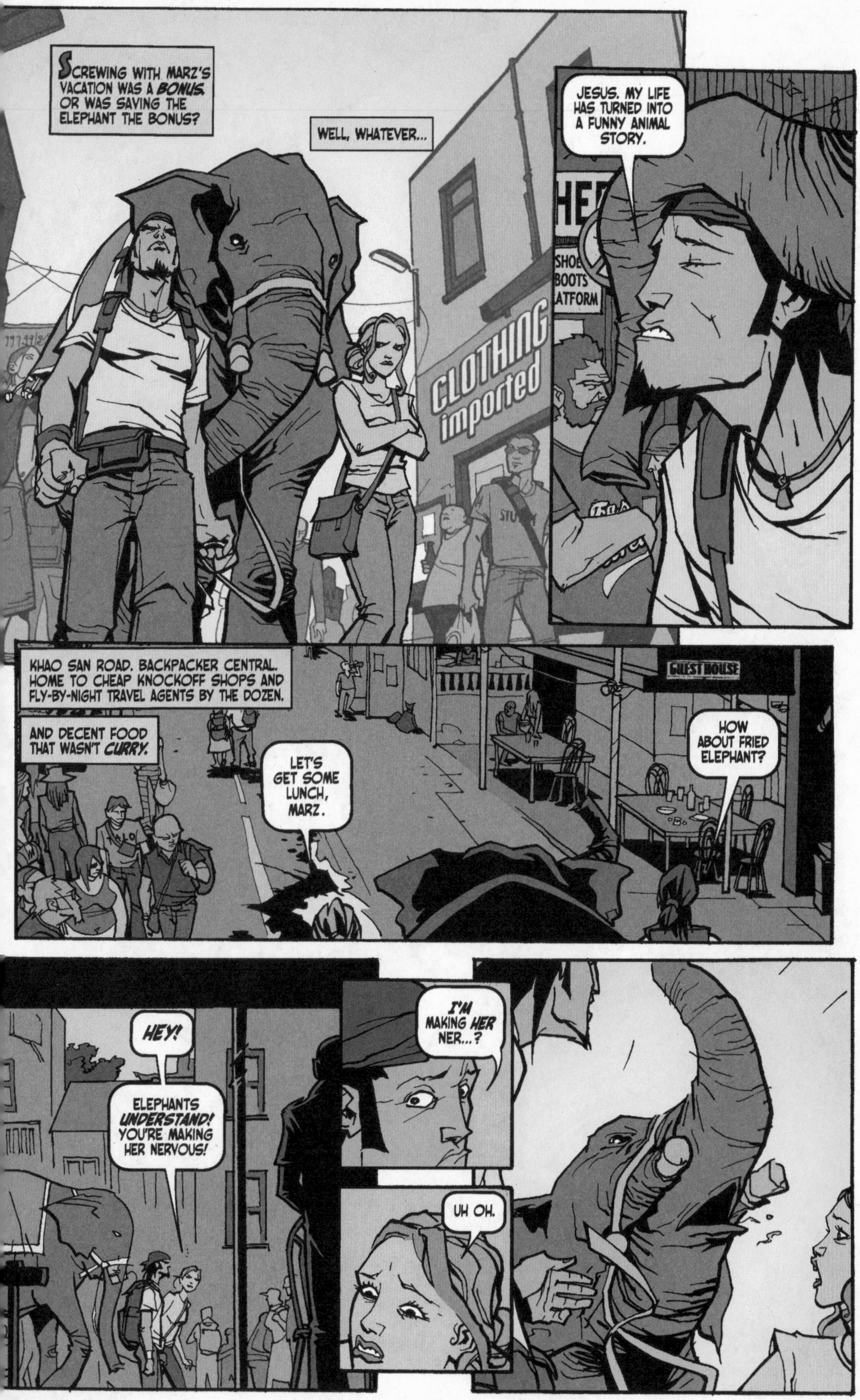
SCREWING WITH MARZ'S VACATION WAS A BONUS. OR WAS SAVING THE ELEPHANT THE BONUS?
WELL, WHATEVER...
CLOTHING imported
JESUS. MY LIFE HAS TURNED INTO A FUNNY ANIMAL STORY.
SHOE BOOTS ATFORM
KHAO SAN ROAD. BACKPACKER CENTRAL. HOME TO CHEAP KNOCKOFF SHOPS AND FLY-BY-NIGHT TRAVEL AGENTS BY THE DOZEN.
AND DECENT FOOD THAT WASN'T CURRY.
LET'S GET SOME LUNCH, MARZ.
GUEST HOUSE
HOW ABOUT FRIED ELEPHANT?
HEY!
ELEPHANTS UNDERSTAND! YOU'RE MAKING HER NERVOUS!
I'M MAKING HER NER...?
UH OH.

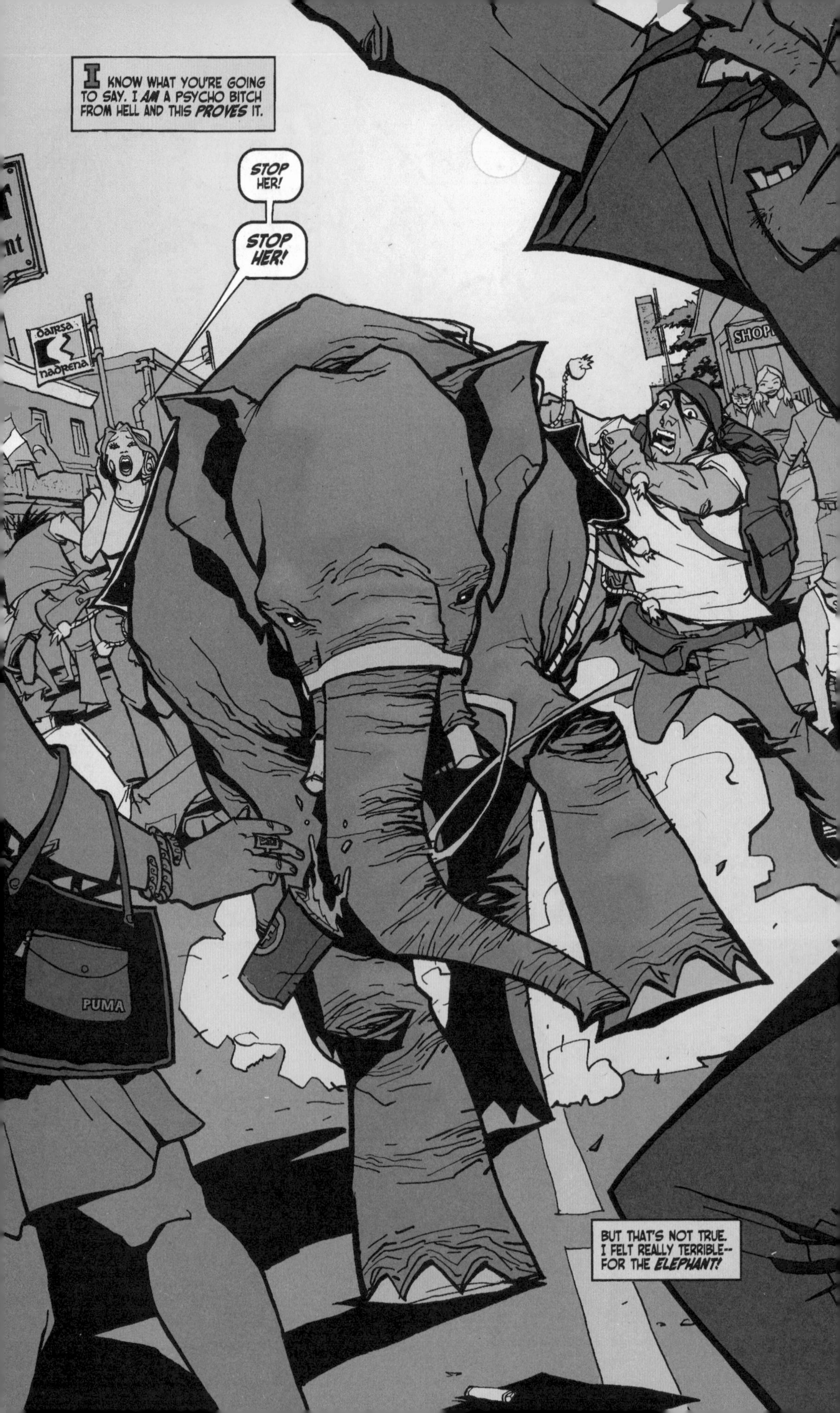
I KNOW WHAT YOU'RE GOING TO SAY. I AM A PSYCHO BITCH FROM HELL AND THIS PROVES IT.
STOP HER!
STOP HER!
BUT THAT'S NOT TRUE. I FELT REALLY TERRIBLE-- FOR THE ELEPHANT!

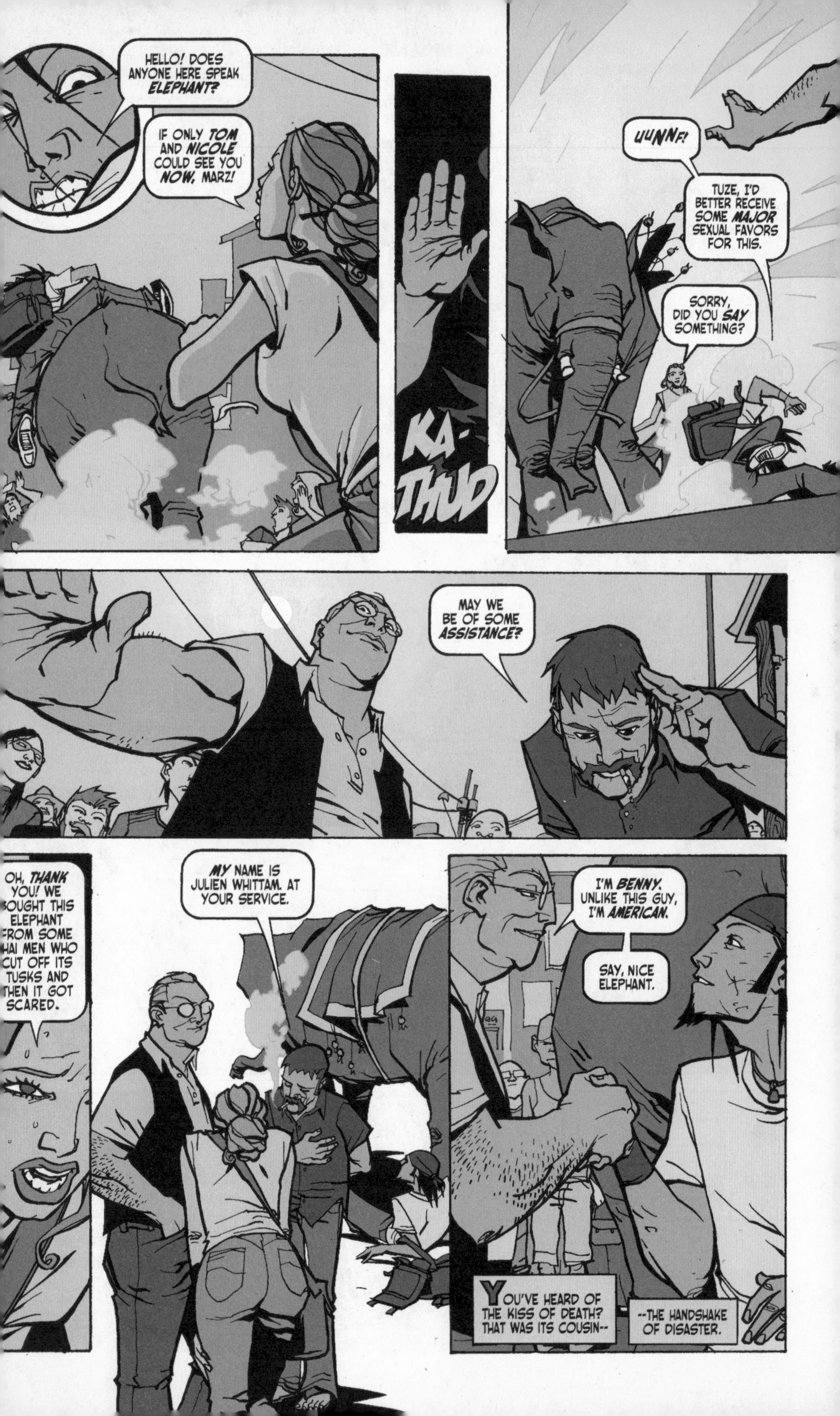
HELLO! DOES ANYONE HERE SPEAK ELEPHANT?
IF ONLY TOM AND NICOLE COULD SEE YOU NOW, MARZ!
KA-THUD
UUNNF!
TUZE, I'D BETTER RECEIVE SOME MAJOR SEXUAL FAVORS FOR THIS.
SORRY, DID YOU SAY SOMETHING?
MAY WE BE OF SOME ASSISTANCE?
OH, THANK YOU! WE BOUGHT THIS ELEPHANT FROM SOME THAI MEN WHO CUT OFF ITS TUSKS AND THEN IT GOT SCARED.
MY NAME IS JULIEN WHITTAM. AT YOUR SERVICE.
I'M BENNY. UNLIKE THIS GUY, I'M AMERICAN.
SAY, NICE ELEPHANT.
YOU'VE HEARD OF THE KISS OF DEATH? THAT WAS ITS COUSIN--
--THE HANDSHAKE OF DISASTER.

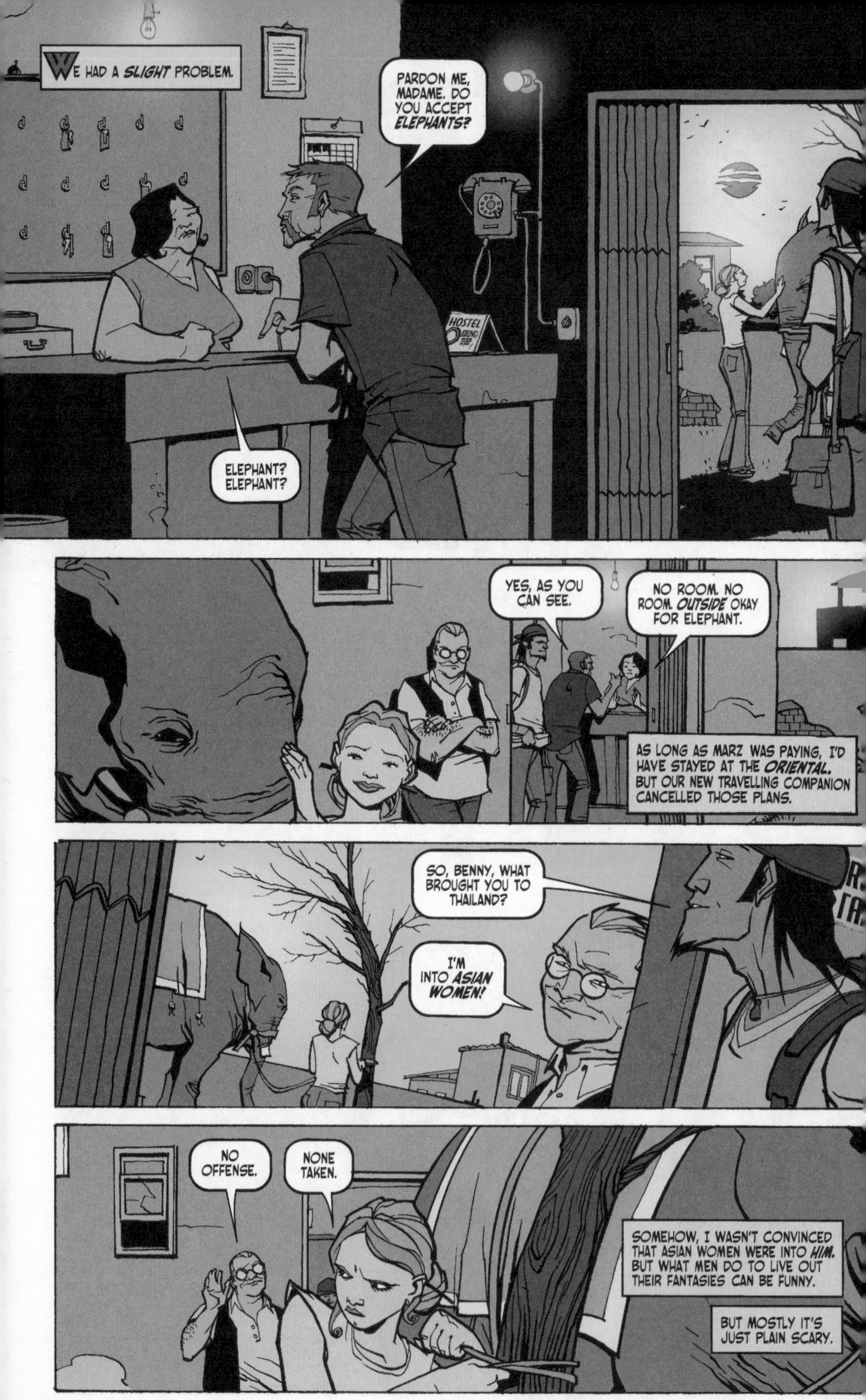
WE HAD A SLIGHT PROBLEM.
PARDON ME, MADAME. DO YOU ACCEPT ELEPHANTS?
HOSTEL
ELEPHANT? ELEPHANT?
YES, AS YOU CAN SEE.
NO ROOM. NO ROOM. OUTSIDE OKAY FOR ELEPHANT.
AS LONG AS MARZ WAS PAYING, I'D HAVE STAYED AT THE ORIENTAL. BUT OUR NEW TRAVELLING COMPANION CANCELLED THOSE PLANS.
SO, BENNY, WHAT BROUGHT YOU TO THAILAND?
I'M INTO ASIAN WOMEN!
NO OFFENSE.
NONE TAKEN.
SOMEHOW, I WASN'T CONVINCED THAT ASIAN WOMEN WERE INTO HIM. BUT WHAT MEN DO TO LIVE OUT THEIR FANTASIES CAN BE FUNNY.
BUT MOSTLY IT'S JUST PLAIN SCARY.

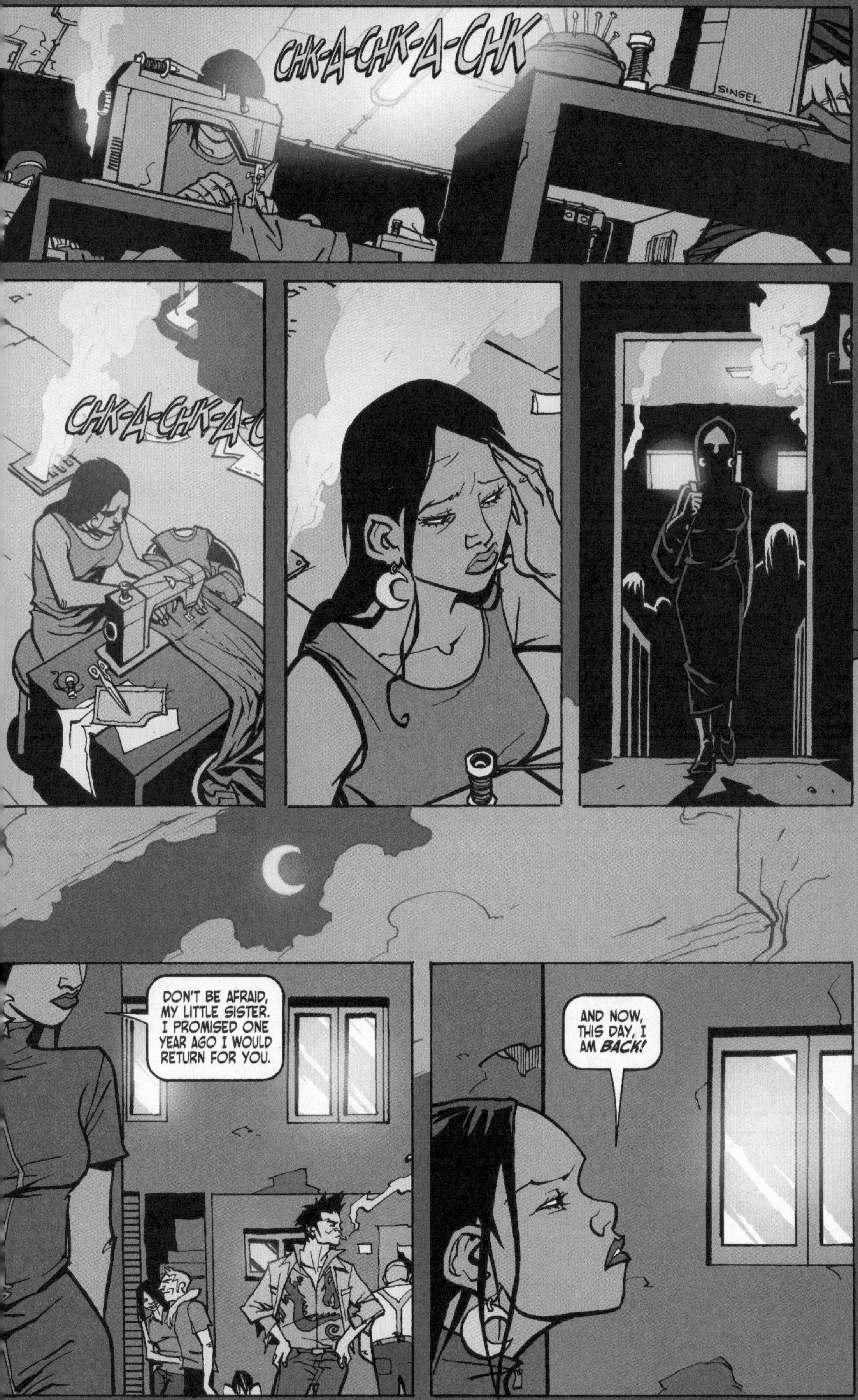
CHK-A-CHK-A-CHK
SINGEL
CHK-A-CHK-A-C
DON'T BE AFRAID, MY LITTLE SISTER. I PROMISED ONE YEAR AGO I WOULD RETURN FOR YOU.
AND NOW, THIS DAY, I AM *BACK!*

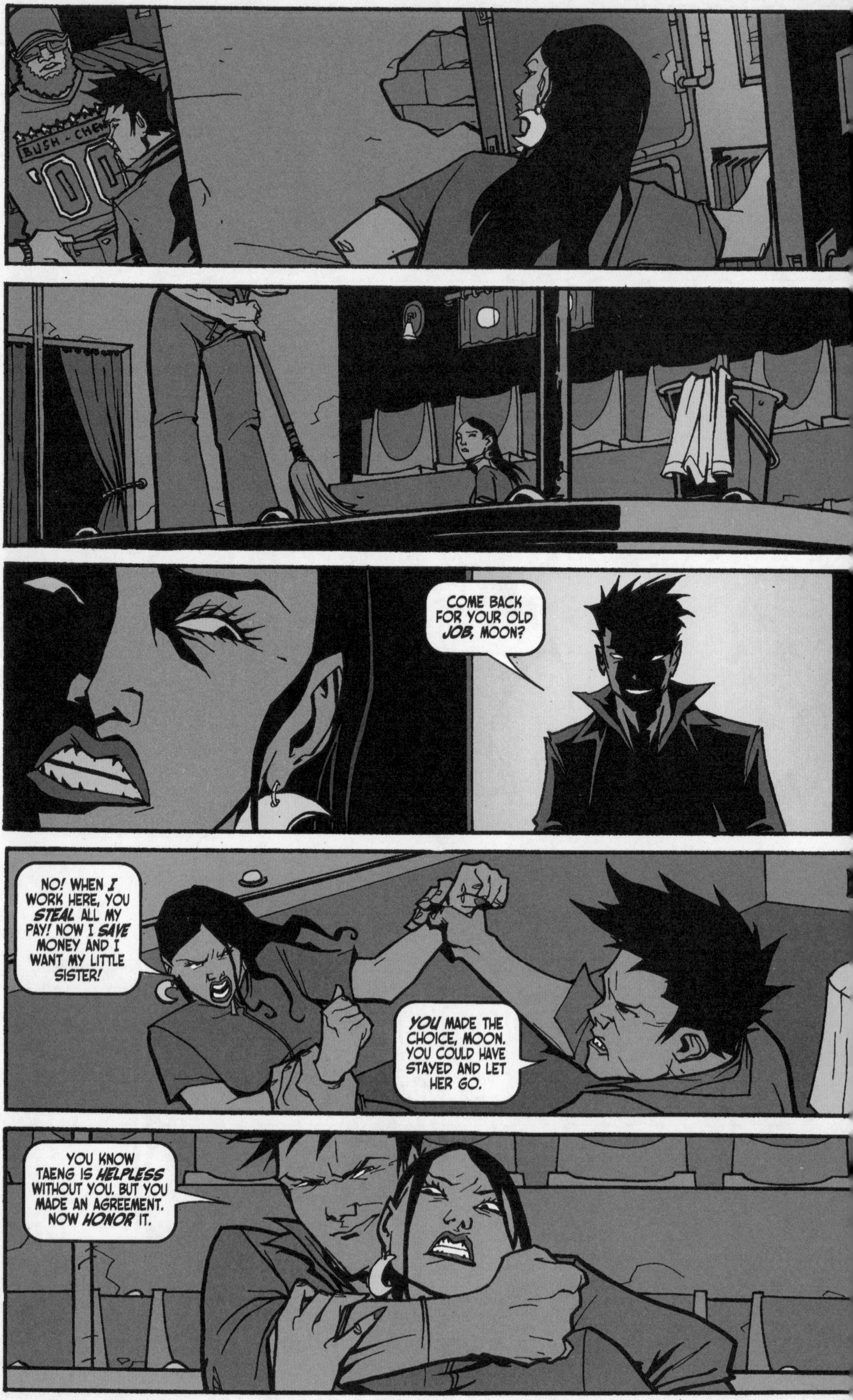
BUSH - CHE
'00
COME BACK FOR YOUR OLD JOB, MOON?
NO! WHEN I WORK HERE, YOU STEAL ALL MY PAY! NOW I SAVE MONEY AND I WANT MY LITTLE SISTER!
YOU MADE THE CHOICE, MOON. YOU COULD HAVE STAYED AND LET HER GO.
YOU KNOW TAENG IS HELPLESS WITHOUT YOU. BUT YOU MADE AN AGREEMENT. NOW HONOR IT.

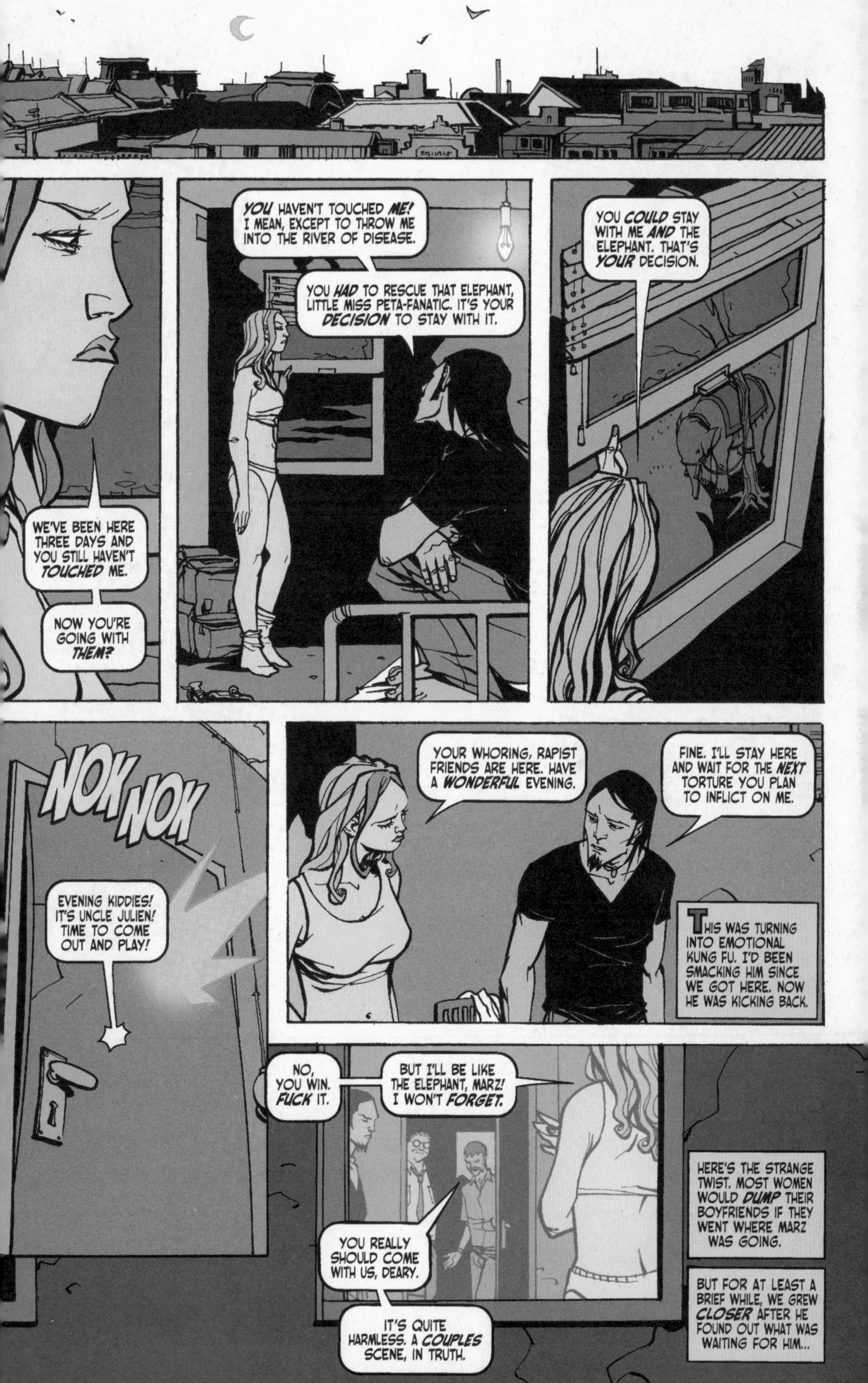
WE'VE BEEN HERE THREE DAYS AND YOU STILL HAVEN'T TOUCHED ME.
NOW YOU'RE GOING WITH THEM?
YOU HAVEN'T TOUCHED ME! I MEAN, EXCEPT TO THROW ME INTO THE RIVER OF DISEASE.
YOU HAD TO RESCUE THAT ELEPHANT, LITTLE MISS PETA-FANATIC. IT'S YOUR DECISION TO STAY WITH IT.
YOU COULD STAY WITH ME AND THE ELEPHANT. THAT'S YOUR DECISION.
NOK NOK
EVENING KIDDIES! IT'S UNCLE JULIEN! TIME TO COME OUT AND PLAY!
YOUR WHORING, RAPIST FRIENDS ARE HERE. HAVE A WONDERFUL EVENING.
FINE. I'LL STAY HERE AND WAIT FOR THE NEXT TORTURE YOU PLAN TO INFLICT ON ME.
THIS WAS TURNING INTO EMOTIONAL KUNG FU. I'D BEEN SMACKING HIM SINCE WE GOT HERE. NOW HE WAS KICKING BACK.
NO, YOU WIN. FUCK IT.
BUT I'LL BE LIKE THE ELEPHANT, MARZ! I WON'T FORGET.
YOU REALLY SHOULD COME WITH US, DEARY.
IT'S QUITE HARMLESS. A COUPLES SCENE, IN TRUTH.
HERE'S THE STRANGE TWIST. MOST WOMEN WOULD DUMP THEIR BOYFRIENDS IF THEY WENT WHERE MARZ WAS GOING.
BUT FOR AT LEAST A BRIEF WHILE, WE GREW CLOSER AFTER HE FOUND OUT WHAT WAS WAITING FOR HIM...

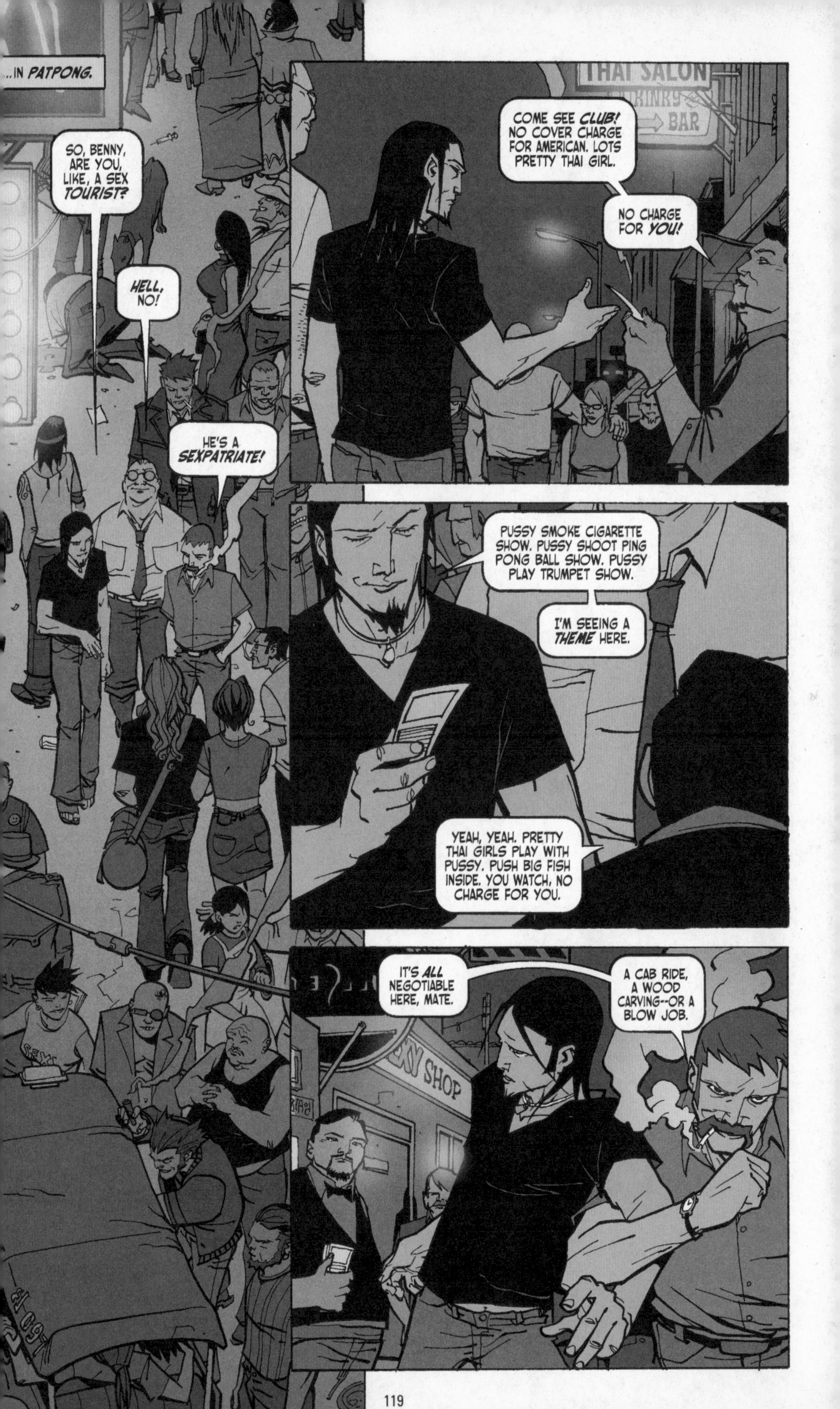
...IN PATPONG.
SO, BENNY, ARE YOU, LIKE, A SEX TOURIST?
HELL, NO!
HE'S A SEXPATRIATE!
THAI SALON
BAR
COME SEE CLUB! NO COVER CHARGE FOR AMERICAN. LOTS PRETTY THAI GIRL.
NO CHARGE FOR YOU!
PUSSY SMOKE CIGARETTE SHOW. PUSSY SHOOT PING PONG BALL SHOW. PUSSY PLAY TRUMPET SHOW.
I'M SEEING A THEME HERE.
YEAH, YEAH. PRETTY THAI GIRLS PLAY WITH PUSSY. PUSH BIG FISH INSIDE. YOU WATCH, NO CHARGE FOR YOU.
IT'S ALL NEGOTIABLE HERE, MATE.
A CAB RIDE, A WOOD CARVING--OR A BLOW JOB.
SHOP

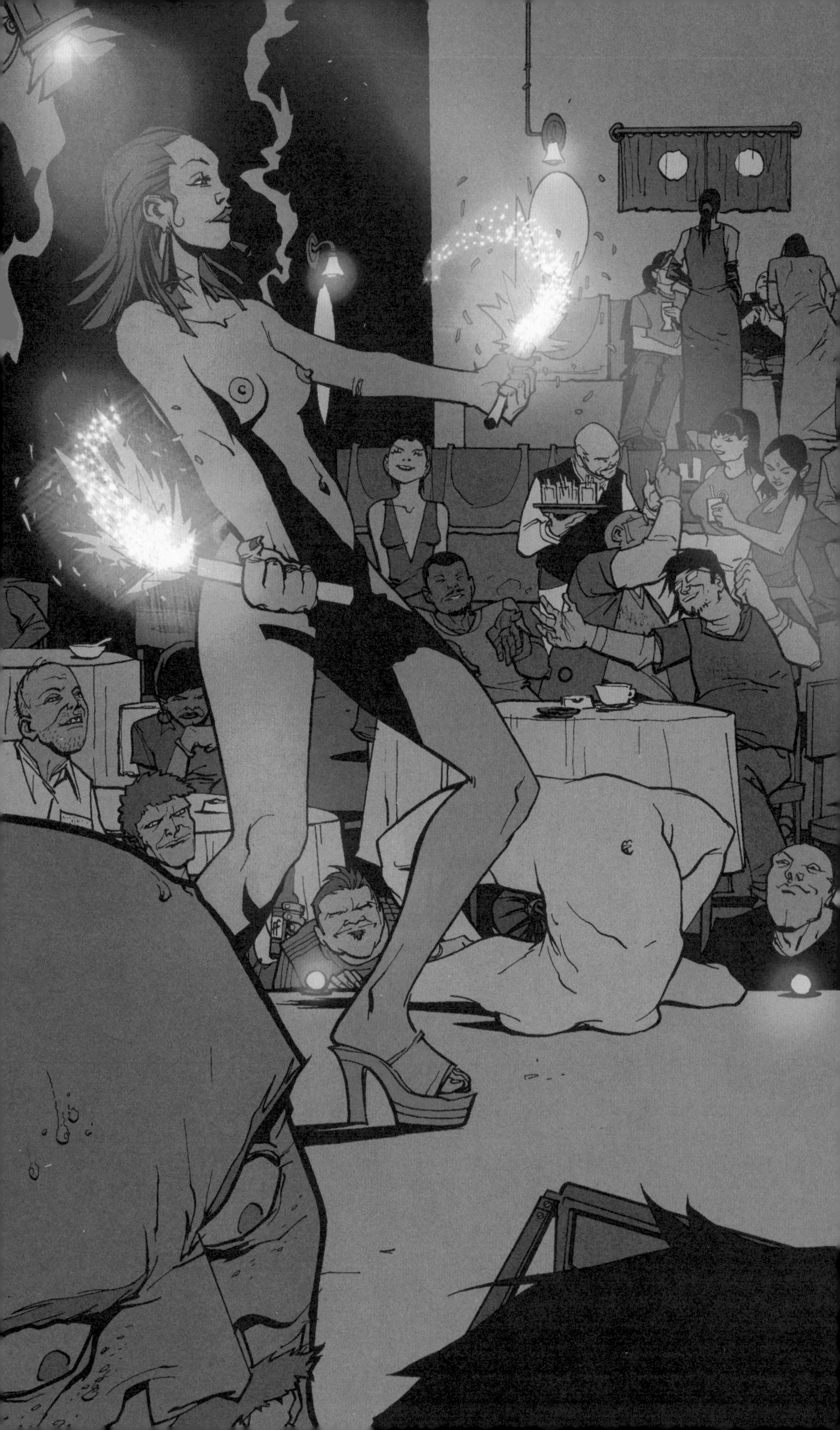

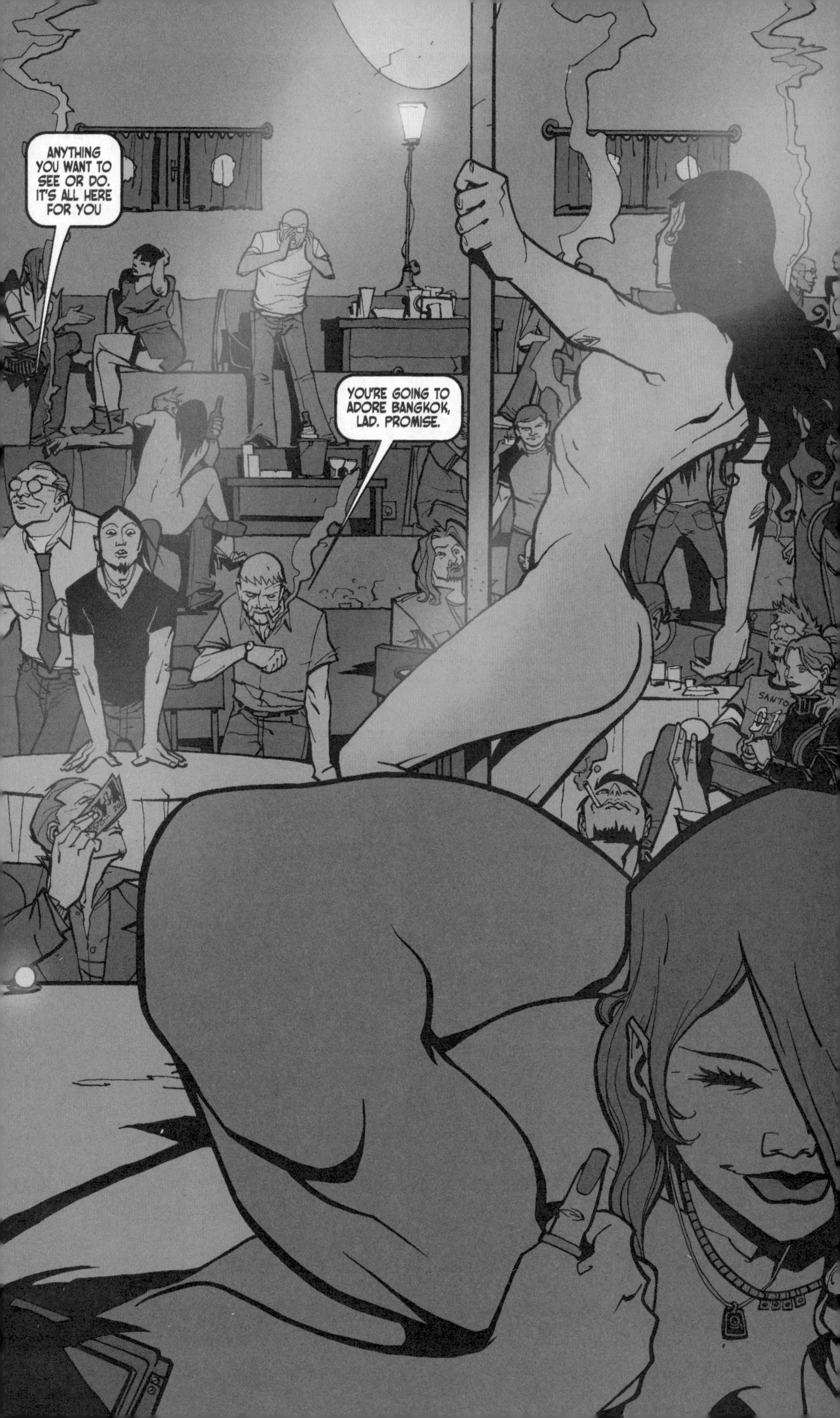
ANYTHING YOU WANT TO SEE OR DO. IT'S ALL HERE FOR YOU
YOU'RE GOING TO ADORE BANGKOK, LAD. PROMISE.

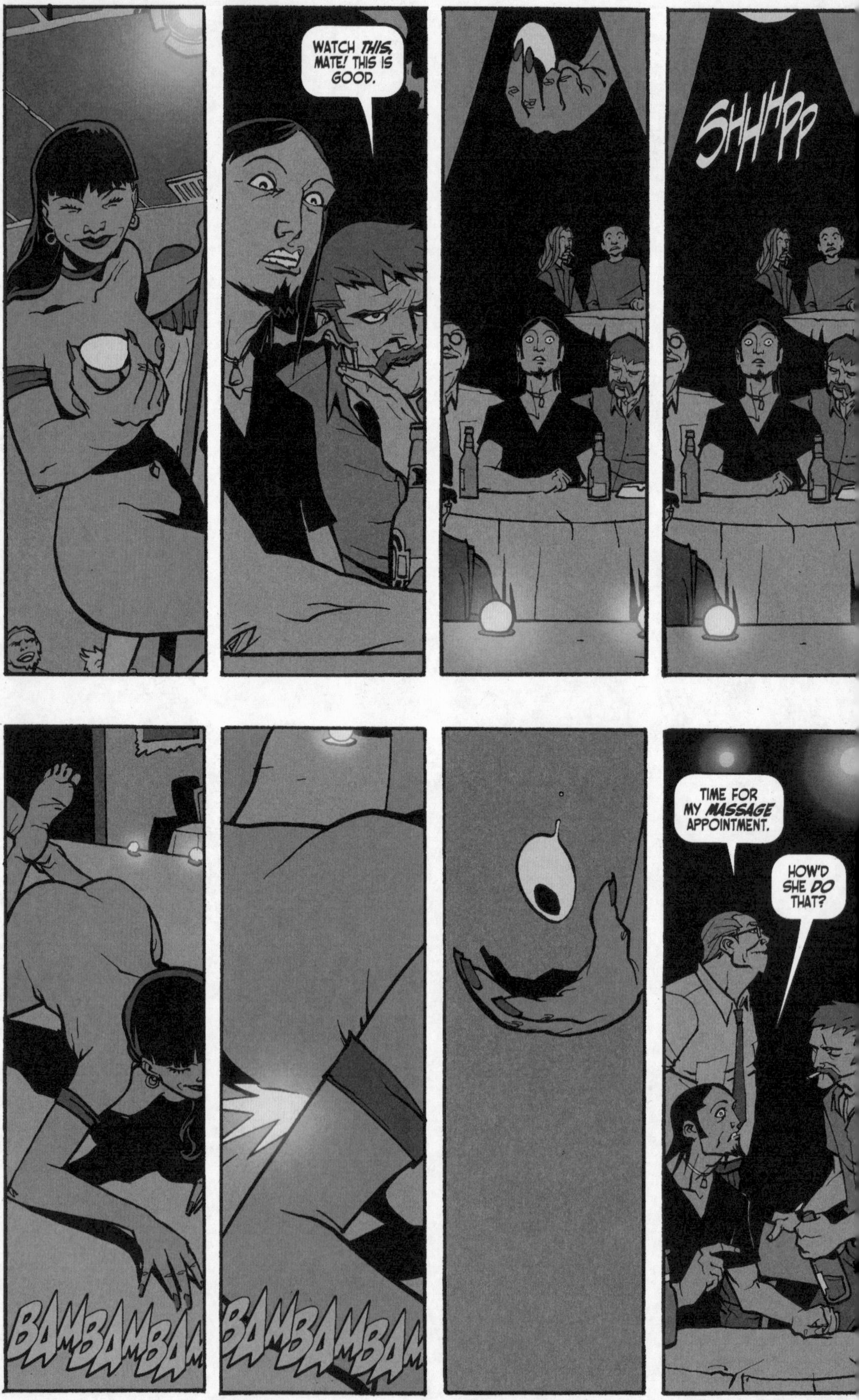
WATCH THIS, MATE! THIS IS GOOD.
SHHHPP
BAMBAMBAM
BAMBAMBAM
TIME FOR MY MASSAGE APPOINTMENT.
HOW'D SHE DO THAT?

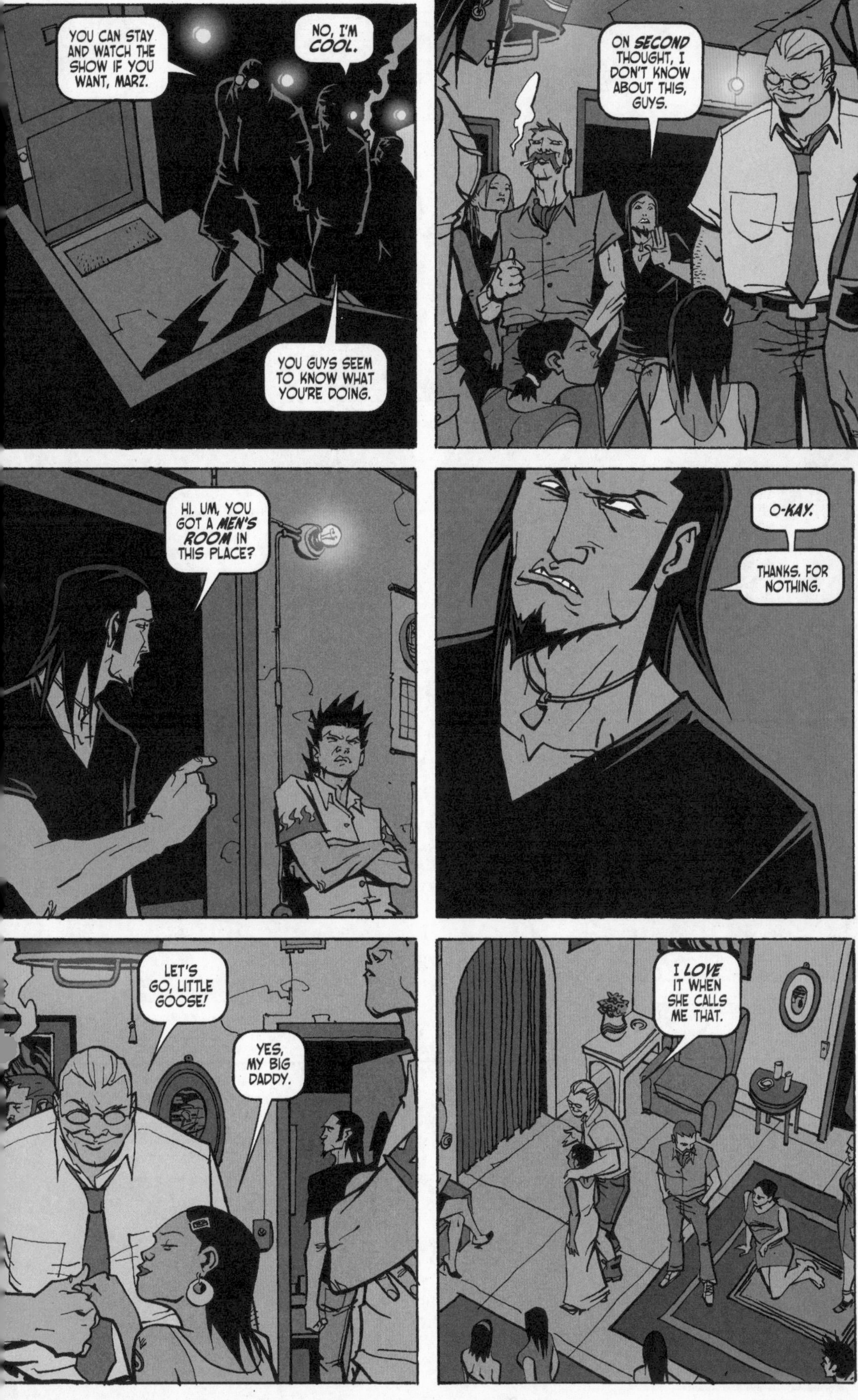

YOU CAN STAY AND WATCH THE SHOW IF YOU WANT, MARZ.
NO, I'M COOL.
YOU GUYS SEEM TO KNOW WHAT YOU'RE DOING.
ON SECOND THOUGHT, I DON'T KNOW ABOUT THIS, GUYS.
HI. UM, YOU GOT A MEN'S ROOM IN THIS PLACE?
O-KAY.
THANKS. FOR NOTHING.
LET'S GO, LITTLE GOOSE!
YES, MY BIG DADDY.
I LOVE IT WHEN SHE CALLS ME THAT.

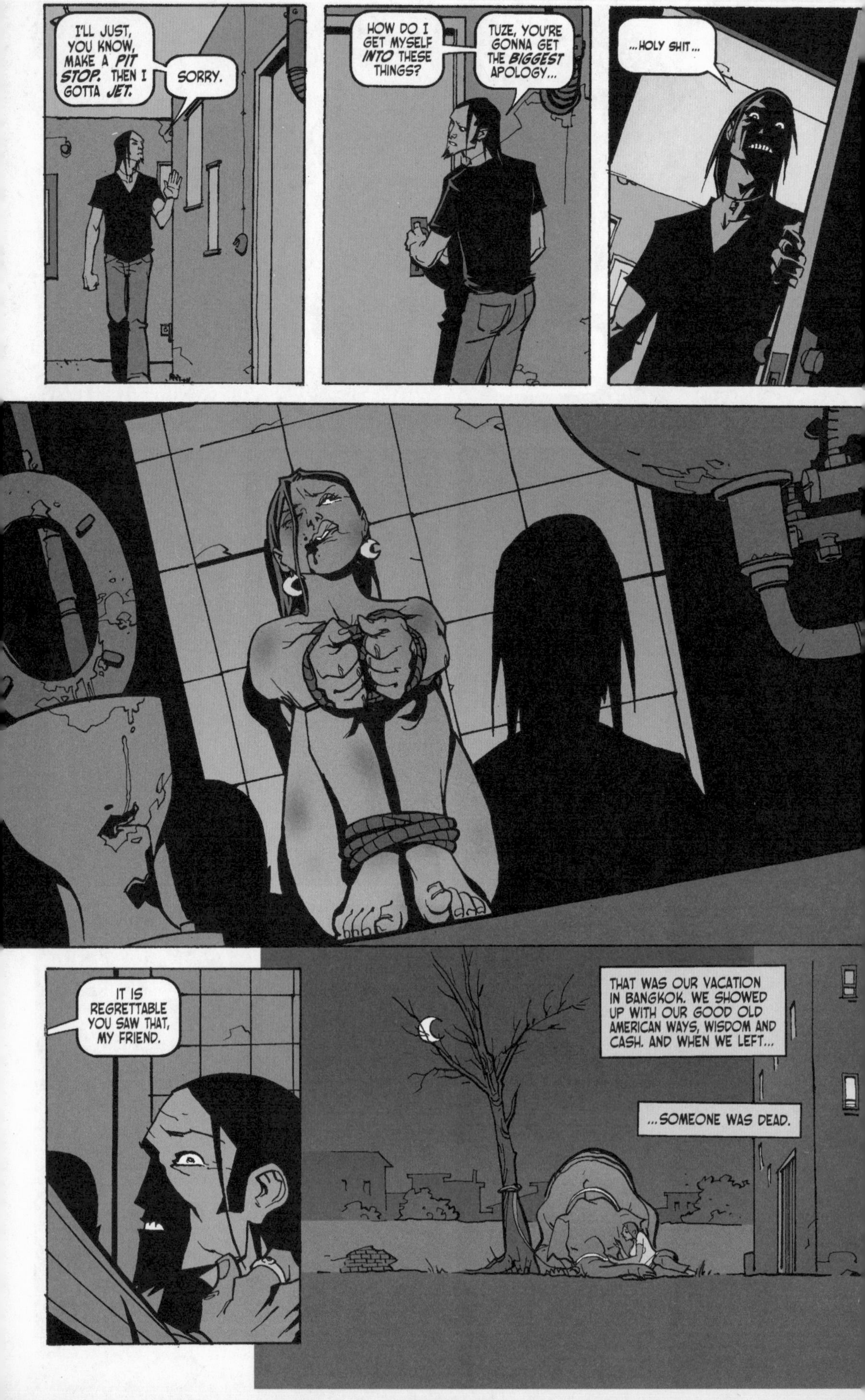
I'LL JUST, YOU KNOW, MAKE A PIT STOP. THEN I GOTTA JET.
SORRY.
HOW DO I GET MYSELF INTO THESE THINGS?
TUZE, YOU'RE GONNA GET THE BIGGEST APOLOGY...
...HOLY SHIT...
IT IS REGRETTABLE YOU SAW THAT, MY FRIEND.
THAT WAS OUR VACATION IN BANGKOK. WE SHOWED UP WITH OUR GOOD OLD AMERICAN WAYS, WISDOM AND CASH. AND WHEN WE LEFT...
...SOMEONE WAS DEAD.

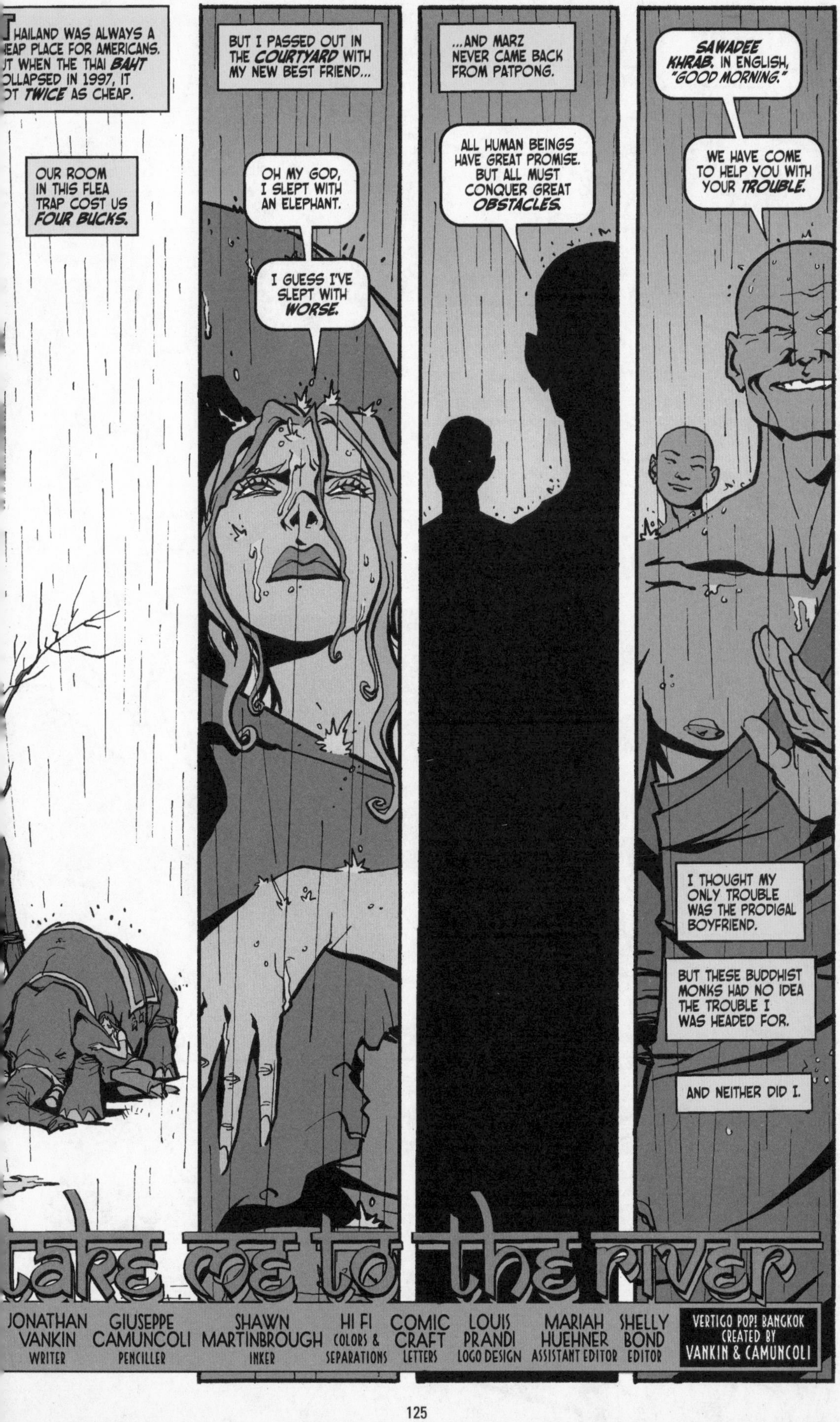

THAILAND WAS ALWAYS A CHEAP PLACE FOR AMERICANS. BUT WHEN THE THAI BAHT COLLAPSED IN 1997, IT GOT TWICE AS CHEAP.
OUR ROOM IN THIS FLEA TRAP COST US FOUR BUCKS.
BUT I PASSED OUT IN THE COURTYARD WITH MY NEW BEST FRIEND...
OH MY GOD, I SLEPT WITH AN ELEPHANT.
I GUESS I'VE SLEPT WITH WORSE.
...AND MARZ NEVER CAME BACK FROM PATPONG.
ALL HUMAN BEINGS HAVE GREAT PROMISE. BUT ALL MUST CONQUER GREAT OBSTACLES.
SAWADEE KHRAB. IN ENGLISH, "GOOD MORNING."
WE HAVE COME TO HELP YOU WITH YOUR TROUBLE.
I THOUGHT MY ONLY TROUBLE WAS THE PRODIGAL BOYFRIEND.
BUT THESE BUDDHIST MONKS HAD NO IDEA THE TROUBLE I WAS HEADED FOR.
AND NEITHER DID I.
TAKE ME TO THE RIVER
JONATHAN VANKIN WRITER
GIUSEPPE CAMUNCOLI PENCILLER
SHAWN MARTINBROUGH INKER
HI FI COLORS & SEPARATIONS
COMIC CRAFT LETTERS
LOUIS PRANDI LOGO DESIGN
MARIAH HUEHNER ASSISTANT EDITOR
SHELLY BOND EDITOR
VERTIGO POP! BANGKOK CREATED BY VANKIN & CAMUNCOLI

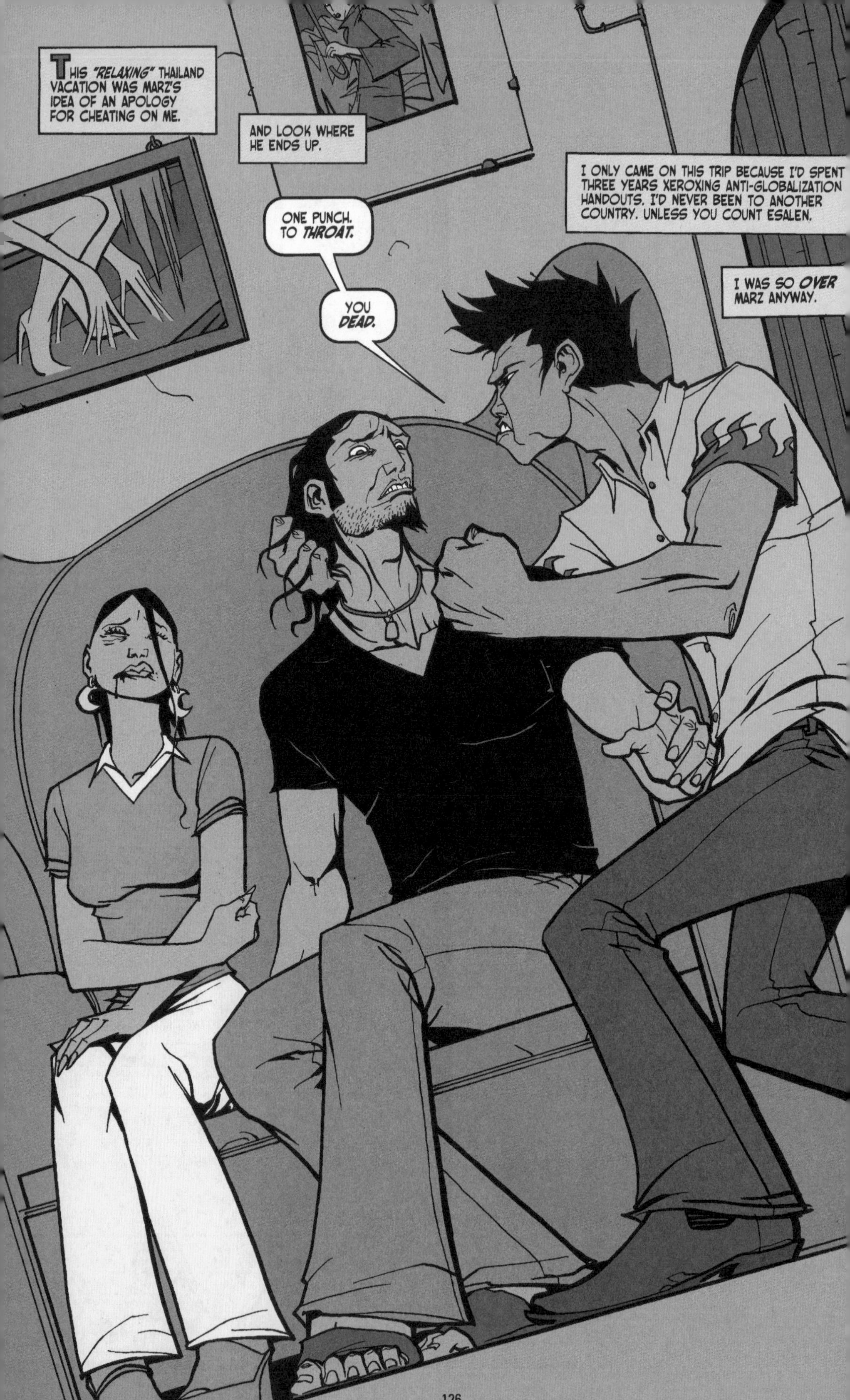
THIS "RELAXING" THAILAND VACATION WAS MARZ'S IDEA OF AN APOLOGY FOR CHEATING ON ME.
AND LOOK WHERE HE ENDS UP.
I ONLY CAME ON THIS TRIP BECAUSE I'D SPENT THREE YEARS XEROXING ANTI-GLOBALIZATION HANDOUTS. I'D NEVER BEEN TO ANOTHER COUNTRY. UNLESS YOU COUNT ESALEN.
ONE PUNCH. TO THROAT.
YOU DEAD.
I WAS SO OVER MARZ ANYWAY.

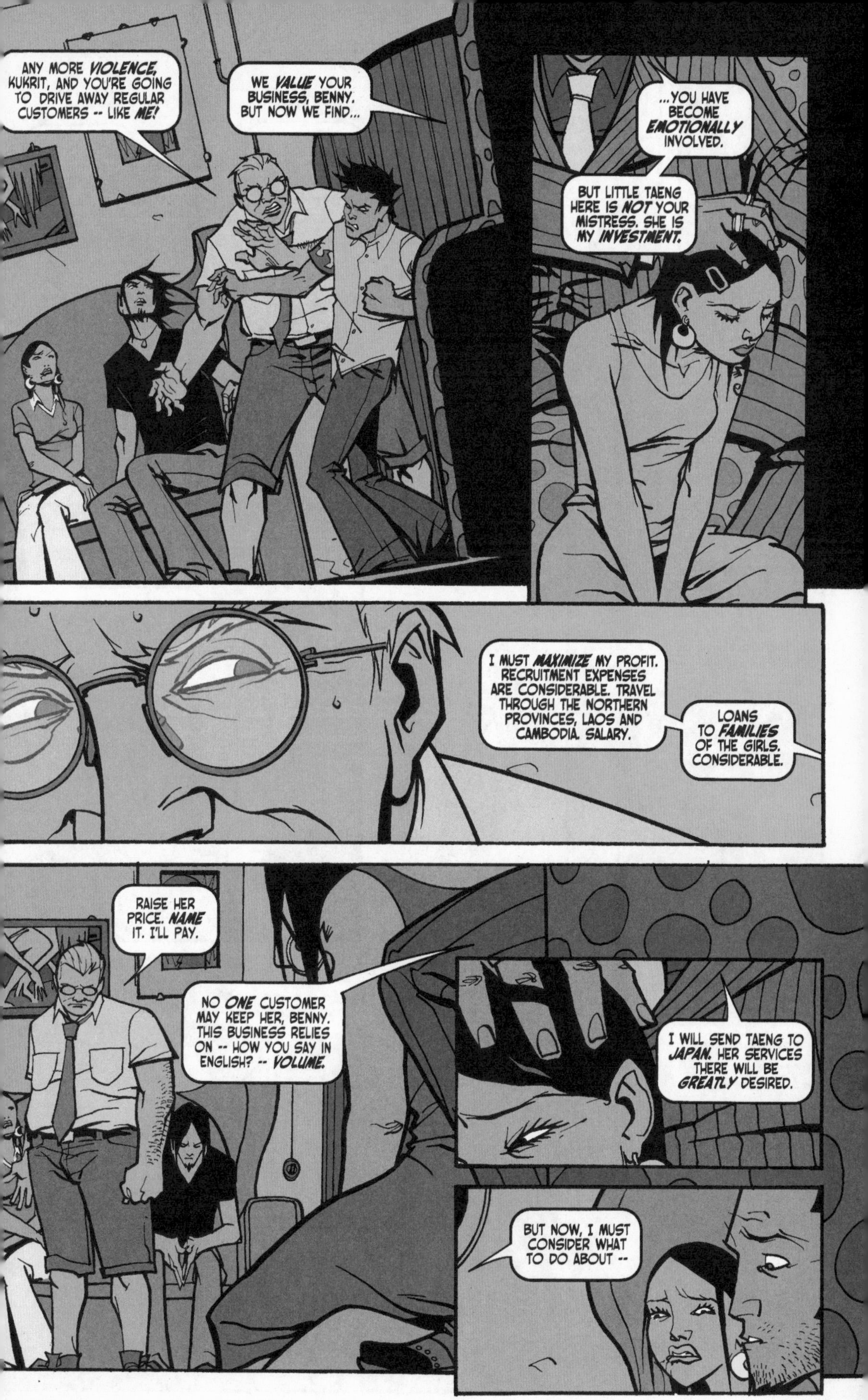
ANY MORE VIOLENCE, KUKRIT, AND YOU'RE GOING TO DRIVE AWAY REGULAR CUSTOMERS -- LIKE ME!
WE VALUE YOUR BUSINESS, BENNY. BUT NOW WE FIND...
...YOU HAVE BECOME EMOTIONALLY INVOLVED.
BUT LITTLE TAENG HERE IS NOT YOUR MISTRESS. SHE IS MY INVESTMENT.
I MUST MAXIMIZE MY PROFIT. RECRUITMENT EXPENSES ARE CONSIDERABLE. TRAVEL THROUGH THE NORTHERN PROVINCES, LAOS AND CAMBODIA. SALARY.
LOANS TO FAMILIES OF THE GIRLS. CONSIDERABLE.
RAISE HER PRICE. NAME IT. I'LL PAY.
NO ONE CUSTOMER MAY KEEP HER, BENNY. THIS BUSINESS RELIES ON -- HOW YOU SAY IN ENGLISH? -- VOLUME.
I WILL SEND TAENG TO JAPAN. HER SERVICES THERE WILL BE GREATLY DESIRED.
BUT NOW, I MUST CONSIDER WHAT TO DO ABOUT --

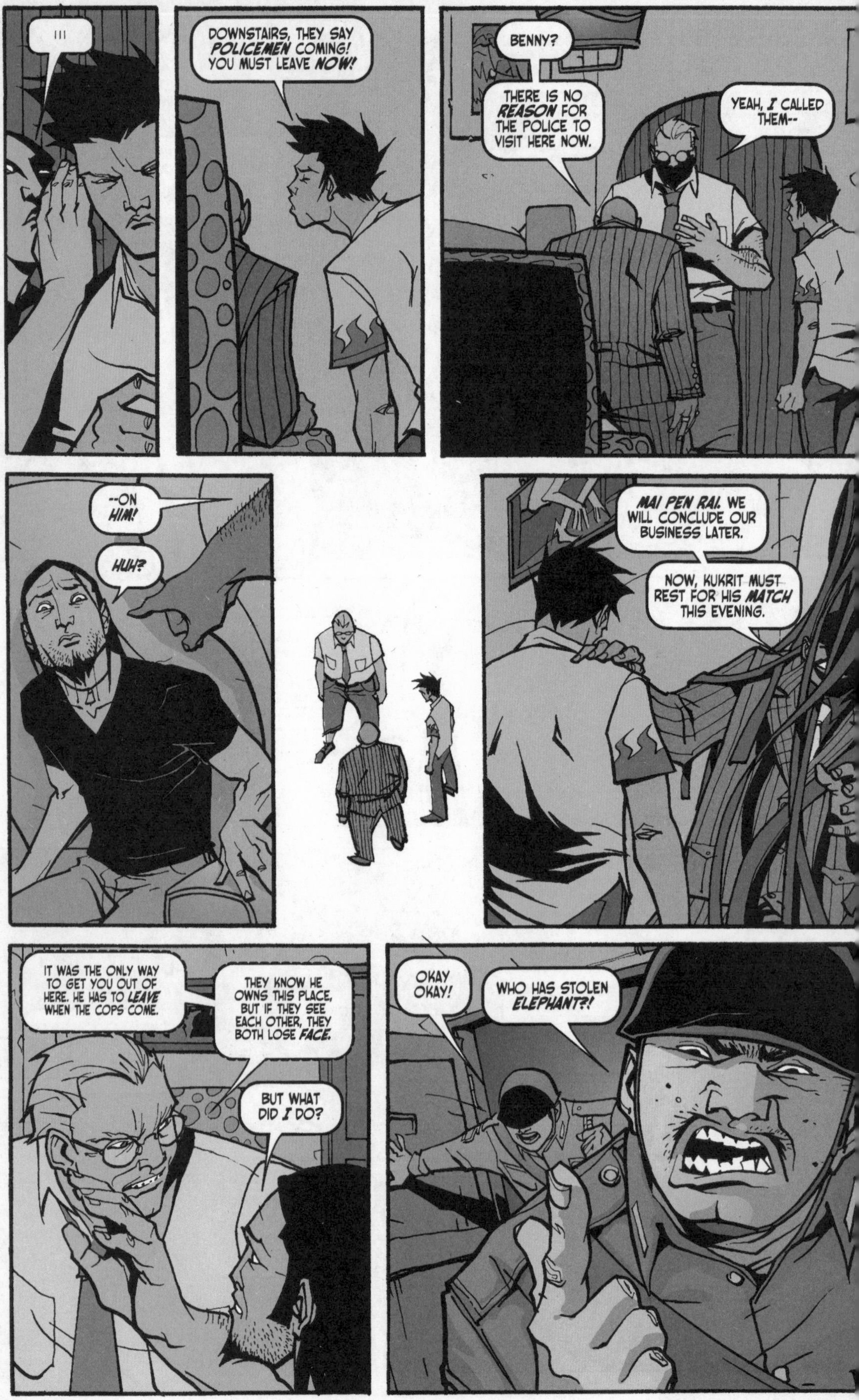
!!!
DOWNSTAIRS, THEY SAY POLICEMEN COMING! YOU MUST LEAVE NOW!
BENNY?
THERE IS NO REASON FOR THE POLICE TO VISIT HERE NOW.
YEAH, I CALLED THEM--
--ON HIM!
HUH?
MAI PEN RAI. WE WILL CONCLUDE OUR BUSINESS LATER.
NOW, KUKRIT MUST REST FOR HIS MATCH THIS EVENING.
IT WAS THE ONLY WAY TO GET YOU OUT OF HERE. HE HAS TO LEAVE WHEN THE COPS COME.
THEY KNOW HE OWNS THIS PLACE, BUT IF THEY SEE EACH OTHER, THEY BOTH LOSE FACE.
BUT WHAT DID I DO?
OKAY OKAY!
WHO HAS STOLEN ELEPHANT?!

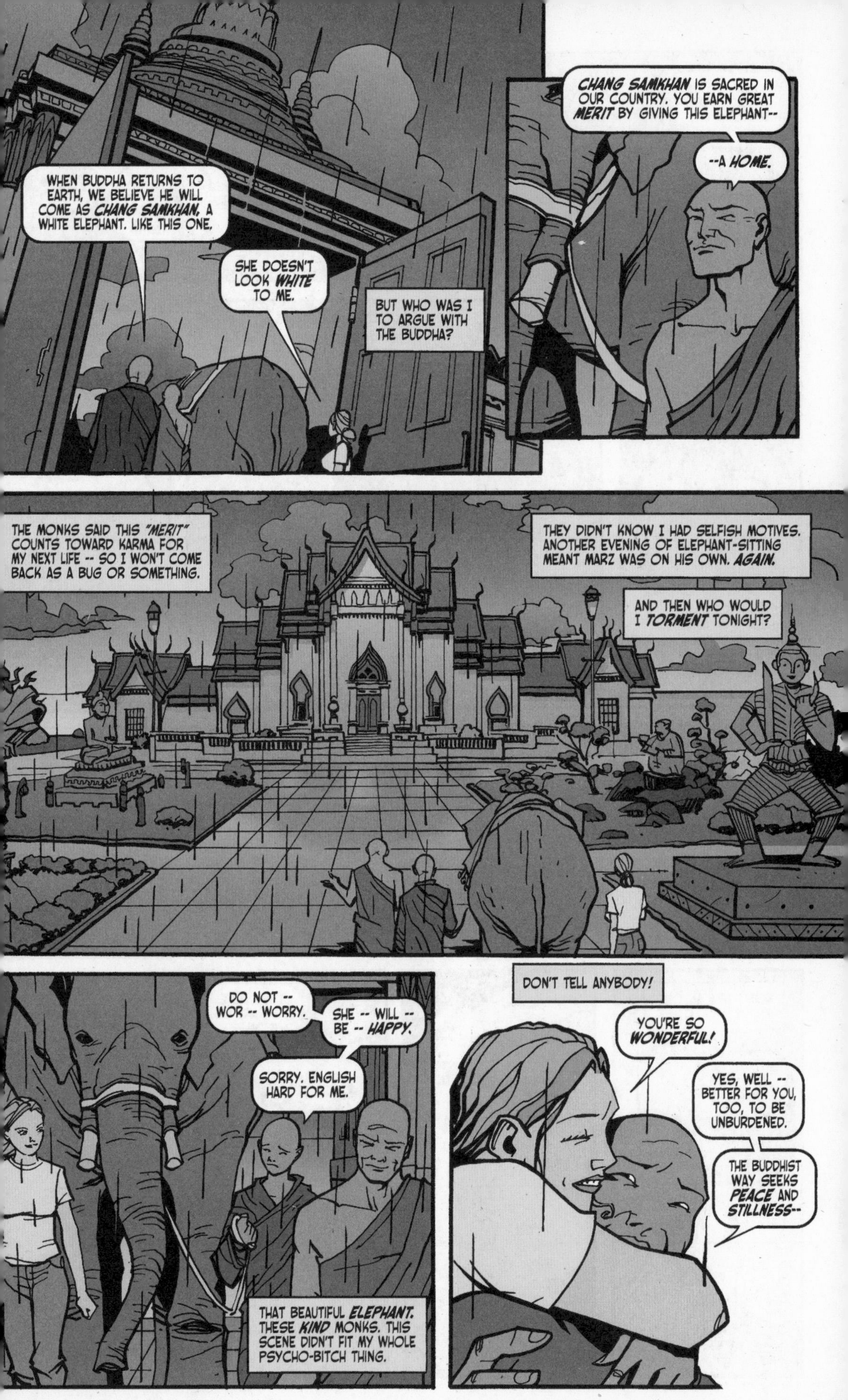
WHEN BUDDHA RETURNS TO EARTH, WE BELIEVE HE WILL COME AS CHANG SAMKHAN, A WHITE ELEPHANT. LIKE THIS ONE.
SHE DOESN'T LOOK WHITE TO ME.
BUT WHO WAS I TO ARGUE WITH THE BUDDHA?
CHANG SAMKHAN IS SACRED IN OUR COUNTRY. YOU EARN GREAT MERIT BY GIVING THIS ELEPHANT--
--A HOME.
THE MONKS SAID THIS "MERIT" COUNTS TOWARD KARMA FOR MY NEXT LIFE -- SO I WON'T COME BACK AS A BUG OR SOMETHING.
THEY DIDN'T KNOW I HAD SELFISH MOTIVES. ANOTHER EVENING OF ELEPHANT-SITTING MEANT MARZ WAS ON HIS OWN. AGAIN.
AND THEN WHO WOULD I TORMENT TONIGHT?
DO NOT -- WOR -- WORRY.
SHE -- WILL -- BE -- HAPPY.
SORRY. ENGLISH HARD FOR ME.
THAT BEAUTIFUL ELEPHANT. THESE KIND MONKS. THIS SCENE DIDN'T FIT MY WHOLE PSYCHO-BITCH THING.
DON'T TELL ANYBODY!
YOU'RE SO WONDERFUL!
YES, WELL -- BETTER FOR YOU, TOO, TO BE UNBURDENED.
THE BUDDHIST WAY SEEKS PEACE AND STILLNESS--

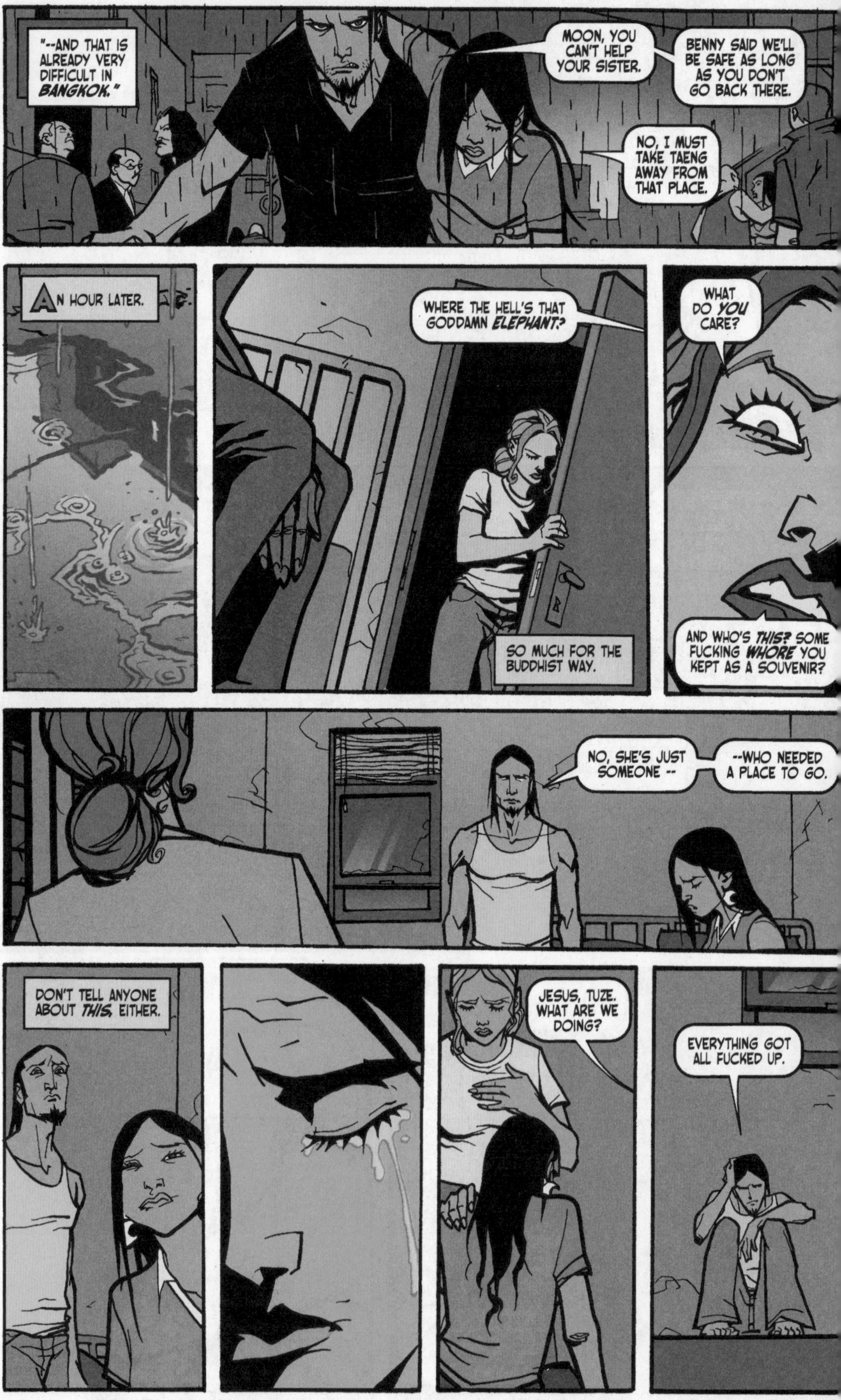
"--AND THAT IS ALREADY VERY DIFFICULT IN BANGKOK."
MOON, YOU CAN'T HELP YOUR SISTER.
BENNY SAID WE'LL BE SAFE AS LONG AS YOU DON'T GO BACK THERE.
NO, I MUST TAKE TAENG AWAY FROM THAT PLACE.
AN HOUR LATER.
WHERE THE HELL'S THAT GODDAMN ELEPHANT?
SO MUCH FOR THE BUDDHIST WAY.
WHAT DO YOU CARE?
AND WHO'S THIS? SOME FUCKING WHORE YOU KEPT AS A SOUVENIR?
NO, SHE'S JUST SOMEONE --
--WHO NEEDED A PLACE TO GO.
DON'T TELL ANYONE ABOUT THIS, EITHER.
JESUS, TUZE. WHAT ARE WE DOING?
EVERYTHING GOT ALL FUCKED UP.

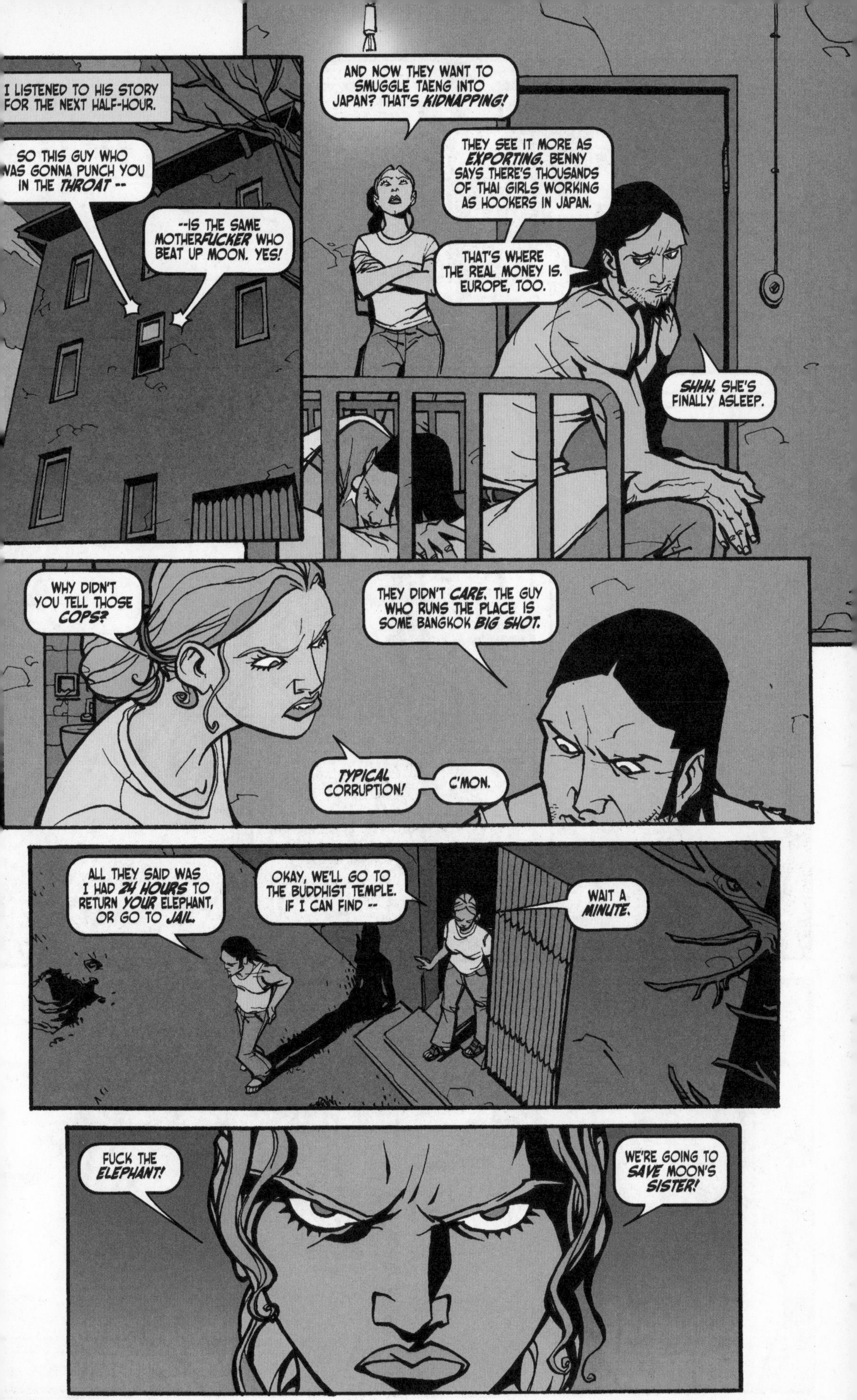
I LISTENED TO HIS STORY FOR THE NEXT HALF-HOUR.
SO THIS GUY WHO WAS GONNA PUNCH YOU IN THE THROAT --
--IS THE SAME MOTHERFUCKER WHO BEAT UP MOON. YES!
AND NOW THEY WANT TO SMUGGLE TAENG INTO JAPAN? THAT'S KIDNAPPING!
THEY SEE IT MORE AS EXPORTING. BENNY SAYS THERE'S THOUSANDS OF THAI GIRLS WORKING AS HOOKERS IN JAPAN.
THAT'S WHERE THE REAL MONEY IS. EUROPE, TOO.
SHHH. SHE'S FINALLY ASLEEP.
WHY DIDN'T YOU TELL THOSE COPS?
THEY DIDN'T CARE. THE GUY WHO RUNS THE PLACE IS SOME BANGKOK BIG SHOT.
TYPICAL CORRUPTION!
C'MON.
ALL THEY SAID WAS I HAD 24 HOURS TO RETURN YOUR ELEPHANT, OR GO TO JAIL.
OKAY, WE'LL GO TO THE BUDDHIST TEMPLE. IF I CAN FIND --
WAIT A MINUTE.
FUCK THE ELEPHANT!
WE'RE GOING TO SAVE MOON'S SISTER!

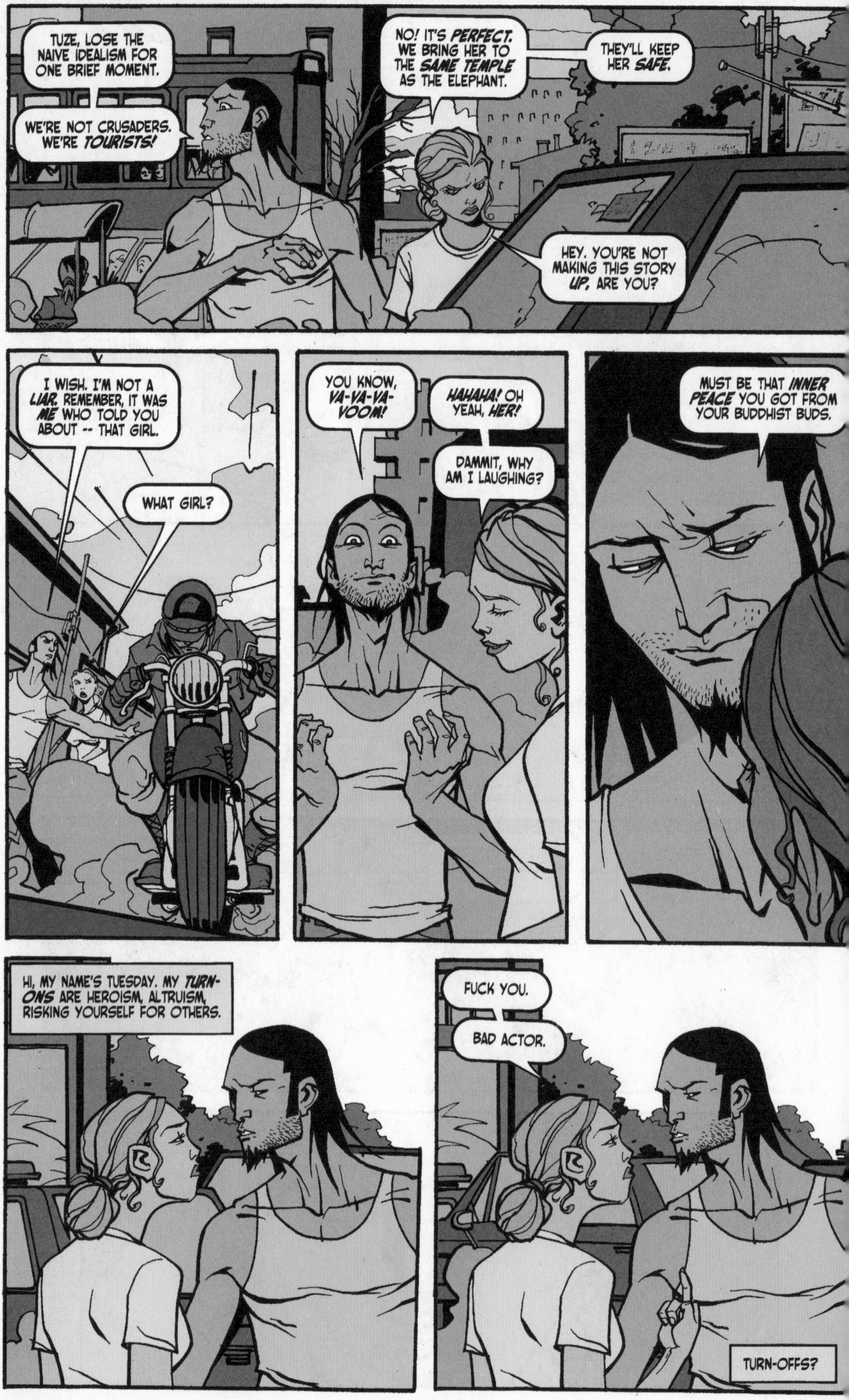
TUZE, LOSE THE NAIVE IDEALISM FOR ONE BRIEF MOMENT.
WE'RE NOT CRUSADERS. WE'RE TOURISTS!
NO! IT'S PERFECT. WE BRING HER TO THE SAME TEMPLE AS THE ELEPHANT.
THEY'LL KEEP HER SAFE.
HEY. YOU'RE NOT MAKING THIS STORY UP, ARE YOU?
I WISH. I'M NOT A LIAR. REMEMBER, IT WAS ME WHO TOLD YOU ABOUT -- THAT GIRL.
WHAT GIRL?
YOU KNOW, VA-VA-VA-VOOM!
HAHAHA! OH YEAH, HER!
DAMMIT, WHY AM I LAUGHING?
MUST BE THAT INNER PEACE YOU GOT FROM YOUR BUDDHIST BUDS.
HI, MY NAME'S TUESDAY. MY TURN-ONS ARE HEROISM, ALTRUISM, RISKING YOURSELF FOR OTHERS.
FUCK YOU.
BAD ACTOR.
TURN-OFFS?

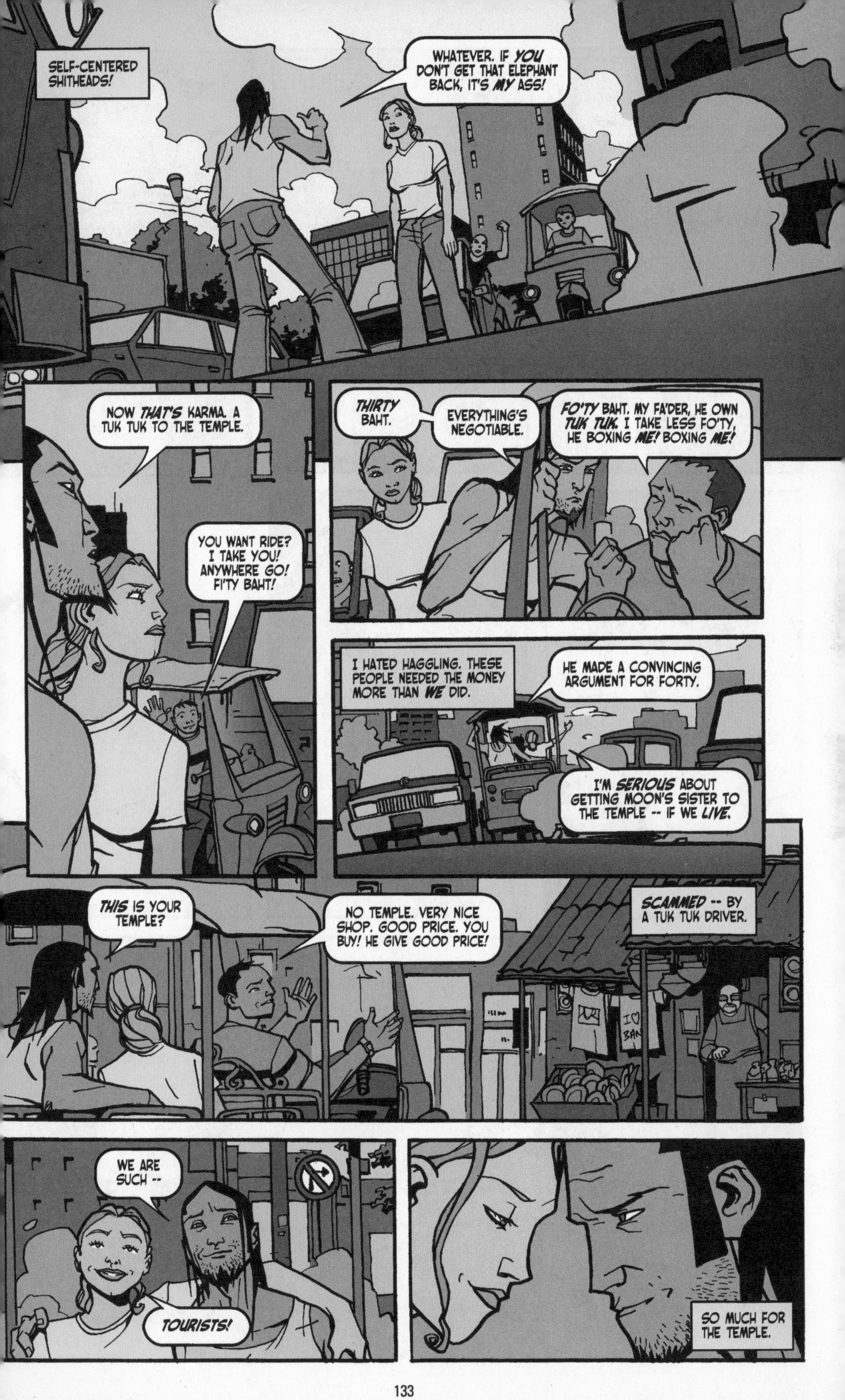

SELF-CENTERED SHITHEADS!
WHATEVER. IF YOU DON'T GET THAT ELEPHANT BACK, IT'S MY ASS!
NOW THAT'S KARMA. A TUK TUK TO THE TEMPLE.
YOU WANT RIDE? I TAKE YOU! ANYWHERE GO! FI'TY BAHT!
THIRTY BAHT.
EVERYTHING'S NEGOTIABLE.
FO'TY BAHT. MY FA'DER, HE OWN TUK TUK. I TAKE LESS FO'TY, HE BOXING ME! BOXING ME!
I HATED HAGGLING. THESE PEOPLE NEEDED THE MONEY MORE THAN WE DID.
HE MADE A CONVINCING ARGUMENT FOR FORTY.
I'M SERIOUS ABOUT GETTING MOON'S SISTER TO THE TEMPLE -- IF WE LIVE.
THIS IS YOUR TEMPLE?
NO TEMPLE. VERY NICE SHOP. GOOD PRICE. YOU BUY! HE GIVE GOOD PRICE!
SCAMMED -- BY A TUK TUK DRIVER.
WE ARE SUCH --
TOURISTS!
SO MUCH FOR THE TEMPLE.

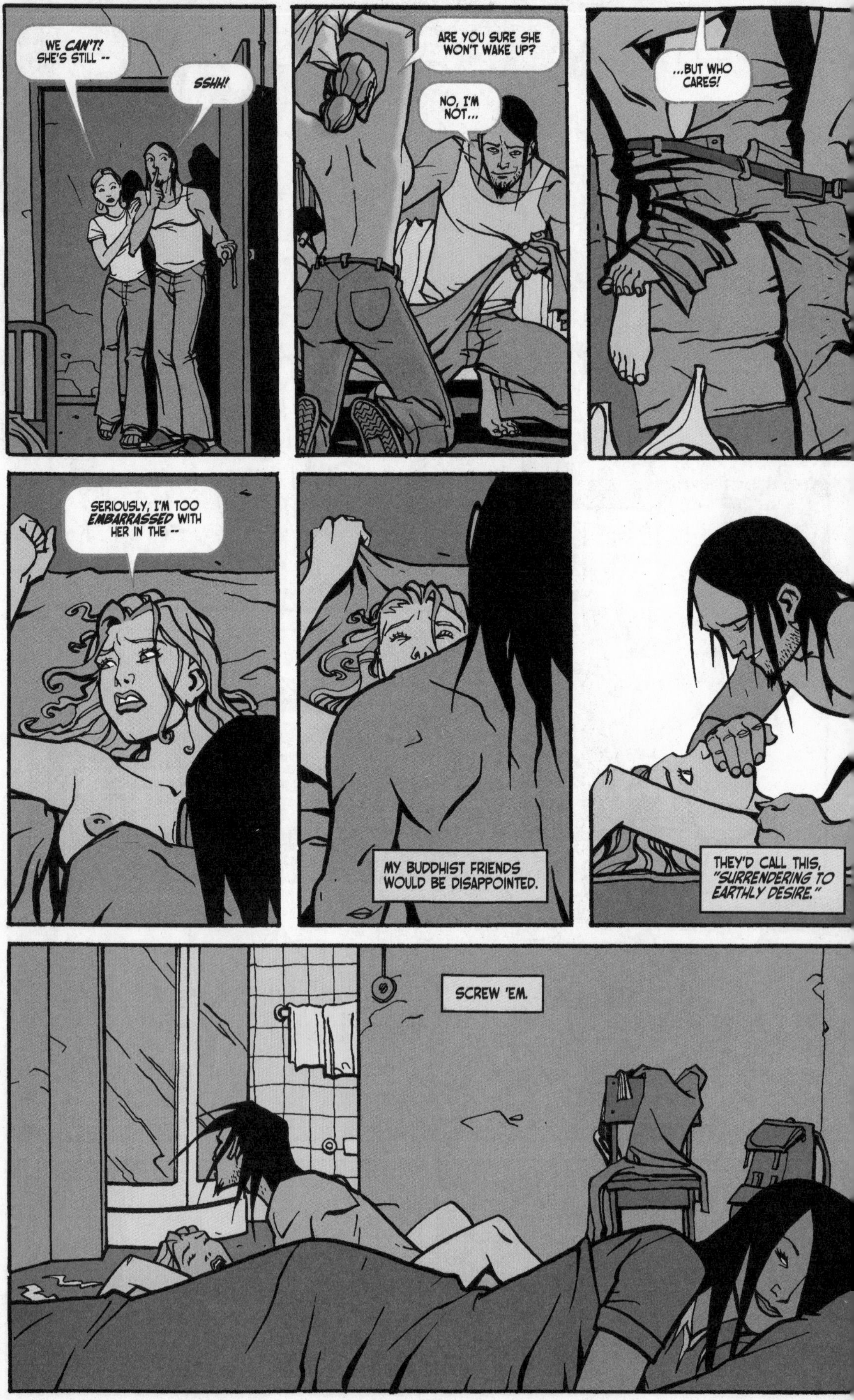
WE CAN'T! SHE'S STILL --
SSHH!
ARE YOU SURE SHE WON'T WAKE UP?
NO, I'M NOT...
...BUT WHO CARES!
SERIOUSLY, I'M TOO EMBARRASSED WITH HER IN THE --
MY BUDDHIST FRIENDS WOULD BE DISAPPOINTED.
THEY'D CALL THIS, "SURRENDERING TO EARTHLY DESIRE."
SCREW 'EM.

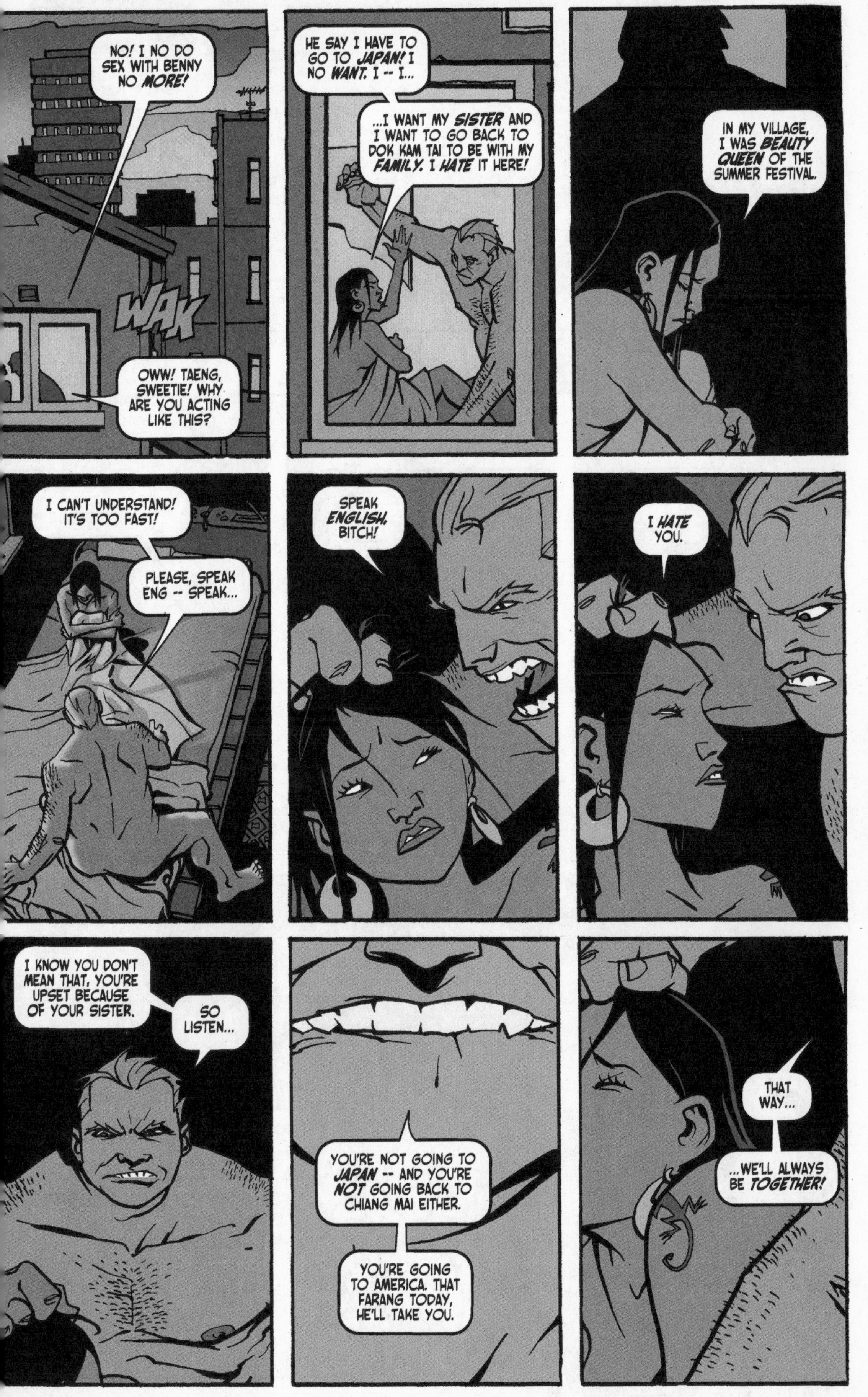
NO! I NO DO SEX WITH BENNY NO MORE!
WAK
OWW! TAENG, SWEETIE! WHY ARE YOU ACTING LIKE THIS?
HE SAY I HAVE TO GO TO JAPAN! I NO WANT. I -- I...
...I WANT MY SISTER AND I WANT TO GO BACK TO DOK KAM TAI TO BE WITH MY FAMILY. I HATE IT HERE!
IN MY VILLAGE, I WAS BEAUTY QUEEN OF THE SUMMER FESTIVAL.
I CAN'T UNDERSTAND! IT'S TOO FAST!
PLEASE, SPEAK ENG -- SPEAK...
SPEAK ENGLISH, BITCH!
I HATE YOU.
I KNOW YOU DON'T MEAN THAT, YOU'RE UPSET BECAUSE OF YOUR SISTER.
SO LISTEN...
YOU'RE NOT GOING TO JAPAN -- AND YOU'RE NOT GOING BACK TO CHIANG MAI EITHER.
YOU'RE GOING TO AMERICA. THAT FARANG TODAY, HE'LL TAKE YOU.
THAT WAY...
...WE'LL ALWAYS BE TOGETHER!

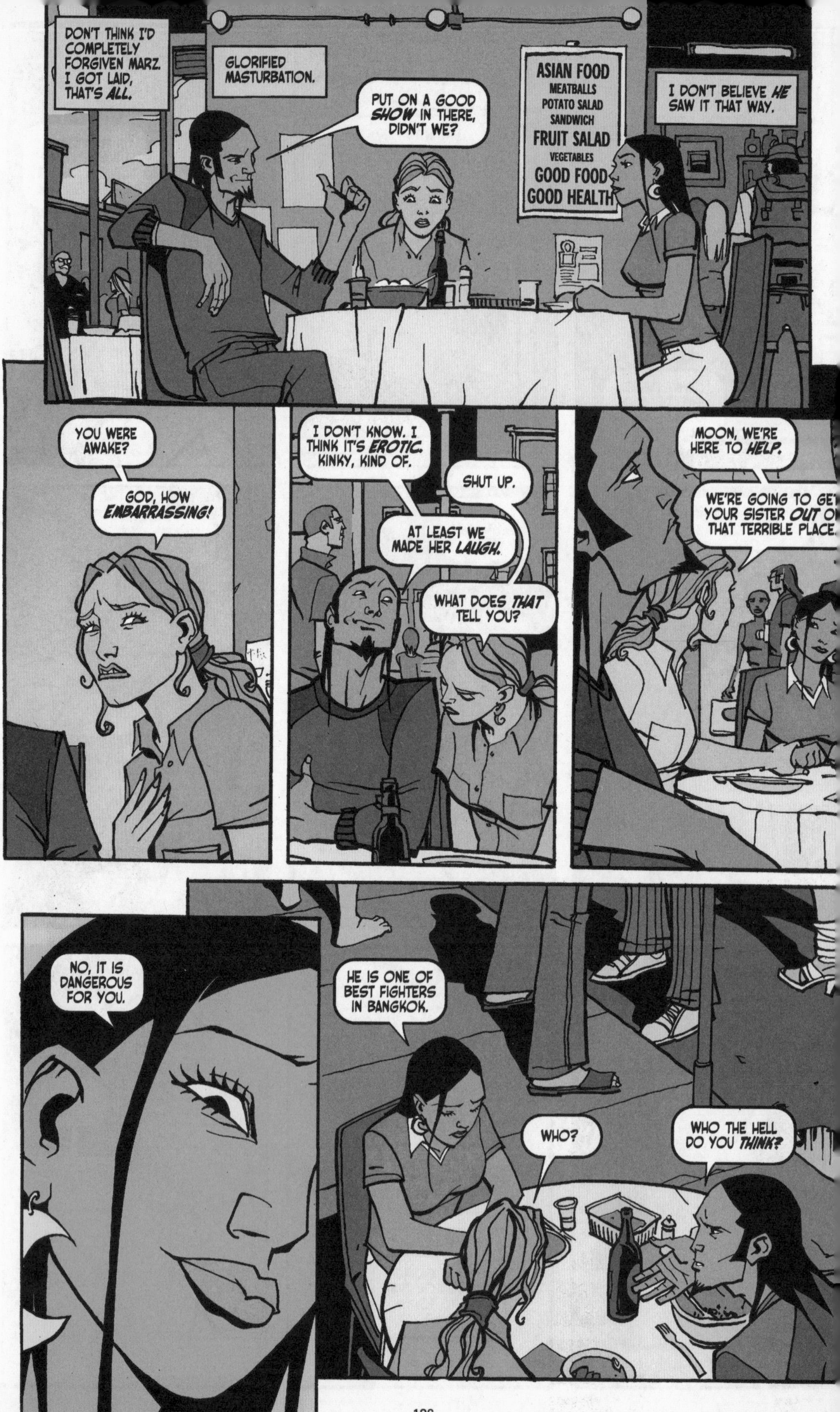
DON'T THINK I'D COMPLETELY FORGIVEN MARZ. I GOT LAID, THAT'S ALL.
GLORIFIED MASTURBATION.
PUT ON A GOOD SHOW IN THERE, DIDN'T WE?
ASIAN FOOD
MEATBALLS
POTATO SALAD
SANDWICH
FRUIT SALAD
VEGETABLES
GOOD FOOD
GOOD HEALTH
I DON'T BELIEVE HE SAW IT THAT WAY.
YOU WERE AWAKE?
GOD, HOW EMBARRASSING!
I DON'T KNOW. I THINK IT'S EROTIC. KINKY, KIND OF.
SHUT UP.
AT LEAST WE MADE HER LAUGH.
WHAT DOES THAT TELL YOU?
MOON, WE'RE HERE TO HELP.
WE'RE GOING TO GET YOUR SISTER OUT OF THAT TERRIBLE PLACE.
NO, IT IS DANGEROUS FOR YOU.
HE IS ONE OF BEST FIGHTERS IN BANGKOK.
WHO?
WHO THE HELL DO YOU THINK?

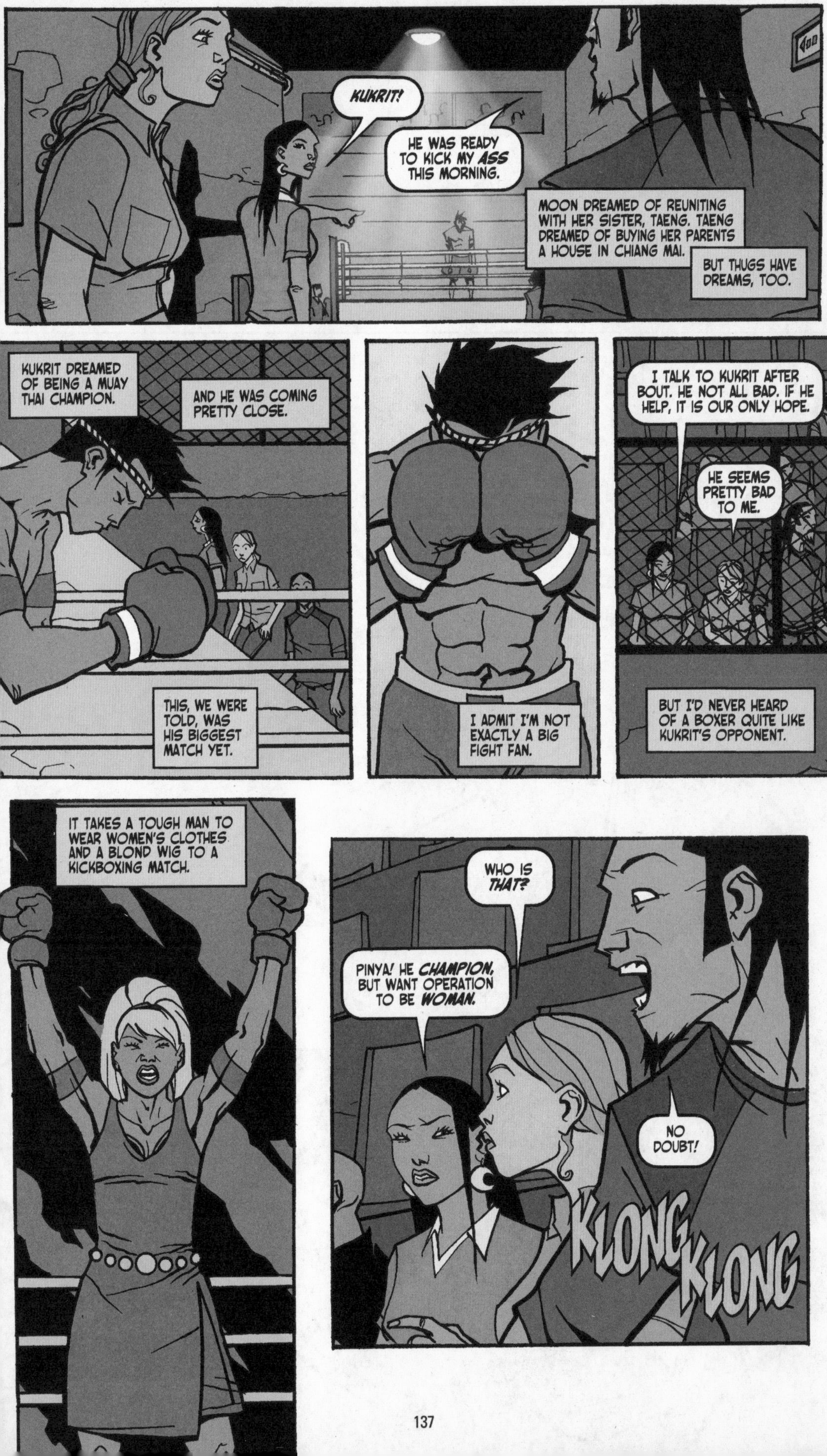
KUKRIT!
HE WAS READY TO KICK MY ASS THIS MORNING.
MOON DREAMED OF REUNITING WITH HER SISTER, TAENG. TAENG DREAMED OF BUYING HER PARENTS A HOUSE IN CHIANG MAI.
BUT THUGS HAVE DREAMS, TOO.
KUKRIT DREAMED OF BEING A MUAY THAI CHAMPION.
AND HE WAS COMING PRETTY CLOSE.
THIS, WE WERE TOLD, WAS HIS BIGGEST MATCH YET.
I ADMIT I'M NOT EXACTLY A BIG FIGHT FAN.
I TALK TO KUKRIT AFTER BOUT. HE NOT ALL BAD. IF HE HELP, IT IS OUR ONLY HOPE.
HE SEEMS PRETTY BAD TO ME.
BUT I'D NEVER HEARD OF A BOXER QUITE LIKE KUKRIT'S OPPONENT.
IT TAKES A TOUGH MAN TO WEAR WOMEN'S CLOTHES AND A BLOND WIG TO A KICKBOXING MATCH.
WHO IS THAT?
PINYA! HE CHAMPION, BUT WANT OPERATION TO BE WOMAN.
NO DOUBT!
KLONG KLONG

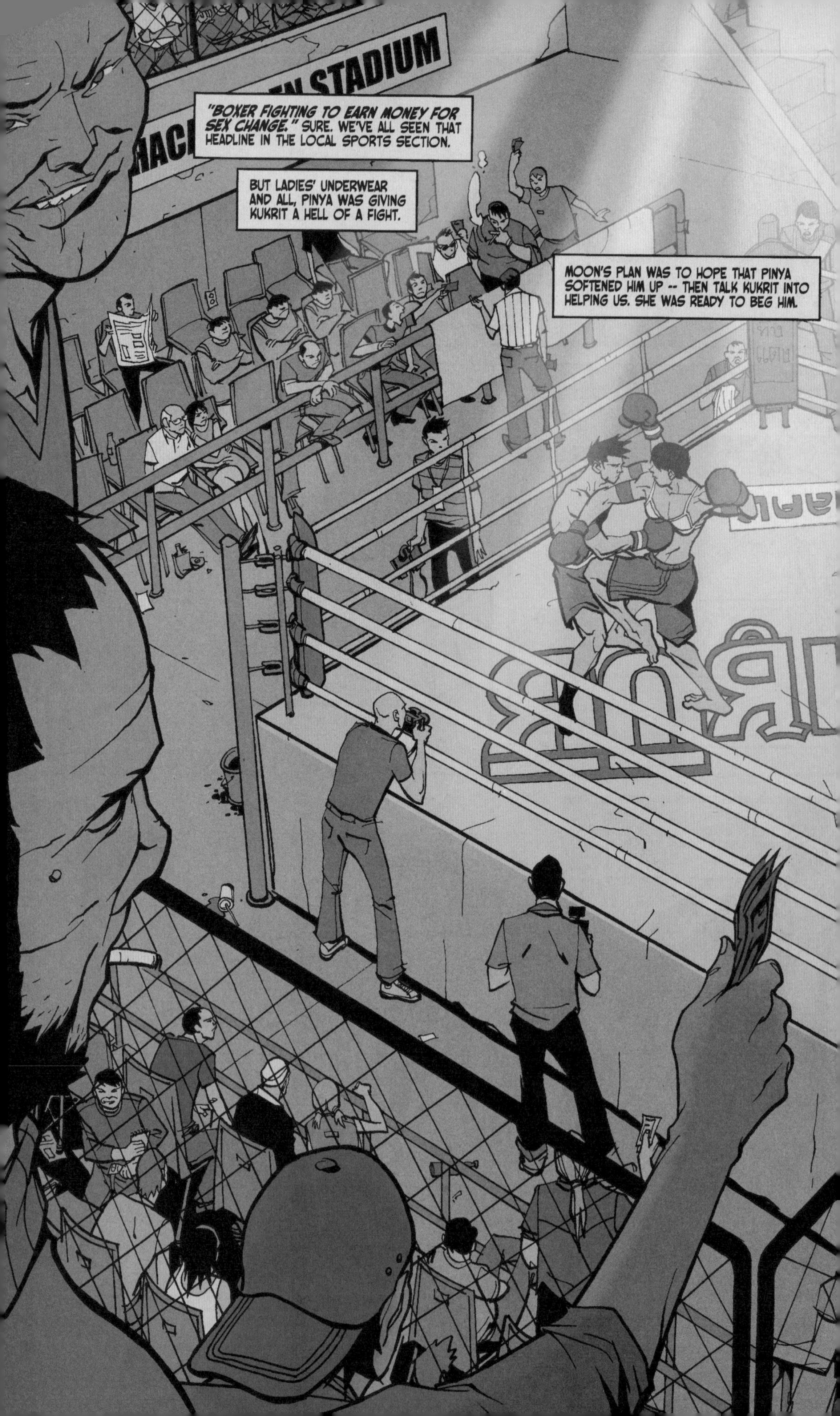

STADIUM
"BOXER FIGHTING TO EARN MONEY FOR SEX CHANGE." SURE. WE'VE ALL SEEN THAT HEADLINE IN THE LOCAL SPORTS SECTION.
BUT LADIES' UNDERWEAR AND ALL, PINYA WAS GIVING KUKRIT A HELL OF A FIGHT.
MOON'S PLAN WAS TO HOPE THAT PINYA SOFTENED HIM UP -- THEN TALK KUKRIT INTO HELPING US. SHE WAS READY TO BEG HIM.

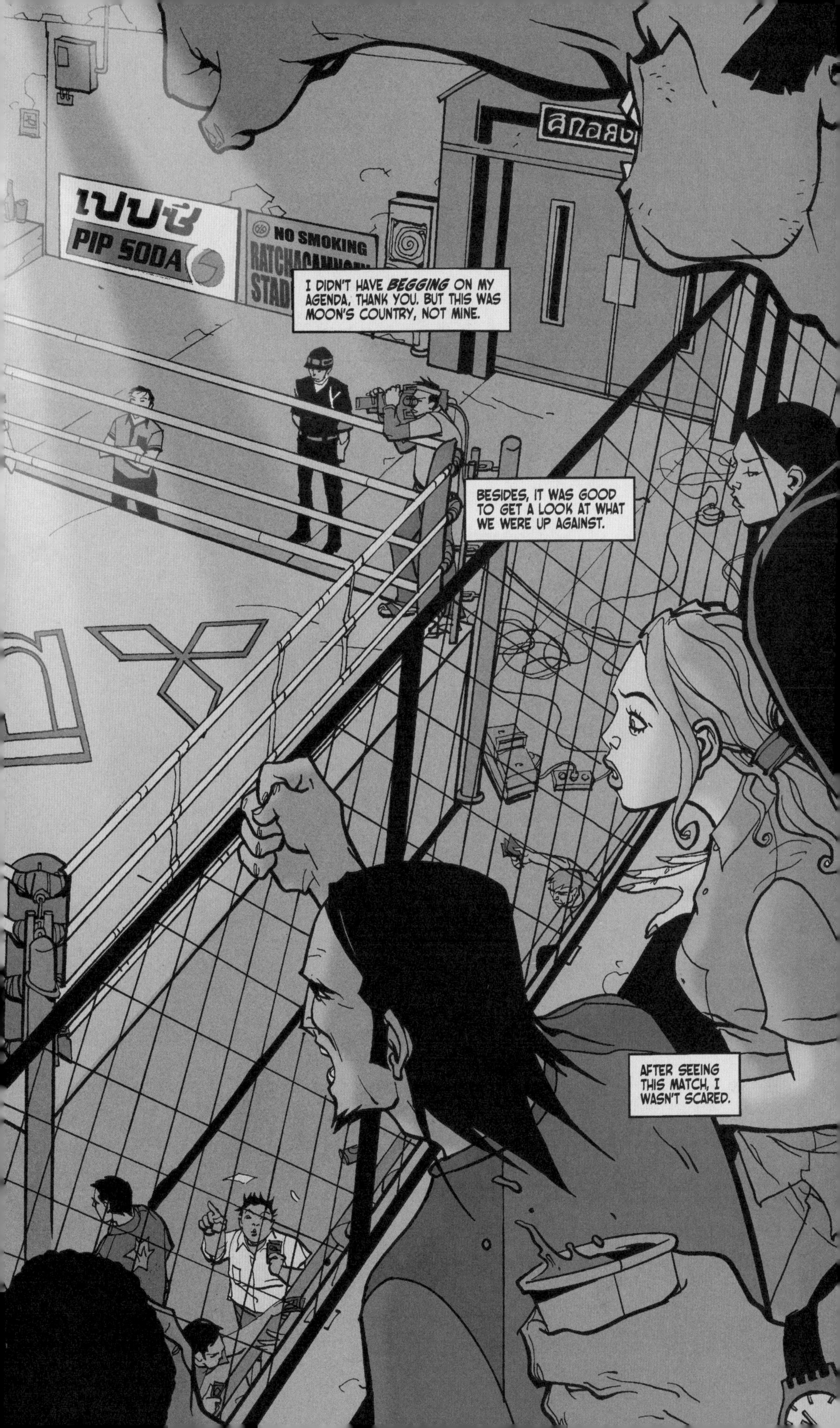

เปปซี่
PIP SODA
NO SMOKING
I DIDN'T HAVE ***BEGGING*** ON MY AGENDA, THANK YOU. BUT THIS WAS MOON'S COUNTRY, NOT MINE.
BESIDES, IT WAS GOOD TO GET A LOOK AT WHAT WE WERE UP AGAINST.
AFTER SEEING THIS MATCH, I WASN'T SCARED.

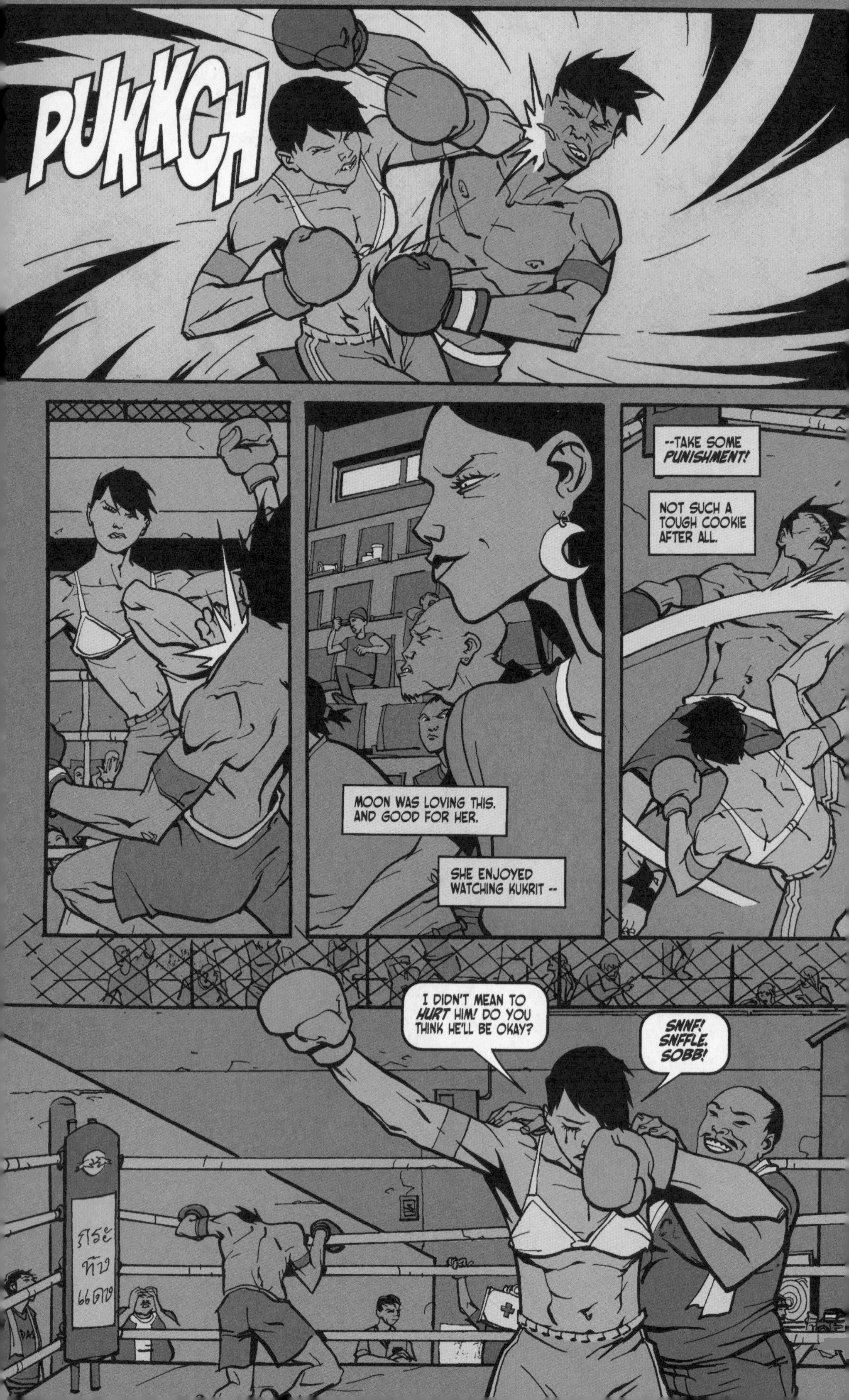
PUKKCH
MOON WAS LOVING THIS. AND GOOD FOR HER.
SHE ENJOYED WATCHING KUKRIT --
--TAKE SOME PUNISHMENT!
NOT SUCH A TOUGH COOKIE AFTER ALL.
I DIDN'T MEAN TO HURT HIM! DO YOU THINK HE'LL BE OKAY?
SNNF! SNFFLE. SOBB!

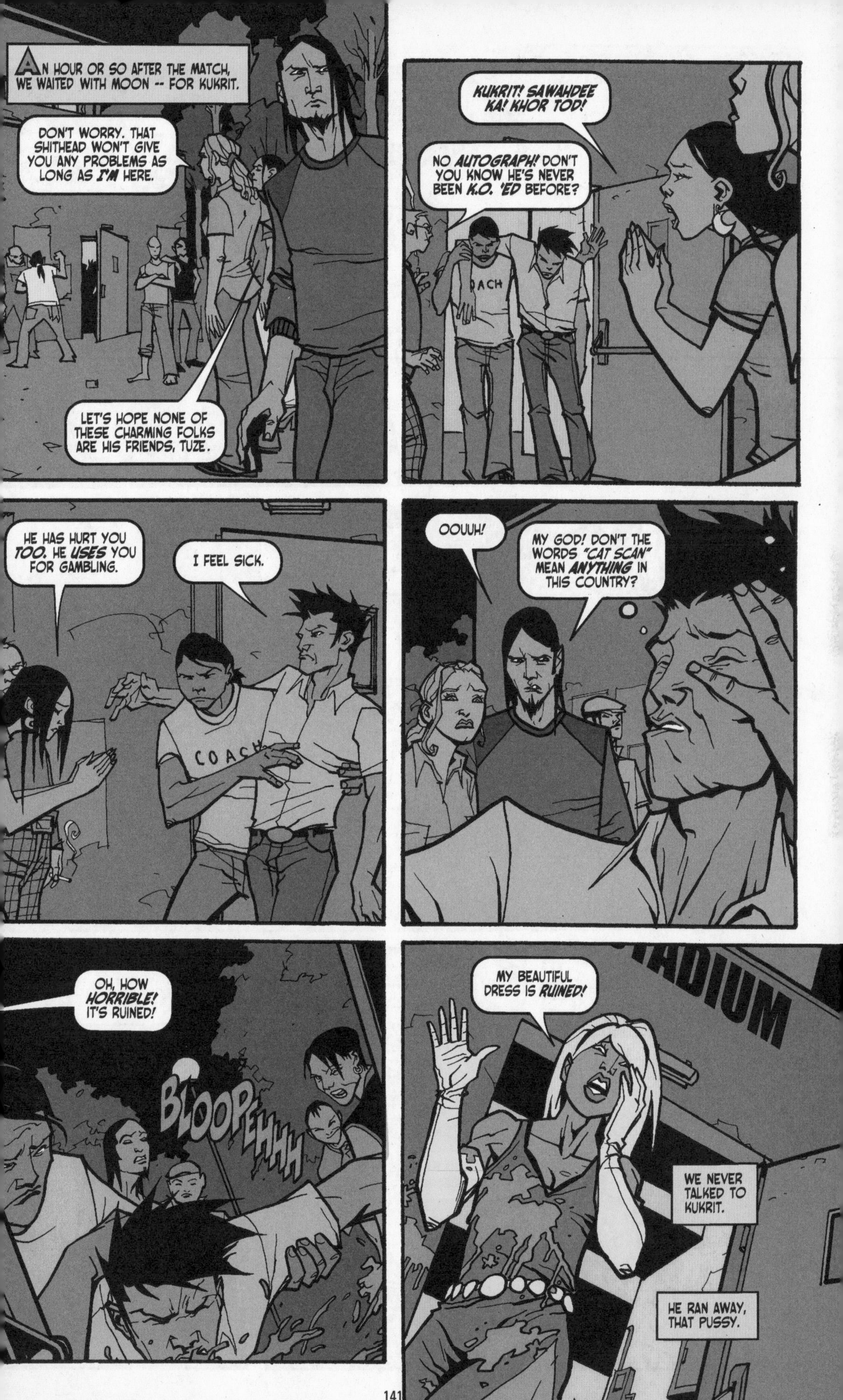
AN HOUR OR SO AFTER THE MATCH, WE WAITED WITH MOON -- FOR KUKRIT.
DON'T WORRY. THAT SHITHEAD WON'T GIVE YOU ANY PROBLEMS AS LONG AS I'M HERE.
LET'S HOPE NONE OF THESE CHARMING FOLKS ARE HIS FRIENDS, TUZE.
KUKRIT! SAWAHDEE KA! KHOR TOD!
NO AUTOGRAPH! DON'T YOU KNOW HE'S NEVER BEEN K.O. 'ED BEFORE?
OACH
HE HAS HURT YOU TOO. HE USES YOU FOR GAMBLING.
I FEEL SICK.
COACH
OOUUH!
MY GOD! DON'T THE WORDS "CAT SCAN" MEAN ANYTHING IN THIS COUNTRY?
OH, HOW HORRIBLE! IT'S RUINED!
BLOOPEHHH
MY BEAUTIFUL DRESS IS RUINED!
ADIUM
WE NEVER TALKED TO KUKRIT.
HE RAN AWAY, THAT PUSSY.

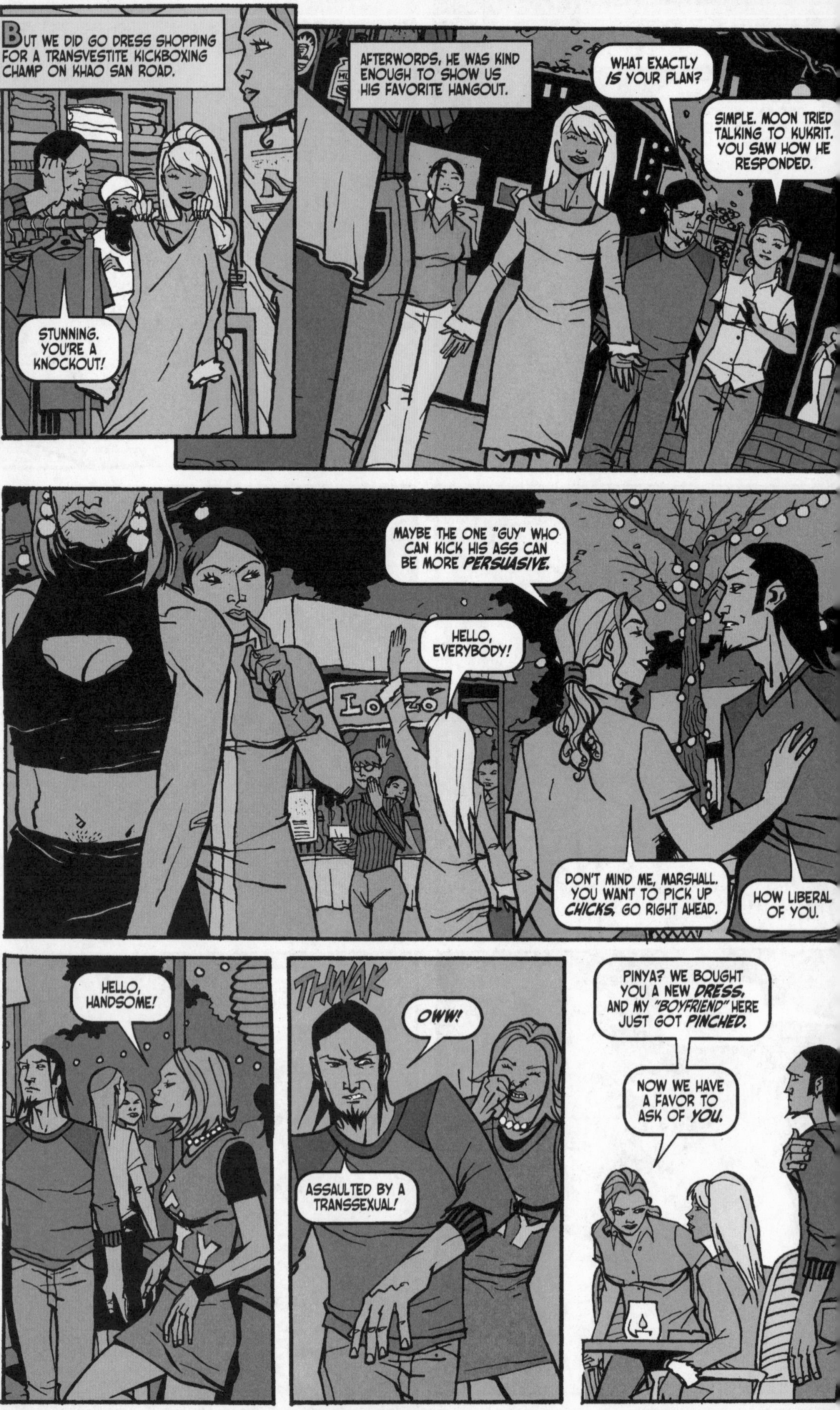
BUT WE DID GO DRESS SHOPPING FOR A TRANSVESTITE KICKBOXING CHAMP ON KHAO SAN ROAD.
STUNNING. YOU'RE A KNOCKOUT!
AFTERWORDS, HE WAS KIND ENOUGH TO SHOW US HIS FAVORITE HANGOUT.
WHAT EXACTLY *IS* YOUR PLAN?
SIMPLE. MOON TRIED TALKING TO KUKRIT. YOU SAW HOW HE RESPONDED.
MAYBE THE ONE "GUY" WHO CAN KICK HIS ASS CAN BE MORE ***PERSUASIVE.***
HELLO, EVERYBODY!
DON'T MIND ME, MARSHALL. YOU WANT TO PICK UP ***CHICKS,*** GO RIGHT AHEAD.
HOW LIBERAL OF YOU.
HELLO, HANDSOME!
THWAK
OWW!
ASSAULTED BY A TRANSSEXUAL!
PINYA? WE BOUGHT YOU A NEW ***DRESS,*** AND MY *"BOYFRIEND"* HERE JUST GOT ***PINCHED.***
NOW WE HAVE A FAVOR TO ASK OF ***YOU.***

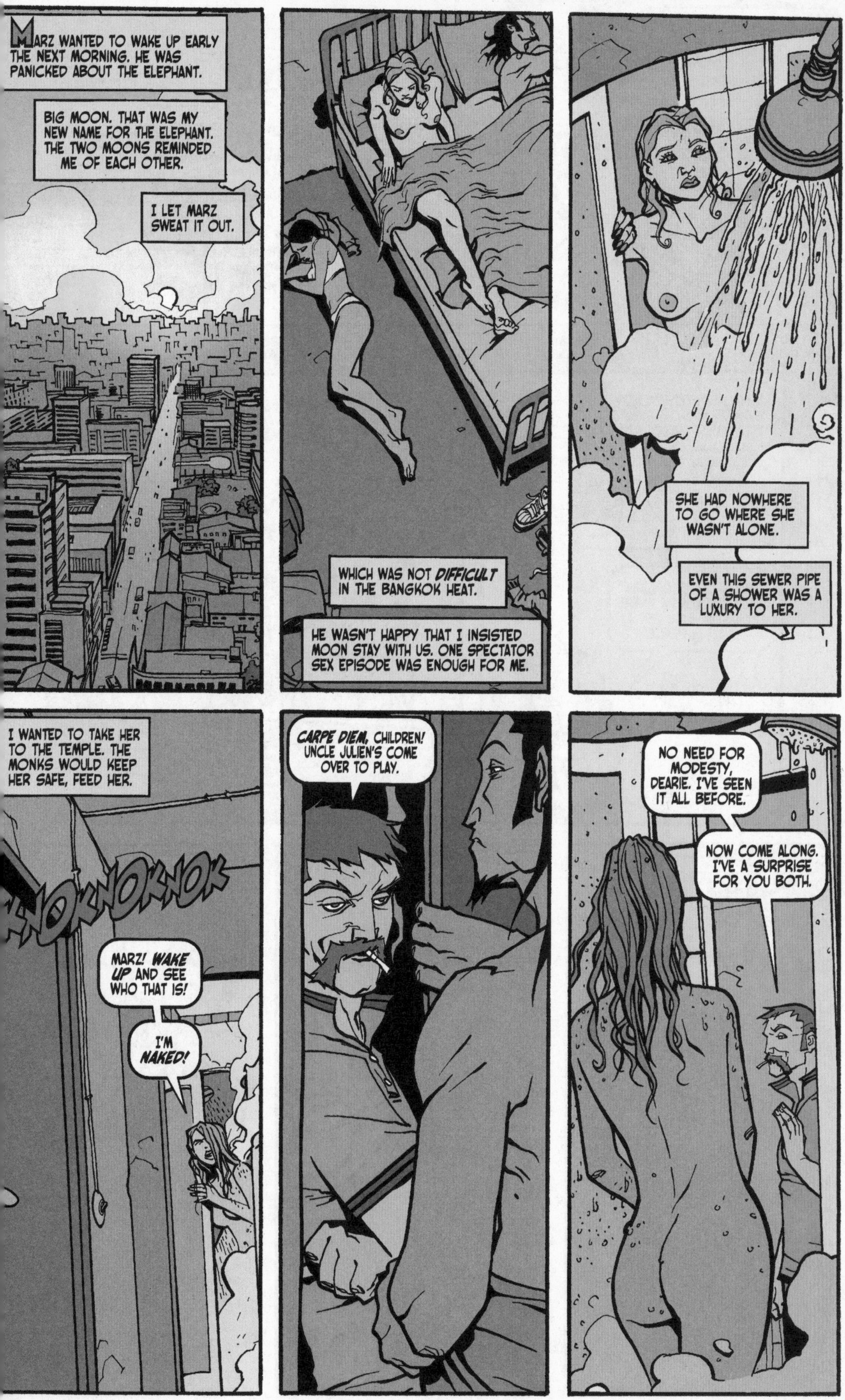
MARZ WANTED TO WAKE UP EARLY THE NEXT MORNING. HE WAS PANICKED ABOUT THE ELEPHANT.
BIG MOON. THAT WAS MY NEW NAME FOR THE ELEPHANT. THE TWO MOONS REMINDED ME OF EACH OTHER.
I LET MARZ SWEAT IT OUT.
WHICH WAS NOT DIFFICULT IN THE BANGKOK HEAT.
HE WASN'T HAPPY THAT I INSISTED MOON STAY WITH US. ONE SPECTATOR SEX EPISODE WAS ENOUGH FOR ME.
SHE HAD NOWHERE TO GO WHERE SHE WASN'T ALONE.
EVEN THIS SEWER PIPE OF A SHOWER WAS A LUXURY TO HER.
I WANTED TO TAKE HER TO THE TEMPLE. THE MONKS WOULD KEEP HER SAFE, FEED HER.
KNOKNOKNOK
MARZ! WAKE UP AND SEE WHO THAT IS!
I'M NAKED!
CARPE DIEM, CHILDREN! UNCLE JULIEN'S COME OVER TO PLAY.
NO NEED FOR MODESTY, DEARIE. I'VE SEEN IT ALL BEFORE.
NOW COME ALONG. I'VE A SURPRISE FOR YOU BOTH.

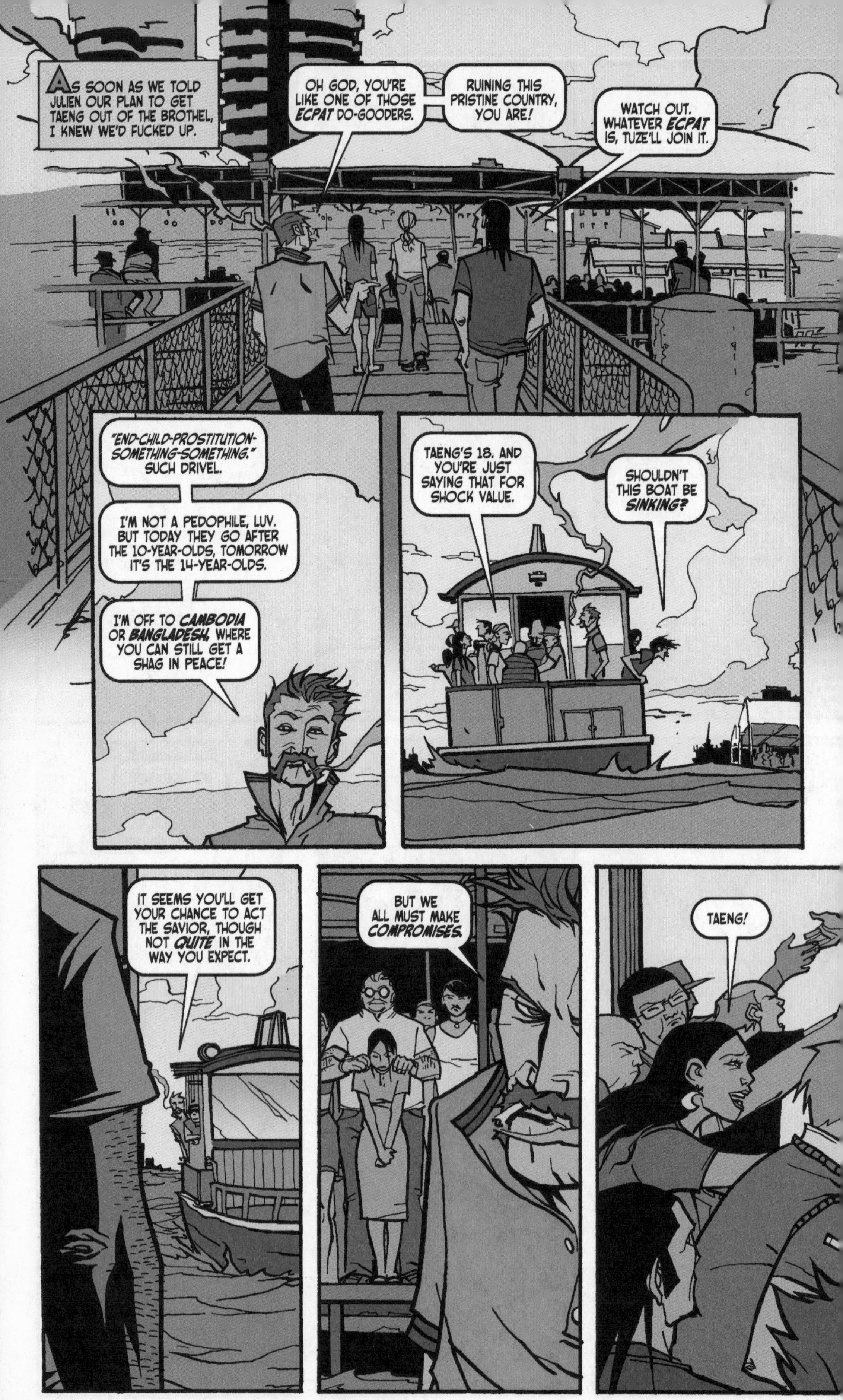
AS SOON AS WE TOLD JULIEN OUR PLAN TO GET TAENG OUT OF THE BROTHEL, I KNEW WE'D FUCKED UP.
OH GOD, YOU'RE LIKE ONE OF THOSE *ECPAT* DO-GOODERS.
RUINING THIS PRISTINE COUNTRY, YOU ARE!
WATCH OUT. WHATEVER *ECPAT* IS, TUZE'LL JOIN IT.
"END-CHILD-PROSTITUTION-SOMETHING-SOMETHING." SUCH DRIVEL.
I'M NOT A PEDOPHILE, LUV. BUT TODAY THEY GO AFTER THE 10-YEAR-OLDS, TOMORROW IT'S THE 14-YEAR-OLDS.
I'M OFF TO *CAMBODIA* OR *BANGLADESH,* WHERE YOU CAN STILL GET A SHAG IN PEACE!
TAENG'S 18. AND YOU'RE JUST SAYING THAT FOR SHOCK VALUE.
SHOULDN'T THIS BOAT BE *SINKING?*
IT SEEMS YOU'LL GET YOUR CHANCE TO ACT THE SAVIOR, THOUGH NOT *QUITE* IN THE WAY YOU EXPECT.
BUT WE ALL MUST MAKE *COMPROMISES.*
TAENG!

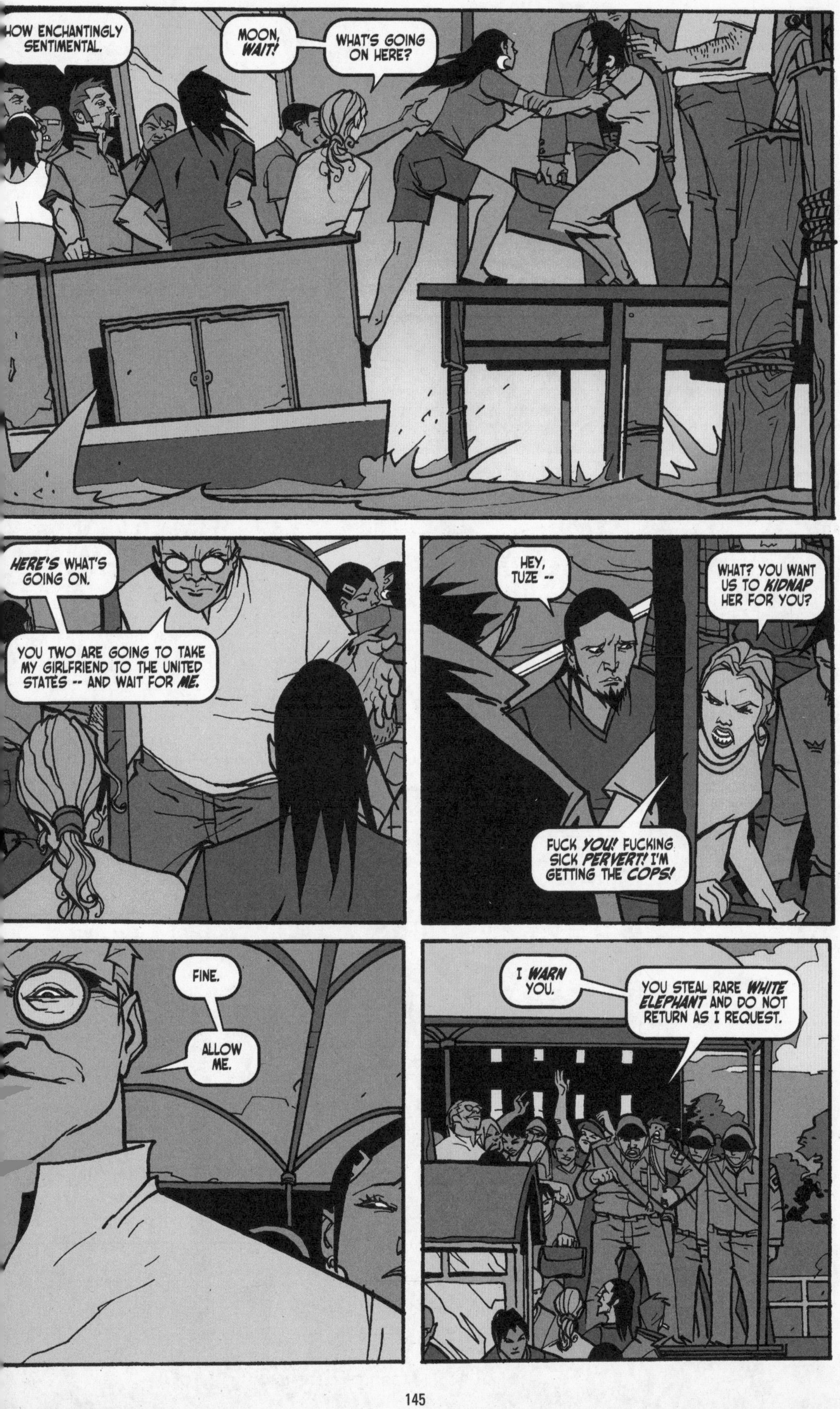
HOW ENCHANTINGLY SENTIMENTAL.
MOON, WAIT!
WHAT'S GOING ON HERE?
HERE'S WHAT'S GOING ON.
YOU TWO ARE GOING TO TAKE MY GIRLFRIEND TO THE UNITED STATES -- AND WAIT FOR ME.
HEY, TUZE --
WHAT? YOU WANT US TO KIDNAP HER FOR YOU?
FUCK YOU! FUCKING SICK PERVERT! I'M GETTING THE COPS!
FINE.
ALLOW ME.
I WARN YOU.
YOU STEAL RARE WHITE ELEPHANT AND DO NOT RETURN AS I REQUEST.

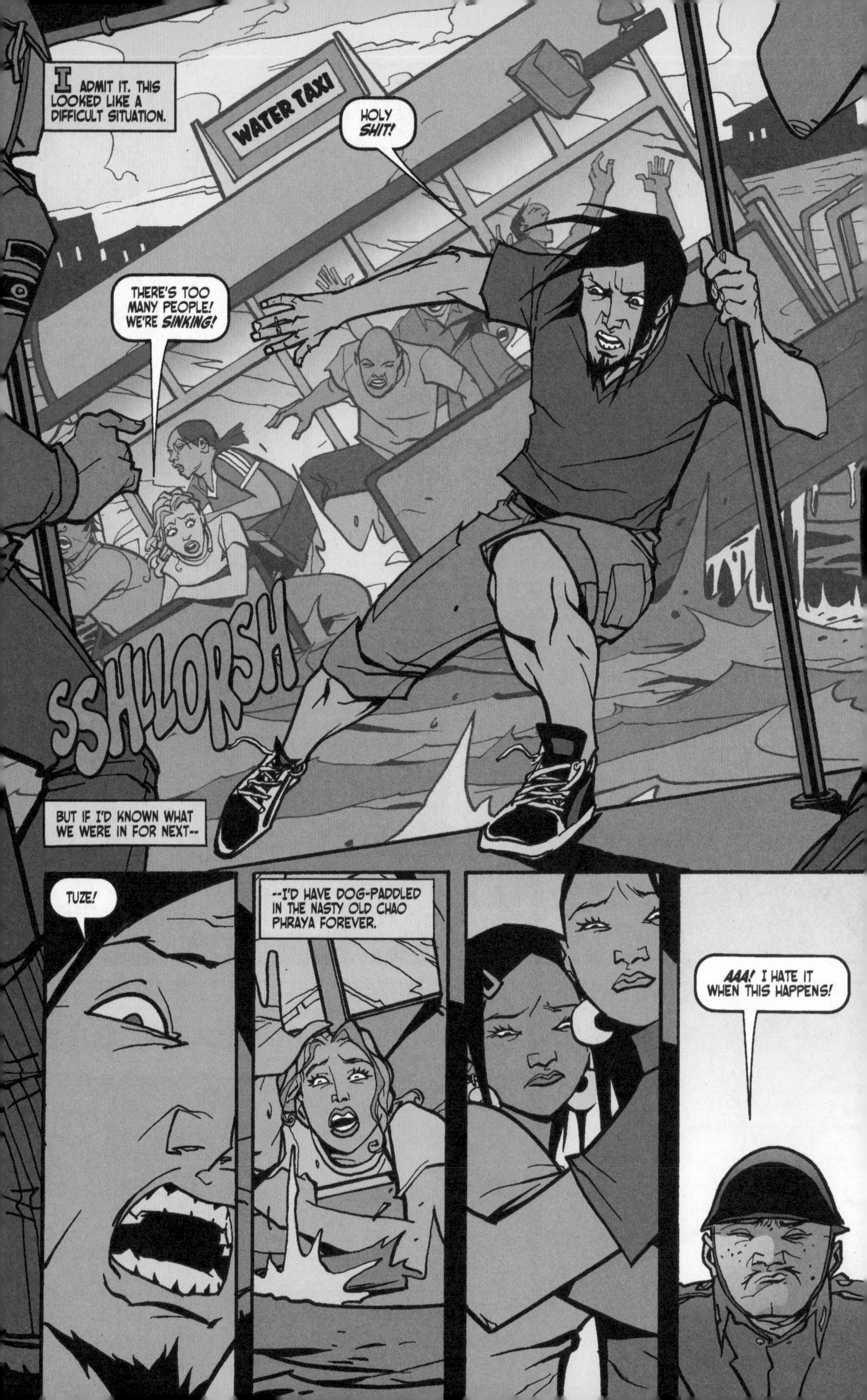
I ADMIT IT. THIS LOOKED LIKE A DIFFICULT SITUATION.
WATER TAXI
HOLY SHIT!
THERE'S TOO MANY PEOPLE! WE'RE SINKING!
SSHLLORSH
BUT IF I'D KNOWN WHAT WE WERE IN FOR NEXT--
TUZE!
--I'D HAVE DOG-PADDLED IN THE NASTY OLD CHAO PHRAYA FOREVER.
AAA! I HATE IT WHEN THIS HAPPENS!

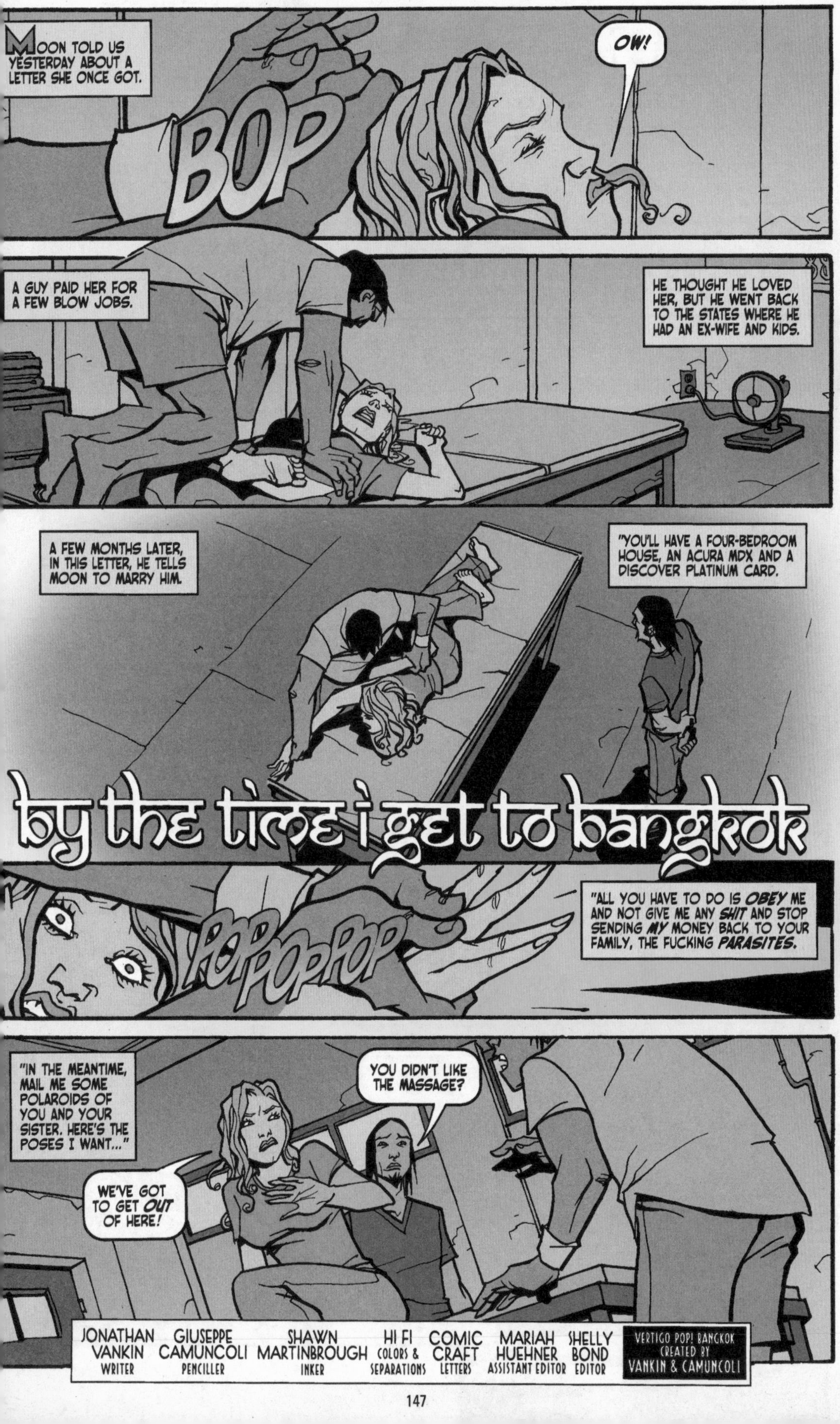
MOON TOLD US YESTERDAY ABOUT A LETTER SHE ONCE GOT.
BOP
OW!
A GUY PAID HER FOR A FEW BLOW JOBS.
HE THOUGHT HE LOVED HER, BUT HE WENT BACK TO THE STATES WHERE HE HAD AN EX-WIFE AND KIDS.
A FEW MONTHS LATER, IN THIS LETTER, HE TELLS MOON TO MARRY HIM.
"YOU'LL HAVE A FOUR-BEDROOM HOUSE, AN ACURA MDX AND A DISCOVER PLATINUM CARD.
by the time i get to bangkok
"ALL YOU HAVE TO DO IS OBEY ME AND NOT GIVE ME ANY SHIT AND STOP SENDING MY MONEY BACK TO YOUR FAMILY, THE FUCKING PARASITES.
POP POP POP
"IN THE MEANTIME, MAIL ME SOME POLAROIDS OF YOU AND YOUR SISTER. HERE'S THE POSES I WANT..."
YOU DIDN'T LIKE THE MASSAGE?
WE'VE GOT TO GET OUT OF HERE!
JONATHAN VANKIN WRITER
GIUSEPPE CAMUNCOLI PENCILLER
SHAWN MARTINBROUGH INKER
HI FI COLORS & SEPARATIONS
COMIC CRAFT LETTERS
MARIAH HUEHNER ASSISTANT EDITOR
SHELLY BOND EDITOR
VERTIGO POP! BANGKOK CREATED BY VANKIN & CAMUNCOLI

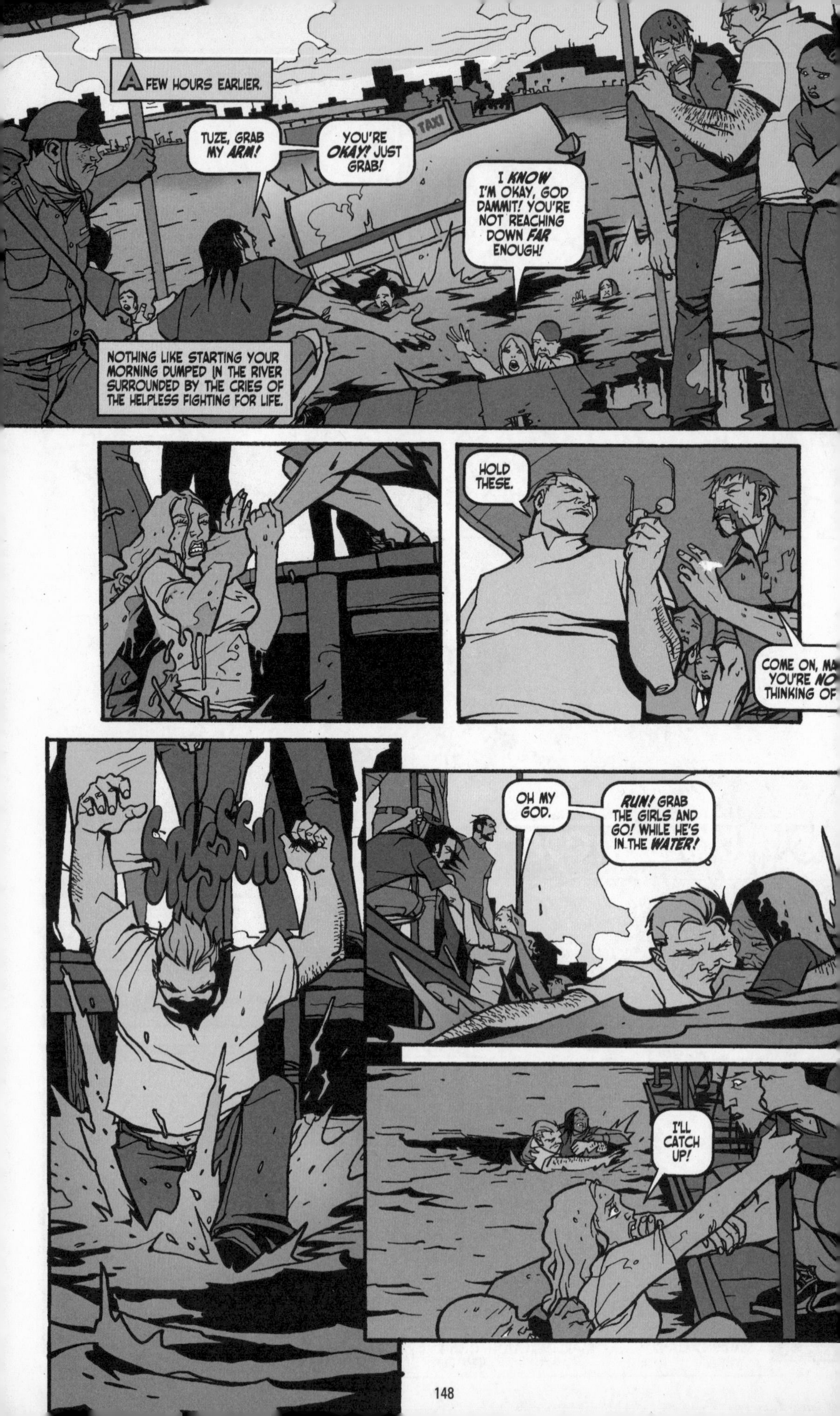
A FEW HOURS EARLIER.
TUZE, GRAB MY ARM!
YOU'RE OKAY! JUST GRAB!
I KNOW I'M OKAY, GOD DAMMIT! YOU'RE NOT REACHING DOWN FAR ENOUGH!
NOTHING LIKE STARTING YOUR MORNING DUMPED IN THE RIVER SURROUNDED BY THE CRIES OF THE HELPLESS FIGHTING FOR LIFE.
TAXI
HOLD THESE.
COME ON, MA
YOU'RE NO
THINKING OF
SPLSSSH
OH MY GOD.
RUN! GRAB THE GIRLS AND GO! WHILE HE'S IN THE WATER!
I'LL CATCH UP!

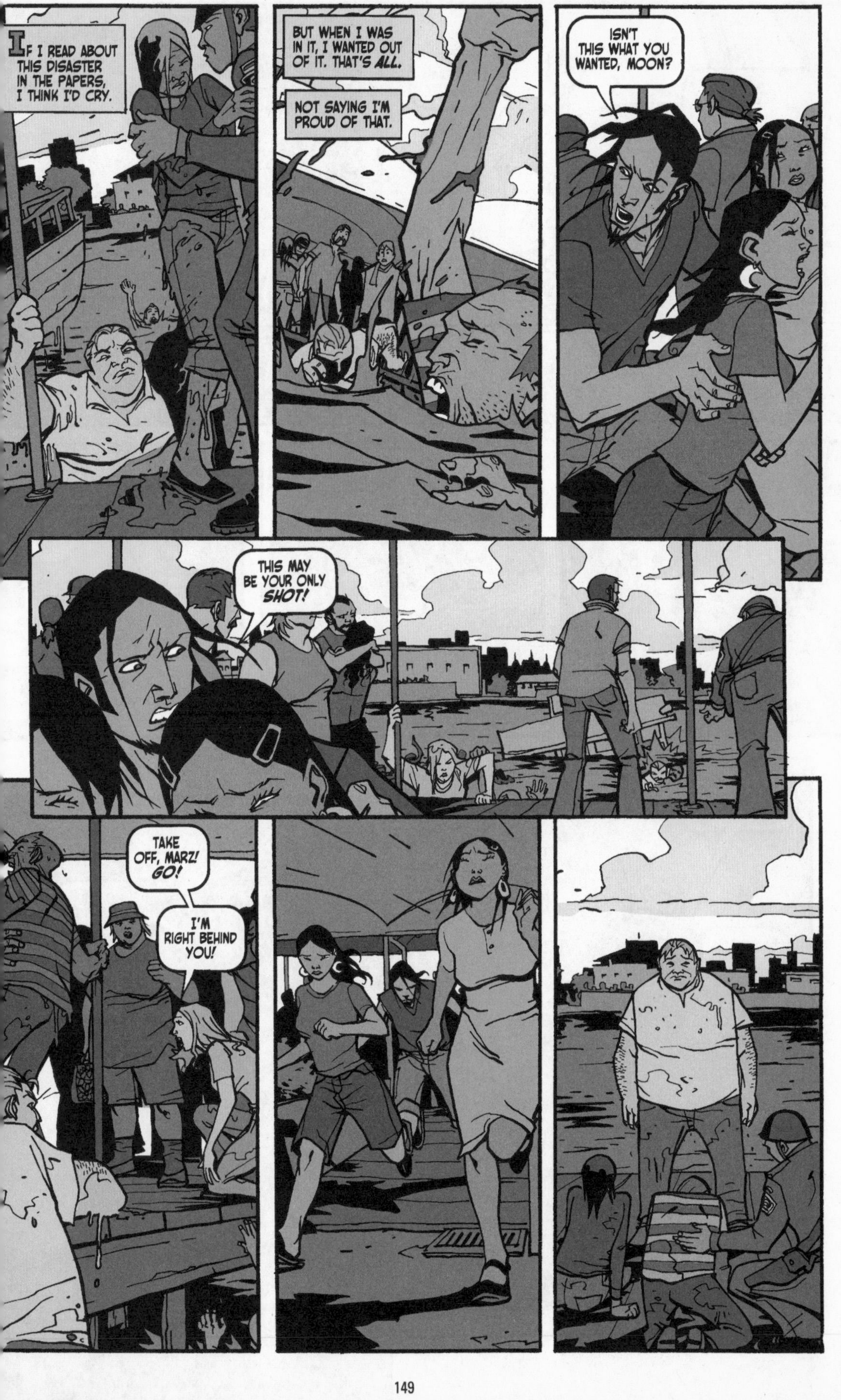
IF I READ ABOUT THIS DISASTER IN THE PAPERS, I THINK I'D CRY.
BUT WHEN I WAS IN IT, I WANTED OUT OF IT. THAT'S ALL.
NOT SAYING I'M PROUD OF THAT.
ISN'T THIS WHAT YOU WANTED, MOON?
THIS MAY BE YOUR ONLY SHOT!
TAKE OFF, MARZ! GO!
I'M RIGHT BEHIND YOU!

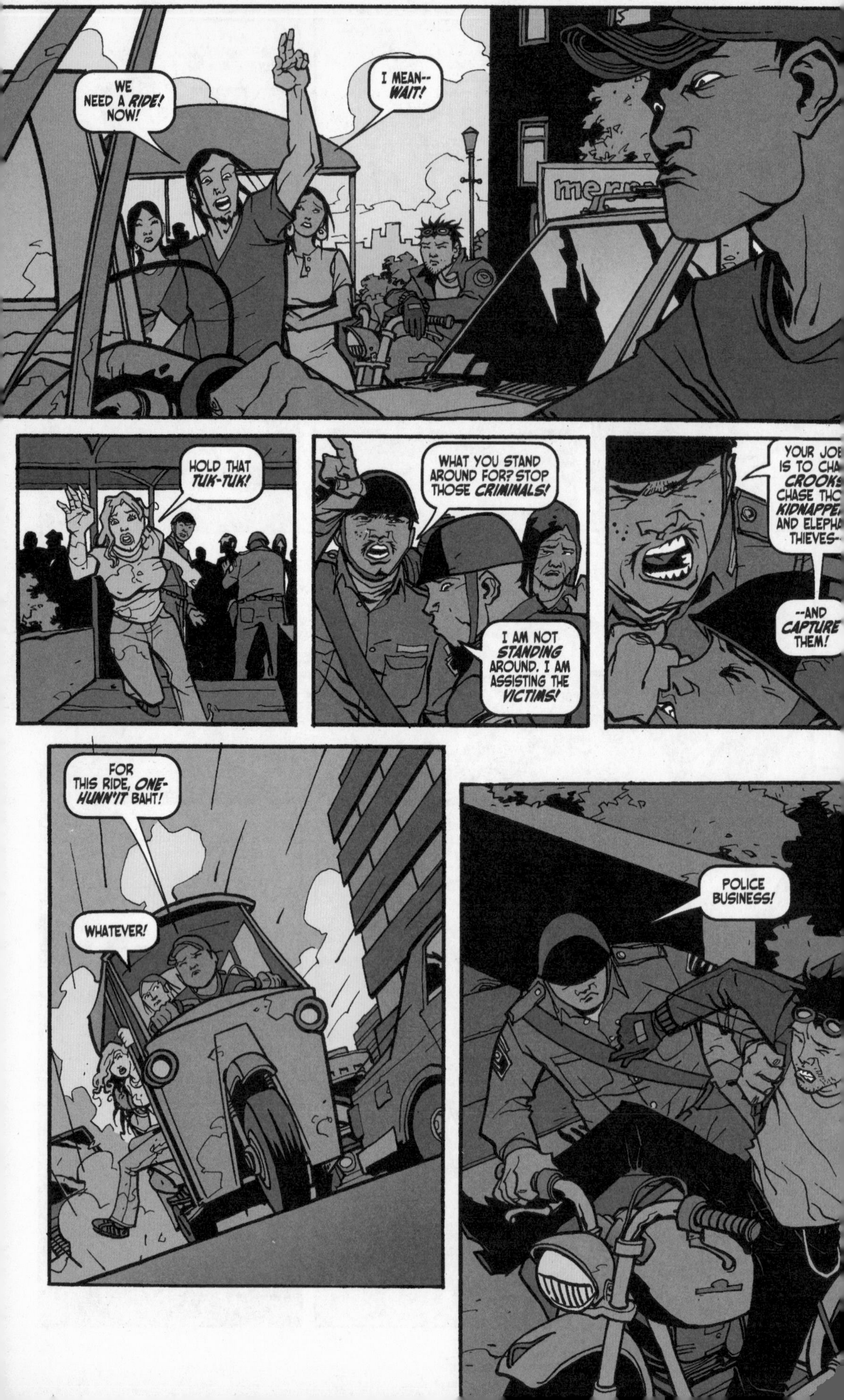
WE NEED A RIDE! NOW!
I MEAN-- WAIT!
HOLD THAT TUK-TUK!
WHAT YOU STAND AROUND FOR? STOP THOSE CRIMINALS!
I AM NOT STANDING AROUND. I AM ASSISTING THE VICTIMS!
YOUR JOB IS TO CHA CROOKS CHASE THO KIDNAPPE AND ELEPHA THIEVES--
--AND CAPTURE THEM!
FOR THIS RIDE, ONE-HUNN'IT BAHT!
WHATEVER!
POLICE BUSINESS!

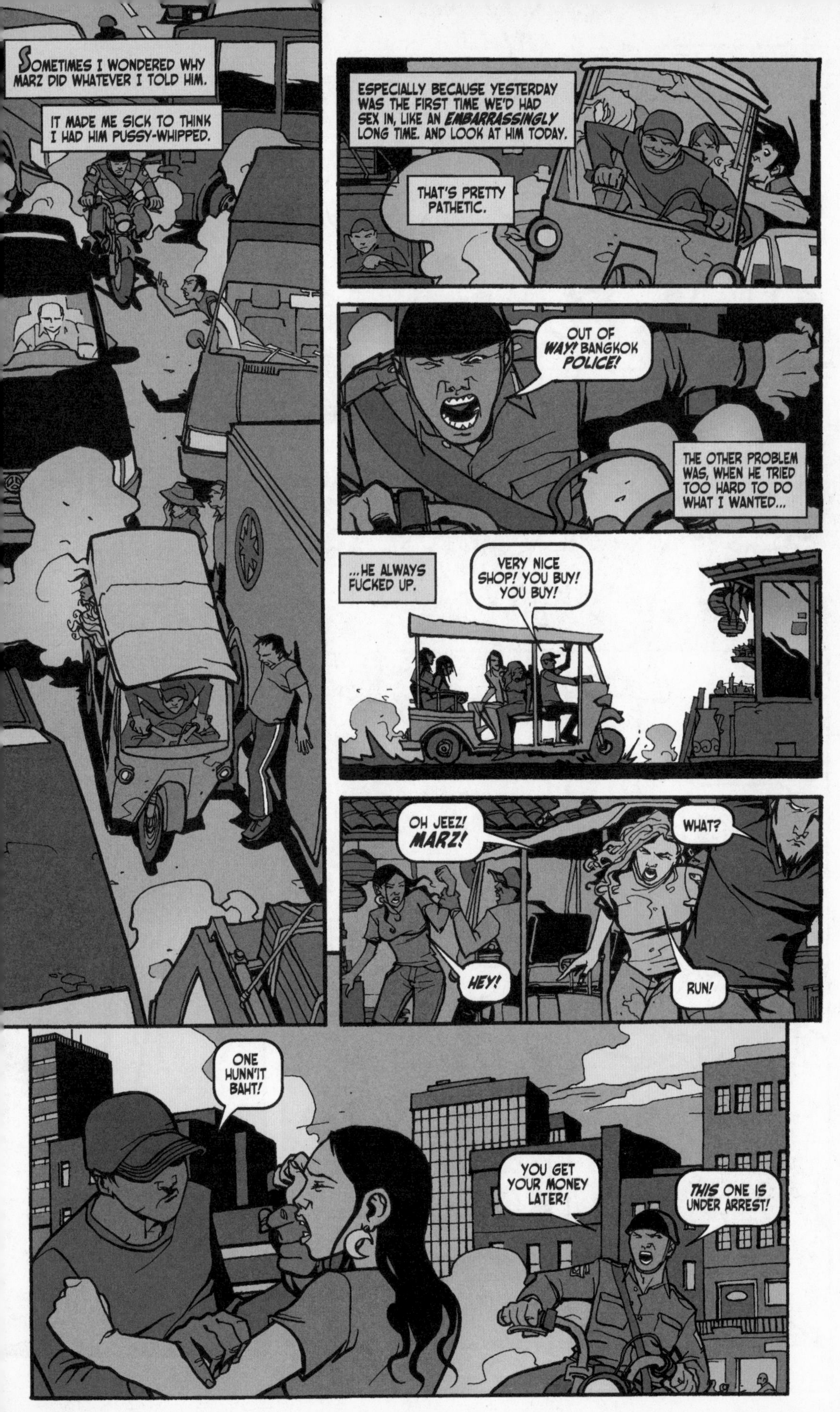
SOMETIMES I WONDERED WHY MARZ DID WHATEVER I TOLD HIM.
IT MADE ME SICK TO THINK I HAD HIM PUSSY-WHIPPED.
ESPECIALLY BECAUSE YESTERDAY WAS THE FIRST TIME WE'D HAD SEX IN, LIKE AN *EMBARRASSINGLY* LONG TIME. AND LOOK AT HIM TODAY.
THAT'S PRETTY PATHETIC.
OUT OF *WAY!* BANGKOK *POLICE!*
THE OTHER PROBLEM WAS, WHEN HE TRIED TOO HARD TO DO WHAT I WANTED...
...HE ALWAYS FUCKED UP.
VERY NICE SHOP! YOU BUY! YOU BUY!
OH JEEZ! *MARZ!*
WHAT?
HEY!
RUN!
ONE HUNN'IT BAHT!
YOU GET YOUR MONEY LATER!
THIS ONE IS UNDER ARREST!

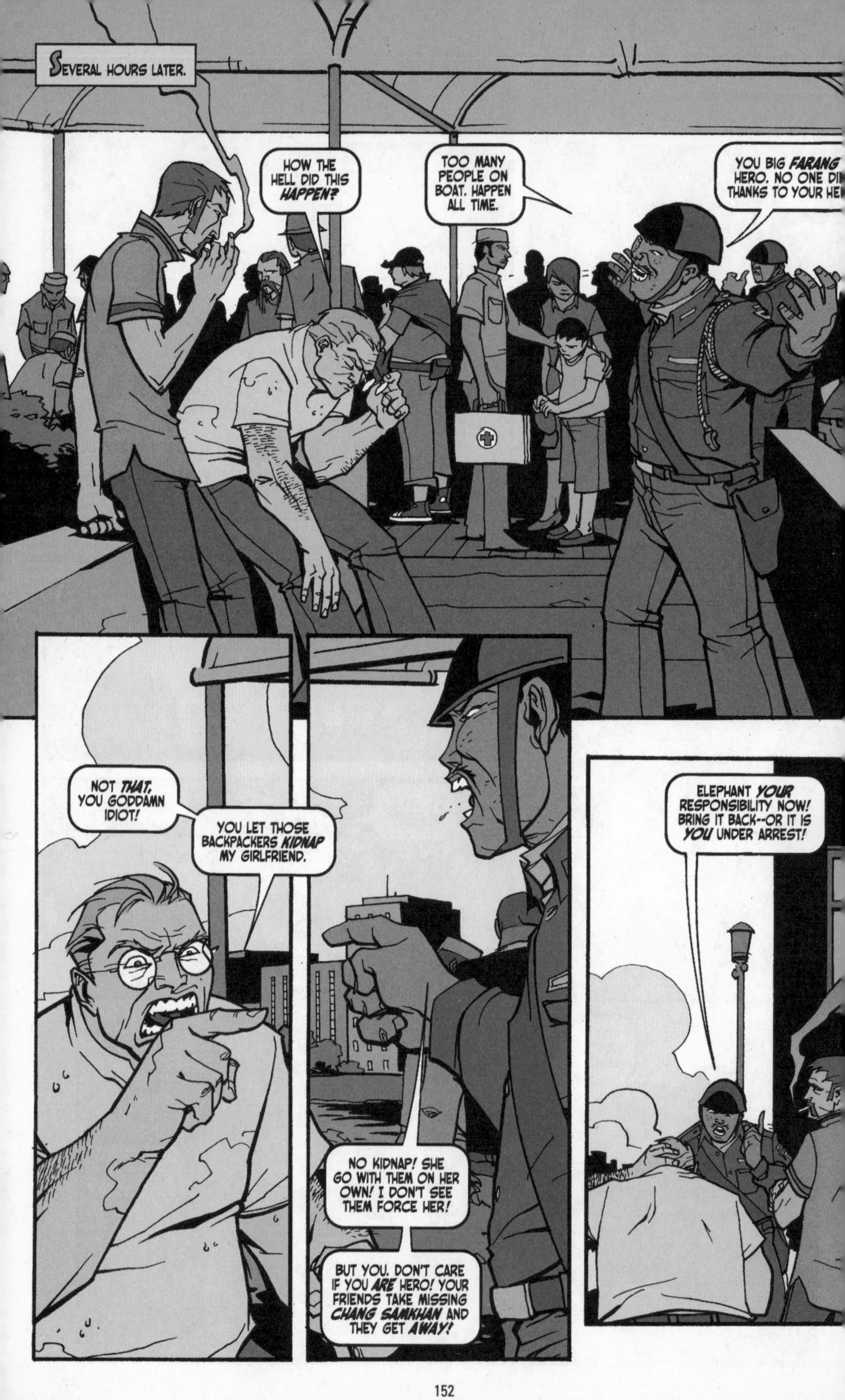
SEVERAL HOURS LATER.
HOW THE HELL DID THIS HAPPEN?
TOO MANY PEOPLE ON BOAT. HAPPEN ALL TIME.
YOU BIG FARANG HERO. NO ONE DI THANKS TO YOUR HE
NOT THAT, YOU GODDAMN IDIOT!
YOU LET THOSE BACKPACKERS KIDNAP MY GIRLFRIEND.
NO KIDNAP! SHE GO WITH THEM ON HER OWN! I DON'T SEE THEM FORCE HER!
BUT YOU. DON'T CARE IF YOU ARE HERO! YOUR FRIENDS TAKE MISSING CHANG SAMKHAN AND THEY GET AWAY!
ELEPHANT YOUR RESPONSIBILITY NOW! BRING IT BACK--OR IT IS YOU UNDER ARREST!

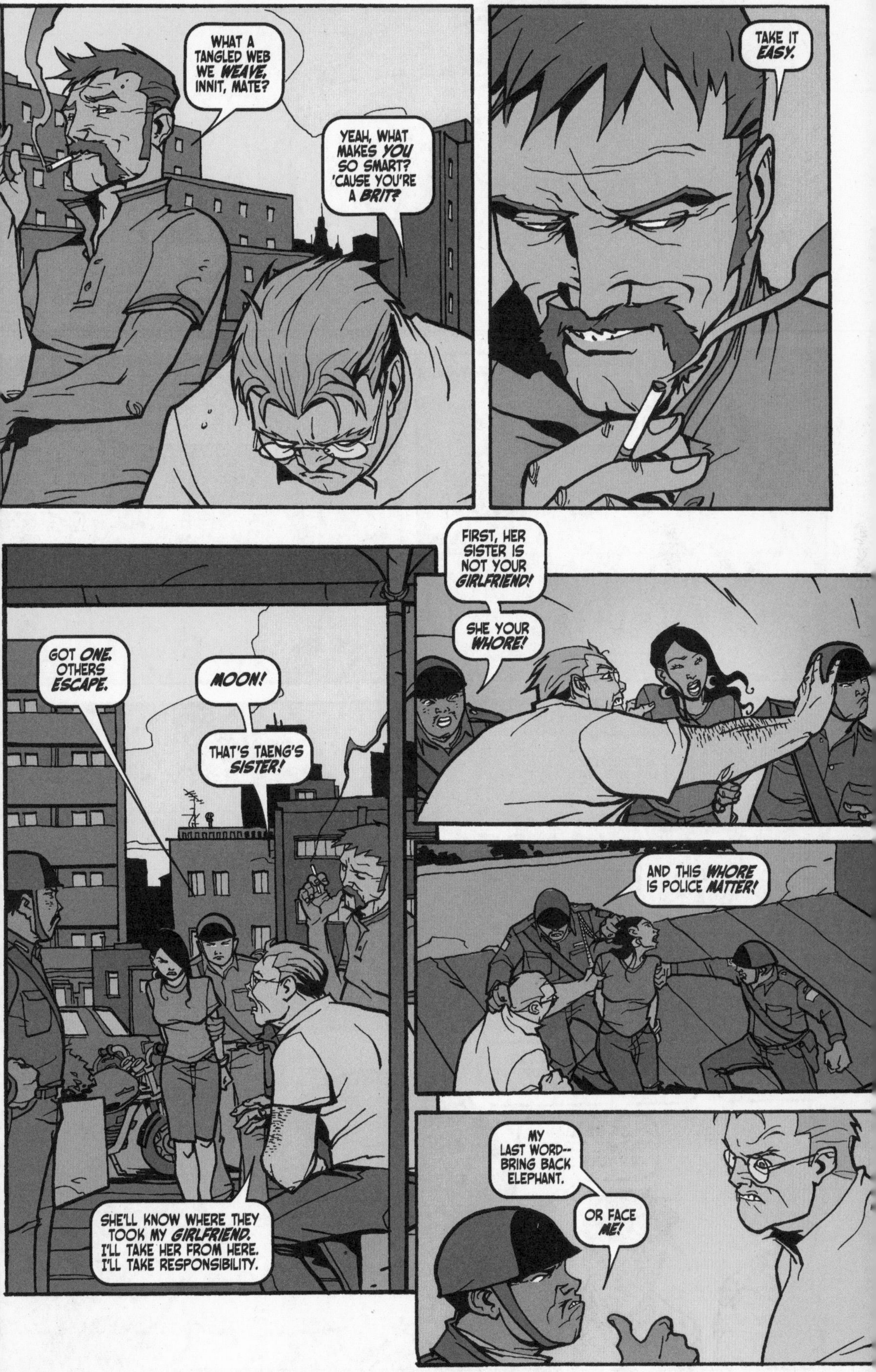
WHAT A TANGLED WEB WE WEAVE, INNIT, MATE?
YEAH, WHAT MAKES YOU SO SMART? 'CAUSE YOU'RE A BRIT?
TAKE IT EASY.
GOT ONE. OTHERS ESCAPE.
MOON!
THAT'S TAENG'S SISTER!
SHE'LL KNOW WHERE THEY TOOK MY GIRLFRIEND. I'LL TAKE HER FROM HERE. I'LL TAKE RESPONSIBILITY.
FIRST, HER SISTER IS NOT YOUR GIRLFRIEND!
SHE YOUR WHORE!
AND THIS WHORE IS POLICE MATTER!
MY LAST WORD-- BRING BACK ELEPHANT.
OR FACE ME!

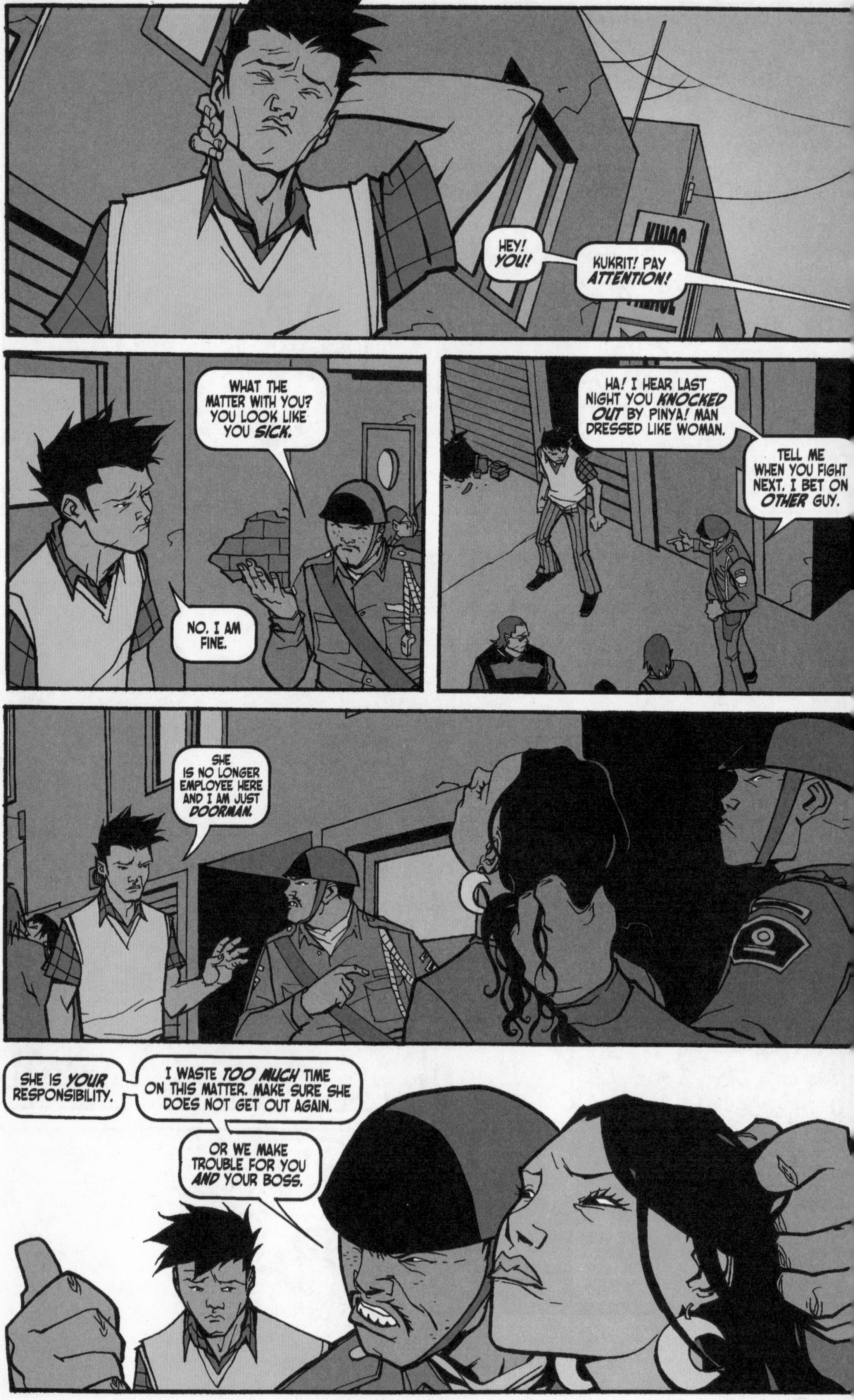
HEY! YOU!
KUKRIT! PAY ATTENTION!
WHAT THE MATTER WITH YOU? YOU LOOK LIKE YOU SICK.
NO. I AM FINE.
HA! I HEAR LAST NIGHT YOU KNOCKED OUT BY PINYA! MAN DRESSED LIKE WOMAN.
TELL ME WHEN YOU FIGHT NEXT. I BET ON OTHER GUY.
SHE IS NO LONGER EMPLOYEE HERE AND I AM JUST DOORMAN.
SHE IS YOUR RESPONSIBILITY.
I WASTE TOO MUCH TIME ON THIS MATTER. MAKE SURE SHE DOES NOT GET OUT AGAIN.
OR WE MAKE TROUBLE FOR YOU AND YOUR BOSS.

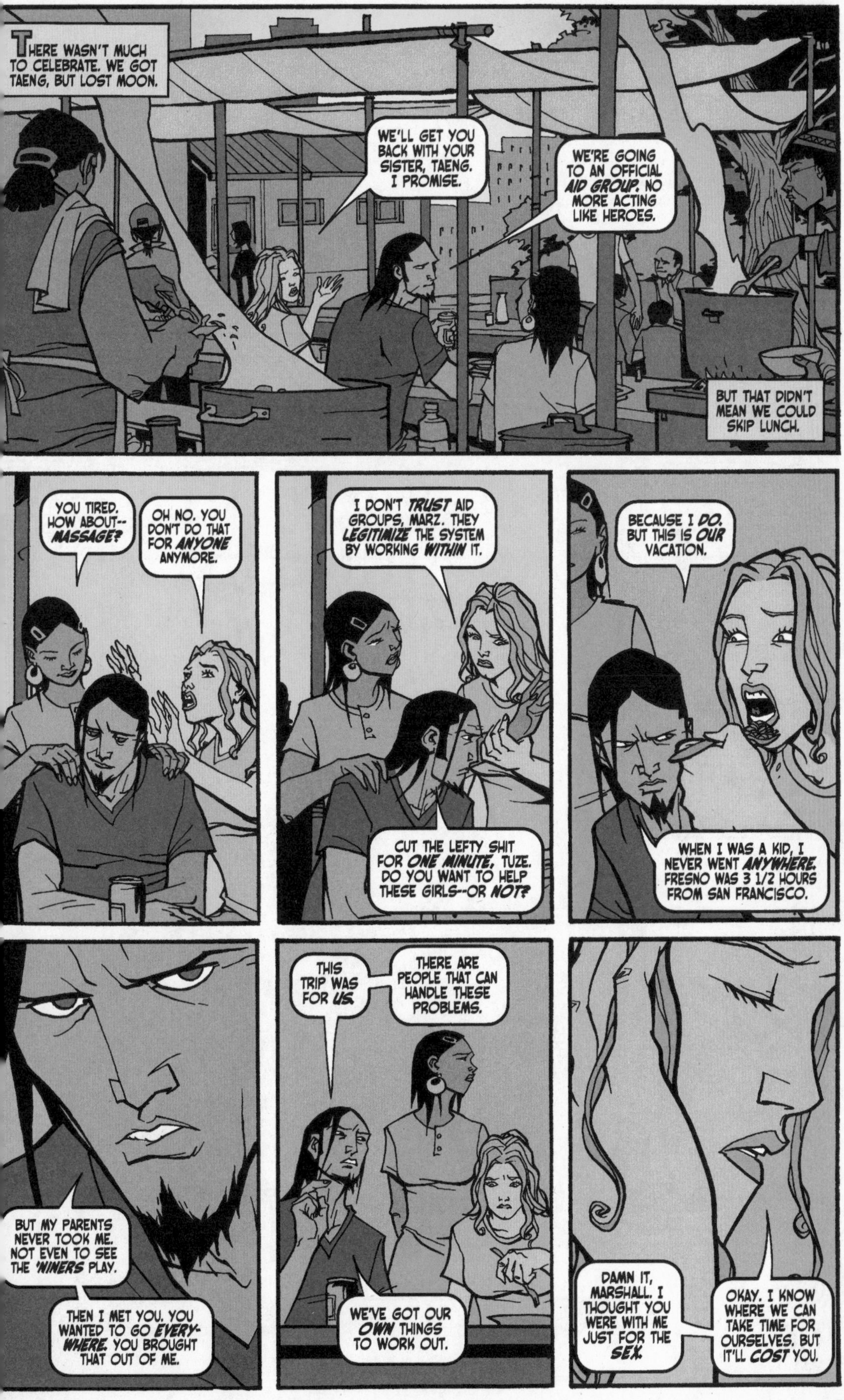
THERE WASN'T MUCH TO CELEBRATE. WE GOT TAENG, BUT LOST MOON.
WE'LL GET YOU BACK WITH YOUR SISTER, TAENG. I PROMISE.
WE'RE GOING TO AN OFFICIAL AID GROUP. NO MORE ACTING LIKE HEROES.
BUT THAT DIDN'T MEAN WE COULD SKIP LUNCH.
YOU TIRED. HOW ABOUT--MASSAGE?
OH NO. YOU DON'T DO THAT FOR ANYONE ANYMORE.
I DON'T TRUST AID GROUPS, MARZ. THEY LEGITIMIZE THE SYSTEM BY WORKING WITHIN IT.
CUT THE LEFTY SHIT FOR ONE MINUTE, TUZE. DO YOU WANT TO HELP THESE GIRLS--OR NOT?
BECAUSE I DO. BUT THIS IS OUR VACATION.
WHEN I WAS A KID, I NEVER WENT ANYWHERE. FRESNO WAS 3 1/2 HOURS FROM SAN FRANCISCO.
BUT MY PARENTS NEVER TOOK ME. NOT EVEN TO SEE THE 'NINERS PLAY.
THEN I MET YOU. YOU WANTED TO GO EVERYWHERE. YOU BROUGHT THAT OUT OF ME.
THIS TRIP WAS FOR US.
THERE ARE PEOPLE THAT CAN HANDLE THESE PROBLEMS.
WE'VE GOT OUR OWN THINGS TO WORK OUT.
DAMN IT, MARSHALL. I THOUGHT YOU WERE WITH ME JUST FOR THE SEX.
OKAY. I KNOW WHERE WE CAN TAKE TIME FOR OURSELVES. BUT IT'LL COST YOU.

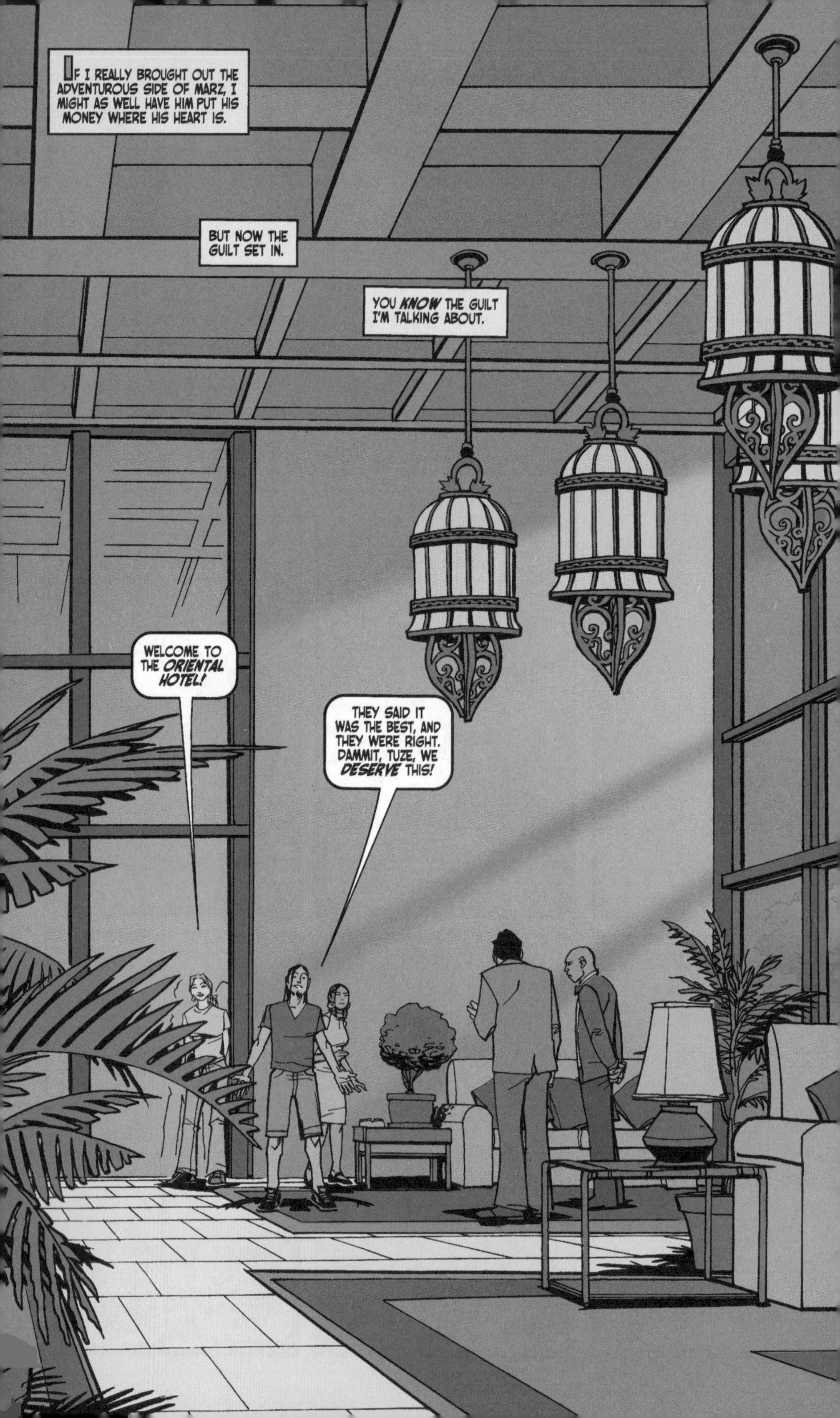
IF I REALLY BROUGHT OUT THE ADVENTUROUS SIDE OF MARZ, I MIGHT AS WELL HAVE HIM PUT HIS MONEY WHERE HIS HEART IS.
BUT NOW THE GUILT SET IN.
YOU *KNOW* THE GUILT I'M TALKING ABOUT.
WELCOME TO THE *ORIENTAL HOTEL!*
THEY SAID IT WAS THE BEST, AND THEY WERE RIGHT. DAMMIT, TUZE, WE *DESERVE* THIS!

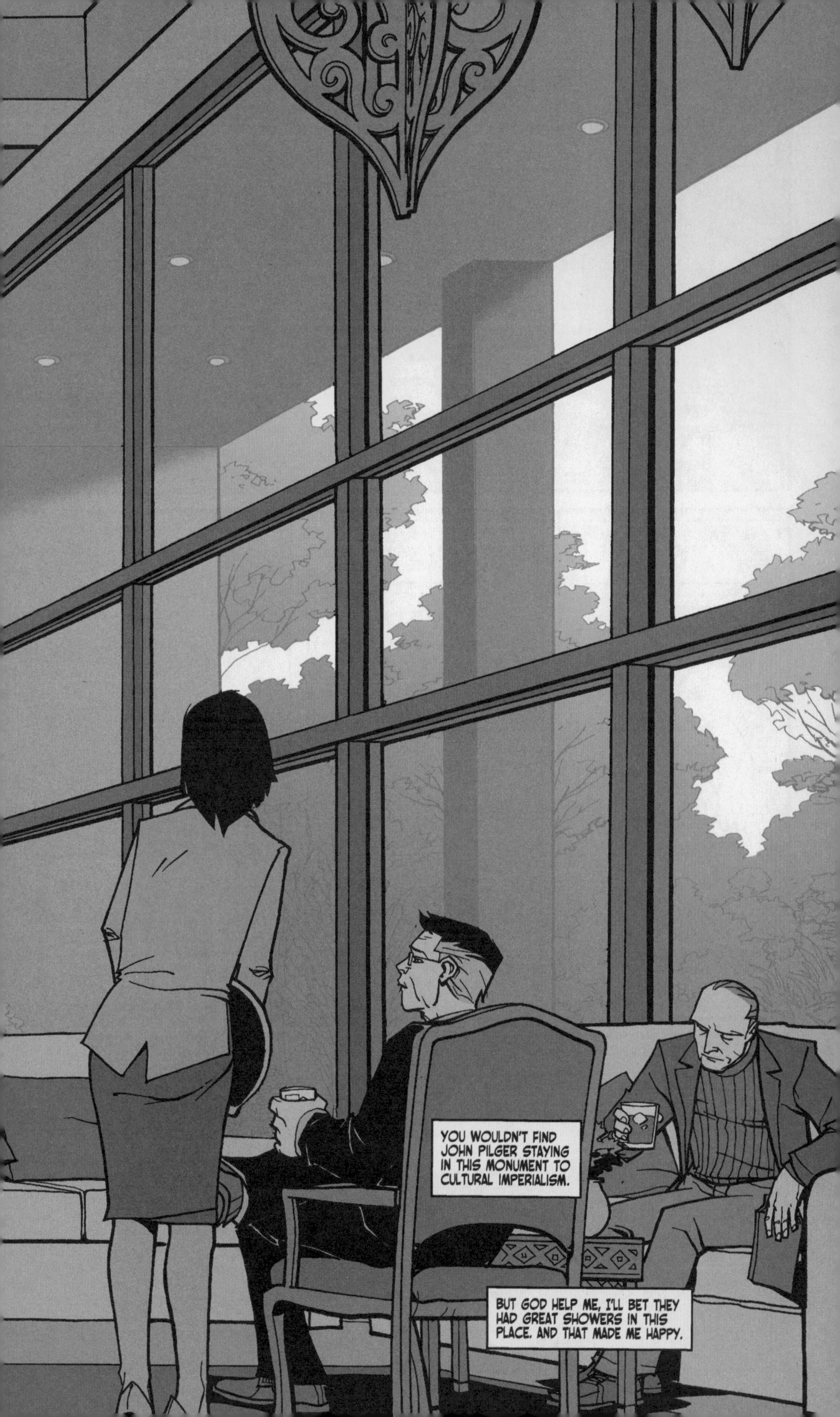
YOU WOULDN'T FIND JOHN PILGER STAYING IN THIS MONUMENT TO CULTURAL IMPERIALISM.
BUT GOD HELP ME, I'LL BET THEY HAD GREAT SHOWERS IN THIS PLACE. AND THAT MADE ME HAPPY.

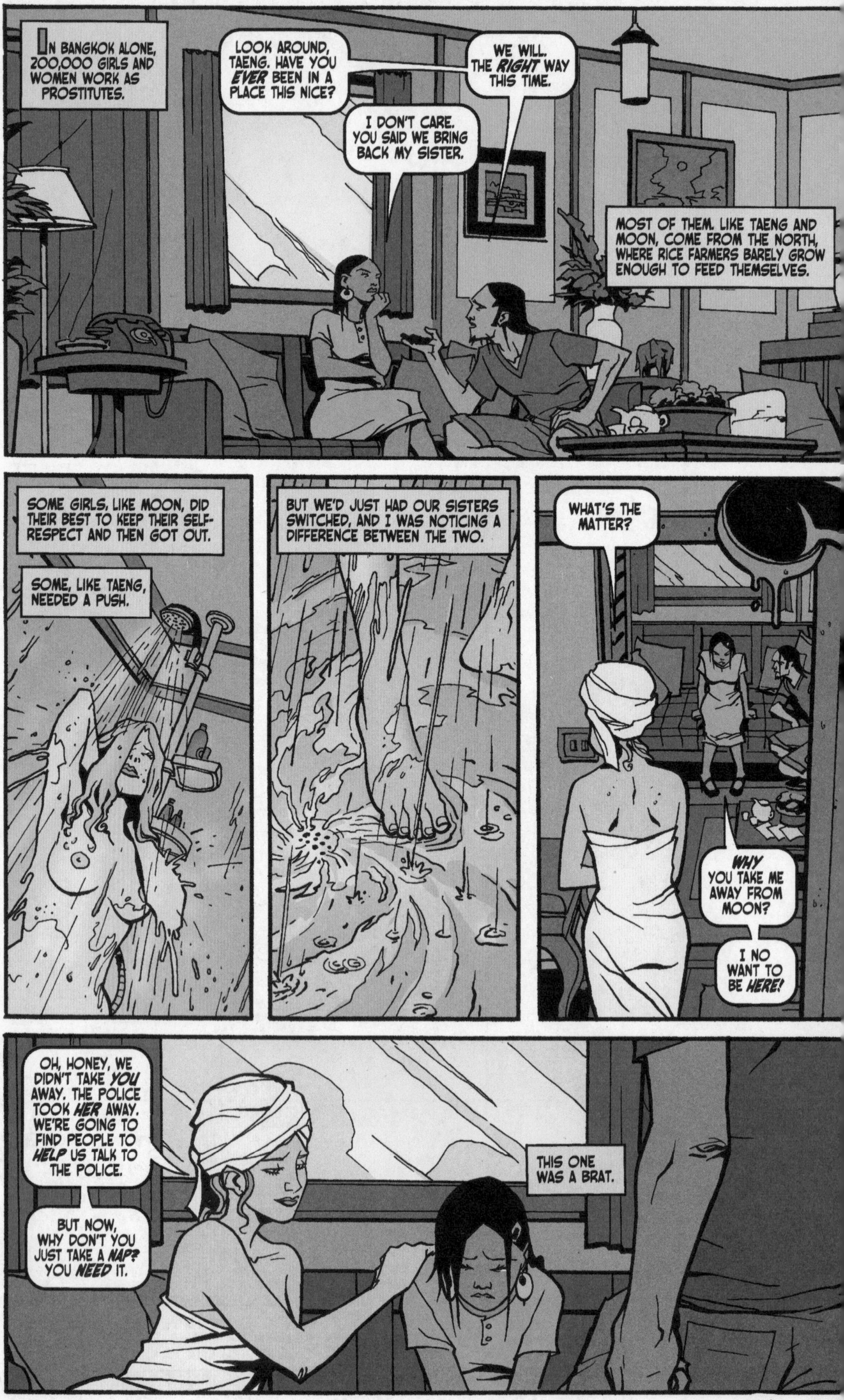

IN BANGKOK ALONE, 200,000 GIRLS AND WOMEN WORK AS PROSTITUTES.
LOOK AROUND, TAENG. HAVE YOU EVER BEEN IN A PLACE THIS NICE?
I DON'T CARE. YOU SAID WE BRING BACK MY SISTER.
WE WILL. THE RIGHT WAY THIS TIME.
MOST OF THEM. LIKE TAENG AND MOON, COME FROM THE NORTH, WHERE RICE FARMERS BARELY GROW ENOUGH TO FEED THEMSELVES.
SOME GIRLS, LIKE MOON, DID THEIR BEST TO KEEP THEIR SELF-RESPECT AND THEN GOT OUT.
SOME, LIKE TAENG, NEEDED A PUSH.
BUT WE'D JUST HAD OUR SISTERS SWITCHED, AND I WAS NOTICING A DIFFERENCE BETWEEN THE TWO.
WHAT'S THE MATTER?
WHY YOU TAKE ME AWAY FROM MOON?
I NO WANT TO BE HERE!
OH, HONEY, WE DIDN'T TAKE YOU AWAY. THE POLICE TOOK HER AWAY. WE'RE GOING TO FIND PEOPLE TO HELP US TALK TO THE POLICE.
BUT NOW, WHY DON'T YOU JUST TAKE A NAP? YOU NEED IT.
THIS ONE WAS A BRAT.

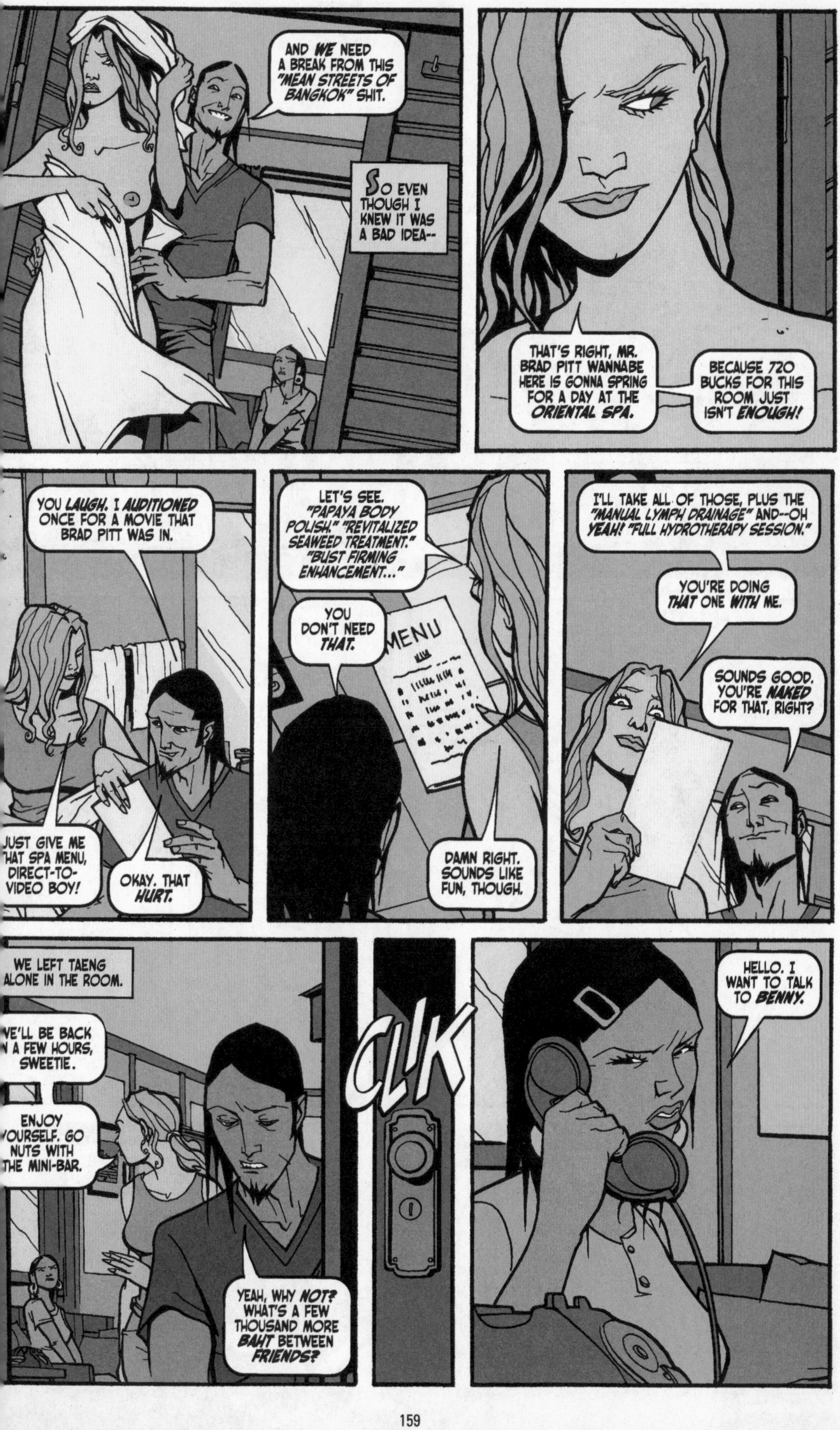
AND WE NEED A BREAK FROM THIS "MEAN STREETS OF BANGKOK" SHIT.
SO EVEN THOUGH I KNEW IT WAS A BAD IDEA--
THAT'S RIGHT, MR. BRAD PITT WANNABE HERE IS GONNA SPRING FOR A DAY AT THE ORIENTAL SPA.
BECAUSE 720 BUCKS FOR THIS ROOM JUST ISN'T ENOUGH!
YOU LAUGH. I AUDITIONED ONCE FOR A MOVIE THAT BRAD PITT WAS IN.
JUST GIVE ME THAT SPA MENU, DIRECT-TO-VIDEO BOY!
OKAY. THAT HURT.
LET'S SEE. "PAPAYA BODY POLISH." "REVITALIZED SEAWEED TREATMENT." "BUST FIRMING ENHANCEMENT..."
YOU DON'T NEED THAT.
MENU
DAMN RIGHT. SOUNDS LIKE FUN, THOUGH.
I'LL TAKE ALL OF THOSE, PLUS THE "MANUAL LYMPH DRAINAGE" AND--OH YEAH! "FULL HYDROTHERAPY SESSION."
YOU'RE DOING THAT ONE WITH ME.
SOUNDS GOOD. YOU'RE NAKED FOR THAT, RIGHT?
WE LEFT TAENG ALONE IN THE ROOM.
WE'LL BE BACK IN A FEW HOURS, SWEETIE.
ENJOY YOURSELF. GO NUTS WITH THE MINI-BAR.
YEAH, WHY NOT? WHAT'S A FEW THOUSAND MORE BAHT BETWEEN FRIENDS?
CL'K
HELLO. I WANT TO TALK TO BENNY.

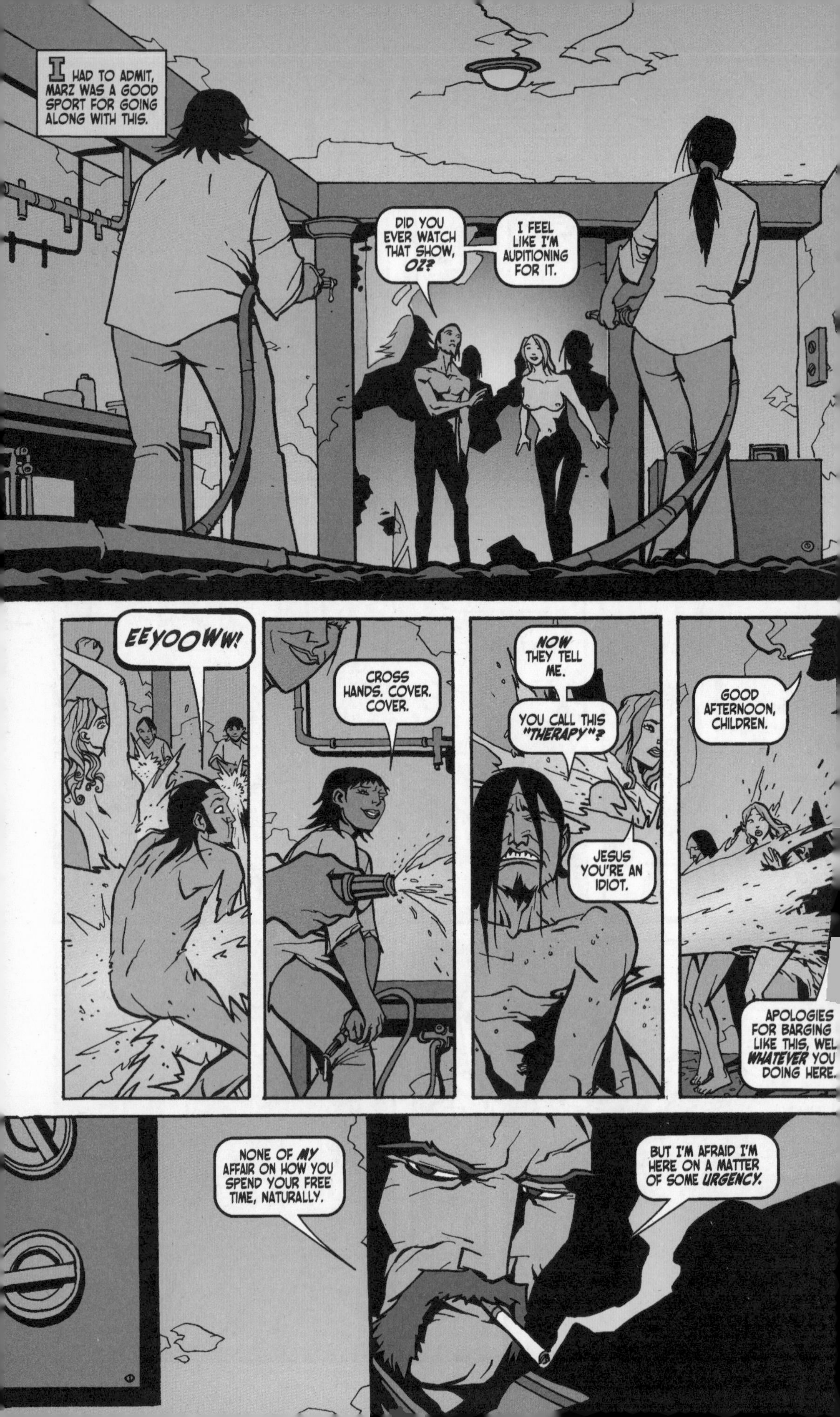
I HAD TO ADMIT, MARZ WAS A GOOD SPORT FOR GOING ALONG WITH THIS.
DID YOU EVER WATCH THAT SHOW, *OZ?*
I FEEL LIKE I'M AUDITIONING FOR IT.
EEYOOWW!
CROSS HANDS. COVER. COVER.
NOW THEY TELL ME.
YOU CALL THIS *"THERAPY"?*
JESUS YOU'RE AN IDIOT.
GOOD AFTERNOON, CHILDREN.
APOLOGIES FOR BARGING LIKE THIS, WEL *WHATEVER* YOU DOING HERE.
NONE OF *MY* AFFAIR ON HOW YOU SPEND YOUR FREE TIME, NATURALLY.
BUT I'M AFRAID I'M HERE ON A MATTER OF SOME *URGENCY.*

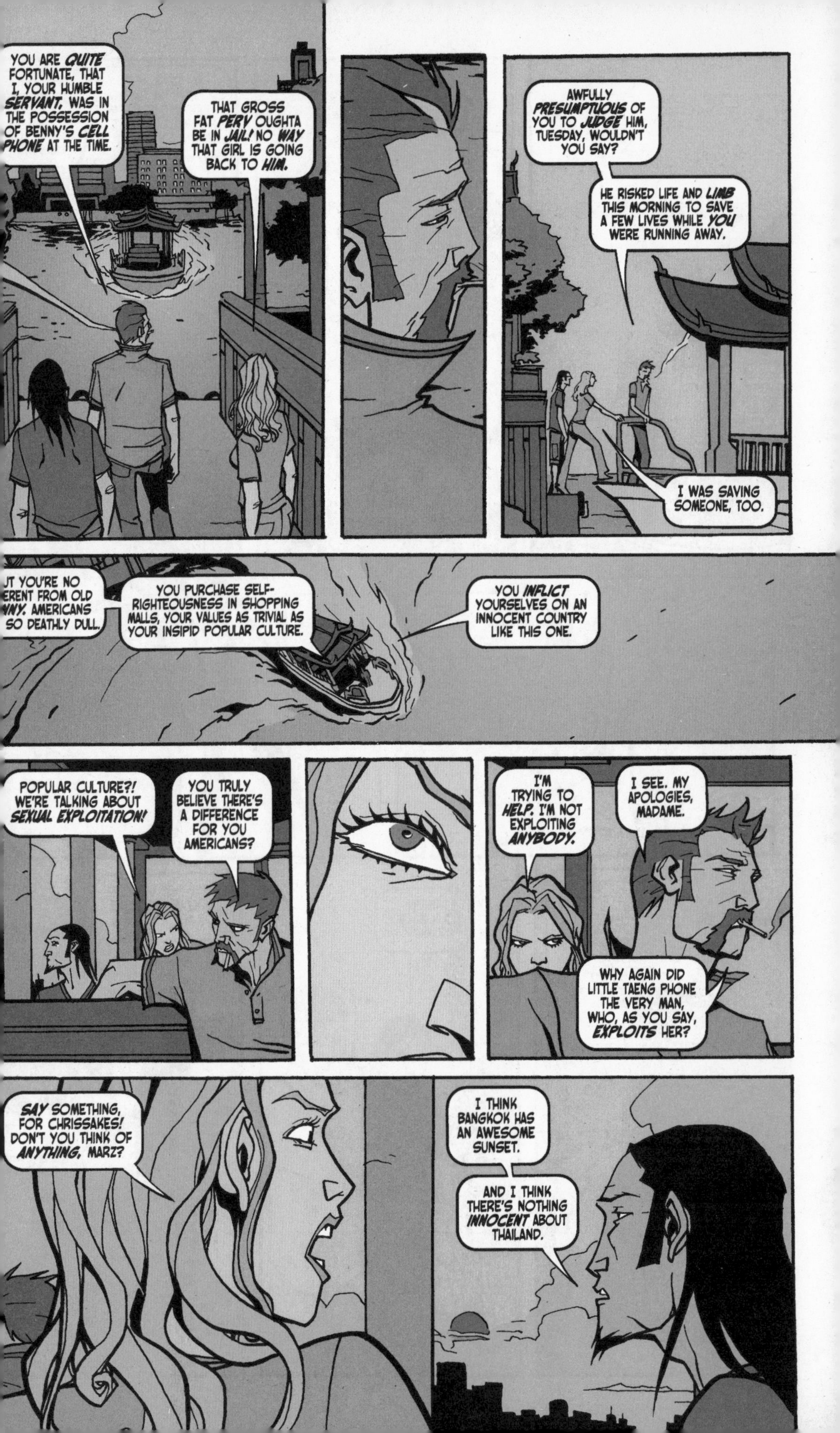
YOU ARE QUITE FORTUNATE, THAT I, YOUR HUMBLE SERVANT, WAS IN THE POSSESSION OF BENNY'S CELL PHONE AT THE TIME.
THAT GROSS FAT PERV OUGHTA BE IN JAIL! NO WAY THAT GIRL IS GOING BACK TO HIM.
AWFULLY PRESUMPTUOUS OF YOU TO JUDGE HIM, TUESDAY, WOULDN'T YOU SAY?
HE RISKED LIFE AND LIMB THIS MORNING TO SAVE A FEW LIVES WHILE YOU WERE RUNNING AWAY.
I WAS SAVING SOMEONE, TOO.
UT YOU'RE NO ERENT FROM OLD NNY. AMERICANS SO DEATHLY DULL.
YOU PURCHASE SELF-RIGHTEOUSNESS IN SHOPPING MALLS, YOUR VALUES AS TRIVIAL AS YOUR INSIPID POPULAR CULTURE.
YOU INFLICT YOURSELVES ON AN INNOCENT COUNTRY LIKE THIS ONE.
POPULAR CULTURE?! WE'RE TALKING ABOUT SEXUAL EXPLOITATION!
YOU TRULY BELIEVE THERE'S A DIFFERENCE FOR YOU AMERICANS?
I'M TRYING TO HELP. I'M NOT EXPLOITING ANYBODY.
I SEE. MY APOLOGIES, MADAME.
WHY AGAIN DID LITTLE TAENG PHONE THE VERY MAN, WHO, AS YOU SAY, EXPLOITS HER?
SAY SOMETHING, FOR CHRISSAKES! DON'T YOU THINK OF ANYTHING, MARZ?
I THINK BANGKOK HAS AN AWESOME SUNSET.
AND I THINK THERE'S NOTHING INNOCENT ABOUT THAILAND.

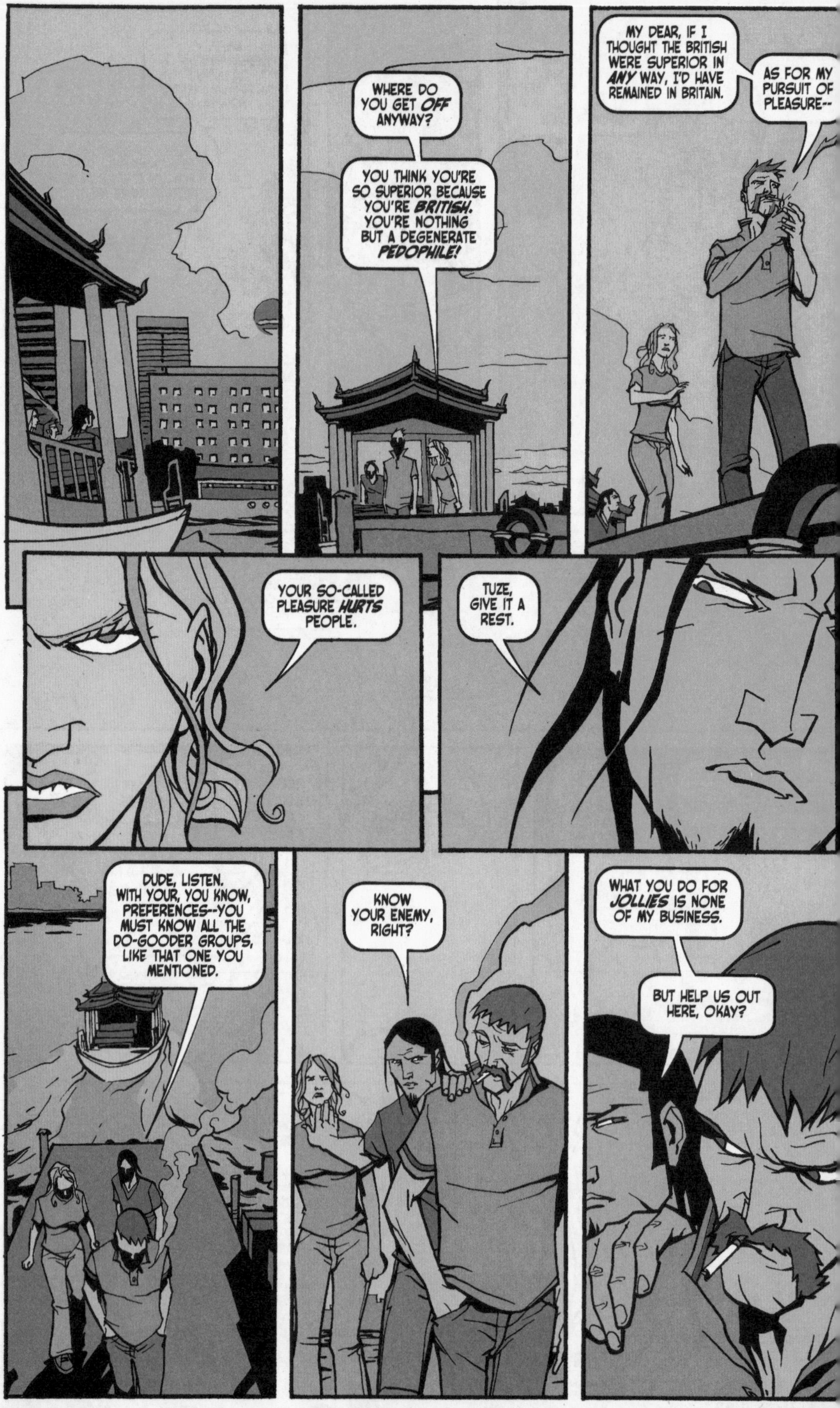
WHERE DO YOU GET OFF ANYWAY?
YOU THINK YOU'RE SO SUPERIOR BECAUSE YOU'RE BRITISH. YOU'RE NOTHING BUT A DEGENERATE PEDOPHILE!
MY DEAR, IF I THOUGHT THE BRITISH WERE SUPERIOR IN ANY WAY, I'D HAVE REMAINED IN BRITAIN.
AS FOR MY PURSUIT OF PLEASURE--
YOUR SO-CALLED PLEASURE HURTS PEOPLE.
TUZE, GIVE IT A REST.
DUDE, LISTEN. WITH YOUR, YOU KNOW, PREFERENCES--YOU MUST KNOW ALL THE DO-GOODER GROUPS, LIKE THAT ONE YOU MENTIONED.
KNOW YOUR ENEMY, RIGHT?
WHAT YOU DO FOR JOLLIES IS NONE OF MY BUSINESS.
BUT HELP US OUT HERE, OKAY?

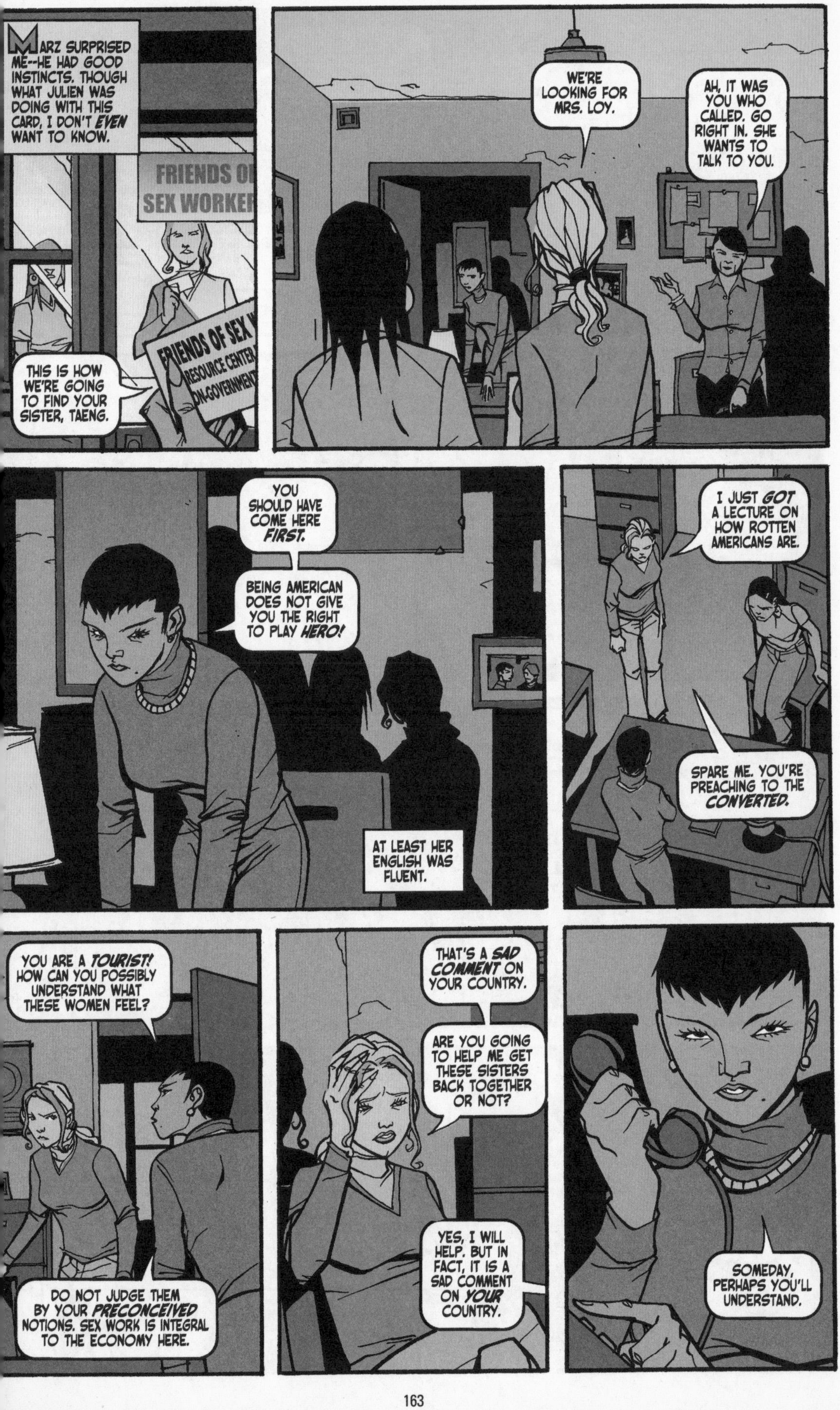

MARZ SURPRISED ME--HE HAD GOOD INSTINCTS. THOUGH WHAT JULIEN WAS DOING WITH THIS CARD, I DON'T *EVEN* WANT TO KNOW.
FRIENDS OF SEX WORKER
FRIENDS OF SEX
RESOURCE CENTER
THIS IS HOW WE'RE GOING TO FIND YOUR SISTER, TAENG.
WE'RE LOOKING FOR MRS. LOY.
AH, IT WAS YOU WHO CALLED. GO RIGHT IN. SHE WANTS TO TALK TO YOU.
YOU SHOULD HAVE COME HERE *FIRST.*
BEING AMERICAN DOES NOT GIVE YOU THE RIGHT TO PLAY *HERO!*
AT LEAST HER ENGLISH WAS FLUENT.
I JUST *GOT* A LECTURE ON HOW ROTTEN AMERICANS ARE.
SPARE ME. YOU'RE PREACHING TO THE *CONVERTED.*
YOU ARE A *TOURIST!* HOW CAN YOU POSSIBLY UNDERSTAND WHAT THESE WOMEN FEEL?
DO NOT JUDGE THEM BY YOUR *PRECONCEIVED* NOTIONS. SEX WORK IS INTEGRAL TO THE ECONOMY HERE.
THAT'S A *SAD COMMENT* ON YOUR COUNTRY.
ARE YOU GOING TO HELP ME GET THESE SISTERS BACK TOGETHER OR NOT?
YES, I WILL HELP. BUT IN FACT, IT IS A SAD COMMENT ON *YOUR* COUNTRY.
SOMEDAY, PERHAPS YOU'LL UNDERSTAND.

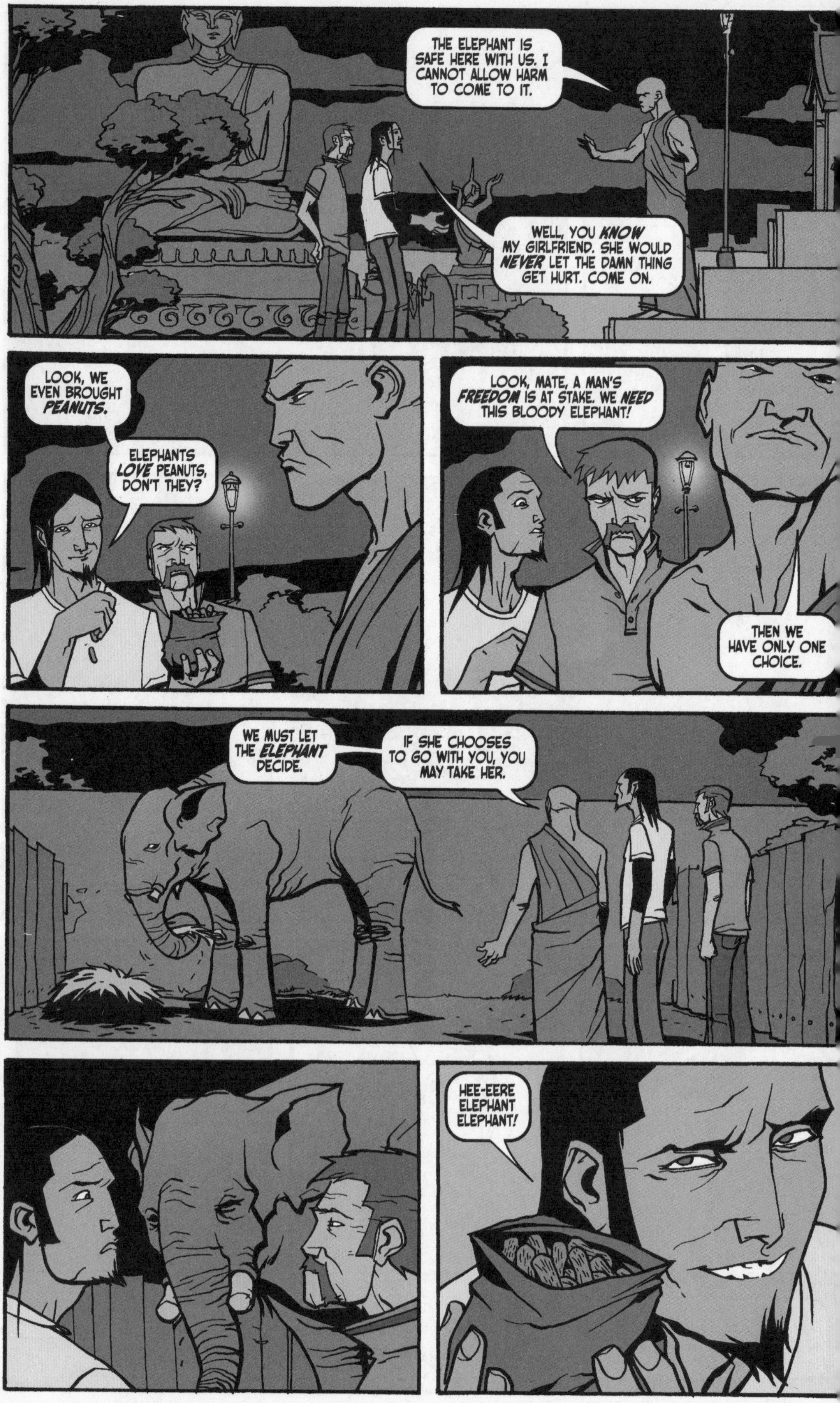
THE ELEPHANT IS SAFE HERE WITH US. I CANNOT ALLOW HARM TO COME TO IT.
WELL, YOU KNOW MY GIRLFRIEND. SHE WOULD NEVER LET THE DAMN THING GET HURT. COME ON.
LOOK, WE EVEN BROUGHT PEANUTS.
ELEPHANTS LOVE PEANUTS, DON'T THEY?
LOOK, MATE, A MAN'S FREEDOM IS AT STAKE. WE NEED THIS BLOODY ELEPHANT!
THEN WE HAVE ONLY ONE CHOICE.
WE MUST LET THE ELEPHANT DECIDE.
IF SHE CHOOSES TO GO WITH YOU, YOU MAY TAKE HER.
HEE-EERE ELEPHANT ELEPHANT!

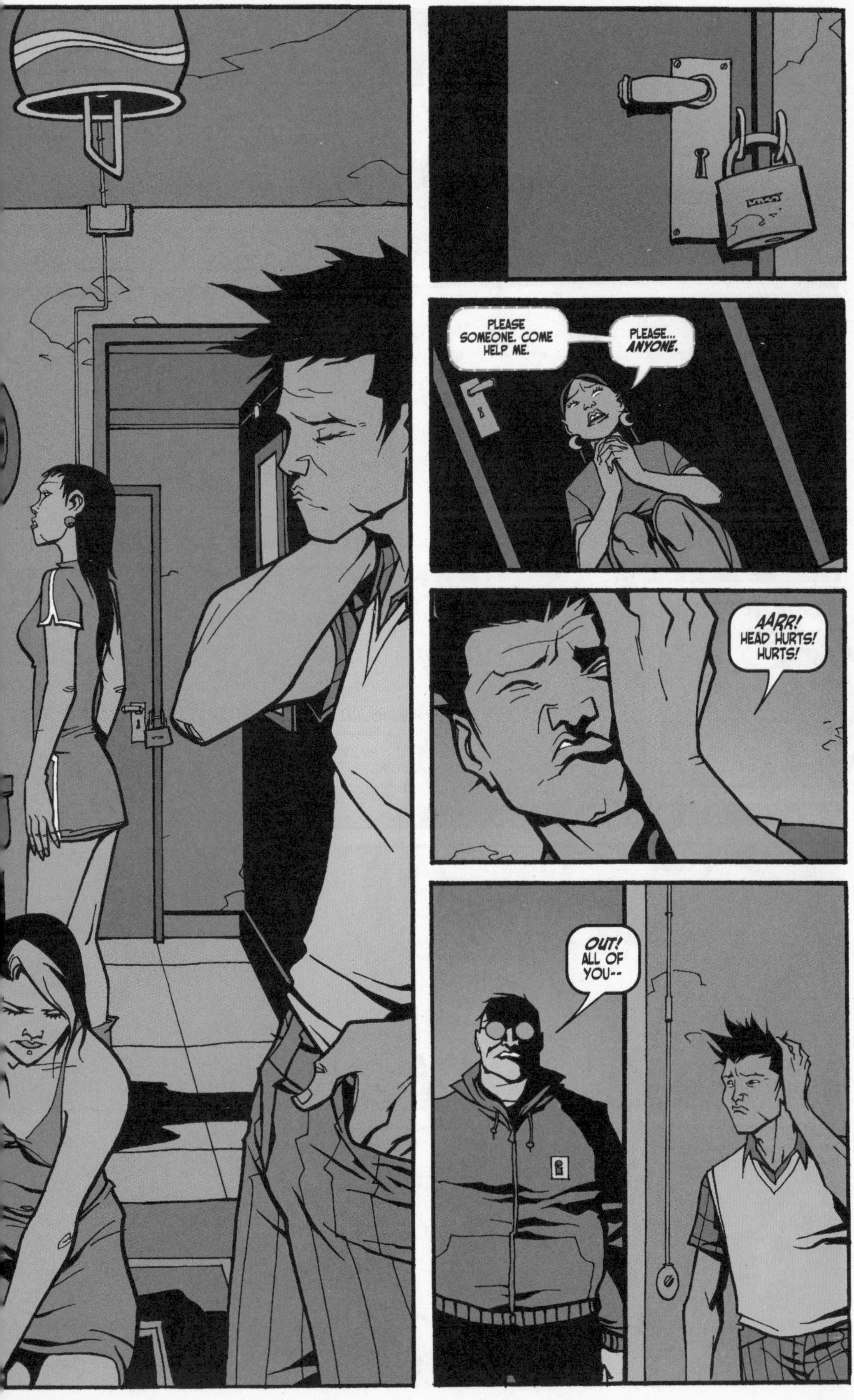
PLEASE SOMEONE. COME HELP ME.
PLEASE... ANYONE.
AARR! HEAD HURTS! HURTS!
OUT! ALL OF YOU--

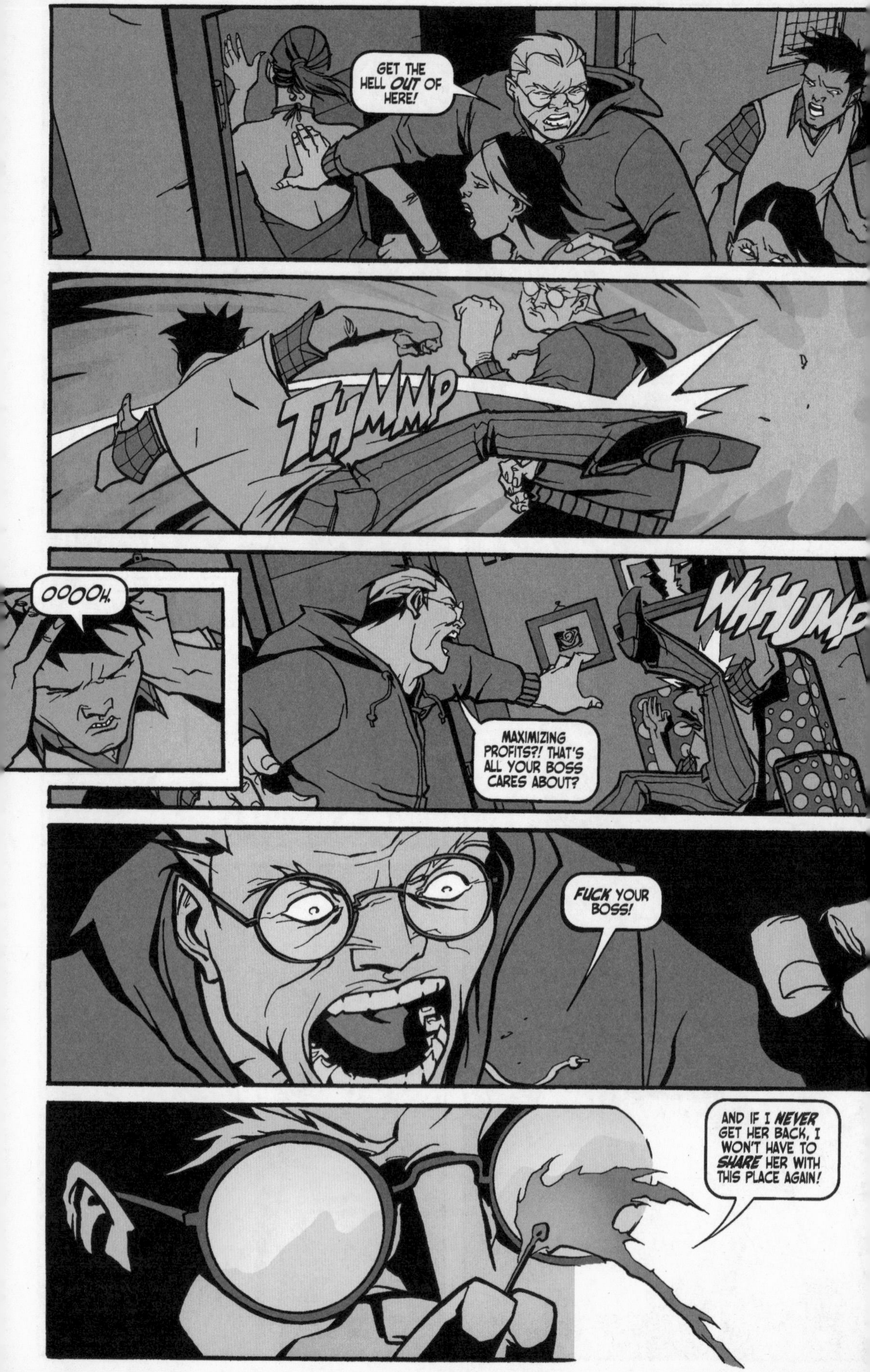
GET THE HELL OUT OF HERE!
THMMP
OOOOH.
WHHUMP
MAXIMIZING PROFITS?! THAT'S ALL YOUR BOSS CARES ABOUT?
FUCK YOUR BOSS!
AND IF I NEVER GET HER BACK, I WON'T HAVE TO SHARE HER WITH THIS PLACE AGAIN!

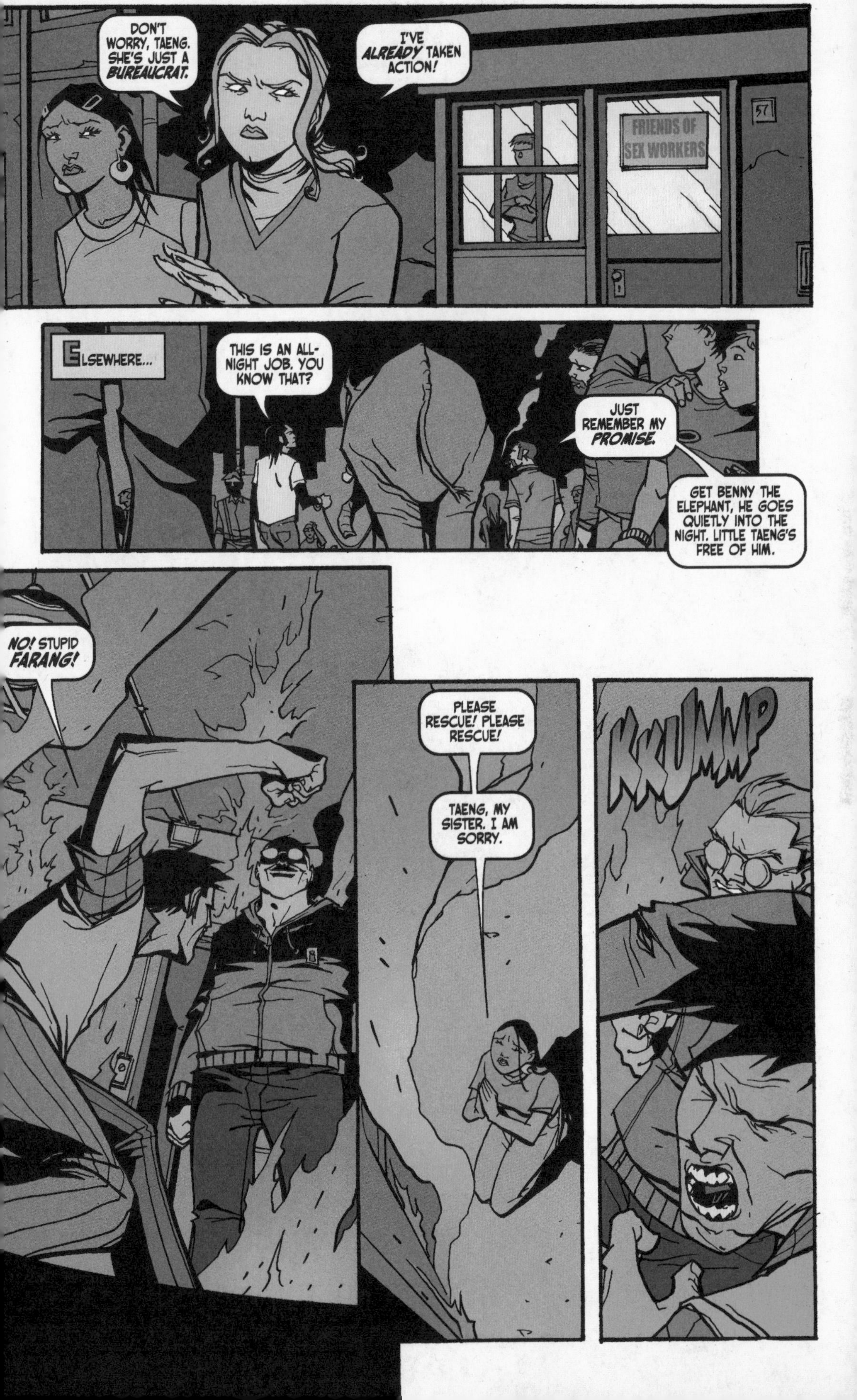

DON'T WORRY, TAENG. SHE'S JUST A BUREAUCRAT.
I'VE ALREADY TAKEN ACTION!
57
FRIENDS OF SEX WORKERS
ELSEWHERE...
THIS IS AN ALL-NIGHT JOB. YOU KNOW THAT?
JUST REMEMBER MY PROMISE.
GET BENNY THE ELEPHANT, HE GOES QUIETLY INTO THE NIGHT. LITTLE TAENG'S FREE OF HIM.
NO! STUPID FARANG!
PLEASE RESCUE! PLEASE RESCUE!
TAENG, MY SISTER. I AM SORRY.
KKUMMP

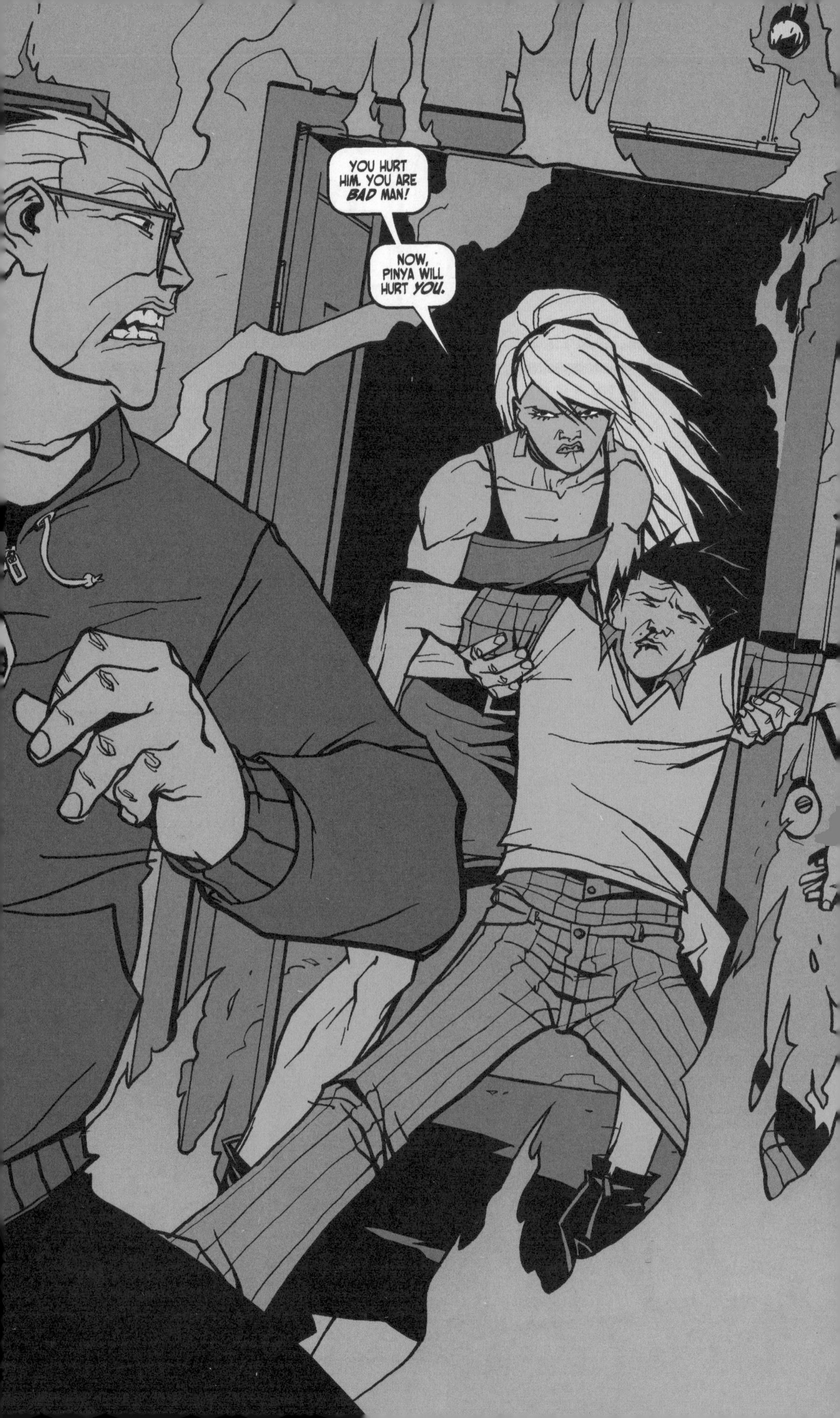
YOU HURT HIM. YOU ARE *BAD* MAN!
NOW, PINYA WILL HURT *YOU*.

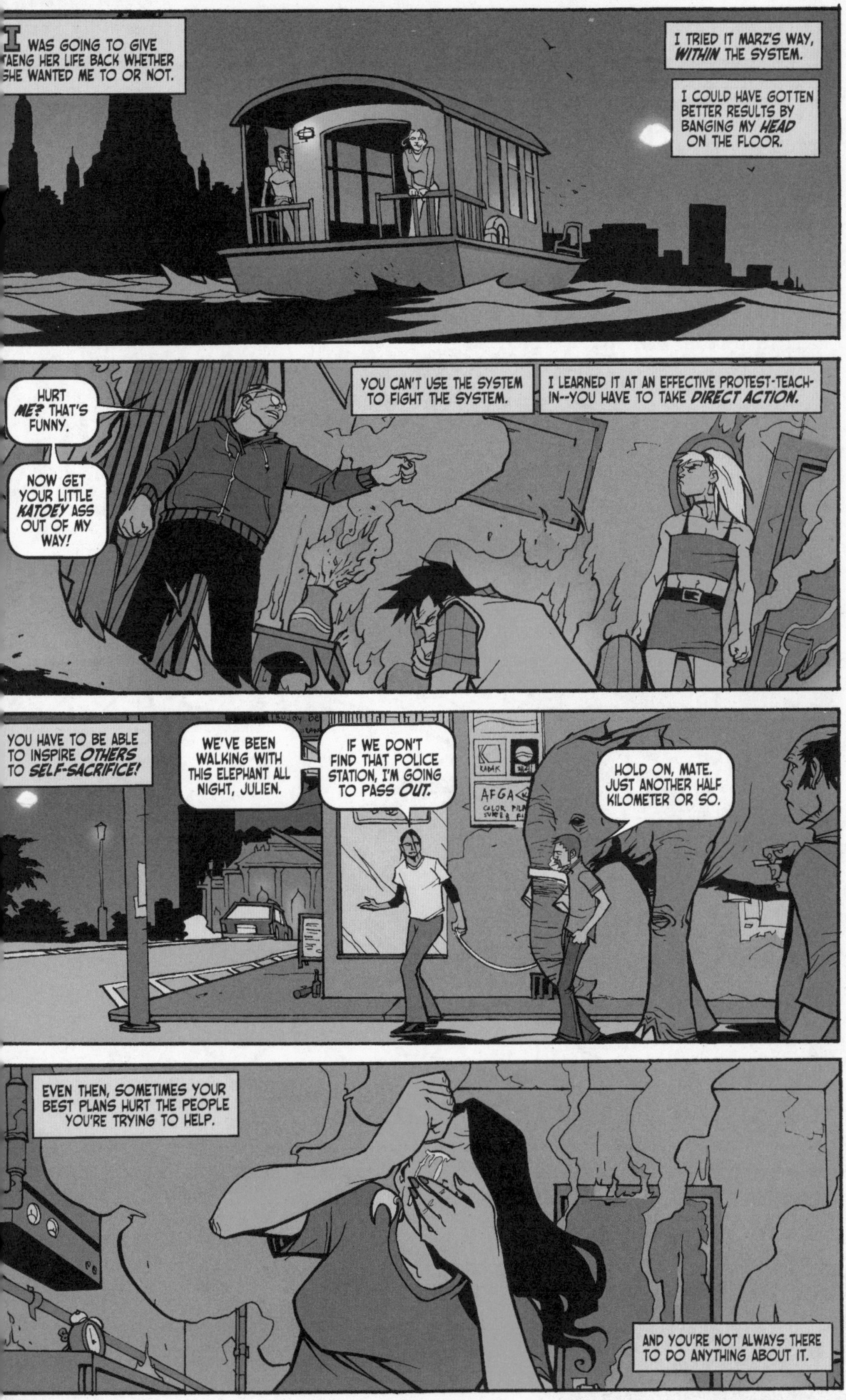
I WAS GOING TO GIVE TAENG HER LIFE BACK WHETHER SHE WANTED ME TO OR NOT.
I TRIED IT MARZ'S WAY, WITHIN THE SYSTEM.
I COULD HAVE GOTTEN BETTER RESULTS BY BANGING MY HEAD ON THE FLOOR.
HURT ME? THAT'S FUNNY.
NOW GET YOUR LITTLE KATOEY ASS OUT OF MY WAY!
YOU CAN'T USE THE SYSTEM TO FIGHT THE SYSTEM.
I LEARNED IT AT AN EFFECTIVE PROTEST-TEACH-IN--YOU HAVE TO TAKE DIRECT ACTION.
YOU HAVE TO BE ABLE TO INSPIRE OTHERS TO SELF-SACRIFICE!
WE'VE BEEN WALKING WITH THIS ELEPHANT ALL NIGHT, JULIEN.
IF WE DON'T FIND THAT POLICE STATION, I'M GOING TO PASS OUT.
HOLD ON, MATE. JUST ANOTHER HALF KILOMETER OR SO.
AFGA
EVEN THEN, SOMETIMES YOUR BEST PLANS HURT THE PEOPLE YOU'RE TRYING TO HELP.
AND YOU'RE NOT ALWAYS THERE TO DO ANYTHING ABOUT IT.

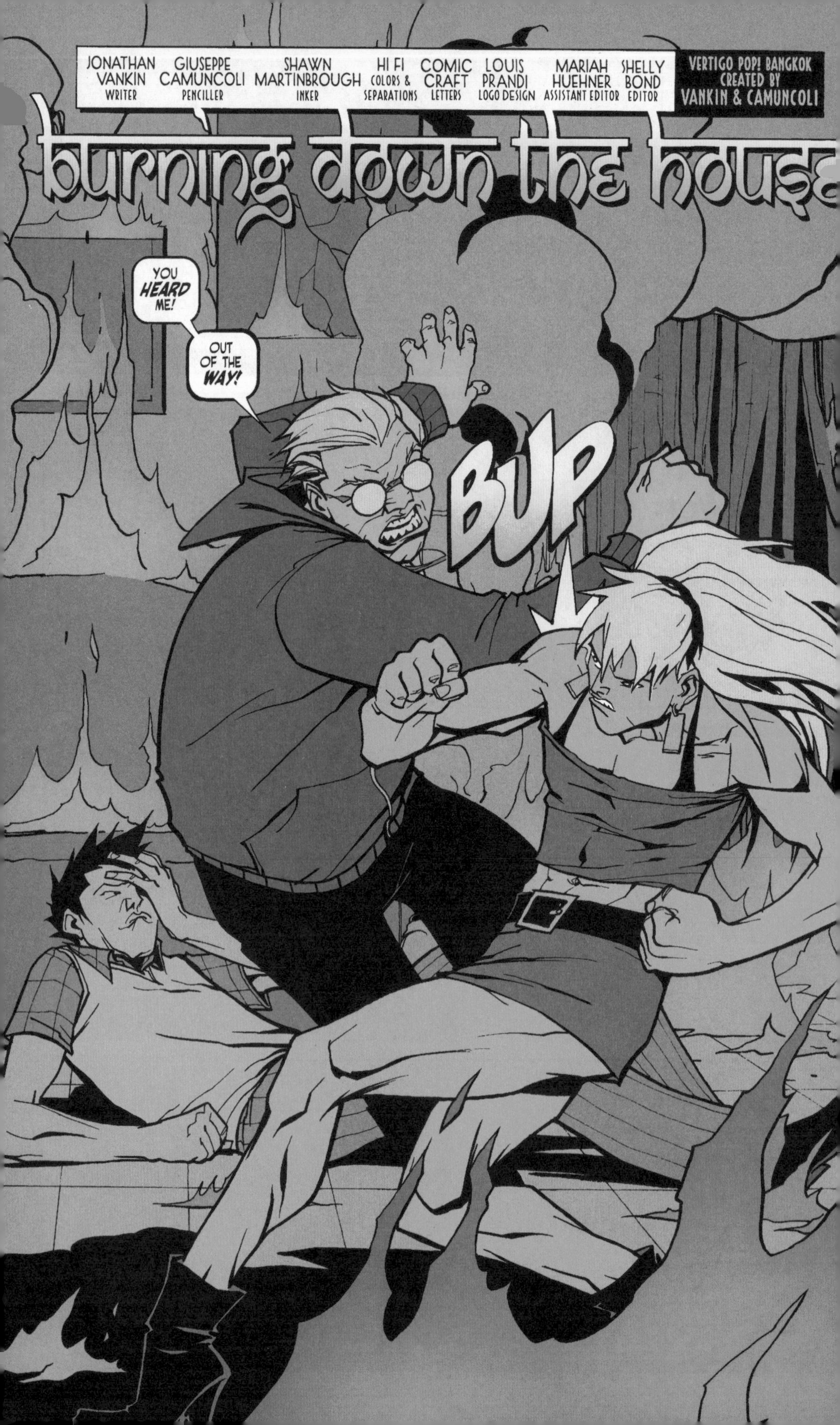
JONATHAN VANKIN WRITER
GIUSEPPE CAMUNCOLI PENCILLER
SHAWN MARTINBROUGH INKER
HI FI COLORS & SEPARATIONS
COMIC CRAFT LETTERS
LOUIS PRANDI LOGO DESIGN
MARIAH HUEHNER ASSISTANT EDITOR
SHELLY BOND EDITOR
VERTIGO POP! BANGKOK CREATED BY VANKIN & CAMUNCOLI
burning down the house
YOU HEARD ME!
OUT OF THE WAY!
BUP

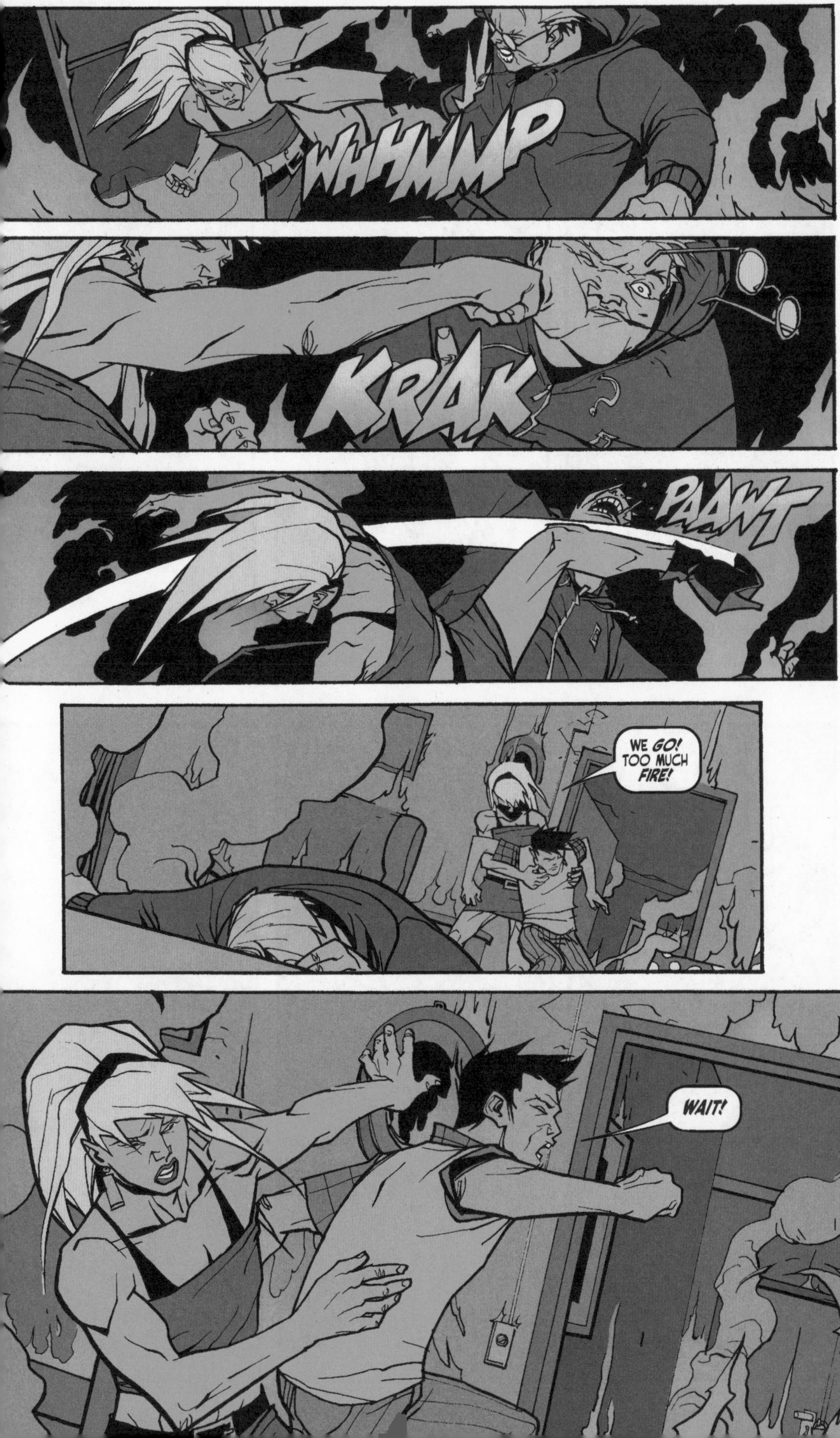
WHHMMP
KRAK
PAAWT
WE GO! TOO MUCH FIRE!
WAIT!

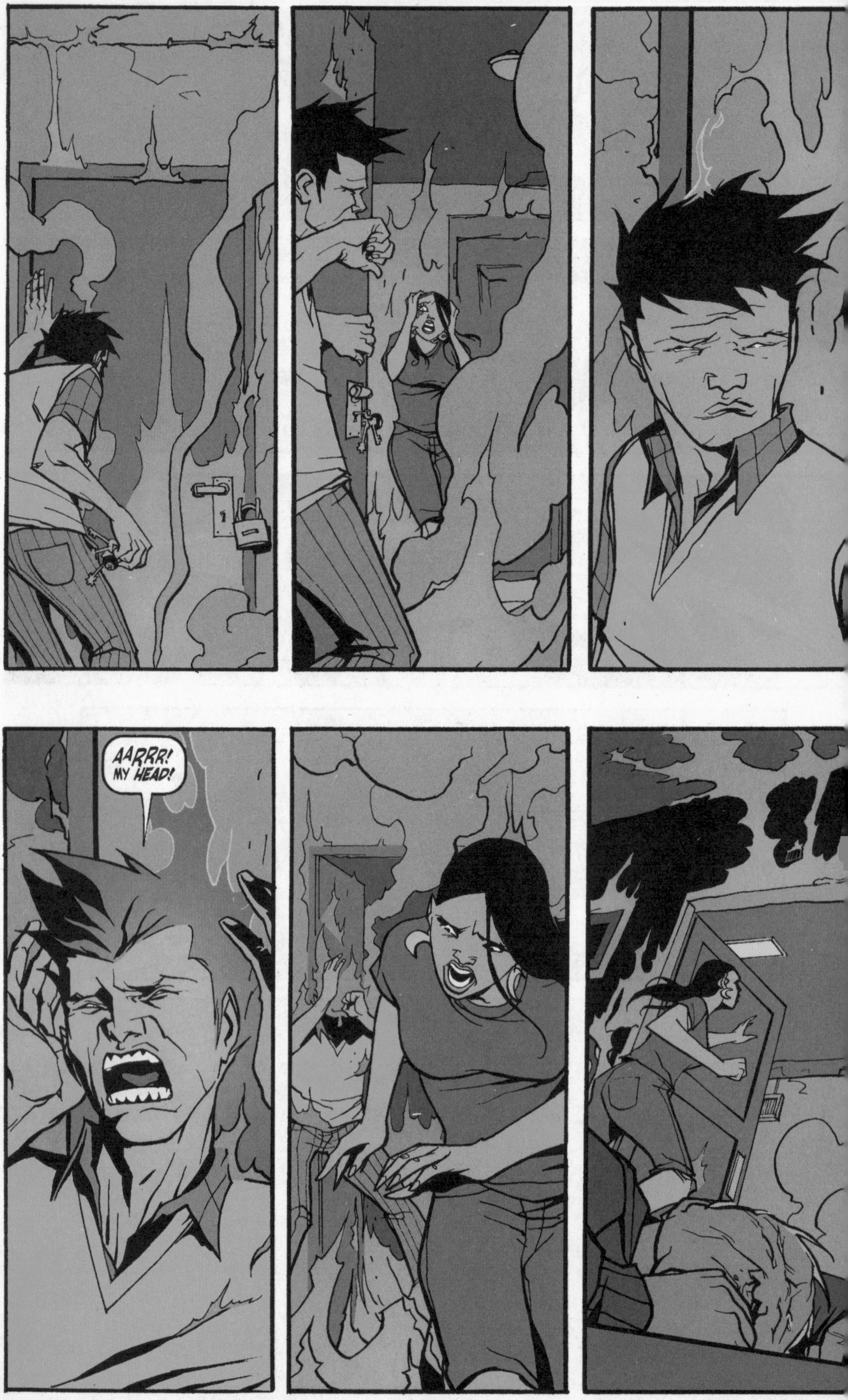
AARRR! MY HEAD!

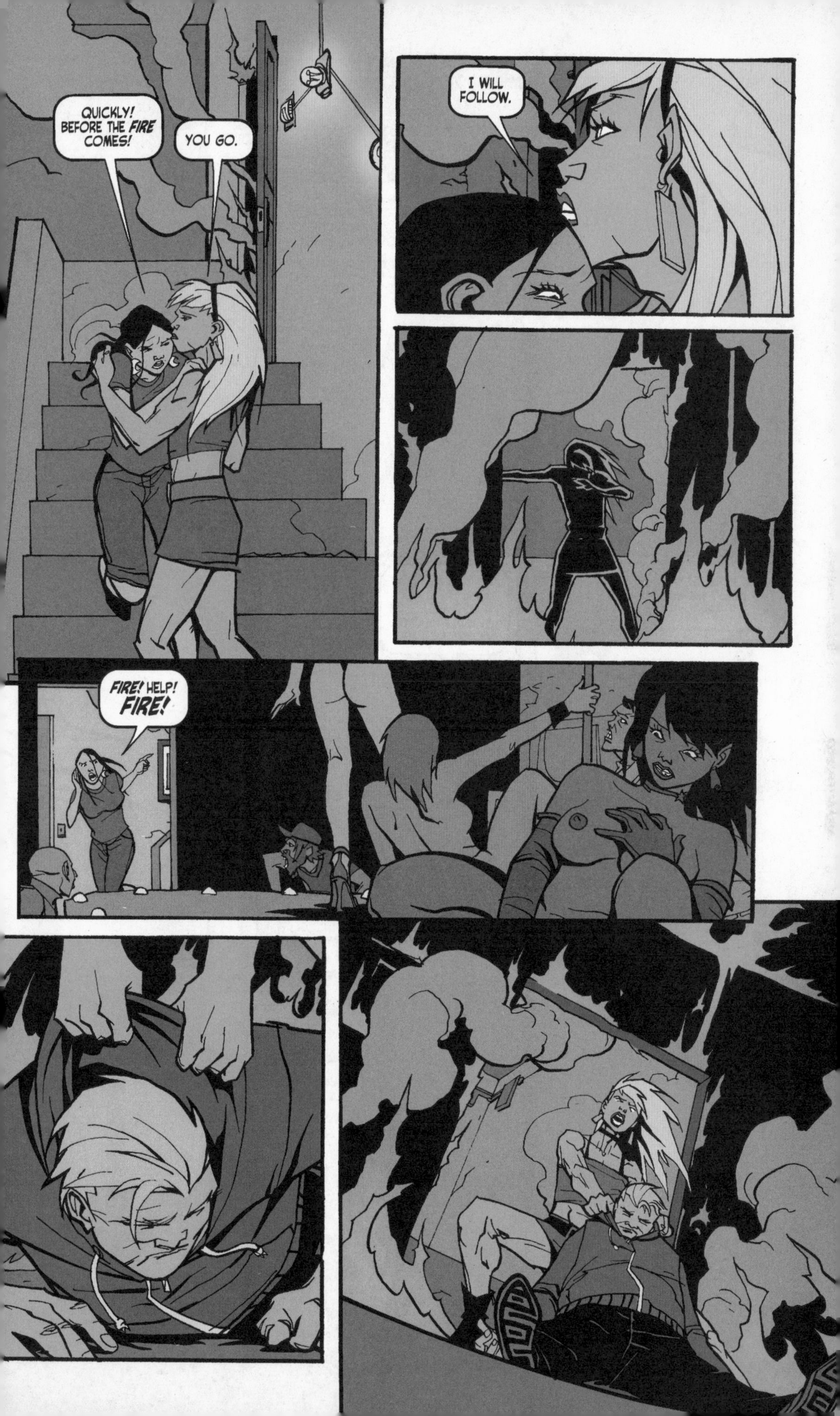
QUICKLY! BEFORE THE FIRE COMES!
YOU GO.
I WILL FOLLOW.
FIRE! HELP! FIRE!

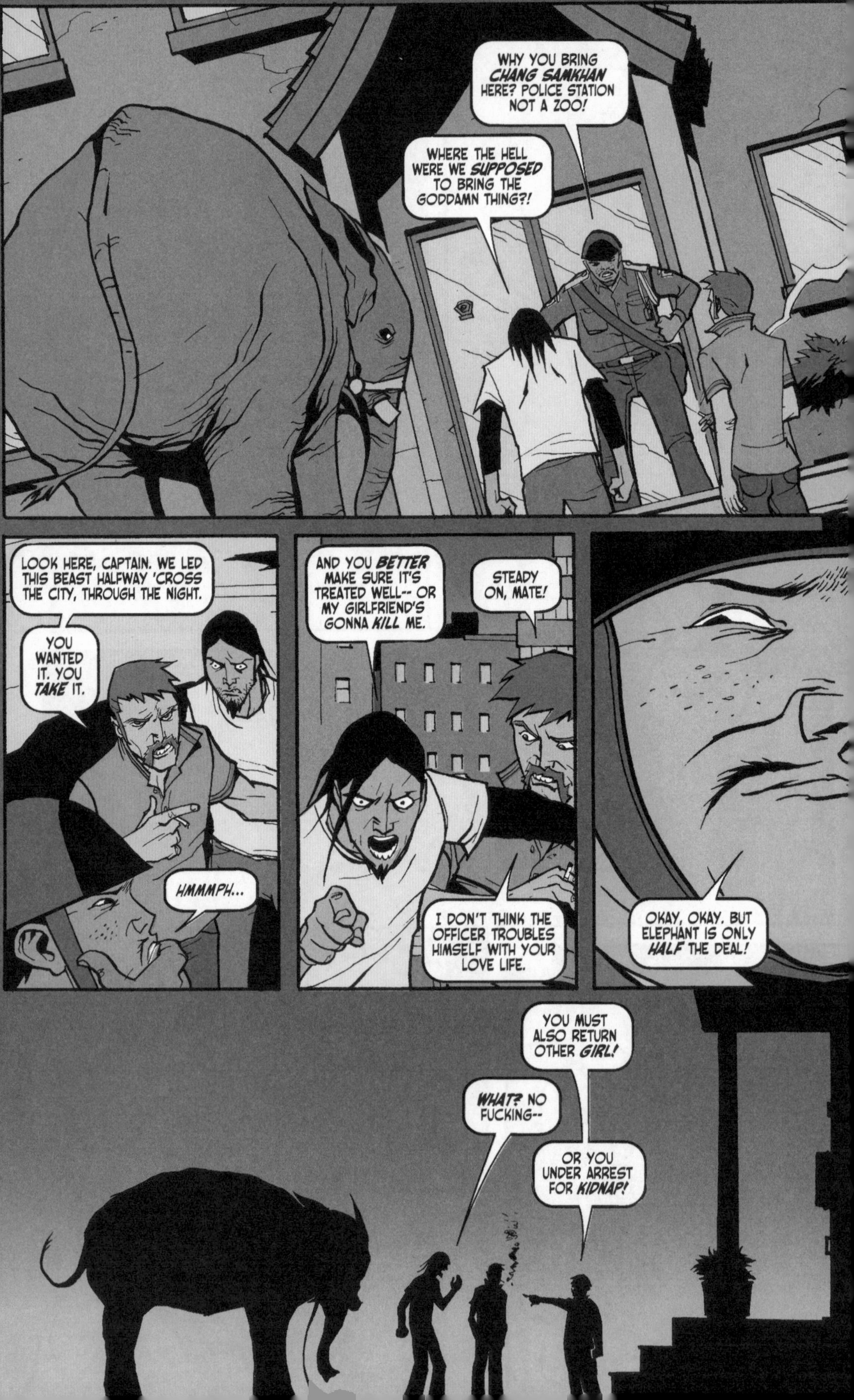
WHY YOU BRING CHANG SAMKHAN HERE? POLICE STATION NOT A ZOO!
WHERE THE HELL WERE WE SUPPOSED TO BRING THE GODDAMN THING?!
LOOK HERE, CAPTAIN. WE LED THIS BEAST HALFWAY 'CROSS THE CITY, THROUGH THE NIGHT.
YOU WANTED IT. YOU TAKE IT.
HMMMPH...
AND YOU BETTER MAKE SURE IT'S TREATED WELL-- OR MY GIRLFRIEND'S GONNA KILL ME.
STEADY ON, MATE!
I DON'T THINK THE OFFICER TROUBLES HIMSELF WITH YOUR LOVE LIFE.
OKAY, OKAY. BUT ELEPHANT IS ONLY HALF THE DEAL!
YOU MUST ALSO RETURN OTHER GIRL!
WHAT? NO FUCKING--
OR YOU UNDER ARREST FOR KIDNAP!

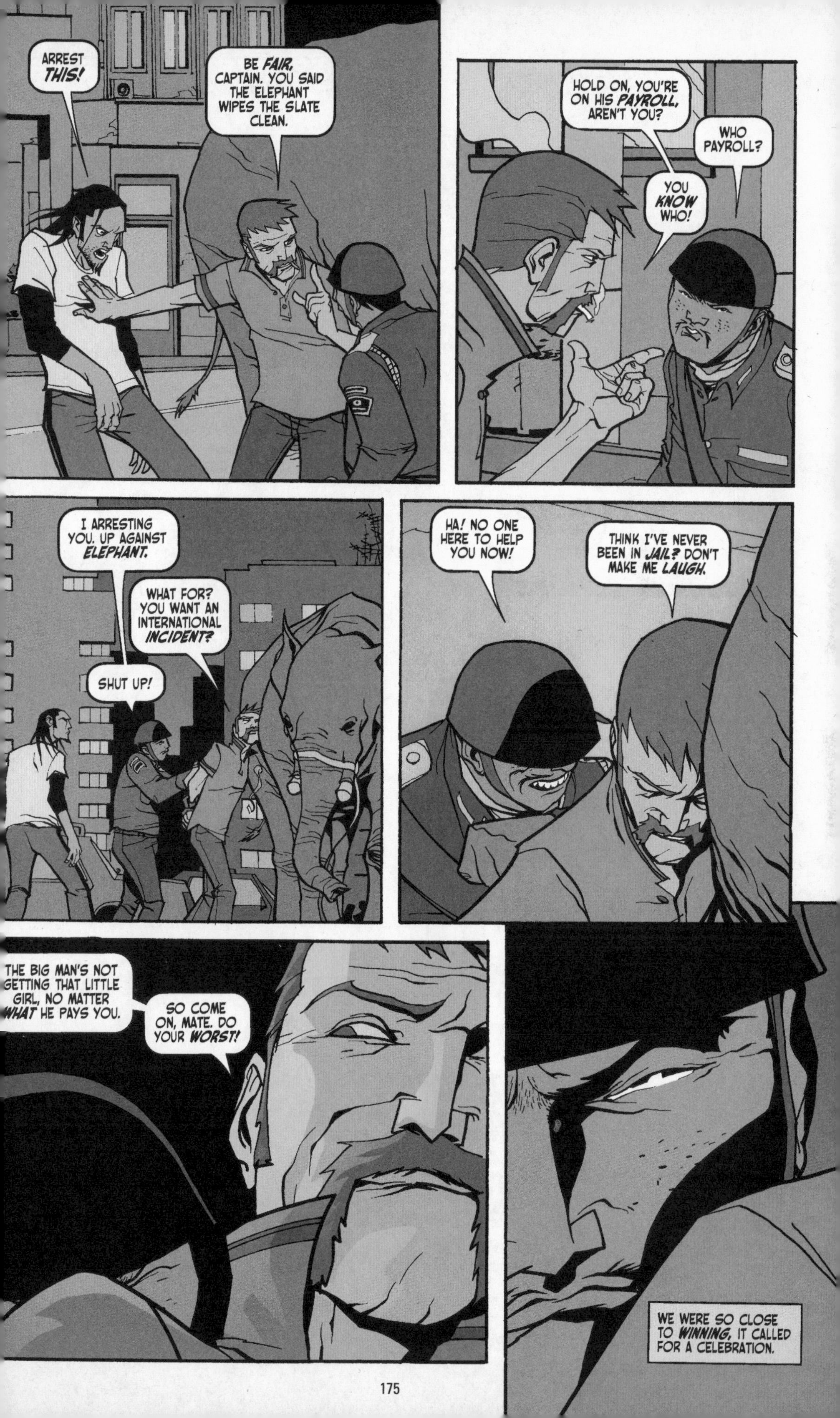
ARREST THIS!
BE FAIR, CAPTAIN. YOU SAID THE ELEPHANT WIPES THE SLATE CLEAN.
HOLD ON, YOU'RE ON HIS PAYROLL, AREN'T YOU?
WHO PAYROLL?
YOU KNOW WHO!
I ARRESTING YOU. UP AGAINST ELEPHANT.
WHAT FOR? YOU WANT AN INTERNATIONAL INCIDENT?
SHUT UP!
HA! NO ONE HERE TO HELP YOU NOW!
THINK I'VE NEVER BEEN IN JAIL? DON'T MAKE ME LAUGH.
THE BIG MAN'S NOT GETTING THAT LITTLE GIRL, NO MATTER WHAT HE PAYS YOU.
SO COME ON, MATE. DO YOUR WORST!
WE WERE SO CLOSE TO WINNING, IT CALLED FOR A CELEBRATION.

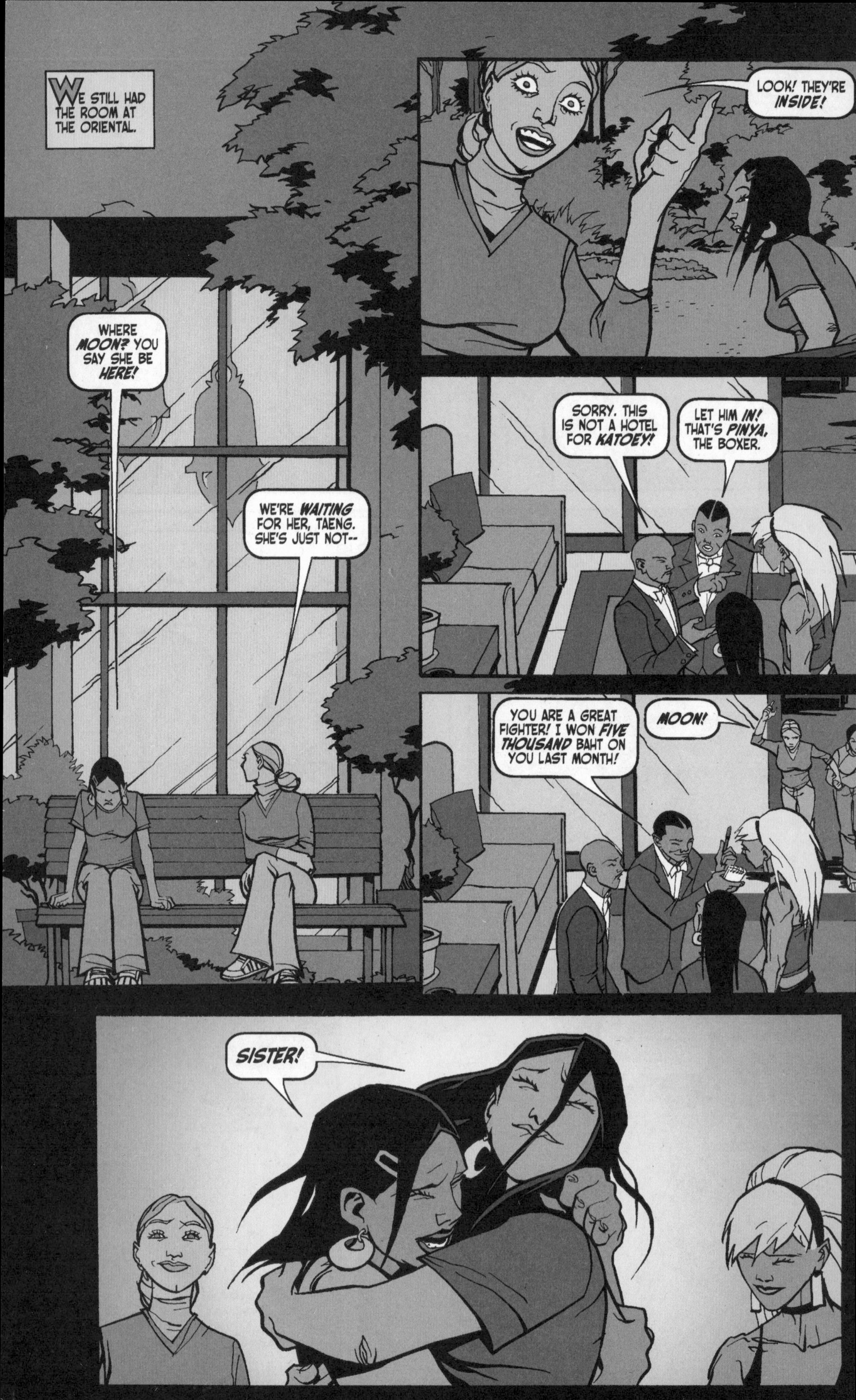
WE STILL HAD THE ROOM AT THE ORIENTAL.
LOOK! THEY'RE INSIDE!
WHERE MOON? YOU SAY SHE BE HERE!
WE'RE WAITING FOR HER, TAENG. SHE'S JUST NOT--
SORRY. THIS IS NOT A HOTEL FOR KATOEY!
LET HIM IN! THAT'S PINYA, THE BOXER.
YOU ARE A GREAT FIGHTER! I WON FIVE THOUSAND BAHT ON YOU LAST MONTH!
MOON!
SISTER!

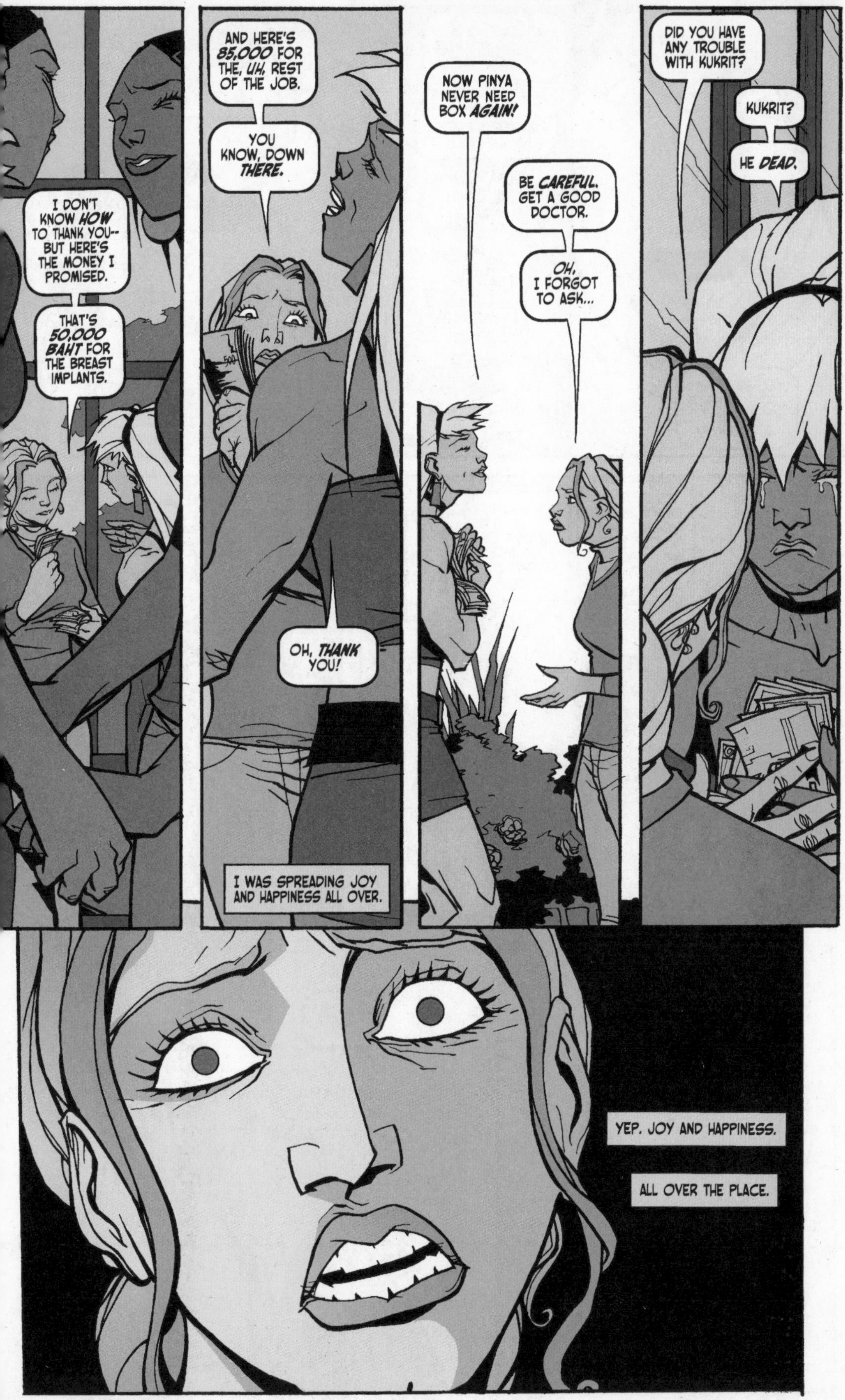
I DON'T KNOW HOW TO THANK YOU-- BUT HERE'S THE MONEY I PROMISED.
THAT'S 50,000 BAHT FOR THE BREAST IMPLANTS.
AND HERE'S 85,000 FOR THE, UH, REST OF THE JOB.
YOU KNOW, DOWN THERE.
OH, THANK YOU!
I WAS SPREADING JOY AND HAPPINESS ALL OVER.
NOW PINYA NEVER NEED BOX AGAIN!
BE CAREFUL. GET A GOOD DOCTOR.
OH, I FORGOT TO ASK...
DID YOU HAVE ANY TROUBLE WITH KUKRIT?
KUKRIT?
HE DEAD.
YEP. JOY AND HAPPINESS.
ALL OVER THE PLACE.

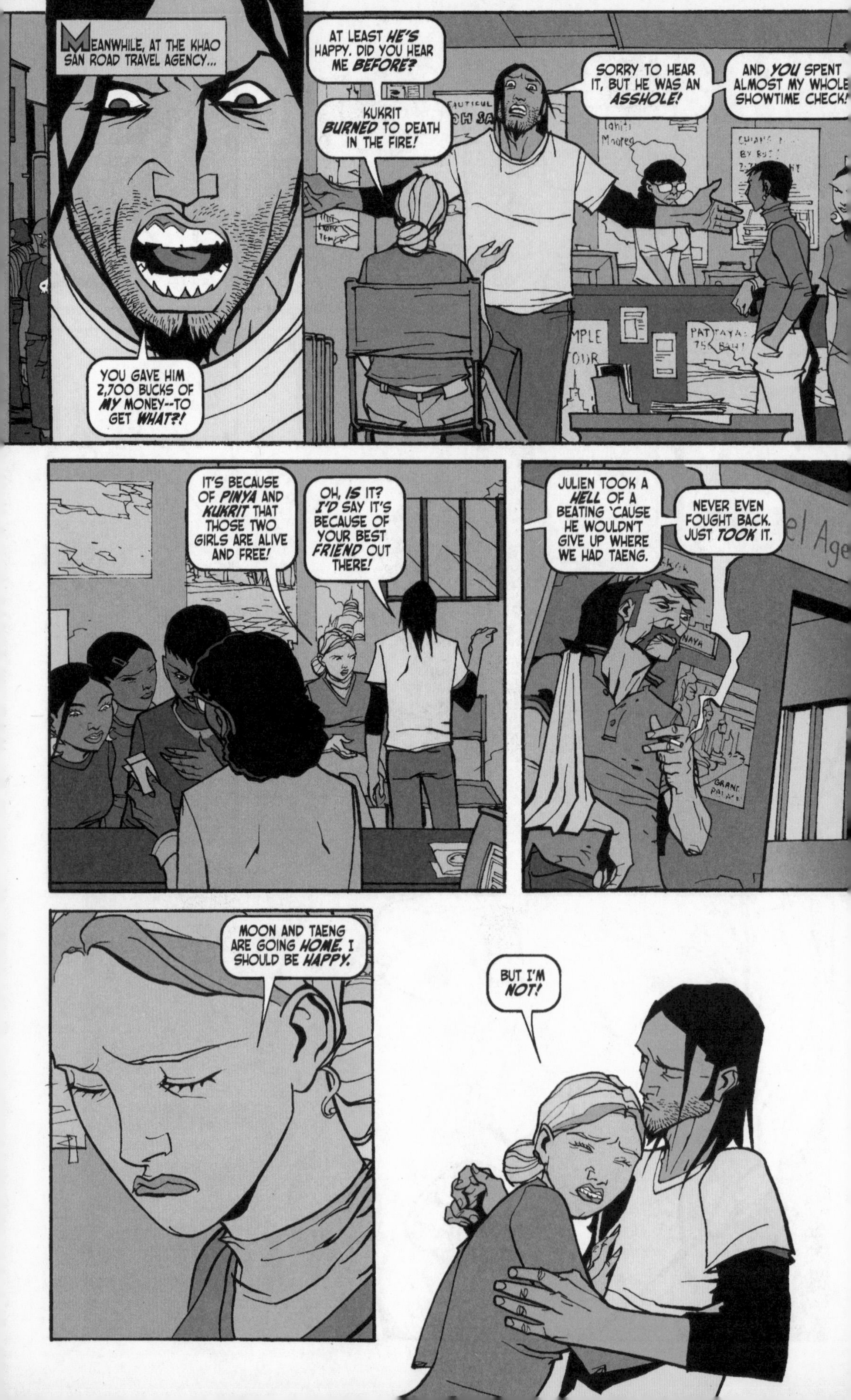
MEANWHILE, AT THE KHAO SAN ROAD TRAVEL AGENCY...
YOU GAVE HIM 2,700 BUCKS OF MY MONEY--TO GET WHAT?!
AT LEAST HE'S HAPPY. DID YOU HEAR ME BEFORE?
KUKRIT BURNED TO DEATH IN THE FIRE!
SORRY TO HEAR IT, BUT HE WAS AN ASSHOLE!
AND YOU SPENT ALMOST MY WHOLE SHOWTIME CHECK!
IT'S BECAUSE OF PINYA AND KUKRIT THAT THOSE TWO GIRLS ARE ALIVE AND FREE!
OH, IS IT? I'D SAY IT'S BECAUSE OF YOUR BEST FRIEND OUT THERE!
JULIEN TOOK A HELL OF A BEATING 'CAUSE HE WOULDN'T GIVE UP WHERE WE HAD TAENG.
NEVER EVEN FOUGHT BACK. JUST TOOK IT.
MOON AND TAENG ARE GOING HOME. I SHOULD BE HAPPY.
BUT I'M NOT!

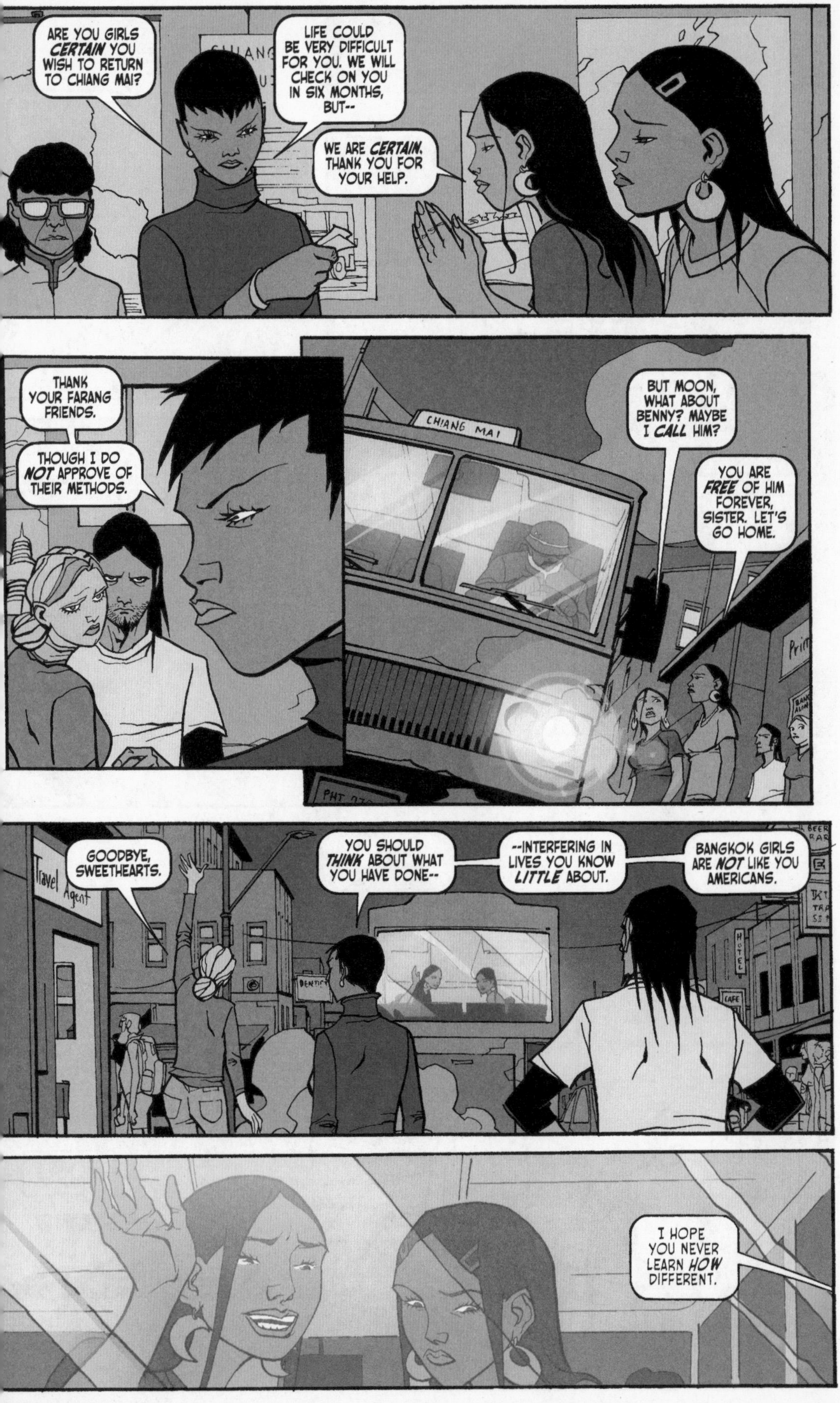

ARE YOU GIRLS CERTAIN YOU WISH TO RETURN TO CHIANG MAI?
LIFE COULD BE VERY DIFFICULT FOR YOU. WE WILL CHECK ON YOU IN SIX MONTHS, BUT--
WE ARE CERTAIN. THANK YOU FOR YOUR HELP.
THANK YOUR FARANG FRIENDS.
THOUGH I DO NOT APPROVE OF THEIR METHODS.
CHIANG MAI
BUT MOON, WHAT ABOUT BENNY? MAYBE I CALL HIM?
YOU ARE FREE OF HIM FOREVER, SISTER. LET'S GO HOME.
Travel Agent
GOODBYE, SWEETHEARTS.
YOU SHOULD THINK ABOUT WHAT YOU HAVE DONE--
--INTERFERING IN LIVES YOU KNOW LITTLE ABOUT.
BANGKOK GIRLS ARE NOT LIKE YOU AMERICANS.
HOTEL
CAFE
I HOPE YOU NEVER LEARN HOW DIFFERENT.

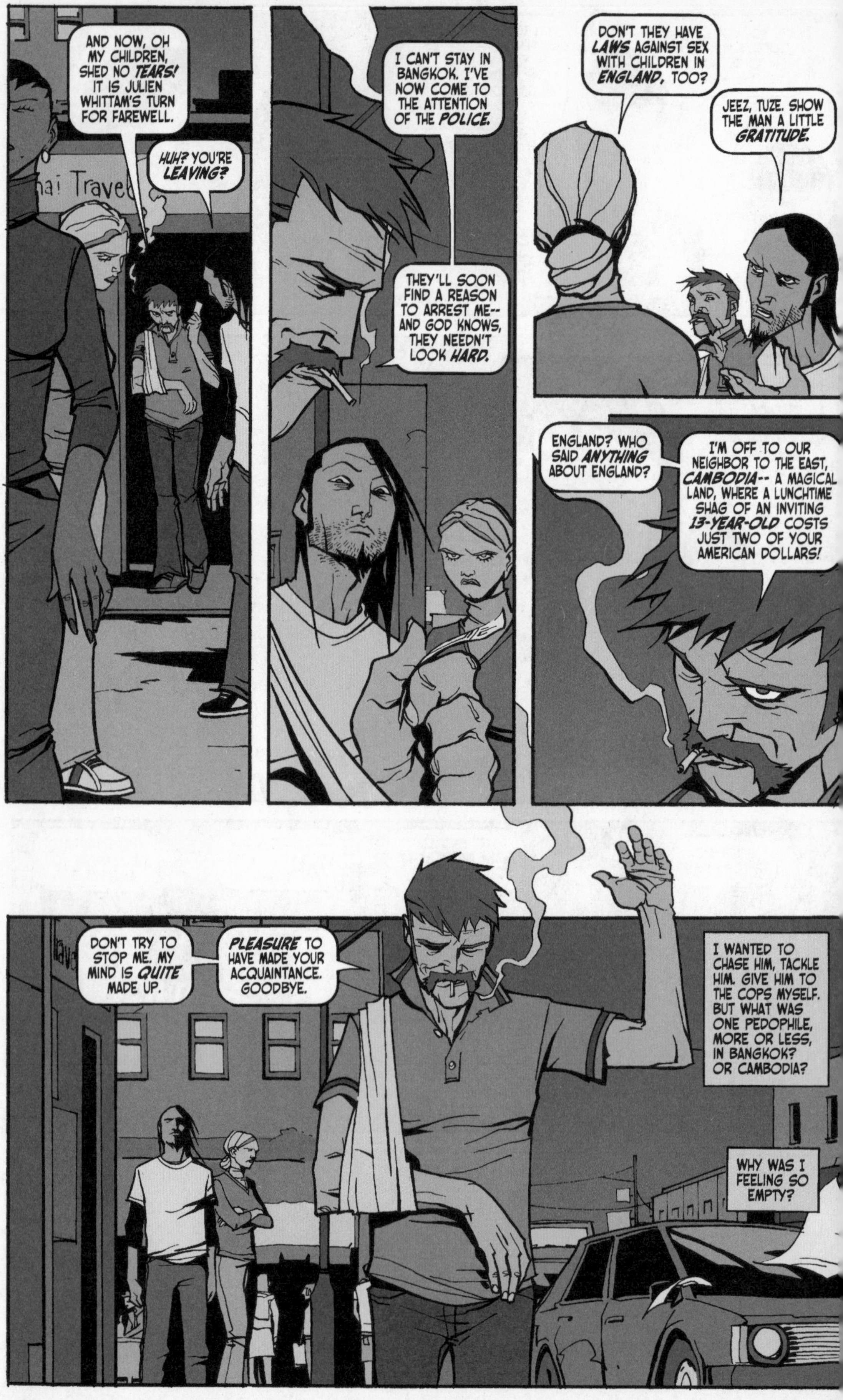
AND NOW, OH MY CHILDREN, SHED NO TEARS! IT IS JULIEN WHITTAM'S TURN FOR FAREWELL.
HUH? YOU'RE LEAVING?
I CAN'T STAY IN BANGKOK. I'VE NOW COME TO THE ATTENTION OF THE POLICE.
THEY'LL SOON FIND A REASON TO ARREST ME-- AND GOD KNOWS, THEY NEEDN'T LOOK HARD.
DON'T THEY HAVE LAWS AGAINST SEX WITH CHILDREN IN ENGLAND, TOO?
JEEZ, TUZE. SHOW THE MAN A LITTLE GRATITUDE.
ENGLAND? WHO SAID ANYTHING ABOUT ENGLAND?
I'M OFF TO OUR NEIGHBOR TO THE EAST, CAMBODIA-- A MAGICAL LAND, WHERE A LUNCHTIME SHAG OF AN INVITING 13-YEAR-OLD COSTS JUST TWO OF YOUR AMERICAN DOLLARS!
DON'T TRY TO STOP ME. MY MIND IS QUITE MADE UP.
PLEASURE TO HAVE MADE YOUR ACQUAINTANCE. GOODBYE.
I WANTED TO CHASE HIM, TACKLE HIM. GIVE HIM TO THE COPS MYSELF. BUT WHAT WAS ONE PEDOPHILE, MORE OR LESS, IN BANGKOK? OR CAMBODIA?
WHY WAS I FEELING SO EMPTY?

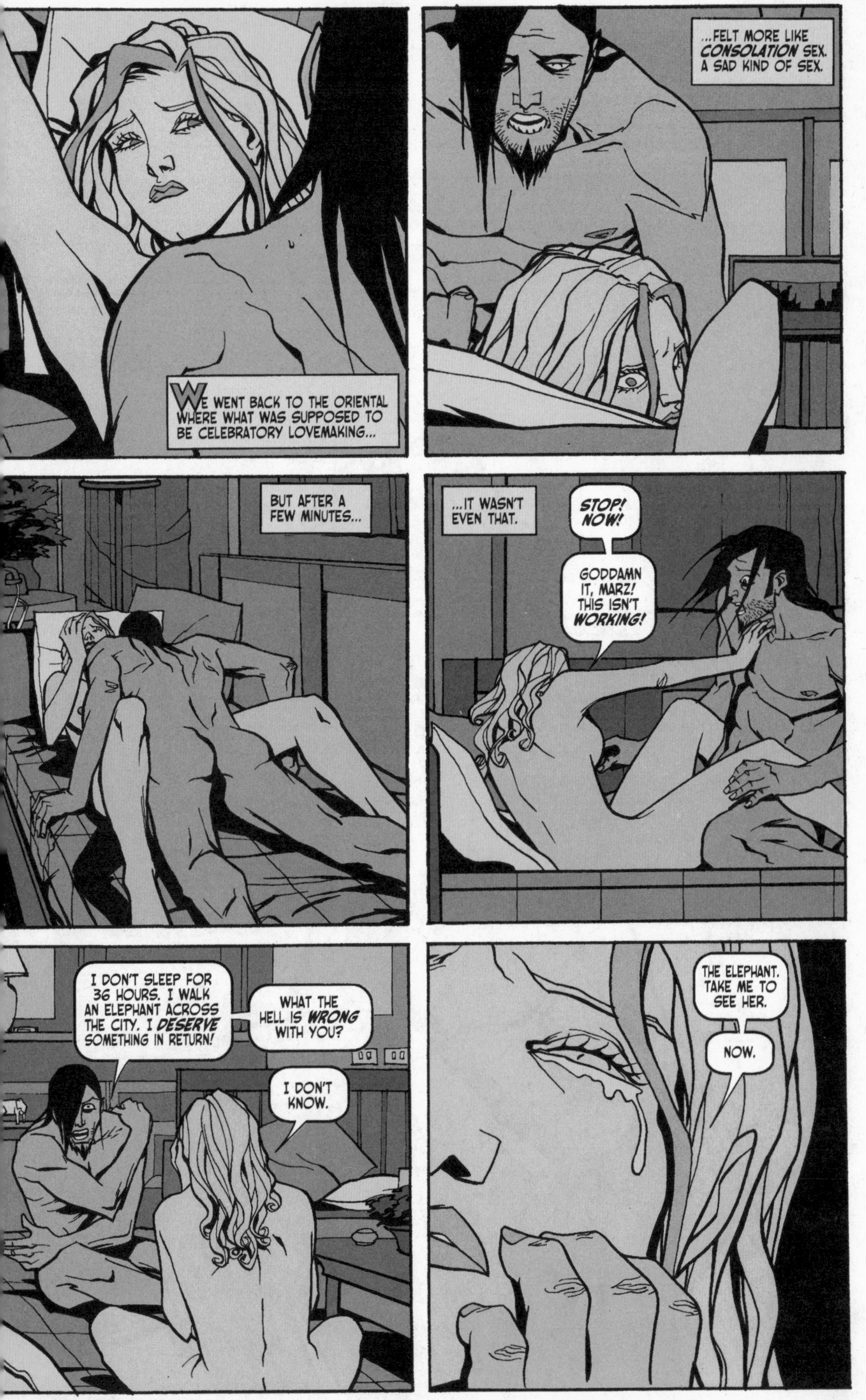

WE WENT BACK TO THE ORIENTAL WHERE WHAT WAS SUPPOSED TO BE CELEBRATORY LOVEMAKING...
...FELT MORE LIKE CONSOLATION SEX. A SAD KIND OF SEX.
BUT AFTER A FEW MINUTES...
...IT WASN'T EVEN THAT.
STOP! NOW!
GODDAMN IT, MARZ! THIS ISN'T WORKING!
I DON'T SLEEP FOR 36 HOURS. I WALK AN ELEPHANT ACROSS THE CITY. I DESERVE SOMETHING IN RETURN!
WHAT THE HELL IS WRONG WITH YOU?
I DON'T KNOW.
THE ELEPHANT. TAKE ME TO SEE HER.
NOW.

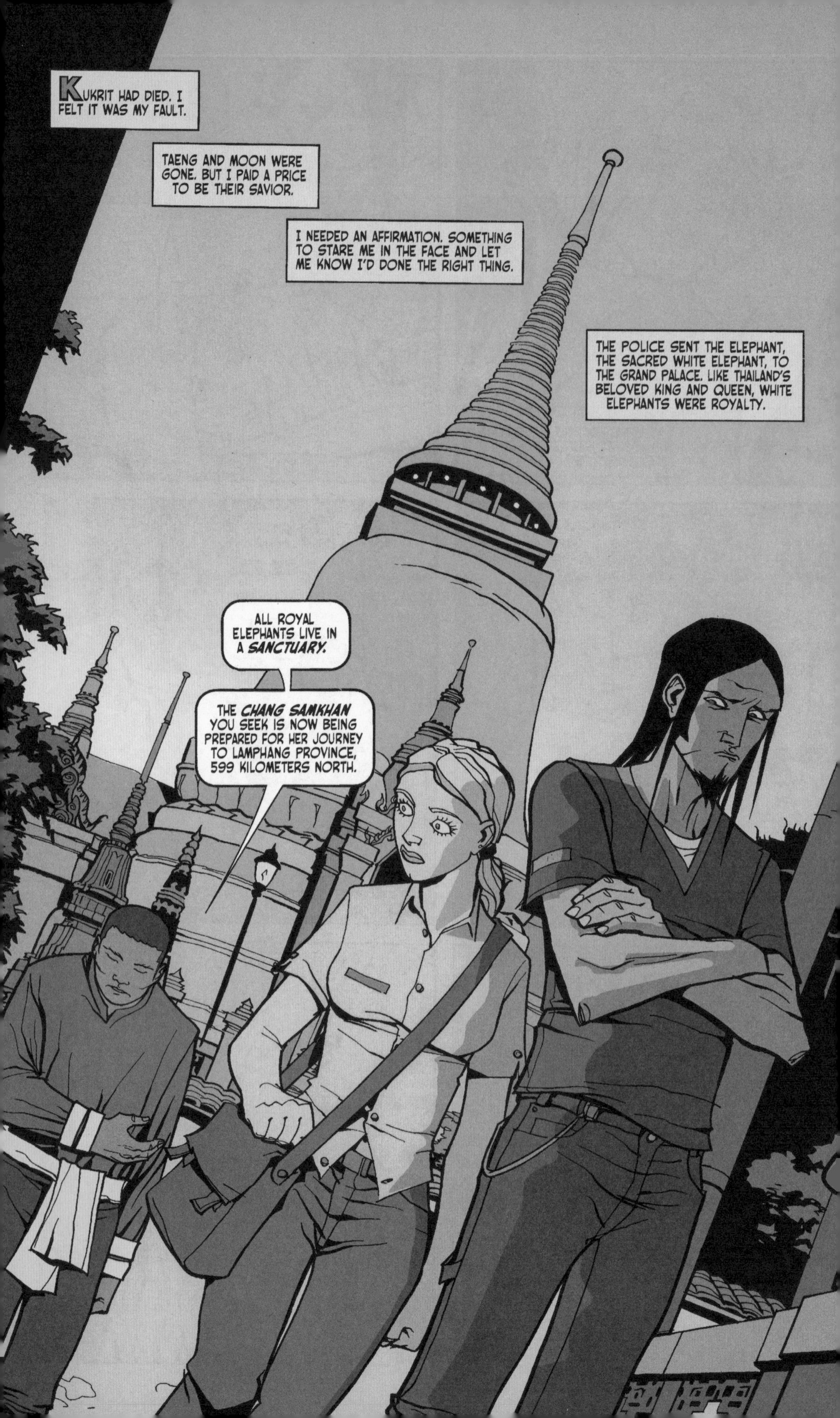

KUKRIT HAD DIED. I FELT IT WAS MY FAULT.
TAENG AND MOON WERE GONE. BUT I PAID A PRICE TO BE THEIR SAVIOR.
I NEEDED AN AFFIRMATION. SOMETHING TO STARE ME IN THE FACE AND LET ME KNOW I'D DONE THE RIGHT THING.
THE POLICE SENT THE ELEPHANT, THE SACRED WHITE ELEPHANT, TO THE GRAND PALACE. LIKE THAILAND'S BELOVED KING AND QUEEN, WHITE ELEPHANTS WERE ROYALTY.
ALL ROYAL ELEPHANTS LIVE IN A *SANCTUARY.*
THE *CHANG SAMKHAN* YOU SEEK IS NOW BEING PREPARED FOR HER JOURNEY TO LAMPHANG PROVINCE, 599 KILOMETERS NORTH.

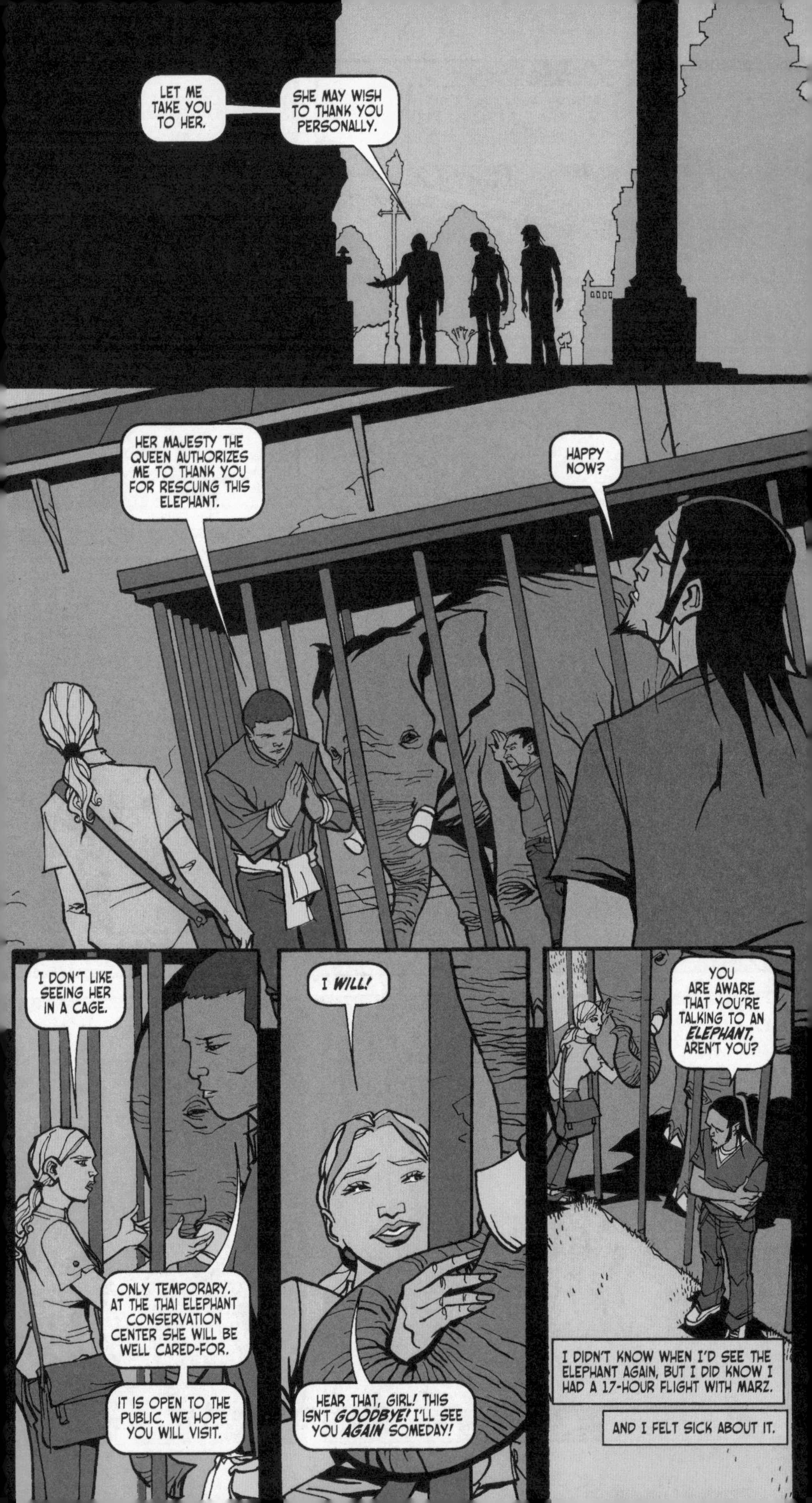

LET ME TAKE YOU TO HER.
SHE MAY WISH TO THANK YOU PERSONALLY.
HER MAJESTY THE QUEEN AUTHORIZES ME TO THANK YOU FOR RESCUING THIS ELEPHANT.
HAPPY NOW?
I DON'T LIKE SEEING HER IN A CAGE.
ONLY TEMPORARY. AT THE THAI ELEPHANT CONSERVATION CENTER SHE WILL BE WELL CARED-FOR.
IT IS OPEN TO THE PUBLIC. WE HOPE YOU WILL VISIT.
I *WILL!*
HEAR THAT, GIRL! THIS ISN'T *GOODBYE!* I'LL SEE YOU *AGAIN* SOMEDAY!
YOU ARE AWARE THAT YOU'RE TALKING TO AN *ELEPHANT,* AREN'T YOU?
I DIDN'T KNOW WHEN I'D SEE THE ELEPHANT AGAIN, BUT I DID KNOW I HAD A 17-HOUR FLIGHT WITH MARZ.
AND I FELT SICK ABOUT IT.

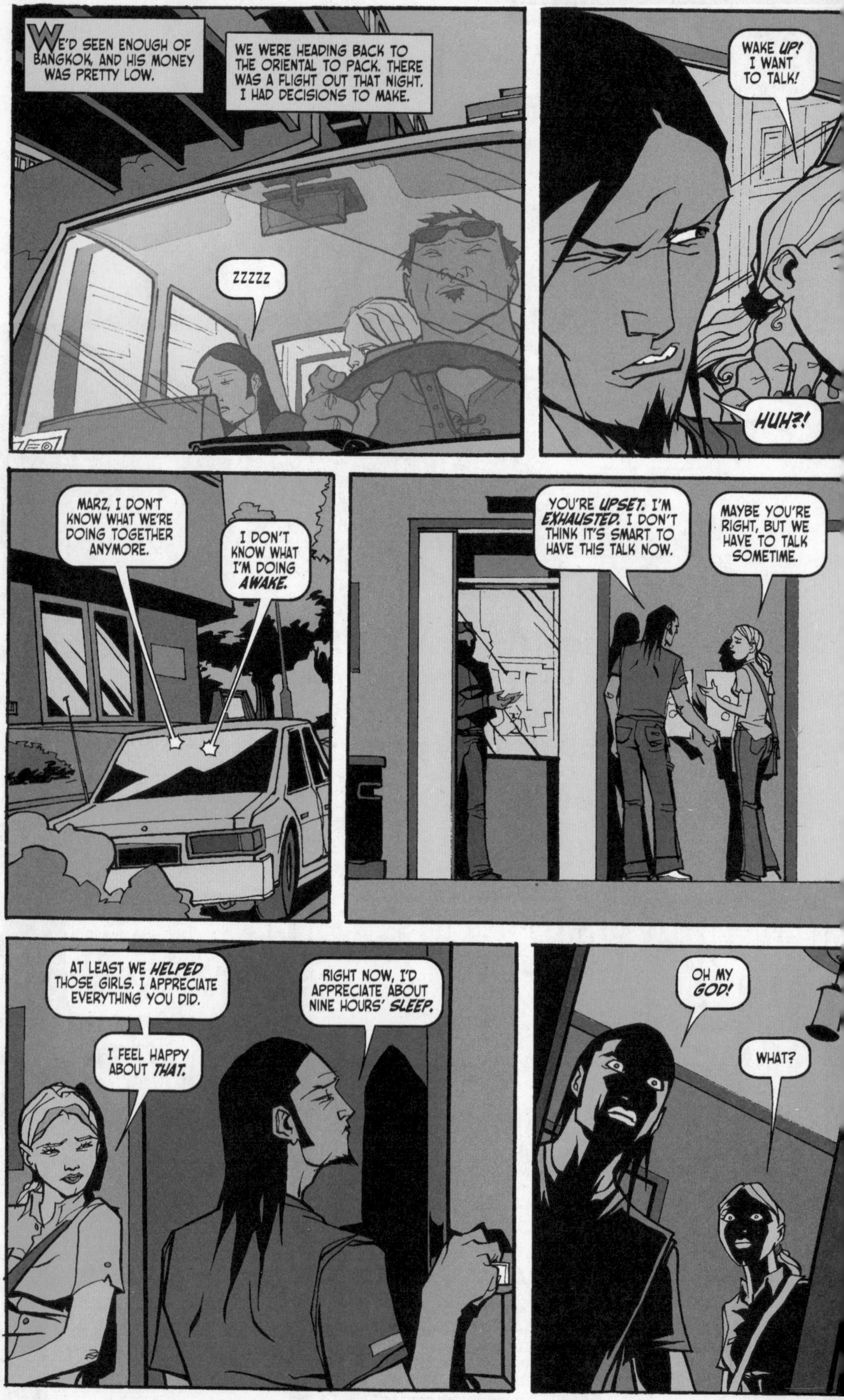

WE'D SEEN ENOUGH OF BANGKOK, AND HIS MONEY WAS PRETTY LOW.
WE WERE HEADING BACK TO THE ORIENTAL TO PACK. THERE WAS A FLIGHT OUT THAT NIGHT. I HAD DECISIONS TO MAKE.
ZZZZZ
WAKE UP! I WANT TO TALK!
HUH?!
MARZ, I DON'T KNOW WHAT WE'RE DOING TOGETHER ANYMORE.
I DON'T KNOW WHAT I'M DOING AWAKE.
YOU'RE UPSET. I'M EXHAUSTED. I DON'T THINK IT'S SMART TO HAVE THIS TALK NOW.
MAYBE YOU'RE RIGHT, BUT WE HAVE TO TALK SOMETIME.
AT LEAST WE HELPED THOSE GIRLS. I APPRECIATE EVERYTHING YOU DID.
I FEEL HAPPY ABOUT THAT.
RIGHT NOW, I'D APPRECIATE ABOUT NINE HOURS' SLEEP.
OH MY GOD!
WHAT?

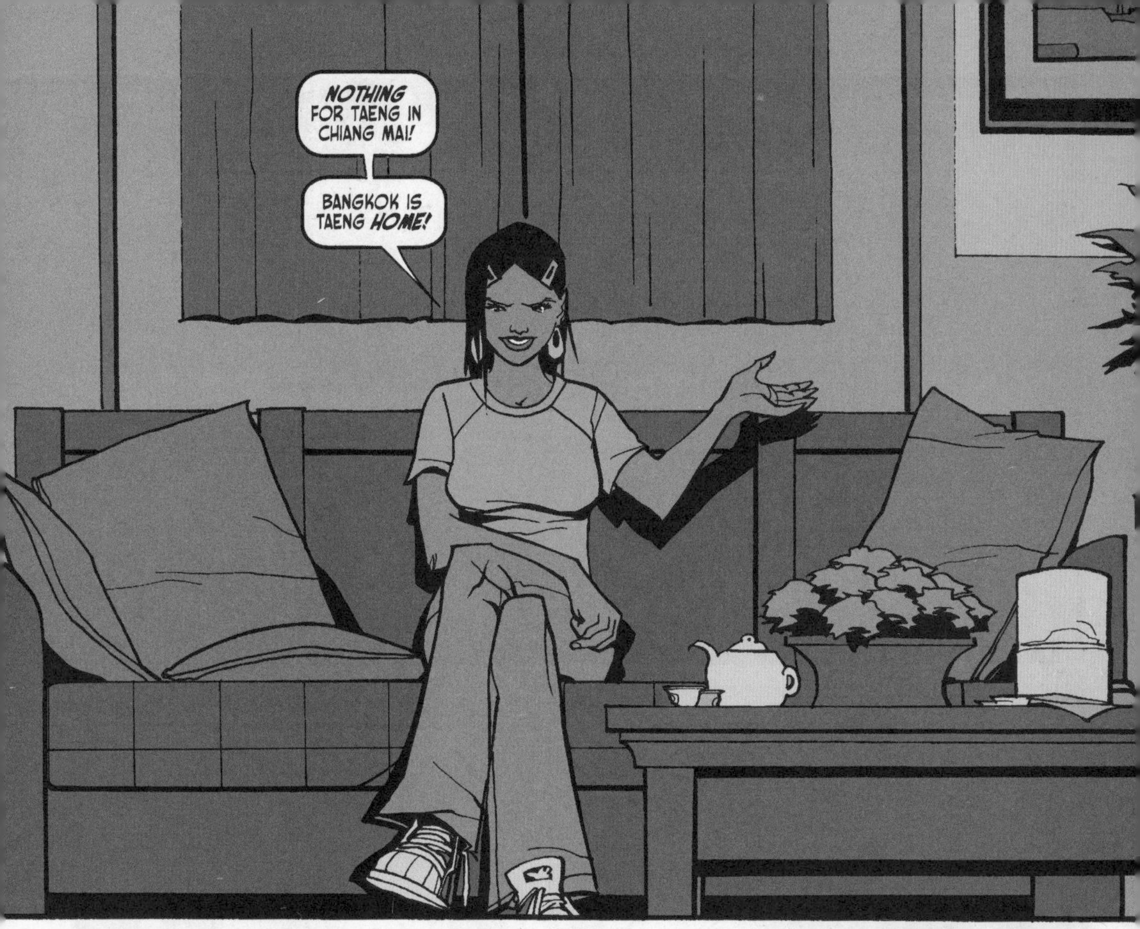
NOTHING FOR TAENG IN CHIANG MAI!
BANGKOK IS TAENG HOME!

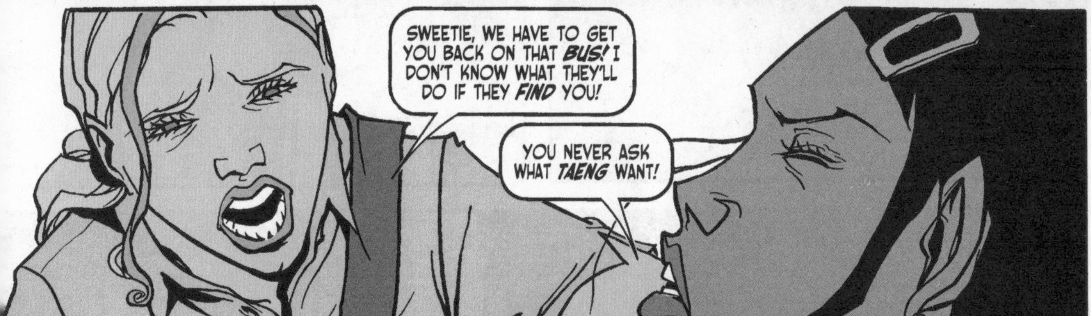
SWEETIE, WE HAVE TO GET YOU BACK ON THAT BUS! I DON'T KNOW WHAT THEY'LL DO IF THEY FIND YOU!
YOU NEVER ASK WHAT TAENG WANT!

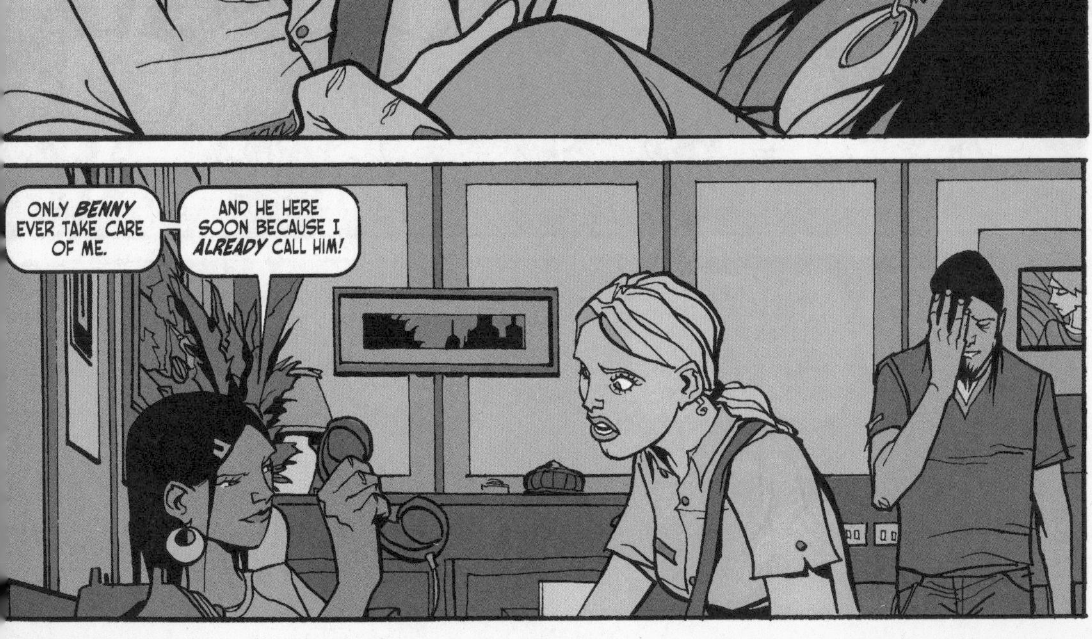
ONLY BENNY EVER TAKE CARE OF ME.
AND HE HERE SOON BECAUSE I ALREADY CALL HIM!

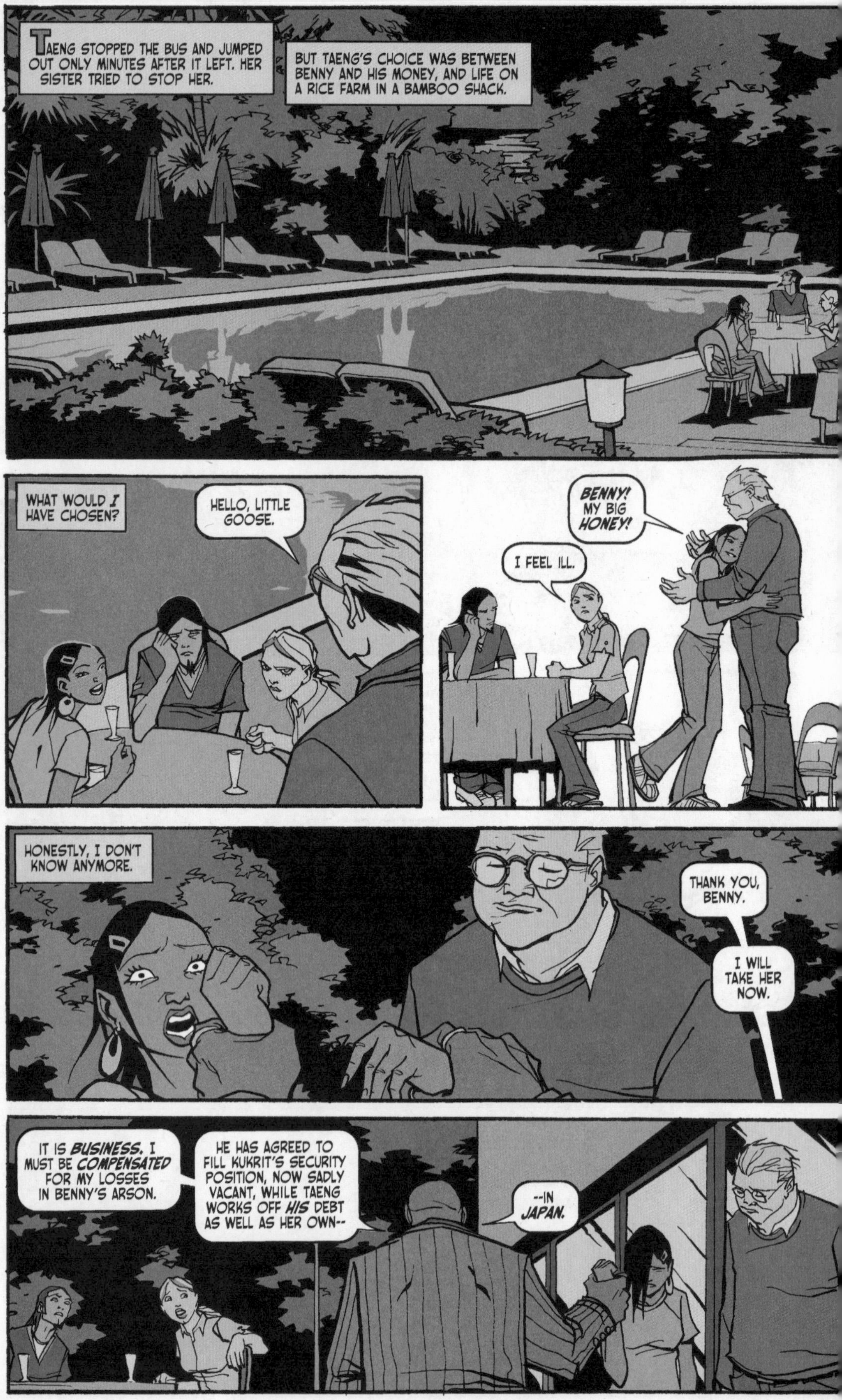
TAENG STOPPED THE BUS AND JUMPED OUT ONLY MINUTES AFTER IT LEFT. HER SISTER TRIED TO STOP HER.
BUT TAENG'S CHOICE WAS BETWEEN BENNY AND HIS MONEY, AND LIFE ON A RICE FARM IN A BAMBOO SHACK.
WHAT WOULD *I* HAVE CHOSEN?
HELLO, LITTLE GOOSE.
BENNY! MY BIG *HONEY!*
I FEEL ILL.
HONESTLY, I DON'T KNOW ANYMORE.
THANK YOU, BENNY.
I WILL TAKE HER NOW.
IT IS *BUSINESS.* I MUST BE *COMPENSATED* FOR MY LOSSES IN BENNY'S ARSON.
HE HAS AGREED TO FILL KUKRIT'S SECURITY POSITION, NOW SADLY VACANT, WHILE TAENG WORKS OFF *HIS* DEBT AS WELL AS HER OWN--
--IN *JAPAN.*

BENNY?

BUT THERE IS *GOOD* NEWS.

AT JAPANESE RATES, I ESTIMATE TAENG'S OBLIGATION WILL BE FULFILLED IN UNDER *FIVE YEARS.*

YOU CORRUPT *PIG!* LET HER GO!

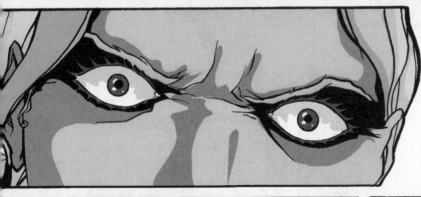

I *HATE* YOU AND YOUR WHOLE FUCKING *COUNTRY!*

MARZ! *DO SOMETHING!*

LET IT *GO,* TUESDAY.

IT'S OVER NOW. WE'RE DONE HERE.

FIVE *YEARS!*

FIVE *YEARS* OF GETTING FUCKED BY JAPANESE BUSINESSMEN! IT'S NOT RIGHT.

NO WORSE THAN BEING *FUCKED*, AS YOU SAY, BY AMERICANS, OR BRITISH. OR THAI.

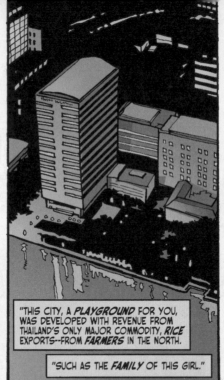

"THIS CITY, A *PLAYGROUND* FOR YOU, WAS DEVELOPED WITH REVENUE FROM THAILAND'S ONLY MAJOR COMMODITY, *RICE* EXPORTS--FROM *FARMERS* IN THE NORTH.

"SUCH AS THE *FAMILY* OF THIS GIRL."

TO COMPETE WE MUST KEEP RICE PRICES *LOW*. OUR PATRIOTIC FARMERS SUPPORT OUR GROWTH--YET THEY REMAIN IN POVERTY.

WHAT OTHER REVENUE SOURCE IS THEIRS *ALONE?*

THEIR *DAUGHTERS!*

WE HAVE A *RIGHT* TO PROSPERITY! WHY SHOULD THIS BE PERMITTED ONLY FOR THE WEST?

OUR SYSTEM BENEFITS EVERYONE. EVEN TAENG.

SHE *CHOSE* TO RETURN, DID SHE NOT?

YOU SAY I AM CORRUPT. BUT IT IS *YOU* WHO TRIED TO UNDERMINE OUR WAYS.

HAVE A PLEASANT JOURNEY BACK TO AMERICA. GOOD BYE.

MARZ WAS RIGHT TIME. IT WAS OVER

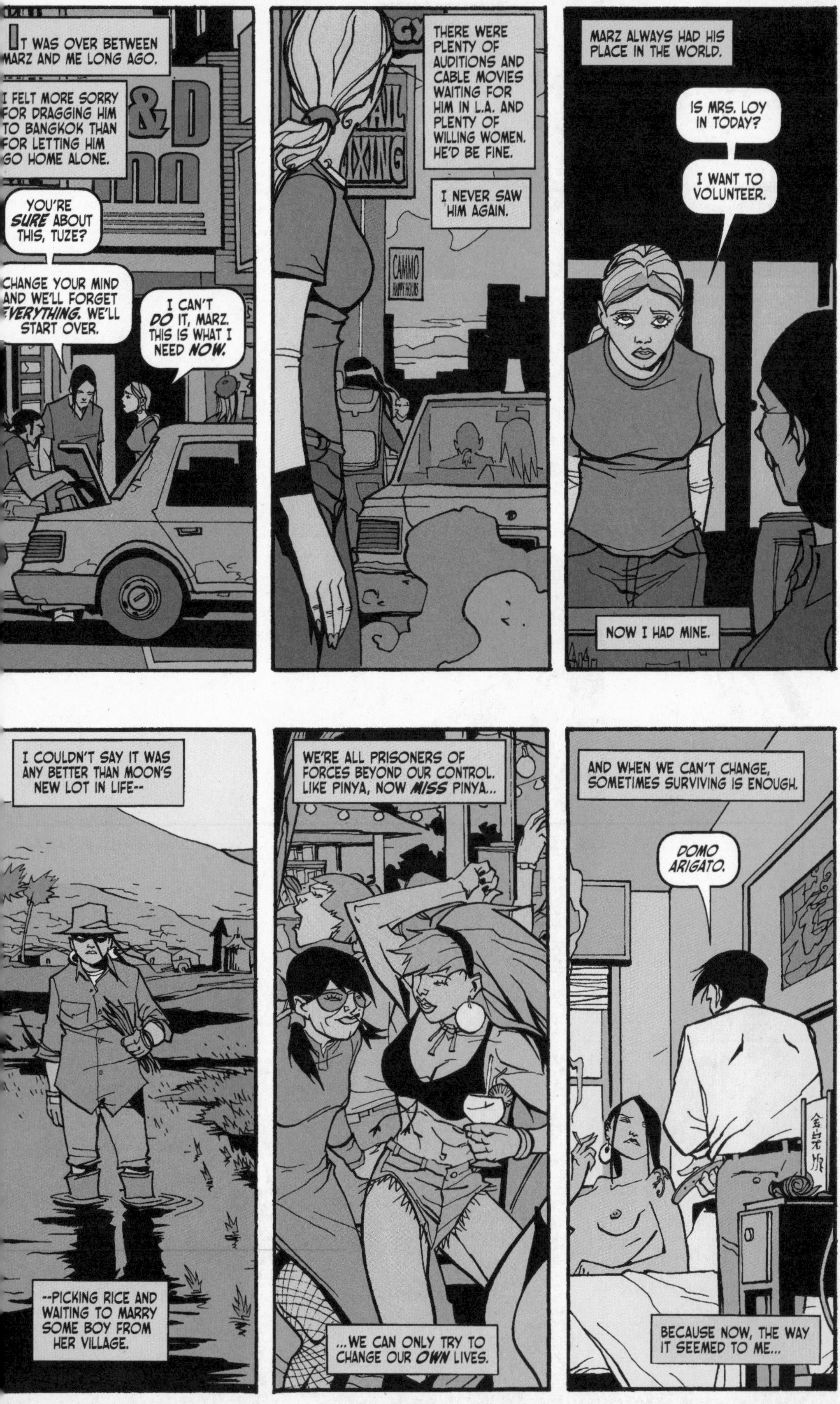
IT WAS OVER BETWEEN MARZ AND ME LONG AGO.
I FELT MORE SORRY FOR DRAGGING HIM TO BANGKOK THAN FOR LETTING HIM GO HOME ALONE.
YOU'RE *SURE* ABOUT THIS, TUZE?
CHANGE YOUR MIND AND WE'LL FORGET *EVERYTHING.* WE'LL START OVER.
I CAN'T *DO* IT, MARZ. THIS IS WHAT I NEED *NOW.*
THERE WERE PLENTY OF AUDITIONS AND CABLE MOVIES WAITING FOR HIM IN L.A. AND PLENTY OF WILLING WOMEN. HE'D BE FINE.
I NEVER SAW HIM AGAIN.
CAMMO
MARZ ALWAYS HAD HIS PLACE IN THE WORLD.
IS MRS. LOY IN TODAY?
I WANT TO VOLUNTEER.
NOW I HAD MINE.
I COULDN'T SAY IT WAS ANY BETTER THAN MOON'S NEW LOT IN LIFE--
--PICKING RICE AND WAITING TO MARRY SOME BOY FROM HER VILLAGE.
WE'RE ALL PRISONERS OF FORCES BEYOND OUR CONTROL. LIKE PINYA, NOW *MISS* PINYA...
...WE CAN ONLY TRY TO CHANGE OUR *OWN* LIVES.
AND WHEN WE CAN'T CHANGE, SOMETIMES SURVIVING IS ENOUGH.
DOMO ARIGATO.
BECAUSE NOW, THE WAY IT SEEMED TO ME...

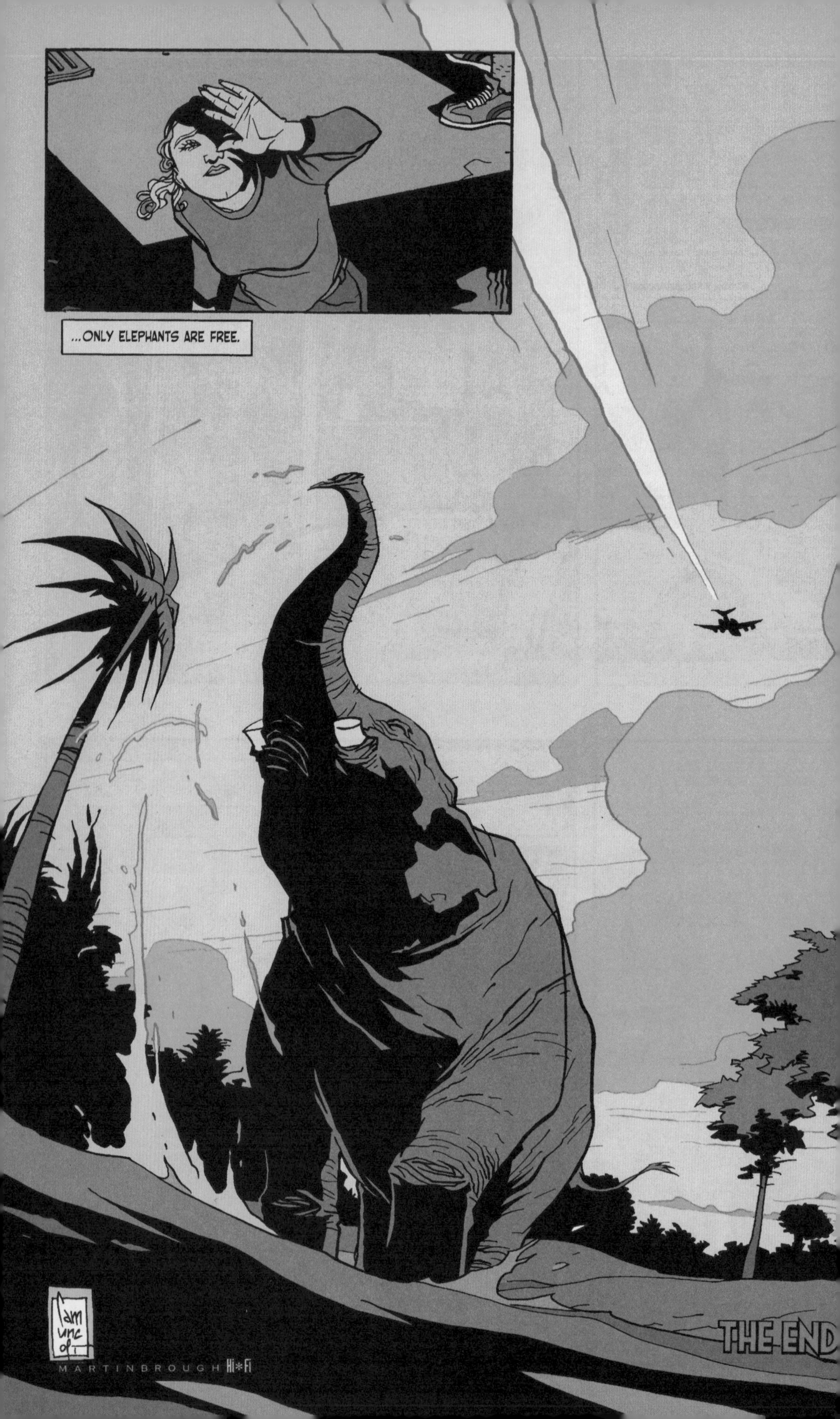

...ONLY ELEPHANTS ARE FREE.
THE END
MARTINBROUGH Hi*Fi

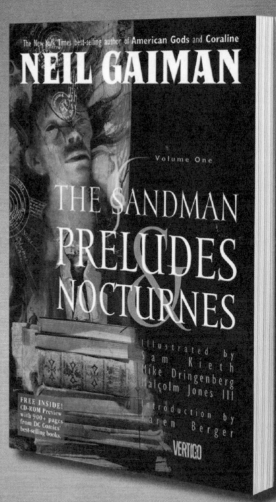

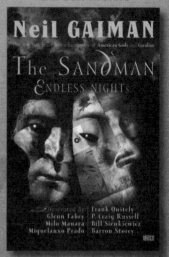